The Sikh Separatist Insurgency in India

Political Leadership and Ethnonationalist Movements

Jugdep S. Chima

⑤SAGE www.sagepublications.com
Los Angeles • London • New Delhi • Singapore • Washington DC

First published in 2010 by

 SAGE Publications India Pvt Ltd
B 1/I-1 Mohan Cooperative Industrial Area
Mathura Road, New Delhi 110044, India
www.sagepub.in

SAGE Publications Inc
2455 Teller Road
Thousand Oaks, California 91320, USA

SAGE Publications Ltd
1 Oliver's Yard, 55 City Road
London EC1Y 1SP, United Kingdom

SAGE Publications Asia-Pacific Pte Ltd
33 Pekin Street
#02-01 Far East Square
Singapore 048763

Published by Vivek Mehra for SAGE Publications India Pvt Ltd, typeset in 10/12 pt Minion by Star Compugraphics Private Limited, Delhi and printed at Chaman Enterprises, New Delhi.

Library of Congress Cataloging-in-Publication Data Available

ISBN: 978-81-321-0302-8 (HB)

The SAGE Team: Rekha Natarajan, Pranab Jyoti Sarma, Amrita Saha and Trinankur Banerjee

For my three little sources of daily frustration (Navkiran, Noorkaran, and Gurmehar), and the wonderful woman (Mandeep) who blessed me with them.

Contents

List of Tables

List of Abbreviations

AD	Akali Dal
AD(A)	Akali Dal (Amritsar)
AD(B)	Akali Dal (Badal)
AD(Baba)	Akali Dal (Baba)
AD(Babbar)	Akali Dal (Babbar)
AD(K)	Akali Dal (Kabul)
AD(L)	Akali Dal (Longowal)
AD(M)	Akali Dal (Mann)
AD(Manjit)	Akali Dal (Manjit)
AD(P)	Akali Dal (Panthic)
AD(T)	Akali Dal (Talwandi)
AD(U)	Akali Dal (United)
AISSF	All India Sikh Students Federation
AISSF(B)	All India Sikh Students Federation (Bittu)
AISSF(B/B)	All India Sikh Students Federation (Bundala/Buttar)
AISSF(G)	All India Sikh Students Federation (Gurjit)
AISSF(K)	All India Sikh Students Federation (Kahlon)
AISSF(M)	All India Sikh Students Federation (Manjit)
AKJ	Akhand Kirtani Jatha
BJP	Bharatiya Janata Party
BSP	Bahujan Samaj Party
BK	Babbar Khalsa
BTFK	Bhindranwale Tiger Force of Khalistan
BTFK(C)	Bhindranwale Tiger Force of Khalistan (Chhandra)
BTFK(M)	Bhindranwale Tiger Force of Khalistan (Manochahal)
BTFK(S)	Bhindranwale Tiger Force of Khalistan (Sangha)
CP(I)	Communist Party of India
CP(M)	Communist Party (Marxist)
DK	Dal Khalsa

DT	Damdami Taksal
INC	Indian National Congress
JD	Janata Dal
KCF	Khalistan Commando Force
KCF(P)	Khalistan Commando Force (Panjwar)
KCF(R)	Khalistan Commando Force (Rajasthani)
KCF(S)	Khalistan Commando Force (Sultanwind)
KCF(Z)	Khalistan Commando Force (Zafferwal)
KLF	Khalistan Liberation Force
KLF(E)	Khalistan Liberation Force (Engineer)
KLF(S)	Khalistan Liberation Force (Sekhon)
MLA	Member of Legislative Assembly
MP	Member of Parliament
NCK	National Council of Khalistan
PC	Panthic Committee
SSF	Sikh Students Federation
SSF(B)	Sikh Students Federation (Bittu)
SSF(M/C)	Sikh Students Federation (Mehta/Chawla)
SYL	Sutlej Yamuna Link Canal
UAD	United Akali Dal
UAD(B)	United Akali Dal (Baba)
UAD(M)	United Akali Dal (Mann)
UAD(T)	United Akali Dal (Talwandi)

Foreword

Terrorist violence results essentially from ethnic, religious, and ideological motivations. Violence in Punjab, India in the later part of the 20th century took the form of an ethnonationalist movement for an independent Sikh state. Sikh content and context added the religious elements as a force multiplier, thereby increasing the scope and intensity of the violence.

Jugdep S. Chima is a third-generation Sikh, who was born and raised in the Sikh diaspora in northern California. Punjabi and American cultures provided him with a passion for understanding and doing something about the human tragedy that encompassed his ancestral homeland. Jugdep began college in California as the movement and state carnage in Punjab increased yearly. He moved in a world of both Khalistan activists and supporters of the Indian state. Above all, he became involved in a scholarly context that increasingly led him to examine micro-political behavior on the one hand and theoretical constructs on the other.

His scholarly interests grew while examining the behavioral patterns of the Sikh insurgency and the larger arena of ethnonationalist and terrorist movements throughout the world. Focusing on a specific case helped inform him about particular patterns and provided avenues to understanding violent behavior in other situations. The reverse also is true with the comparative perspectives assisting him in understanding the "Punjab problem".

I witnessed these developments and Jugdep's continuing scholarly growth as his major advisor while he earned a PhD in political science. In one graduate seminar focusing on comparative terrorism, he compared and contrasted the Khalistan movement in Punjab with the "troubles" in Northern Ireland. A published article in a major peer-reviewed journal resulted. Scholarly intensity in research and publication marked his academic pursuits at the University of Missouri. Our intellectual exchanges were mutually beneficial.

Scholarly objectivity marks the author and the book that he now presents to the public. It doesn't dwell on "terror" as does so much of what has become a worldwide publishing industry. Political violence is a fact whether committed by a movement or the state. Categorizing a phenomenon as terrorist or as a movement by freedom fighters is a pre-judgment. "Militant" became the acceptable term in Punjab for the armed Khalistani activists.

Jugdep's meticulous research—originally presented in a 1,000 page dissertation—involved the identification of leadership changes from point to point during the Khalistan insurgency and its battles with various state forces. His analysis establishes key points from the beginning to the end in what he terms the trajectory of the movement. Patterns of political leadership and the changes that took place are set forth as the key conceptual framework. His major contribution, therefore, is to the rich political and sociological literature on political elites.

The social sciences critically need a return to this type of focus if they are to deal with real life problems. In a test of his original theoretical formulations, Jugdep applies them to ethnonationalist movements in four other very different contexts. Chechnya's first stage is an ethnic attempt at independence from Russia. It is reinforced in a second stage by Islamic radicalism. Thus, like Punjab, it involves ethnonationalism and religion. Northern Ireland and Kashmir also include both factors, ethnic and religious. Assam's case is more purely based on ethnic/tribal identities. In all these very dissimilar cultures, Jugdep's theoretical constructs provide a major comparative bridge.

Dr Jugdep Chima emerges with his present book as a significant contributor to comparative studies of political violence—read terrorism for the publishing industry—and provides notice that a young scholar is making his mark in the social sciences.

Dr Paul Wallace
Professor Emeritus
Department of Political Science
University of Missouri
Columbia, Missouri
USA

Preface

The researching and writing of this book emanated from two interrelated scholarly frustrations and concerns. First, there had been much written about the "Punjab crisis," but no academic study existed that offered a sufficiently-detailed and systematic political history of the entire movement from its initial emergence in the early-1980s to its demise in the 1990s. Such a work, in my scholarly assessment, was necessary in order to critically understand the evolution of the various organizations and individuals involved in the conflict, their changing motivations and interests over time, and their transitory political interrelationships with each other—not to mention the entire trajectory of the Sikh ethnonationalist insurgency itself. Second, I was intellectually unsatisfied with existing theories in the field that attempted to explain the phenomenon of ethnonationalism, which, much to my chagrin, tended to be ahistorical and relied on underlying abstract variables for explanation. Furthermore, most of these theories explained the factors behind the emergence of ethnonationalist movements but not for their sustenance and/or demise. In contrast, I assumed that the actions of individuals and organizations—including in relation to each other—had a determining effect on the rise, sustenance, and/or fall of ethnonationalist insurgencies. Thus, in the attempt to incorporate observable human agency into the explanation for this phenomenon, I constructed a theory of how "patterns of political leadership" affect the trajectory of ethnonationalist movements. The "theory" forwarded in this book includes empirically-verifiable and testable propositions for each, the rise, sustenance, and/or demise of this phenomenon. Thus, this book provides a unique explanation both for the rise and fall of the Sikh ethnonationalist movement in particular, and for the trajectory of ethnonationalist movements in general. The wider applicability of the propositions formulated in this study is demonstrated in its concluding chapter by critically examining four additional cases of ethnonationalist insurgency—Chechnya, Northern Ireland, Kashmir, and Assam. Thus, this book should be of significant interest to area specialists working on India and the Sikhs, academic theoreticians dealing with the conceptual issues of ethnonationalism and social movements, and also to public policy makers in multiethnic societies.

Jugdep S. Chima, PhD
Berkeley, California
USA

Acknowledgements

Researching and writing a PhD dissertation or a book is never a solo project. One inevitably accumulates a host of intellectual and personal debts whenever doing so. Fortunately, I have had the honor and privilege of working with a number of well-known and emphatic scholars who never made me feel that either I or my project was ever a burden on them. The intellectual exchanges I had with them vastly improved this work, and I hope it also somehow contributed to their own work and academic knowledge as well. In particular, I would like to thank Professor Paul Wallace who has been both a friend and mentor for years. Words cannot describe the personal and intellectual debt I owe him for his guidance and courtesy over the past many years. Paul is the model of a PhD advisor who combines the first-rate academic knowledge of a scholar of his caliber with the helpfulness and sensitivity of a true friend. While a doctoral student at the University of Missouri-Columbia, I also gained immensely from my long conversations with Professor N. Gerald Barrier. In particular, I thank Professor Barrier for emphasizing the importance of human agency and process in determining political outcomes, instead of the abstract variables we political scientists are often trained to focus on. His methodological perspective as a historian helped shape the content and presentation of both the original PhD dissertation and this published book.

I have accumulated many academic, personal, and professional debts while both as an undergraduate student and then as a professional scholar at the University of California, Berkeley. The late Professor Leo E. Rose and Professor Jyotirindra Das Gupta initially led me into the study of South Asian politics while an undergraduate at this institution. Professor Das Gupta, in fact, advised me to undertake my graduate studies at Missouri under Paul Wallace, and remains a readily available and always cheerful source of academic advice even today. I would also like to thank Daisy

Rockwell and Mark Koops Elson, who provided me with institutional affiliation as a postdoctoral researcher and visiting scholar with the Center for South Asia Studies (CSAS) at UC-Berkeley after completing my doctoral degree. This time allowed me to revise and transform the original dissertation into a publishable book manuscript. I also owe a debt of gratitude to my colleagues at *Asian Survey*, including David Fraser, Bonnie Dehler, and Professor Lowell Dittmer. They were always there to provide their input and encouragement, not to mention flexibility in terms of my schedule, while I completed this project. Finally, no one at Berkeley has been as instrumental in the final presentation of this study as Professor Pradeep Chhibber who acted as my postdoctoral advisor while I was affiliated with CSAS. Pradeep's razor-edged and incisive, but always constructive, comments helped me flesh out this book's contribution to the existing theoretical literature in the field. His witty intellect and detailed commentary helped me ponder the implications of the Punjab case to the broader conceptual issues of political leadership and ethnonationalist insurgency. Without his time and input, this study may have looked much different than it does today.

The publication of this book is also the product of the highly responsive and professional editorial team at SAGE Publications India. In particular, I would like to thank Sugata Ghosh, Vice President for Commissioning, who expressed initial interest in publishing this project and then waited patiently while I appropriately revised the dissertation into a book manuscript. Rekha Natarajan, Senior Commissioning Editor, has also always been there to answer my incessant questions and to politely provide me with the cogent editorial advice necessary for the presentation and production of a marketable book. I wish to thank her for her time and professionalism.

Finally, I simply could not have completed this project without the help and support of my family. My father, Lal, waited patiently while I completed this book, often nudging me to get it done. My mother, Kirpal, spent seemingly endless days babysitting my eldest daughter, Navkiran, while I completed my dissertation, and then did the same with Noorkaran and subsequently my son, Gurmehar, while I revised the dissertation into a book manuscript. Without her willingness to watch my children while I worked, I would have probably never finished this book project. Finally, the various debts I owe to my wife, Mandeep, and my three children are too numerous to list. In short, they had to "live" with this book while their husband and father was incessantly distracted, both mentally and emotionally, with issues of Sikh politics, political leadership, and ethnonationalist insurgency. For whatever consolation it may be, this book is lovingly dedicated to them. They are most precious in my life today, and the publication of this book is a testament to their love, strength, and commitment, for which I will eternally remain grateful.

PART I

Introduction

1

"Patterns of Political Leadership" and Ethnonationalist Insurgency

INTRODUCTION

The northwestern Indian state of Punjab was a model of political stability and economic development for India during the late-1960s and early-1970s. The state had been free of communal violence and large-scale political instability since the traumatic events and population transfers associated with the Partition of colonial India into Hindu-majority India and Muslim-majority Pakistan after Independence in 1947. The Indian state had also successfully accommodated a non-violent political mobilization by Punjab's Sikh minority during the late-1950s and early-1960s by creating a truncated Punjabi-speaking state consistent with the principle of linguistic reorganization applied throughout India during this period. Punjab's enterprising and generally prosperous Sikh community seemed well-integrated into the "national mainstream," providing a disproportionate number of recruits into the Indian armed forces and helping turn the state of Punjab into the "granary of India" with the Green Revolution. Punjab was described as being "a model province" and "an object of envy" for the rest of India.[1]

This situation changed dramatically during the early-1980s when a violent Sikh ethnonationalist movement emerged which eventually transformed itself into an openly secessionist struggle for the creation of an independent Sikh state—Khalistan. An estimated 25,000 people died as a result of political violence associated with the "Punjab crisis," tens of thousands were arrested, and an unknown number of Punjab's inhabitants

fled to foreign countries as political refugees.[2] Over a quarter of a million
Indian security force personnel were deployed in Sikh-majority Punjab
during the height of the insurgency to prevent its secession from the Indian
Union.[3] The Sikh separatist insurgency represented the "worst threat" to
India's territorial integrity and unity since Independence and Partition.
Yet, as Figure 1.1 shows, the violent Sikh ethnonationalist movement,
which had escalated precipitously through the late-1980s, declined by
the mid-1990s to the point that no significant militancy-related deaths
occurred after 1993.

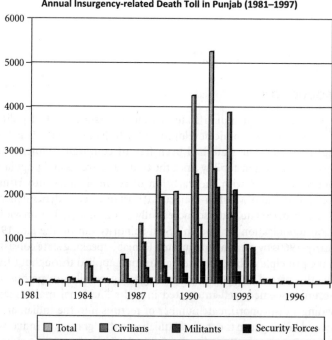

Figure 1.1
Annual Insurgency-related Death Toll in Punjab (1981–1997)

Source: Data accumulated from South Asia Terrorism Portal, Institute for Conflict Man-
        agement (New Delhi), available at http://www.satp.org/satporgtp/countries/india/
        states/punjab/data_sheets/annual_casualties.htm.
Note: The figures for 1984 do not including those killed in Operation Bluestar and in the
        anti-Sikh riots of November 1984.

This puzzling trajectory of the violent Sikh ethnonationalist movement raises a number of important questions: How and why did the

movement emerge in the first place? How was it sustained? And finally, how did it eventually decline? This book provides a unique explanation for these questions focusing on the previously unexamined explanatory variable of "patterns of political leadership."[4] The main argument presented in this study is that *"patterns of political leadership," defined as the dynamic interaction between and amongst state and ethnic elites, significantly affect the trajectory of ethnic subnationalist movements by defining the political relationship between an ethnic group and the central state.* While it focuses primarily on explaining the rise and fall of the Sikh separatist insurgency in India, the conceptual arguments formulated in this book can also help explain the trajectory of ethnic subnationalist movements in general, as demonstrated in the concluding chapter by examining the cases of Chechnya, Northern Ireland, Jammu and Kashmir, and Assam. Thus, this book should be of interest to both area-specialists studying South Asia, and also to academics and policy-practitioners interested in the phenomenon of ethnonationalism, mobilization, and conflict in general.

EXISTING EXPLANATIONS FOR THE RISE AND FALL OF THE SIKH ETHNONATIONALIST MOVEMENT

As alluded earlier, this study grew out of a general dissatisfaction with the existing explanations for the rise, sustenance, and demise of the Sikh separatist insurgency in Punjab. Five main explanations have emerged for the onset of the "Punjab crisis"—primacy of regional factors, primacy of national factors, Marxist interpretations, conspiracy theories, and Sikh nationalism.[5] Explanations focusing on regional factors contend that changing socio-economic conditions in Punjab emanating from the Green Revolution, including increased unemployment and alienation of the rural youth, provided a fertile breeding ground for Sikh militancy during the early-1980s.[6] Much like the regional factors thesis, a variety of Marxist interpretations formulated by left-of-center scholars also point to how the Green Revolution intensified economic antagonism between various social classes in Punjab, causing heightened potential for conflict.[7] In contrast, scholars analyzing national factors view the "Punjab crisis" as being the result of the changing style of political leadership in the center: from Jawaharlal Nehru's more neutral, decentralized, and accommodative style during the 1950s and early-1960s to the more partisan, centralized, and interventionist style of Indira Gandhi during the 1970s and early-1980s.[8] Conspiracy theorists also contribute to an understanding of the emergence of the "Punjab crisis" by emphasizing the role of Pakistan in supporting extremist Sikh groups in order to weaken and possibly dismember India.[9] Lastly, explanations focusing on Sikh nationalism simply claim that a heightened sense of nationalism within the Sikh community grew during the early-1980s due to increased perceptions of discrimination, thus leading to militancy.[10]

These five categories of explanation contribute significantly to our understanding as to how and why the "Punjab crisis" emerged in the first place, but they cannot successfully explain its demise. In this regard, the first four explanations suffer from one major weakness in common, namely, that they cannot demonstrate that the quantitative or qualitative "value" of their respective explanatory variables changed from the period when the movement first arose to when it eventually declined. For example, explanations relying on regional factors and most Marxist interpretations cannot show that the socio-economic conditions that supposedly contributed to the onset of the "Punjab crisis" in the late-1970s changed during the early-1990s when it declined. It is also uncertain whether the national leaders who presided over the eventual decline of the Sikh separatist movement were any less partisan, interventionist, and centralizing than Mrs Gandhi, as the "primacy of national factors" thesis would suggest. Similarly, conspiracy theorists are correct to assert that Pakistan aided and abetted the emergence of Sikh extremist groups, but they cannot demonstrate that the level of Pakistani support decreased during the early-1990s. In fact, it may have actually increased. Regarding the Sikh nationalism thesis, discrimination and state violence against sections of the Sikh community actually became more intense after 1984 than before when militancy first arose, thus casting doubt on this, somewhat tautological, explanation.

Compared to explanations for the initial emergence of the violent Sikh ethnonationalist movement, less has been written explaining its decline. Three incipient explanations—effective anti-terrorism measures, Punjab's social structure, and "managed disorder"—have emerged.[11] According to the first, a variety of operational, organizational, and technological improvements made by the Punjab police and Indian security forces helped crush Sikh militancy.[12] The second explanation—Punjab's social structure—contends that the Jat Sikh political culture, with its emphasis on personal power and honor, could not sustain a long-term separatist struggle based on an overarching sense of corporate Sikh nationalism.[13] Lastly, the "managed disorder" thesis hypothesizes that many Sikh insurgent groups were actually supported and sustained by elements within the Congress (I) party and agents of the Indian state for their own partisan reasons, and were eliminated when they were no longer useful for serving their interests.

These incipient explanations for the decline of the Sikh separatist movement (especially the first two) carry significant merit, but each (especially the third) also suffer from some major weaknesses. The first focuses almost exclusively on military variables and disregards important political variables in explaining the decline of violent Sikh ethnonationalism. The second explanation—Punjab's social structure—is especially compelling for explaining the decline of the movement, but it cannot explain its emergence because the nature of Punjab's social structure, including the Jat Sikh political culture, did not change from the 1970s to the 1990s. In contrast, the "managed disorder" thesis is a particularly weak explanation. Some of the Sikh "militant" groups may indeed have been supported by elements within the Congress (I) party and the government, but this explanation completely ignores the existence of powerful bona fide Sikh separatist groups which fought a bloody struggle for the creation of Khalistan after 1984.

Thus, extensive research exists which explains either the rise of the violent Sikh ethnonationalist movement or its fall, but not both phases of the phenomenon within a common analytic framework. Furthermore, there is no work that focuses on "patterns of political leadership" as its primary explanatory variable for either phase of the separatist insurgency. This study fills this void by providing a micro-historical account of how "patterns of political leadership" affected the rise, sustenance, and decline of the Sikh separatist movement from its emergence in the late-1970s to its decline in the mid-1990s.[14] Thus, this book also offers a detailed political history of the entire "Punjab crisis," especially of the complex post-1984 period which has been generally under-researched by historians and political scientists alike.

THE BOOK'S CONCEPTUAL ARGUMENTS

Several key terms are used repeatedly throughout this study and must be briefly defined before presenting the book's main conceptual arguments. To begin, the term "state" refers to the governmental structure that has the legal right to impose binding rules over a given territory and population. "Ethnic groups" are self-defined groups with a collective conscious based either on objective cultural characteristics or a subjective sense of "community". An ethnic group is different from a "class" in that the latter is based on economic factors while the former is based on a combination of cultural, racial, or religious ones. The term "elites" refers to a group of people or members of this group who either head a political party or organization, or who have undue influence within one.

The term "nationalism" is defined as being the politicized sense of collective identity shared by members of a polity or ethnic group. The term "politicized" is important in this definition to distinguish between the mere existence of a sense of collective identity and that which forms the basis for political action vis-à-vis other actors. "Ethnonationalism" refers to nationalism based on ethnic identity. This differs from civic nationalism which is a sense of politicized identity based on identification with the central state. The term "subnationalism" is used interchangeably with "ethnonationalism" in this book. "Insurgency" is defined as being a violent struggle between the state and a non-ruling group which tries to establish a competing form of legitimacy to existing state authority. The term "secessionism" refers to a demand for formal withdrawal from a central political authority by an ethnic group and the creation of its own sovereign political status. "Separatism" is also used interchangeably with "secessionism" in this book. Lastly, the term "movement" refers to a systematic, organized effort by individuals to achieve a common political goal.

As stated earlier, this book's central and overarching argument is that *"patterns of political leadership," defined as the dynamic interaction between and amongst state and ethnic elites, significantly affect the trajectory of ethnic subnationalist movements by defining the political relationship between an ethnic group and the central state.* This seems to be a commonsense and straightforward proposition, but determining the effects of "patterns of political leadership" on the trajectory of ethnic movements has not been sufficiently examined by scholars in the field. This argument suggests that both the central state and the ethnic groups are not unitary actors. They invariably contain a number of internal leaders and factions competing against each other for positions of leadership and dominance within their respective spheres of politics. The internal political competition within both the state and ethnic groups revolves around either ideological differences or, more often than not, purely political power struggles in which various leaders and factions adjust their ideologies and policy-positions to enhance their power relative to their internal rivals. The political relationship between an ethnic group and the central state is not only determined by which leaders or factions are dominant within their respective spheres of politics, but also by the changing relationships, often based on mutual convenience, between dissident leaders and factions within both ethnic groups and the state. Thus, the strategic interaction both between and amongst ethnic and state elites influences the nature of ethnic group–central state relations and affects the trajectory of ethnonationalist movements. This book sets forth three specific, but inter-related, propositions about how particular "patterns of political leadership" affect the rise, sustenance, and decline of violent ethnonationalist movements.

Regarding the rise of ethnonationalism, this book argues that *violent subnationalist movements arise when competing ethnic and state elites cannot resolve their political differences and ethnic militants emerge often, but not always, facilitated by either traditional ethnic elites or state elites to use in their respective intra-system struggles or against each other.* This argument points to the centrality of the political interaction between and amongst ethnic and state elites in facilitating the rise of violent ethnonationalist movements. Several interrelated routes for the emergence or escalation of violent subnationalism are identified. First, violent ethnonationalism emerges when competing ethnic and state elites cannot resolve their political differences, and a more extreme, militant ethnic leadership emerges independently from within the ethnic group. Alternatively, violent subnationalist movements can also emerge when the central state facilitates the rise of a more extreme and militant ethnic leadership in order to undermine, weaken, or divide the traditional ethnic leadership for its own partisan purposes. These relatively simple patterns facilitating the emergence or escalation of violent ethnonationalism, while certainly possible, usually occur in combination with other patterns. For example, the rise of violent ethnonationalism often takes a slightly more complex form, involving the internal competition within either state or ethnic elites in addition to the competition between them. To explain, violent subnationalist movements often arise when competing ethnic or state elites facilitate the emergence of a militant ethnic leadership to use in their intra-system struggles against internal rivals. The former is more common, and occurs when a section of the traditional ethnic leadership promotes the emergence of a militant ethnic leadership either to undermine its intra-group competitors or to use it as an ally against them. Thus, most instances of violent ethnonationalism involve a combination of these patterns with the intense political competition between traditional ethnic elites and state elites being a necessary, but often not sufficient, condition for the emergence of violent ethnonationalist movements. Instead, political dynamics within both the state and within the ethnic group also often factor into this equation.

Regarding the sustenance of ethnonationalism, this book argues that *in the absence of a negotiated settlement, violent subnationalist movements persist when ethnic militants remain "united" and retain a viable political front, while state elites become internally-divided and fractionalized traditional ethnic elites engage in competitive "ethnic-outflanking".* This argument pertains to the phase of violent ethnonationalism after its initial emergence or escalation. Negotiated settlements can be devised after the initial onset of violence, but they are unlikely in the short-term because ethnic and/or state elites have themselves facilitated the emergence of militants and violence in the first place. Violent subnationalist movements tend to persist when ethnic militants remain united and retain a viable political front. This "unity" within the ranks of ethnic militants does not necessarily mean that only one militant group exists, but rather that the various militant groups, assuming that there are more than one, do not engage in internally-destructive competition and fratricide. The creation and retention of a viable "political front" is also important for ethnic militants in order to maintain an organizational link between their political ideology and the ethnic masses in general. Without this political link, violent ethnonationalist movements often denigrate into parochial terrorist campaigns without the institutionalized popular support base necessary for maintaining long-term subnationalism. Ethnic militants' "political fronts" usually consist of either dissident traditional ethnic elites who strategically support the militants for their own partisan reasons or, more importantly, extremist political organizations either directly linked to the militants or generally supportive of their ideological goals. The viability of this "political front" is largely predicated on its ability to maintain relative organizational unity without splitting into internally-competitive factions. Fractionalization reduces the movement's overall viability and strength by diminishing its ability to maintain long-term popular support and effectively confront the central state.

In contrast, internal disunity within both state elites and the traditional ethnic leadership contribute to the persistence of violent ethnonationalism. At minimum, the lack of unity between state elites hinders the formulation and implementation of coherent, systematic policies to confront or ameliorate the insurgency. At worse, competing state elites sometimes work at cross-purposes against each other, either directly or indirectly helping to sustain the insurgency for their own partisan reasons vis-a-vis other state elites. Similarly, the internal division and competition between traditional ethnic elites, which often leads to competitive "ethnic-outbidding," also contributes to the sustenance of violent ethnonationalism.[15] Traditional ethnic leaders do not necessarily have to take progressively more extreme positions to contribute to the sustenance of violent ethnonationalism, but rather the actions of one section of the traditional ethnic leadership in "outflanking" another section by aligning with ethnic extremists or militants is often sufficient. Traditional ethnic elites usually engage in ethnic "outbidding" or "outflanking" either to appease the ascending ethnic militants or to align with them in the attempt to compete against another section of the traditional ethnic leadership in intra-system competition.

Regarding the demise of ethnonationalism, this book argues that *in the absence of a negotiated settlement or complete military victory, violent subnationalist movements decline when ethnic militants "fractionalize" and lose a viable political front, and unified state elites pursue coordinated policies prompting traditional ethnic elites to unite, moderate, and re-enter the "normal" political process.* Negotiated settlements for ethnonationalist conflicts are most likely after an extended period of confrontation, especially when both sides foresee continued military and political stalemate. Yet, not all negotiated settlements succeed in ending ethnonationalist movements. After all, such agreements cannot always be implemented, and a section of either the ethnic or state leadership may refuse to support the negotiated settlement. In the absence of an overt military victory by one side or the other, violent subnationalism declines when political dynamics change within both the ethnic group and the state. In particular, "fractionalization" of ethnic militants and an erosion of their "political front" contribute to the demise of violent ethnonationalist movements. The erosion of unity within the ranks of ethnic militants and their internal fratricide reduces the movement's overall military and political effectiveness, and also allows state and traditional ethnic elites to more easily exploit rivalries between militant groups to their own advantage. Similarly, the erosion of the militants' "political front" contributes to the demise of violent ethnonationalism. This erosion can occur either when traditional ethnic elites withdraw support to the militants, when the militants' political front organizations themselves fractionalize and begin to compete against each other, or when a schism develops between the militants and their extremist political front organizations. Erosion of the militants' "political front," regardless of which form it may take, reduces the movement's overall ability to retain popular support and confront the central state, and also allows traditional ethnic elites to more forcefully reassert themselves in the attempt to regain their positions of political dominance within the ethnic group.

The internal dynamics both within state political elites and ethnic elites also affect the trajectory of ethnonationalist movements. In much the same way that internal disunity and competition between state elites often contributes to the rise of the violent ethnonationalism, their internal unity and coordinated action can conversely help dampen violent ethnonationalist movements. To explain, unity between governmental elites allows the state to formulate more coherent and effective strategies against ethnic militants and also implement policies designed to strengthen the traditional, usually more moderate, ethnic leadership. Similarly, unity forged between traditional ethnic elites and their moderation contributes to the decline of violent ethnonationalism. Yet, traditional ethnic elites usually cannot forge "unity" themselves after a period of extended "ethnic-flanking" and insurgency. Instead, this must be facilitated by a concurrent weakening of the ethnic militants either as a result of their internal fractionalization or through effective state action by unified governmental elites. After all, traditional ethnic elites feel more secure in engaging in a process of gradual ethnic "under-bidding" only after the militants have become politically and/or militarily weakened. The strategic, as opposed to unequivocal, holding of democratic elections by the state, especially once the militants have become even marginally weakened, is often effective in prompting traditional ethnic elites to begin uniting, moderating, and consider re-entering more "normal" modes of politics. After all, traditional ethnic elites do not want to become permanently marginalized in the wider political process once even a semblance of "normalcy" appears to be re-emerging after a period of extended insurgency. In essence, the same traditional ethnic elites who may have been "pushed" into competitive "ethnic-outbidding" can also be "pulled" back into more normal modes of politics. This process, if it occurs, contributes to the decline of violent ethnonationalist movements and the eventual cementing of political "normalcy."

THE BOOK'S THEORETICAL CONTRIBUTION

In addition to offering a unique explanation for the rise and fall of the Sikh separatist insurgency in particular, the conceptual arguments formulated in this book also contribute significantly to existing theoretical accounts of ethnonationalism, mobilization, and conflict in general. Several characteristics stand out about the existing theoretical explanations for these political phenomena. First, there are many theories that claim to explain either the rise or the fall of ethnonationalist movements, but relatively few which explain both phases of this phenomenon within a unified analytical framework. Second, most explanations for the rise of ethnonationalism focus primarily on underlying permissive conditions instead of the actual proximate political processes that catalyze mobilization and conflict at a given time. Third, virtually no theoretical work exists that uses "patterns of political leadership" as its primary explanatory variable to explain the rise, sustenance, and demise of ethnonationalist movements. A brief illustrative overview of the existing theoretical literature helps delineate the exact contribution this book makes to a general understanding of the trajectory of violent subnationalist movements.

First, only a few theories exist that attempt to explain both the rise and fall of this political phenomenon within a unified analytical framework. For example, Atul Kohli argues that the level of institutionalization of central authority, and whether the central leadership is accommodating or unaccommodating explains the trajectory of "self-determination" movements.[16] For his part, Ashutosh Varshney focuses on the combination of "value-rationality" (emotional, non-material motivations and goals) and "instrumental-rationality" (calculated, material motivations and goals) to explain the sustenance of political movements.[17] This thesis is somewhat akin to that of Subrata Mitra who contends that the sustenance of subnationalism is predicated on the successful transformation of normal "transactional" politics involving material interests into "transcendental" issues involving identity, community, and dignity.[18] Finally, Doug McAdam hypothesizes that the trajectory of "social insurgencies" is determined by the interplay of broad socio-economic processes, the structure of political opportunities, indigenous organizational strength, and the ideological salience of symbolic appeals.[19] While all of these works contribute to a general understanding of the trajectory of ethnonationalist movements, none of them uses "patterns of political leadership" as its primary explanatory variable. This represents a significant gap in the existing theory on the trajectory of ethnonationalist movements.

Second, most of the existing theoretical explanations for the emergence of ethnonationalism focus on underlying *permissive* conditions instead of immediate and *proximate* political processes which catalyze it at given points in time. Four underlying conditions are identified in the literature explaining the rise of violent ethnonationalism—structural factors, political factors, economic/social factors, and cultural factors.[20] Explanations based on structural factors contend that conflict is most prone in "weak states" in which governmental authority is not well-institutionalized.[21]

It is argued that ethnic groups are more likely to mobilize in "weak states" because the potential consequences of mobilizing (that is, facing effective state repression) are low and the chances of gaining increased political power are high. In contrast, scholars focusing on political factors argue that ethnonationalism emerges when a state's discriminatory or exclusionary practices against an ethnic group leads to a crisis of legitimacy and subsequent mobilization.[22] For their part, economic/social theorists contend that "discriminatory economic systems…can generate feelings of resentment and levels of frustration prone to the generation of violence [and mobilization]."[23] In contrast, other economic/social theorists argue that development and modernization are the basis for ethnic mobilization because these processes heighten ethnic awareness and increase economic competition between groups.[24] Lastly, cultural theorists point to a history of inter-group animosity and distrust as being a potential basis for conflict.[25] As stated earlier, all of these explanations tend to focus on underlying *permissive* conditions generally conducive to mobilization and conflict, but neglect to identify the *proximate* political processes that actually catalyze ethnonationalist movements at given points in time.

Finally, existing explanations for the decline of ethnonationalist movements also leave wide theoretical holes unfilled. Most of these works offer either conceptual frameworks that measure the internal sustainability of insurgencies and their comparative strength vis-à-vis the state, or broad political strategies that the states use to try to end ethnonationalist conflicts. Regarding the former, Bard O'Neil identifies several variables that help determine the success or failure of an insurgency—its level of popular support, the effectiveness of its organization, its degree of internal cohesion, the external support it receives, the geographical environment in which it exists, and the effectiveness of the governmental response.[26] John R. Wood and others also point to similar variables.[27] In terms of the latter, theories of conflict resolution generally delineate specific strategies and mechanisms that the state can use to try to end a conflict without a military victory. These include government by grand coalition and power-sharing, proportional representation, mutual veto, purposive depoliticization of issues, federalism, and compromises and concessions.[28] The role of political leadership is implicit in many of these conceptual frameworks and political strategies, but none of them explicitly focus on "patterns of political leadership" as their primary explanatory variable.

This omission is also present in theories of collective mobilization, including rational-choice theory and social constructivism. These theories do incorporate the role of political leadership into their explanations, but they do so in a vastly different way than conceptualized in this book. Instead of analyzing the dynamic interaction between and amongst ethnic and state elites, these theories tend to focus on the relationship between ethnic leaders and their followers. For example, rational-choice theorists argue that leaders mobilize their followers by offering them either immediate or deferred material rewards, and social constructivists focus on the symbolic and psychological link between leaders and followers.[29] The instrumentalist theory of ethnic identity and mobilization also combines both material and symbolic appeals into its explanatory framework, but it too neglects an examination of the effects of "patterns of political leadership"—that is, the dynamic interaction between and amongst state and ethnic elites—on the trajectory of ethnonationalist movements as specifically conceptualized in this study.[30]

Thus, the foregoing discussion points to the fact that existing theories for the rise, sustenance, and fall of ethnonationalist movements are "thin" in terms of explaining this phenomenon within a unified conceptual framework. Scholarly work that uses "patterns of political leadership" as its primary variable is, in particular, especially "thin" if not virtually non-existent. This is unfortunate because analytical attention to the variable of political leadership in general, and "patterns of political leadership" in specific, is well-warranted in helping explain the trajectory of ethnonationalist movements. As Michael E. Brown writes, the existing theory is:

> …weak in its understanding of the roles played by elites and leaders… [T]he decisions and actions of domestic elites often determine whether political disputes veer toward war or peace. Leaving elite decisions and actions out of the equation, as many social scientists do, is analytically misguided.[31]

James Fearon and David Laitin also concur by writing that "large-scale ethnic violence is provoked by elites seeking to gain, maintain, or increase their hold on power."[32] Furthermore they observe that "an interesting feature…is that internal conflicts between extremists and moderates belonging to a single group spur leaders or dissidents to provoke violence [and mobilization]."[33] Thus, the paucity of theory in these areas leaves an important part of "the entire picture" of how and why violent ethnonationalist movements rise and fall untheorized. This book fills this analytical gap by offering a general theory of how "patterns of political leadership," defined as the dynamic political interaction between and amongst state and ethnic elites, affect the course of violent ethnonationalist movements.

More importantly, the specific arguments presented in this book also incorporate the central role of *human agency* into their explanation, and thus offer a proximate *theory of action* instead of relying on underlying permissive conditions and abstract variables for explanation. An important conclusion emerging out of this book is that ethnonationalist movements are not inevitable. Instead, *the emergence and decline of violent subnationalist movements are largely predicated on the interaction between self-interested political elites who not only react to the structural choices they face, but whose purposeful actions and decisions affect the larger political environment and the course of ethnic group–state relations.* In essence, political leaders and their dynamic interaction, not only underlying permissive conditions, are ultimately responsible for the rise, sustenance, and/or fall of violent ethnonationalist conflicts so endemic in the world today.

THE REST OF THIS STUDY

The remainder of this book examines the trajectory of the Sikh ethnonationalist movement and develops the overarching argument that *"patterns of political leadership," defined as the dynamic interaction between and amongst state and ethnic elites, significantly affect the trajectory of ethnic subnationalist movements by defining the political relationship between an ethnic group and the central state.* The methodological approach used is a micro-historical case-study involving detailed "process-tracing."[34] The purpose of "analytic narratives" that emerge from such case-studies is to "cut deeply into the specifics of a time and place, and to locate the processes that generate the outcome of interest" which, in this case, is the rise and fall of the Sikh ethnonationalist movement.[35] Yet, the narratives produced by such case-studies are also "analytic" because they extract "explicit and formal lines of reasoning" which provide the basis for generalizable theories and models.[36]

Chapter 2 of this book provides a wider political context for and historical background to the violent Sikh ethnonationalist movement in Punjab. In particular, it discusses the historical and sociological bases for Sikh ethnic identity, the institutionalization of Sikh identity into contemporary political organizations, and Punjab's political party system. This chapter also provides a brief overview of Sikh politics from Independence to the late-1970s, before the emergence of the violent "Punjab crisis."

Chapters 3 through 5 examine the political dynamics that gave rise to violent Sikh ethnonationalism from 1978 to 1984. These chapters develop the argument that *violent subnationalist movements arise when competing ethnic and state elites cannot resolve their political differences and ethnic militants emerge often, but not always, facilitated by either traditional ethnic elites or state elites to use in their respective intra-system struggles or against each other.* Chapter 3 focuses on the period from 1978 to 1981. During this period, radicals within the main Sikh political party—the Akali Dal—began challenging the leadership of the dominant moderates, and Sikh extremist groups and leaders also emerged, partially supported by the Congress (I) in its attempt to weaken the Akali Dal. The political relationship between the Akali Dal and the central government also changed from being cooperative to becoming competitive after the disintegration of the Janata coalition and the Congress (I)'s coming into power, thus setting the stage for potential ethnic group–state conflict. After going out of power, the traditional Akali leadership split and individual Akali leaders began engaging in competitive "ethnic-flanking," often allying with the extremists in their intra-system struggles against each other. Chapter 4 analyzes the period from 1981 to 1983 during which the Akali Dal launched a massive agitation against the central government demanding increased autonomy for Punjab. During these years, continuing factionalism within the traditional Akali leadership greatly enhanced the power of extremists in Sikh politics. In addition, competing Congress (I) leaders also aided and abetted Sikh extremists in their attempt to undermine each other in their own intra-party struggles in Punjab. In essence, Sikh extremists were used as allies or pawns by both internally-competing Akali and Congress (I) leaders in their respective intra-party struggles, and also by both the Akali Dal and the Congress (I) in their bitter political confrontation against each other. As a result, the extremists quickly emerged as a powerful political force in Sikh politics. Chapter 5 examines the period from 1983 to 1984. During this period, the traditional Akali leaders and the central government were unable to resolve their political impasse, and the extremist Sikh leadership rose to a position of dominance within the community. The central state—with the possible acquiescence of the traditional Akali leadership—responded to the ascendance of the extremists/militants and the emergence of armed insurgency by ordering the Indian Army to storm the Sikhs' holiest shrine, the Golden Temple complex, to root-out Sikh extremists/militants in Operation Bluestar. This military action alienated Sikhs throughout India and the world.

Chapters 6 through 9 analyze the re-escalation and sustenance of the violent Sikh ethnonationalist movement from 1984 to 1992. An examination of this period develops the argument that *in the absence of a negotiated settlement, violent subnationalist movements persist when ethnic militants remain "united" and retain a viable political front, while state elites become internally-divided and fractionalized traditional ethnic elites engage in competitive "ethnic-outflanking."* Chapter 6 analyzes the immediate post-Bluestar period from 1984 to 1986 during which the central state and the traditional Akali leadership sought to negotiate a settlement to their enduring political impasse after the supposed "elimination" of the extremists/militants. A political compromise was formulated and a moderate Akali government voted into power in Punjab, but the central government eventually proved unwilling or unable to implement key provisions of the accord. This weakened the Sikh moderates and strengthened the surviving extremists, who subsequently began challenging the traditional Akalis for community leadership. Chapter 7 examines the period from 1986 to 1988. During this period, the violent Sikh ethnonationalist movement became resurrected after Sikh extremists reorganized, armed Sikh militant groups emerged, and the traditional Akali leadership fractionalized into two competing blocs. The emerging militants also officially declared the launching of an armed separatist struggle for the creation of Khalistan, and a section of the divided Akali leadership aligned with the extremists and militants against fellow Akalis, thus further reinvigorating the conflict. Chapter 8 analyzes the period from 1988 to 1990. During this period, internally-divided state elites failed to implement coherent political initiatives to curtail the rise of violent Sikh ethnonationalism, and the largely united militants and extremists once again became dominant in Sikh politics over the divided Akali leadership. Levels of political violence also rose markedly. Towards the end of this period, extremist-led and militant-supported candidates swept parliamentary elections in Punjab giving the impression that the state was lost from the Indian Union. Chapter 9 examines the period from 1990 to 1992. During these critical and complex years, multifaceted factionalism within the ranks of both the extremists and the militants emerged and escalated for the first time in the post-1984 period. A schism between the armed militants and their political front—the extremists—also began to develop as the militants, although internally-divided themselves, became collectively dominant over all other groups within Sikh politics.

Chapters 10 and 11 analyze the decline of the violent Sikh eth-nonationalist movement and explain the eventual return of political "normalcy" to both Sikh and Punjab politics. These chapters develop the argument that *in the absence of a negotiated settlement or complete military victory, violent subnationalist movements decline when ethnic militants "fractionalize" and lose a viable political front, and unified state elites pursue coordinated policies prompting traditional ethnic elites to unite, moderate, and re-enter the "normal" political process.* Chapter 10 examines the period from 1992 to 1993. During this period, the armed militants became weakened as a result of effective state repression, internal disunity, and their schism with the extremists. The governmental leadership also united and concurrently implemented policies to systematically restart the democratic political process at the local and state levels in Punjab. This prompted all sections of the traditional Akali leadership, and even the extremists, to cautiously start re-entering more "normal" modes of politics to avoid being politically marginalized. They also began breaking free from the militants to whom they had become subservient, and the violent Sikh ethnonationalist movement began to subside. Chapter 11 examines the period from 1993 to 1997. During this period, the militants were routed and unified state authorities continued to reinvigorate the "normal" democratic political process in the state. The crippling of the militants and the reemergence of competitive political activity prompted the divided traditional Akali leadership to gradually unite, moderate, and completely re-enter "normal" modes of politics in the state. The united and moderated traditional Akali leadership also emerged clearly dominant over the extremists within internal Sikh politics, and "normalcy" returned to Punjab and Sikh politics after nearly 20 years of political strife and violence, thus ending the "Punjab crisis".

Finally, the last chapter of this book—Chapter 12—summarizes how each of the book's three main conceptual arguments emerged through an in-depth, microhistorical analysis of the rise, sustenance, and fall of the violent Sikh ethnonationalist movement. It also explains the continuing maintenance of peace in Punjab by briefly analyzing the predominant "patterns of political leadership" in the post-militancy era of 1997 to the present. This chapter concludes by applying the book's central arguments to help explain the comparative trajectories of the ethnonationalist insurgencies in Chechnya, Northern Ireland, Kashmir and Assam, and offers final insights into the overall importance of "patterns of political leadership" on ethnonationalist movements.

NOTES

1. Cited in J.S. Grewal, *The Sikhs of the Punjab* (New Delhi: Cambridge University Press, 1994), 209.
2. Gurharpal Singh, *Ethnic Conflict in India: A Case-Study of Punjab* (New York: St. Martin's Press, 2000), 205.

3. Calculated by adding up figures presented in Manoj Joshi, "Combating Terrorism in Punjab: Indian Democracy in Crisis," in *Rivalry and Revolution in South and East Asia,* ed. Partha S. Ghosh (Brookfield, VT: Ashgate Publishing, 1997), 198.

4. This is not to suggest that other variables, such as socio-economic or other political ones, are not important, but that, *ceteris paribus,* changing "patterns of political leadership" have a significant impact on the trajectory of ethnonationalist movements and thus deserve to be theorized in their own right.

5. These five general categories of explanations are offered by Gurharpal Singh, "Understanding the 'Punjab Problem'," *Asian Survey* 27, no.12 (December 1987): 1268–77.

6. See Murray J. Leaf, "The Punjab Crisis," *Asian Survey* 25:5 (May 1985): 478–98; and Hamish Teleford, "The Political Economy of Punjab: Creating Space for Sikh Militancy," *Asian Survey* 32, no.11 (November 1992): 969–87.

7. For example, see Sucha Singh Gill and K.C. Singhal, "The Punjab Problem: Its Historical Roots," *Economic and Political Weekly* 19, no.14 (April 7, 1984): 603–08.

8. The best example in this vein of literature is Paul R. Brass, "The Punjab Crisis and the Unity of India," in *India's Democracy: An Analysis of Changing State-Society Relations,* ed. Atul Kohli (Princeton: Princeton University Press, 1988), 169–213.

9. An example is Balraj Madhok, *Punjab Problem: The Muslim Connection* (New Delhi: Hindu World Publications, 1985).

10. Joyce Pettigrew, "Take Not Arms Against Thy Sovereign," *South Asia Research* 4:2 (November 1984): 102–23.

11. Gurharpal Singh, "Punjab Since 1984: Disorder, Order, and Legitimacy," *Asian Survey* 36, no.4 (April 1996): 410–21. It should be noted that Gurharpal Singh subsequently forwarded another explanation for the demise of the "Punjab crisis" in which he credits the Indian state's shift from "hegemonic control" to "violent control" for effectively crushing the Sikh ethnonationalist movement. For details see Gurharpal Singh, *Ethnic Conflict in India: A Case-Study of Punjab* (New York: St. Martin's Press, 2000). While a fascinating conceptualization, I find this explanation to be largely descriptive and an inadequate substitute for a detailed micro-historical analysis of the period in question.

12. For example, see K.P.S. Gill, "Endgame in Punjab: 1988–93," in *Terror and Containment: Perspectives of India's Internal Security,* ed. K.P.S. Gill (New Delhi: Gyan Publishing House), 23–84.

13. Joyce Pettigrew, *The Sikhs of the Punjab: Unheard Voices of State and Guerilla Violence* (London: Zed Books, 1995).

14. To his credit, Brass examines both intra-Akali and intra-governmental elite politics in the pre-1984 period in his "The Punjab Crisis" chapter. Yet, he does not extend his analysis into the post-1984 period, nor does he examine the politics internal to extremist groups in either the pre- or post-Bluestar period.

15. The concept of "ethnic outbidding" was first formulated in Alvin Rabushka and Kenneth Shepsle, *Politics in Plural Societies: A Theory of Democratic Instability* (Columbus, OH: Charles E. Merrill Publishing, 1972).

16. Atul Kohli, "Can Democracies Accommodate Ethnic Nationalism? Rise and Decline of Self-Determination Movements in India," *The Journal of Asian Studies* 56, no.2 (May 1997): 325–44.

17. Ashutosh Varshney, "Nationalism, Ethnic Conflict, and Rationality," *Perspectives on Politics* 1, no. 1 (March 2003): 85–99.

18. Subrata K. Mitra, "The Rational Politics of Cultural Nationalism: Subnational Movements of South Asia in a Comparative Perspective," *British Journal of Political Science* 25, no.1 (January 1995): 57–77.
19. Doug McAdam, *Political Process and the Development of Black Insurgency, 1930–1970* (Chicago: University of Chicago Press, 1982).
20. These four categories are found in Michael E. Brown, "The Causes of Internal Conflict: An Overview," in *Nationalism and Ethnic Conflict,* eds, Michael E. Brown, Owen R. Cote Jr., Sean M. Lynn-Jones and Steven E. Miller (Cambridge, MA: The MIT Press, 1997), 5.
21. For example, see Gerald B. Helman and Steven R. Ratner, "Saving Failed States," *Foreign Policy* 89 (Winter 1992–1993), 3–20; and Barry R. Posen, "The Security Dilemma and Ethnic Conflict," *Survival,* 35, no.1 (Spring 1993), 27–47.
22. Brown, "The Causes of Internal Conflict," 8.
23. Ibid.: 11.
24. For example, see Benedict Anderson, *Imagined Communities: Reflections on the Origin and Spread of Nationalism* (London: Verso, 1983). Also see Saul Newman, "Does Modernization Breed Ethnic Political Conflict?" *World Politics* 43, no.3 (April 1991), 451–78 for an overview of this literature.
25. Brown, "The Causes of Internal Conflict," 12–13
26. Bard E. O'Neill, "Insurgency: A Framework for Analysis," in *Insurgency in the Modern,* eds, Bard E. O'Neill, William R. Heaton, and Donald J. Alberts (Boulder, CO.: Westview Press, 1980), 1–26.
27. John R. Wood, "Secession: A Comparative Analytical Framework," *Canadian Journal of Political Science* 14, no.1 (March 1981): 107–34. Also see, Syed Serajul Islam, "The Islamic Independence Movements in Patani of Thailand and Mindanao of the Philippines," *Asian Survey* 38, no.5 (May 1998): 441–56.
28. Eric A. Nordlinger, *Conflict Regulation in Divided Societies* (Cambridge, MA: Center for International Affairs-Harvard University, 1972), 20–33.
29. Examples of works in the rational-choice framework include Albert Breton, Gianluigi Galeotti, Pierre Salmon and Ronald Wintrobe (eds), *Nationalism and Rationality* (Cambridge: Cambridge University Press, 1995); and Samuel L. Popkin, *The Rational Peasant: The Political Economy of Rural Society in Vietnam* (Berkeley: University of California Press, 1979); The social constructivist perspective is contained in Aldon D. Morris and Carol McClurg Mueller, eds, *Frontiers in Social Movement Theory* (New Haven: Yale University Press, 1992).
30. For example, see Paul R. Brass, "Ethnic Groups and Ethnic Identity Formation," in *Ethnicity and Nationalism: Theory and Comparison,* ed. Paul R. Brass (New Delhi: Sage Publications, 1991), 18–40.
31. Brown, "The Causes of Internal Conflict," 17.
32. James D. Fearon and David D. Laitin, "Violence and the Social Construction of Ethnic Identity," *International Organization* 54, no.4 (Autumn 2000): 846.
33. Ibid.
34. For a discussion of "process-tracing," see Alexander L. George and Timothy J. McKeown, "Case Studies and Theories of Organizational Decision Making," in *Advances in Information Processing in Organizations,* Volume 2, eds Robert F. Coulam and Richard A. Smith (Greenwich, CT: JAI Press, 1985), 21–58.
35. Robert H. Bates, Avner Greif, Margaret Levi, Jean-Laurent Rosenthal and Barry Weingast, *Analytic Narratives* (Princeton: Princeton University Press, 1998), 12.
36. Ibid.: 10.

2

Sikh Ethnic Identity and Early Post-Independence Politics in Punjab

The Political Institutionalization and Symbolic Content of Sikh Ethnic Identity

Sikhs today view Guru Nanak (1465–1539) as being the founder of their religion, a prophet with a divine revelation. Historians generally agree that Nanak was influenced by the *bhakti* (devotion) movement in north india that criticized the religious leadership and many of the beliefs of both Hinduism and Islam of the contemporary times. A new religion eventually emerged from his teachings and also from the teachings of his successors. Nanak's main beliefs included the belief in a single God, the equality of mankind, a repudiation of the caste system, and rejection of idol worship. Through the succession of nine other *gurus* (religious teachers) over two centuries, what is now called Sikhism took a more distinct form.[1] This process involved the establishment of a separate religious script (Gurmukhi), a separate religious text (the *Adi Granth* or the *Granth Sahib*) embodying the teachings of the Sikh *gurus* and other saints, and the emergence of separate religious and cultural rituals.

A particular form of Sikh ethnic identity was codified by the 10th Sikh *guru*, Gobind Singh, on the *Baisakhi* Day in April 1699. At a large gathering at Anandpur, Gobind Singh initiated the order of the Khalsa. He instructed all Sikhs to become baptized through a new ceremony called *khande ki pahul*. After being baptized, all adherents to the Khalsa order were required to keep five religious symbols, the five "K's".[2] These are *kesh* (unshorn hair), *kirpan* (a ceremonial dagger), *kara* (a steel bracelet), *kacchara* (a military-style underpant), and *kanga* (a wooden comb). Baptized Sikh males were instructed to carry the last name *Singh* (lion) and baptized females the name *Kaur* (lioness or princess). This gave the Khalsa Sikhs a distinct ethnic or religious identity.

Yet, Sikh identity is somewhat paradoxical. On one hand, "of all the ethnic groups and peoples of the north, the Sikhs come the closest to satisfying the definition of a nationality or nation."[3] This is because Punjabi-speaking Sikhs are a people with a largely distinct religion, who have managed to acquire a high degree of internal social and political cohesion and subjective self-awareness (sense of "peoplehood"). On the other hand, "though there is a strong solidary core to contemporary Sikh nationality, the boundaries of the Sikh people remain flexible and uncertain."[4] In addition to unclear boundaries between the Sikhs and other religious groups, Sikh identity is also complicated by the existence of cross-cutting cleavages, including caste, class, and partisan affiliation. This is further complicated by the existence of overarching identities such as the regional "Punjabi" identity or the national "Indian" identity. These cross-cutting cleavages and overarching identities often moderate a reified construction of Sikh ethnic identity.

Even though Sikh theology does not subscribe to the existence of caste, four major sociological caste categories—the Jats, the merchant and trading castes, the intermediate artisan castes, and the lower castes—still exist within the Sikh society in Punjab.[5] The traditionally agriculturalist Jat caste is considered to be the most dominant in the Sikh society, and *they* are assumed to be about one-half to two-thirds of the total Sikh population.[6] Another category comprises the urban merchant and trading castes such as the Aroras and Khatris, who often consider themselves superior to the rural Jats. The artisan castes, including the Tarkans, Lohars, Kambos, Malis, and Sainis, form the intermediate castes. On the lowest strata, there are the Chuhras and Chamars, also known as the Mazhabis and Adharmis, who form a vast majority of the so-called official "Scheduled Castes".[7]

At its most basic level, Sikh religious identity consists of four different categories—*amritdhari Khalsa* Sikhs, *keshdhari* Sikhs, *sahajdhari* Sikhs, and various "Hindu-Sikh" sects.[8] At the central core of Sikh religious identity, there are the *amritdhari Khalsa* Sikhs who have taken *amrit* (the baptismal nectar) and wear the five K's. *Amritdhari* Sikhs comprise only a small portion of the total Sikh population. Moving away from this solidary core, there are *keshdhari* Sikhs who have not taken *amrit* but still keep unshorn hair. *Keshdhari* Sikhs, according to one estimate, constitute anywhere from two-thirds to three-quarters of the Sikh population in India.[9] Moving even further from the core of Sikh religious identity, there are the *sahajdhari* Sikhs. The term *sahajdhari* translated literally means "those who take the slow path." *Sahajdhari* Sikhs do not keep unshorn hair but most identify exclusively with the Sikh religion. At the outer edges of Sikh religious identity, there are a variety of Hindu-Sikh sects such as the Nanakpanthis or new reformist sects such as Radha Swamis and Nirankaris. Many orthodox Sikhs consider these sects as being "hetrodoxical," and their status in Sikhism is questionable.

Political Institutionalization of Sikh Identity

While the Khalsa model has long been at the core of Sikh ethnic identity, its institutionalization as the clearly dominant construction of Sikh identity has evolved over time, including during the 19th and the 20th centuries. After the British annexation of Maharaja Ranjit Singh's kingdom in 1848, the main Sikh political organizations in Punjab were the Singh Sabhas and the Chief Khalsa Diwan. The Singh Sabhas were originally formed in the 1870s, and the Chief Khalsa Diwan was created in 1902 to serve as an umbrella organization for the Singh Sabhas. These organizations performed three main functions—promoting the Khalsa Sikh identity through schools and publications, countering the proselytizing efforts of both Christian missionaries and Hindu organizations such as the Arya Samaj, and representing Sikh political interests to the British Crown while remaining loyal to Her Majesty.[10]

This loyalty to the Crown eventually became questioned during the early-1920s as a result of the Gurdwara Reform Movement. This movement started when Khalsa Sikhs demanded control of historical Sikh shrines that were being managed by "Hinduized" *mahants* (custodians). The *mahants* were accused of introducing Hindu practices into the Sikh religion, including idol worship and barring members of the lower castes from entering Sikh temples. After British authorities upheld the legal right of the *mahants* to control the shrines, Khalsa Sikhs began to forcibly capture and occupy them. Two important Sikh institutions and organizations emerged from the Gurdwara Reform Movement that further institutionalized the Khalsa Sikh identity—the Shiromani Gurdwara Prabandhak Committee (SGPC) and the Akali Dal political party.

The SGPC was originally created in November 1920 to be a representative Sikh body to manage the newly-captured Sikh shrines. The Akali Dal formally came into being a month later to coordinate the activities of bands of Khalsa Sikh volunteers (called the *akalis* or immortals) who captured these shrines. The SGPC eventually received official recognition in November 1925 from the British authorities with the signing of the Sikh Gurdwaras Act. The SGPC and Akali Dal even today form the central core of the modern "Sikh political system" in Punjab.[11]

The SGPC is a corporate body with 175 members, out of which 140 are directly elected in popular elections from an exclusively Sikh electorate every five years.[12] In addition, there is a 15-member executive committee led by the president of the SGPC, who is elected annually by the general house. All adult Sikhs who are not "apostate" can vote in these elections, but all members of the SGPC's general house must be *amritdharis*.[13] This protects the institution from interference of "non-Sikhs". The SGPC has either direct or indirect jurisdiction over all "historical" Sikh *gurdwaras* (temples) in Punjab and even some *gurdwaras* in other north Indian states as well. Its primary source of income is the daily offerings given by devotees to *gurdwaras* estimated to be Rs 600 million in 1993, up from only Rs 9.5 million in 1966.[14] This money is used for a variety of purposes, including the maintenance of the Sikh shrines and propagating the Sikh religion.

The SGPC is considered to be "the largest and the most important non-government bureaucratic organization in Punjab and the pre-eminent institution in the Sikh community."[15] It is a permanent, legally-sanctioned institution, which has been described as being a "mini-Parliament of the Sikhs"[16] or even a "state within a state".[17] Since the SGPC is a representative institution, the Akali faction which gains a majority within the SGPC general house is considered to be the premier leadership of the Sikh community in Punjab. It also provides the dominant Akali faction with a source of funding and access to its huge networks of Sikh shrines for political campaigning.

While the SGPC is the main forum for internal Sikh politics, the Akali Dal political party represents Sikh interests in the secular democratic political systems of Punjab and India. Three main features underpin the Akali Dal's ideology. First, the Akali Dal views religion and politics as being inseparable, and espouses the notion that Sikhs should act as a separate and unified political entity.[18] Second, the Akali Dal beholds the goal of "creating such an environment, wherein the manifestation of national aspirations and nationality of the Sikh Panth may find complete realization".[19] Third, the Akali Dal espouses an ideology of "regionalism" by which it represents the interests of the state of Punjab and supports the decentralization of power from the center to the states.[20] Since the Akali Dal competes in the "secular" and democratic political systems of Punjab and India, it is compelled to moderate its purely ethnic message and, instead, also appeal to the various "producer classes" in Punjab, especially large and middle-range farmers who form an influential part of the Sikh population.[21]

In addition to the SGPC and Akali Dal, another important Sikh political institution is the Akal Takht ("immortal throne"). The Akal Takht is a shrine located in the Golden Temple complex in the city of Amritsar. The Akal Takht is considered to be the "primary seat of Sikh religious authority and the central altar for Sikh political assembly".[22] Its religious authority and significance in Sikh political affairs emanates from the popular Sikh tradition which teaches that the sixth Sikh *guru*, Hargobind, wore two swords—one representing *miri* (spiritual authority) and the other representing *piri* (temporal power)—when ordering the construction of the Akal Takht.[23] Thus, the Akal Takht represents the synthesis of spiritual authority and temporal power for the Sikh community. The Akal Takht's authority is exerted through its *jathedar* (head of the shrine), who can issue a *hukamnama* (edict) to provide guidance or clarification on religious and, sometimes, political matters.[24] The Akal Takht's role in politics has been significant in various periods of Sikh history without a clearly dominant Sikh leader—including during the "*misl* period" (1708–1769)—but very limited at most other times.[25] Since the early-1920s, the Akal Takht has come under the purview of the SGPC which is empowered to appoint the Akal Takht *jathedar*.[26]

A fourth source of leadership and authority within the Sikh community are the numerous Sikh civic and religious organizations and institutions that exist throughout Punjab. These include Sikh study circles, various *Nihang* (a Khalsa sub-sect) orders, historical Sikh seminaries, and the *deras* (headquarters) of various Sikh saints who tend to have significant religious and political influence in their respective locales. The SGPC often consults with these various Sikh civic and religious organizations and institutions on religious matters, and sometimes tries to use them to disseminate the SGPC's religious and political messages. In turn, these various Sikh civic and religious organizations and institutions often influence the decisions made by the SGPC and the Akali Dal through informal channels.

Symbolic Content of Sikh Ethnic Indentity

Sikhs have acquired "a high degree of internal social and political cohesion and subjective self-awareness."[27] This high degree of subjective self-awareness (sense of "peoplehood") has been important for the Akali Dal in mobilizing large sections of the Sikh community. Three sets of religious or ethnic symbols have been particularly important in the development of Sikh communal consciousness—the symbols derived from Sikh history, including from the Sikh kingdoms before the British annexation of Punjab, the religious symbols used to differentiate between Sikhs and Hindus, and the resonance of the Punjabi language written in the Gurmukhi script.[28]

Sikh history, as disseminated by the SGPC and popular historians, is replete with warriors and "martyrs" who purportedly gave their lives defending the Sikh religion and the cause of "righteousness". Several of the Sikh *gurus* and many of their followers were, in fact, heroically "martyred" during the "*guru* period" and beyond.[29] British historians also contributed to this consciousness-building after the annexation of Punjab by describing the Sikh people as being a unified nation and a brave martial race.[30] Maharaja Ranjit Singh's 19th century kingdom has given modern Sikh leaders a particularly salient pool of historical ethnic symbols from which to draw, including the notion of Sikhs being an exceptionally courageous fighting force that once controlled a vast empire in north India. Yet, Sikh political elites ironically avoid alluding to historical dynamics that dilute this conception of a unified, courageous nation, including factionalism and internecine violence within Sikhs throughout their history.[31]

Second, the processes of "boundary definition and boundary maintenance" in relation to the Hindu community have also contributed to the consolidation of internal Sikh solidarity.[32] Sikhism is partially an outgrowth of Hinduism and, through the 1880s, intermarriage between Sikhs and Hindus was common. Thus, boundaries between the two religious "communities" were quite permeable and, in fact, often overlapped. The historical tendency for differentiation became more pronounced in the late 19th and early 20th centuries with the rise of aggressive communally-based associations such as the Punjab Hindu Sabha, the Punjab Muslim League, and the Chief Khalsa Diwan.[33] Sikh fears of reabsorption into the Hindu fold were exacerbated when Hindu political organizations opposed the Gurdwara Reform Movement and engaged in *shuddi* (repurification) campaigns in which scheduled castes Sikhs were convinced to publicly discard their Sikh symbols and rejoin the Hindu faith.[34] Since then, there has been a constant fear amongst Sikhs of being reabsorbed into Hinduism. This has led to the perceived need to reaffirm the uniqueness of Sikh ethnic identity, and the status of Sikhs as a separate social and political collectivity in India.

Third, the Punjabi language written in the Gurmukhi script has been an important symbol in the development of Sikh communal consciousness.

The "language controversy" in colonial Punjab began in the late 19th century when urban Hindus demanded that both English and Urdu in the Persian script should be replaced with Hindi in the Devanagri script as the official language in schools and for governmental administration.[35] Hindu communal organizations viewed Urdu as being a foreign language imposed on them by Muslim invaders several centuries ago. This controversy turned into a three-way split between Muslim, Hindu, and Sikh political elites. For their part, Sikh political organizations demanded equal status for Punjabi in the Gurmukhi script if Urdu was discarded in favor of Hindi. A part of this controversy ended with the partition of the province in 1947 and the creation of Pakistan, but this still left the controversy between Punjabi in the Gurmukhi script and Hindi in the Devanagri script unresolved in post-Independence India. The fact that Sikh religious scriptures were written in the Gurmukhi script made it an especially salient symbol for Sikhs, while many Hindus viewed Hindi in the Devanagri script as being the central core of a post-Independence "Indian" identity.

THE STRUCTURE OF SIKH POLITICS

Sikh politics in Punjab has five major focal points of power or influence. At the core of the "Sikh political system" are the SGPC and the Akali Dal political party. Factionalism within this institutionalized "Sikh political system" revolves around three separate wings—the presidentship of the SGPC (the temple system), the presidentship of the Akali Dal political party (organizational wing), and leadership of Akali legislators in the state legislative assembly (the ministerial or legislative wing). The Akal Takht *jathedar* is a fourth potential focal point of power in the wider "Sikh political system". Lastly, various Sikh civic and religious groups and organizations also often have significant influence on Sikh politics, even though they are not institutionally a part of the "Sikh political system".

This "Sikh political system" is contained within two broader "secular" political systems. The first is the state-level Punjab political system which includes a number of political parties competing for seats in the Punjab legislative assembly, called the *Vidhan Sabha*. Major political parties in Punjab include the bi-communal and "catch-all" Congress party, the Sikh-based Akali Dal, the Hindu-nationalist Bharatiya Janata Party (BJP, previously known as the Jan Sangh), the two communist parties, and other minor political parties, including the scheduled-caste-based Bahujan Samaj Party (BSP). Both the "Sikh political system" and Punjab's "secular" political system are further contained within the national political system of India, which includes numerous national and regional political parties who compete to win seats in the national parliament called the *Lok Sabha* and form the government in the center. Thus, the relational structure of Sikh politics, the political system of Punjab, and the national Indian political system can be conceptualized as three concentric circles as exemplified in Figure 2.1.

Figure 2.1
Sikh Political System in Relation to Punjab and Indian Politics

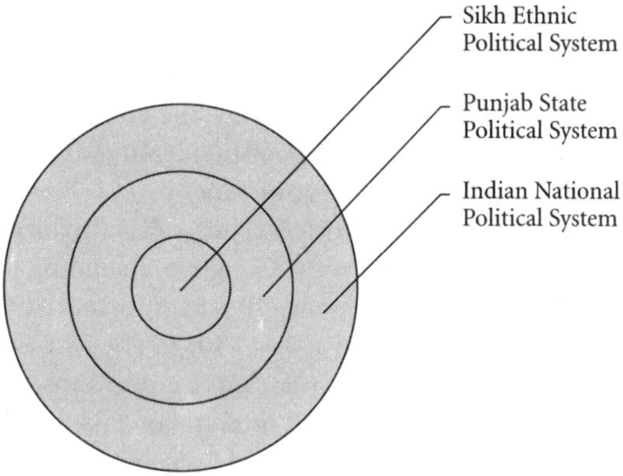

Sikh Ethnic
Political System

Punjab State
Political System

Indian National
Political System

Source: Author.

OVERVIEW OF POST-INDEPENDENCE POLITICS IN PUNJAB (1947–1978)

At the onset of Independence in August 1947, the Sikh community found itself living in secular, democratic India. Before Independence, the composition of religious "communities" in the colonial province of Punjab was about 61 percent Muslim, 26 percent Hindu, and 13 percent Sikh.[36] After Independence and Partition, the population of Indian Punjab became approximately 61 percent Hindu and 35 percent Sikh, with almost the entire Muslim population going to Pakistan.[37] Unlike during British rule, there were no separate communal electorates or reservation of seats for Sikhs in the elected political bodies of independent India. Such arrangements had been instrumental in reaffirming Sikh ethnic identity and providing Sikhs with significant group power in the political process during the British Raj. Thus, the status of ethnic minorities in a Hindu-majority India took on special significance for Sikh leaders in the immediate post-Independence period.

The Akali Dal had two main political goals after Independence—one proximate and the other more long-term. The Akali Dal's immediate goal was to extract maximum protections and benefits for the Sikh community from the central government, and its eventual goal was to try to form a Sikh-majority state in north India. For achieving its immediate goal, the Akali Dal initially adopted an "infiltrational" strategy, whereas an "agitational" approach was preferred for its long-term goal.[38] Regarding the former, the premier Sikh leader, Master Tara Singh, strategically placed Akali legislators into Punjab's Congress party, which was afflicted with bi-factionalism at the time. This allowed the Akali Dal to hold the balance of power between the two competing Congress factions, thus maximizing its leverage and influence. A portion of the Akali Dal also periodically "merged" with the Congress, while another portion of the party strategically maintained its independent identity to continue to press for Sikh demands from outside the government.

This strategy initially worked very well. The Akali Dal managed to extract several political concessions from the Congress, including the "services formula," the "parity formula," and, most importantly, the "Sachar Formula" during the period from 1947 to 1951. The first established an undisclosed proportion of government service positions for Sikhs, the second guaranteed an equal number of seats for Sikhs and Hindus in the state ministry, and the third demarcated Punjab into separate Punjabi-speaking and Hindi-speaking areas in which their respective language was to be the medium for education up to high school and the other would be taught after the fourth grade.[39] Hindu-based organizations such as the Arya Samaj opposed all of these concessions to the Akali Dal.

These concessions aside, the Akali Dal performed "poorly" in the 1952 state assembly elections, winning only 13 out of 126 seats in contrast to the Congress which won 98 seats.[40] For the Akali Dal, this mediocre performance reinforced that it needed a smaller, Sikh-majority state if it wanted to compete effectively with the Congress in electoral politics and ever form the state government in Punjab. For this reason, the Akali Dal reverted to an "agitational strategy" in May 1955 and launched a *morcha* (agitation) for the creation of a Punjabi-speaking state, which it hoped would also contain a larger Sikh population. Tens of thousands of Akali workers courted arrest in this *morcha*, but the States Reorganization Commission still rejected the demand for the *Punjabi Suba*.[41]

Nonetheless, the high levels of political mobilization demonstrated popular Sikh support for the Akali Dal's demands, thus prompting the Congress party's chief minister of Punjab, Pratap Singh Kairon, to offer concessions to the Akali Dal in the form of the "Regional Formula". The Regional Formula merged some Sikh-majority areas into Punjab, and purposely excluded Hindu-majority areas, thus resulting in a slightly increased Sikh population in the state.[42] It also divided the state into separate Punjabi-speaking and Hindi-speaking regions with two separate committees in the legislature. The Regional Formula mandated that legislation would have to be approved by both of the two regional committees and, in case of a disagreement, the Governor's decision would be final and binding. After this political compromise, a section of the Akali leadership once again "infiltrated" or merged into the Congress party, and Kairon reciprocated by inducting several Akali legislators into his ministry. This gave Kairon's Congress ministry the appearance of being a "Panthic" (Sikh) government.

Yet, the Regional Formula failed to solve the communal problem in Punjab. Hindu nationalist organizations such as the Hindi Raksha Samiti, the Jan Sangh, and the Arya Samaj reacted sharply to Kairon's concessions to the Akalis, and started the "Save Hindi" agitation demanding that compulsory teaching of any language be stopped.[43] This agitation ended without any official concessions, but Kairon did begin informally slowing-down implementation of the Regional Formula in his attempt to maintain Hindu support in the state. This angered Master Tara Singh who launched a new *morcha* for the *Punjabi Suba* in 1960 in which about 60,000 Akalis courted arrest, but the government still refused to relent.[44]

The Akali Dal once again polled "poorly" in the February 1962 general elections, winning only 19 seats in comparison to the Congress which won 90 seats.[45] After these elections, Master Tara Singh's repeated inability to force the central government to concede to the *Punjabi Suba* took its toll on his reputation, and Sant Fateh Singh and other Sikh leaders rebelled against his leadership, forming their own separate Akali party. Thus, the Akali Dal split into two factions—the Akali Dal (Sant) and the Akali Dal (Master). It was suspected that Kairon and the Congress party engineered this split in their attempt to bolster the more moderate Sant Fateh Singh over Master Tara Singh.[46] After all, Sant Fateh Singh emphasized that the *Punjabi Suba* demand was purely a linguistic one, in contrast to Master Tara Singh who publicly admitted that it was designed to create a Sikh-majority state. The latter conception was against Nehru's stated principle of "secularism."

The Sant faction narrowly gained control of the SGPC in 1962, thus making it the most dominant Akali faction (or party) in Punjab.[47] Over the next two years, Sant Fateh Singh further consolidated his position as the premier Sikh leader over Master Tara Singh, and subsequently announced that he would lead a new agitation for the creation of the *Punjabi Suba* if the central government failed to accede to this demand.[48] On the eve of the proposed agitation, the Indo-Pakistan war broke out in September 1965 and the Akali Dal postponed its plans in order to fully cooperate in the nation's war effort against Pakistan. The patriotic role played by the Akali Dal and Sikhs during this war helped to reaffirm their nationalist credentials and loyalty to India. After the war ended, the Congress central government endorsed a plan to allow Punjab to be bifurcated into two states and, in essence, conceded to the creation of the *Punjabi Suba*. Leaders in the Hindu-majority Haryana region of Punjab also agreed to this bifurcation for their own partisan political reasons. Nonetheless, the official explanation given by the government for acceding to the Akali Dal's demand was that the *Punjabi Suba* conformed to the same principle of linguistic reorganization under which other states had been reorganized during the 1950s.[49]

The *Punjabi Suba* was officially created in the fall of 1966.[50] Thus, the Akali Dal had finally secured a separate Punjabi-speaking state that also contained a Sikh-majority after nearly 20 years of periodic agitation. The population of the new, truncated Punjab was 60.22 percent Sikh and 37.54 percent Hindu.[51] Yet, the creation of the *Punjabi Suba* did not completely ameliorate tension between the Akali Dal and the central government. The manner in which Punjab was bifurcated created a number of inter-state disputes between Punjab and its neighbors, and also between Punjab and the central government. These disputes included the central government's decision to take control of the Bhakra and Beas dam projects, its decision to give Chandigarh the status of Union Territory instead of granting it to Punjab, and its unwillingness to incorporate certain Punjabi-speaking areas into the state.

In the first state assembly elections after the creation of the *Punjabi Suba*, the Congress won 48 seats, the Akali Dal (Sant) won 24, and the Akali Dal (Master) secured only two seats out of a possible 104.[52] These results demonstrated that the Congress continued to be the dominant party in the state, but that the Akali Dal's political competitiveness had increased in the truncated, Sikh-majority Punjab. In fact, these elections marked that, for the first time in post-Independence history, the Congress party failed to secure a majority of seats in the state legislative assembly of Punjab. As a result, the Akali Dal (Sant) and its allies formed the first non-Congress ministry in the state called the "United Front" in 1967. Yet, this government fell within eight months after the Congress engineered the defection of dissident Akali legislators from the ministry.[53] These Akali dissidents subsequently formed a new coalition ministry with outside support from the Congress party, but this ministry also fell in less than a year when the Congress withdrew support in mid-1968.

The fall of two consecutive non-Congress ministries after the formation of the *Punjabi Suba* prompted the Akali Dal (Sant) and the fledgling Akali Dal (Master) to temporarily unite against the Congress party. This unity proved effective when the united Akali Dal won 43 seats, the Congress 38, and the Jan Sangh eight in the February 1969 mid-term elections for the Punjab state assembly.[54] As a result, another United Front ministry was formed between the Akalis and Jan Sangh in Punjab, and this government remained in power for three years.[55] Congress (I) came back into power in 1972 with Giani Zail Singh as chief minister of Punjab as a part of a "Congress wave" that swept India after the nation's spectacular victory over Pakistan under the leadership of prime minister Indira Gandhi during the 1971 Indo-Pakistan war. Sant Fateh Singh clearly remained the dominant leader within Sikh politics until his death in late-1972.

Through the mid-1970s, the Akali Dal continued its largely confrontational relationship with the Congress (I) central government with controversies over the control of Delhi's Sikh *gurdwaras*, the central government's attempt to unilaterally amend the 1925 Sikh Gurdwara Act, and continued tension over lingering inter-state issues. In 1975, Mrs Gandhi imposed a national Emergency under which democratic rule was suspended throughout India. The Akali Dal responded by launching a "Save Democracy" *morcha* which became the nation's only sustained, large-scale agitation against the Emergency.[56] Mrs Gandhi withdrew the Emergency in 1977 and ordered fresh elections, as a result of which a Janata party-led coalition came into power in the center. This was India's first ever non-Congress national government. This Janata-led ruling coalition in the center also included the Akali Dal. For the first time in the post-Independence era, the Akali Dal had a "sympathetic" government in power in the center. In Punjab, the Akali Dal also swept into power in alliance with the Jan Sangh.

Thus, the Akali Dal had become much more competitive with the Congress in Punjab's "secular" political system after the creation of the *Punjabi Suba*, making political competition between the two parties much more consequential and intense. This trend was exemplified by the fact that the Congress formed every state ministry in Punjab after Independence until 1966, but that the Akali Dal and the Congress alternated in and out of power in the state afterwards. Yet, a fundamental transformation had occurred within internal Sikh politics after the passing away of Master Tara Singh and Sant Fateh Singh—two consecutive hegemonic leaders who had reigned over Sikh politics from Independence to the early-1960s and from the early-1960s to the early-1970s, respectively. In contrast, Sikh politics had became deeply-divided by the mid-1970s with different leaders controlling their own separate spheres of power within the "Sikh political system" instead of one clearly dominant or hegemonic leader as was the case previously. Jagdev Singh Talwandi had become president of the Akali Dal and controlled the organizational wing, Gurcharan Singh Tohra dominated the temple wing as SGPC president, and Parkash Singh Badal was the chief minister of Punjab and the leader of the legislative/ministerial wing. Talwandi and Tohra, both of whom did not have to compete in Punjab's secular political system which also included Hindus, tended to be slightly more radical and ethnically-oriented than Badal. The "Sikh political system" at the beginning of 1978 looked like the following (Table 2.1):

Table 2.1
Sikh Political Spectrum (Early-1978)

Moderates	Radicals
Badal[1]	Tohra[1]
	Talwandi[1]

Source: Author.
Note: [1] Akali Dal leaders.

These changing political dynamics—the increased competitiveness of the Akali Dal and Congress in Punjab, and the emerging factionalism within Sikh politics—would contribute to the initial onset of the "Punjab crisis" only a few years later.

NOTES

1. For a detailed discussion of the entire "guru period" in Sikh history, refer to J.S. Grewal, *The Sikhs of the Punjab* (Cambridge: Cambridge University Press, 1990), 23–81.
2. Ibid.: 77–78.
3. Paul R. Brass, *Language, Religion, and Politics in North India* (Cambridge: Cambridge University Press, 1974), 277.
4. Ibid.
5. This categorization is presented in Shinder Purewal, *Sikh Ethnonationalism and the Political Economy of Punjab* (New Delhi: Oxford University Press, 2000), 4.

6. Ibid.: 5; and Jugdep S. Chima, review of *Ethnic Conflict in India: A Case-Study of Punjab*, by Gurharpal Singh, *Commonwealth and Comparative Politics* 39, no. 1 (March 2001), 142.

7. "Scheduled Castes" is an official administrative term used by the government to classify members of the lowest castes for special government benefits. The Scheduled Caste population in Punjab has been described as being a "floating element" in terms of ethnic identity because a significant portion, but not all, of the schedule caste population cannot clearly be demarcated as being either Hindu or Sikh. The schedule caste population in Punjab is estimated to be about 27 percent. See M.S. Dhami, "Religious-Political Mobilisation and Shifts in the Party Support Base in the 1985 Punjab Assembly Elections", in *Political Dynamics and Crisis in Punjab*, eds. Paul Wallace and Surendra Chopra (Amritsar: Guru Nanak Dev University Press, 1988), 381.

8. In contrast, Gurharpal Singh divides Sikh religious identity into four categories: *amritdhari* Sikhs, *keshdhari* Sikhs, *mona* Sikhs, and *sahajdhari* Sikhs. He essentially refers to *sahajdhari* Sikhs as "*mona* (shorn) Sikhs" and refers to adherents of various Hindu-Sikh sects as being "*sahajdharis.*" See Gurharpal Singh, *Ethnic Conflict in India: A Case-Study of Punjab* (New York: St. Martin's Press, 2000), 86.

9. Ibid.

10. These three functions are delineated by Paul Brass in *Language, Religion, and Politics*, 309.

11. The term "Sikh political system" was originally coined by Paul Wallace, "Religious and Secular Politics in Punjab: The Sikh Dilemma in Competing Political Systems", in *Political Dynamics in Punjab*, eds, Paul Wallace and Surendra Chopra (Amritsar: Guru Nanak Dev University Press, 1981), 1–32.

12. Baldev Raj Nayar, *Minority Politics in the Punjab* (Princeton: Princeton University Press, 1966), 177; and Personal interview by the author with Kabul Singh, former president of SGPC and former president of Akali Dal (Longowal), Yuba City, California, USA, 24 July 1995. Hereafter referred to as "Interview with former SGPC and Akali Dal president, 24 July 1995."

13. The definition of "apostate" has changed several times through amendments to the original Gurdwara Act of 1925. Those allowed to vote in SGPC elections have generally included *amritdhari* Sikhs, *keshdhari* Sikhs, and those *sahajdhari* Sikhs who profess that they did not drink alcohol, did not smoke, and accept only the *Guru Granth Sahib* and Sikhism. *The Tribune* (internet edition), 30 March 2001 and Interview with former SGPC and Akali Dal president, 24 July 1995.

14. Gurharpal Singh, *Ethnic Conflict*, 101.

15. Brass, *Language, Religion, and Politics*, 311.

16. Harish K. Puri, "Akali Politics: Emerging Compulsions," in *Political Dynamics and Crisis in Punjab*, eds, Wallace and Chopra (Amritsar: Guru Nanak University Press, 1988), 301.

17. Nayar, *Minority Politics*, 177.

18. Devinder Singh, *Akali Politics in Punjab, 1964–1985* (New Delhi: National Book Organisation, 1993), 45.

19. Quoted in Ibid.: 46. The original citation refers to the party constitution of the Akali Dal.

20. Ibid.: 49.

21. For a "political economy" explanation for the evolution of Sikh ethnic identity see Purewal, *Sikh Ethnonationalism.*

22. Harbans Singh, ed., *The Encyclopaedia of Sikhism*, volume 1 (Patiala: Punjabi University, 1995), 56.
23. J.S. Grewal, *The Sikhs*, 64.
24. Harbans Singh, *The Encyclopaedia*, 57. It is a matter of contention whether the Akal Takht can issue a *hukamnama* without the consent of the four other Sikh Takhts (Takht Sri Kesgarh Sahib, Takht Sri Patna Sahib, Takht Sri Hazur Sahib, and Takht Sri Damdama Sahib).
25. For a history of the Akal Takht's role in both spiritual and temporal affairs refer to Harjinder Singh Dilgeer, *The Akal Takht* (Jullundur: Punjabi Books Company, 1980), 30–34; 60–73.
26. See Ibid.: 60–73.
27. Brass, *Language, Religion, and Politics*, 277.
28. These three sets of symbols have been identified by Brass in Ibid.: 278.
29. Grewal, *The Sikhs*, 72.
30. Refer to Brass, *Language, Religion, and Politics*, 279.
31. Ibid.: 280.
32. Ibid.: 281–82.
33. Ibid.: 283.
34. See Kenneth W. Jones, "Ham Hindu Nahin: Arya-Sikh Relations, 1877–1905," *Journal of Asian Studies* 32:3 (May 1973), 457–75.
35. Brass, *Language, Religion, and Politics*, 288.
36. Rajiv Kapur, *Sikh Separatism: The Politics of Faith* (New Delhi: World Book Centre, 1988), 208 and 232. Kapur cites the Government of India census report of 1941 as the source for these figures.
37. Ibid., Kapur cites the Government of India census report of 1951 as the source for these figures.
38. Nayar has identified three different strategies used by the Akali Dal—the "constitutional strategy" involving contesting elections, the "infiltrational strategy" involving merging with the Congress party to extract maximum benefits from within, and the "agitational strategy" involving launching non-violent movements. See Nayar, *Minority Politics*, 202–05, 212–14, and 234–36.
39. Ibid.: 217–18.
40. Paul Wallace, "Religious and Ethnic Politics: Political Mobilization in Punjab," in *Dominance and State Power in Modern India: Decline of a Social Order*, vol. 2, eds, Francine R. Frankel and M.S.A. Rao (Delhi: Oxford University Press, 1990), 439.
41. Sangat Singh, *The Sikhs in History* (New Delhi: Uncommon Books, 1996), 302.
42. Nayar, *Minority Politics*, 222.
43. Gur Rattan Pal Singh, *The Illustrated History of the Sikhs, 1947–78* (Chandigarh: Akal Printmatics, 1979), 185.
44. S. Singh, *The Sikhs*, 314. Kairon attempted to emasculate Master Tara Singh by having him replaced as president of the SGPC by more moderate elements loyal to Gian Singh Rarewala and Giani Kartar Singh, but this attempt eventually failed. G.R.P. Singh, *The Illustrated History*, 190.
45. Wallace, "Religious and Ethnic Politics," 438.
46. Kuldeep Kaur, *Akali Dal in Punjab Politics: Splits and Mergers* (New Delhi: Deep and Deep Publications, 1999), 35.
47. Grewal, *The Sikhs*, 200.
48. G.R.P. Singh, *The Illustrated History*, 237.

49. Grewal, *The Sikhs*, 204.

50. Ibid.

51. Figures taken from Government of India census report of 1971 as listed in personal document from Paul Wallace entitled "Religious Composition of the Three Punjabs." In contrast, Rajiv Kapur cites the respective figures as being 54 percent Sikh and 44 per cent Hindu, but he does not offer a source or reference for his figures. See Kapur, *Sikh Separatism*, 216.

52. Grewal, *The Sikhs*, 206.

53. S. Singh, *The Sikhs*, 345. Gurnam Singh, generally a Sant Fateh Singh loyalist, was the United Front chief minister. The defectors were led by Lachman Singh Gill, who became the chief minister of the subsequent government.

54. G.R.P. Singh, *The Illustrated History*, 266.

55. For details, see Grewal, *The Sikhs*, 208–09. Gurnam Singh was replaced by Parkash Singh Badal as the Akali chief minister midway through the United Front ministry.

56. This agitation was led by Sant Harchand Singh Longowal since other Akali leaders were arrested by Mrs Gandhi.

PART II

The Emergence of the Sikh Ethnonationalist Movement (1978–1984)

3

Beginnings of Sikh Extremism (1978–1981)

THE NIRANKARI–SIKH CLASH

When the Akali–Janata coalition government was formed in Punjab in June 1977, it appeared that a more permanent Hindu–Sikh political unity had finally been forged in the state. The Akali Dal was a Sikh-based ethnic political party, and the Jan Sangh—the largest constituent member of the Janata in Punjab—was India's premier Hindu nationalist party. Yet, the unity of this coalition and the internal dynamics of Sikh politics were quickly affected by a religious controversy between Sikhs and a "Hindu–Sikh" sect called the "Nirankaris."

The Nirankaris were one of the several reformist or offshoot sects that had emerged from either Hinduism or Sikhism which blurred the boundaries between the two major religions in Punjab. Many orthodox Sikhs considered the Nirankaris, and members of other such "Hindu–Sikh" sects, as being heretical. The Sikhs' belief in one God, a non-living *guru* (religious teacher or prophet), and opposition to idol worship put them into conflict with the Nirankaris whose faith revolved around a living *guru* and his teachings. The Nirankari sect had began in the mid-19th century, and had bifurcated into two wings in the 1930s when a sub-sect emerged which eventually became known as the Sant Nirankari Mission.[1] It is this wing, the Sant Nirankaris, with which the Sikhs clashed on several occasions beginning in the early-1950s.

Tension between Sikhs and Nirankaris escalated when the Nirankari leader, Baba Avtar Singh, proclaimed himself to be the living *sat guru* (true *guru*) in the presence of the *Guru Granth Sahib*, and declared himself to be an "incarnation of Guru Nanak" in his religious text called *Avtar Bani*.[2]

These actions were considered sacrilege by Sikhs. The Sant Nirankaris also adopted many of the rituals and symbols found in Sikhism but with variations considered "heretical" by many Sikhs. For example, the Khalsa Sikh institution of *Panj Pyare* (the Five Beloved) was retained but changed to the *Sat Pyare* (the Seven Beloved) or *Sat Satara* (the Seven Stars).[3] These *Sat Satara* were baptized with *charan amrit*, the baptismal nectar consisting of the water used to wash the feet of the Nirankari *guru*, and not *khanda ki amrit* as dictated by Guru Gobind Singh.[4]

Sikhs also accused the Sant Nirankaris of directly criticizing their religion and *gurus* in their religious texts, the *Avtar Bani* and *Yug Pursh*. For example, Avtar Singh used the allegory of churning butter, and wrote that he had repeatedly churned the *gurbani* (teaching of the *gurus* contained in the *Granth Sahib*) but found that no cream or butter emerged from it.[5] It was also alleged that the Nirankari *guru* at the time, Baba Gurbachan Singh, narrated a story in the *Yug Pursh* about how prophets of all of the world's major religions refused to go back to earth to spread God's true message except for Avtar, who decided to do so only after God agreed that anyone blessed by him would go to heaven irrespective of any worldly deeds.[6] Many Sikhs viewed this as being direct criticism of their *gurus* and religion, and they characterized the Nirankari faith as being *shakmat* (a questionable religion or cult).[7] The Akalis claimed that the Sant Nirankaris were supported by the Congress Party to divide and undermine the Sikh community, and other more militant Sikhs suspected that the Nirankaris were aided and abetted by the Hindu-dominated central government and the urban-based Hindu elite in Punjab to weaken the power of the Khalsa *Panth* (community).[8]

Religious tension between Sikhs and Nirankaris had simmered since the 1950s and 1960s. During these decades, the Damdami Taksal had come to the forefront of countering the growing influence of the Nirankaris in Punjab. The Damdami Taksal, an important Sikh religious seminary, had been created by Guru Gobind Singh in 1706 with the goal of indoctrinating disciples with the "proper teachings" of Sikhism (for example, Khalsa Sikhism) and the *Guru Granth Sahib*. The Taksal was subsequently led by a succession of 12 other *jathedars* (leaders). During the 1970s, the 13th Damdami Taksal *jathedar*, Sant Kartar Singh, had engaged in aggressive proselytizing to bring Sikh youth back into the Khalsa fold, and to wean them away from both communist ideology and the "hetrodoxical" religious teaching of the Nirankaris.

Tension between Sikhs and Nirankaris exploded in a violent way on Baisakhi day (13 April) 1978. On this day, a procession of Sikhs clashed with the Nirankaris during the latter's convention in the Sikh holy city of Amritsar. As a result of this clash, 13 Sikhs were killed by the Nirankari *guru*'s armed bodyguards. Four of the 13 dead belonged to the Damdami Taksal led by Sant Jarnail Singh Bhindranwale, and the remaining nine were members of another Khalsa Sikh organization—the Akhand Kirtani Jatha.[9] This clash gave the Sikhs their first religious "martyrs" of the post-Independence era and offended Sikh religious sensibilities throughout India.

The Nirankari–Sikh clash of April 1978 also had several important political ramifications. First, it put the Akali Dal and especially Punjab's Akali chief minister, Parkash Singh Badal, in a very precarious political situation. On one side, Sikh radicals and large sections of the community demanded immediate governmental action against the Nirankaris. On the other side, the Akali Dal's Hindu-based Janata allies warned the Akalis not to trample on religious freedoms in the state. Second, the Nirankari–Sikh clash gave Sikh radicals within the "Sikh political system," including Akali Dal president Jagdev Singh Talwandi and SGPC president Gurcharan Singh Tohra, a salient issue with which to assert their power at the expense of the comparatively more moderate Badal. Talwandi and Tohra could afford to be, and actually needed to be, more radical because they were responsible to only the Sikh community. In contrast, Badal had to emphasize communal harmony in order to maintain his position as chief minister because he competed in Punjab's secular political system which included both Hindus and Sikhs. Third, the Nirankari–Sikh clash precipitated the emergence of a number of extremist Sikh groups and leaders who would eventually become willing to use violence against the Sikh Panth's perceived enemies, including the Nirankaris.

AKAL TAKHT'S ANTI-NIRANKARI *HUKAMNAMA*

Sikhs reacted to the killing of their co-religionists by holding massive demonstrations, some violent, in both Punjab and Delhi. This outpouring of Sikh resentment and grief compelled the SGPC—which had always claimed to be the main representative of the Sikhs—to coordinate with Akal Takht *jathedar* Sadhu Singh Bhaura, who issued a *hukamnama* (religious edict) from the Akal Takht specifying the community's unified response to the Nirankari challenge.[10] This *hukamnama* described the Nirankaris as being "enemies of dharma (religion) and Sikhism," and directed Sikhs to use "all appropriate means" to prevent the Sant Nirankaris from "grow[ing] and flourish[ing] in society."[11] Specifically, the *hukamnama* asked all Sikhs to sever social ties with the Nirankaris and threatened those who did not do so with religious punishment. *Jathedar* Bhaura clarified the term "by all appropriate means" as being only normal propaganda and religious teachings, but militant Sikhs interpreted the ambiguous wording of the *hukamnama* as being a justification for violence.

The anti-Nirankari *hukamnama* had several important political effects. First, it caused tension between the Janata central government and the Akali Dal. Other political parties in India, including the Akali Dal's Janata allies, criticized the edict for not respecting the constitutional rights of the Nirankaris. In fact, prime minister Morarji Desai met with Nirankari *guru* Gurbachan Singh and assured him of the Nirankaris' right to free speech and practice of their religion.[12] Major Sikh leaders, including Talwandi and Tohra, responded by warning the press and other political parties not to meddle in the "internal affairs" of the Sikhs by commenting on the *hukamnama*, which they described as being "above the Constitution" for Sikhs.[13]

Second, the *hukamnama* strengthened the power of "the radicals" in Sikh politics and intensified factionalism within the Akali Dal. In particular, the organizational wing led by Talwandi and backed by SGPC president Tohra used the Nirankari issue to assert their supremacy over Badal's ministerial wing. Referring to the Nirankari–Sikh clash, Talwandi publicly proclaimed that state power could be sacrificed at the altar of religion.[14] In contrast, Badal tried desperately to avoid the Nirankari controversy and focus on developmental issues in the state in order to maintain the Akali–Janata coalition. Tohra, who was ideologically closer to Talwandi, took a more "middle-of-the-road" approach by accusing the Badal government of inaction, but also stressing the need to remain a part of the Janata coalition in the center. Tohra also played an important mediation role between Talwandi and Badal, thus preventing the party from splitting and also demonstrating his pivotal role as a potential "king-maker" in Sikh politics.

Third, the anti-Nirankari *hukamnama* gave the Sikh extremists an issue with which to exert their influence in Sikh politics and mold the tenor of Sikh political discourse. In particular, Damdami Taksal *jathedar* Sant Jarnail Singh Bhindranwale announced in August 1978 that he would not allow the Nirankaris to hold *satsang*s (religious gatherings) in Punjab. He also demanded that the Government of Punjab ban the Nirankari texts *Avtar Bani* and *Yug Pursh* as an appropriate means of stopping the "growth and flourishing" of Nirankaris as stipulated in the Akal Takht *hukamnama*.[15] This put the Akali Dal in a difficult position with their Janata allies in both Chandigarh and New Delhi. Bhindranwale, being the *jathedar* of the Damdami Taksal, carried significant respect in Khalsa Sikh circles in the Majha countryside, and also in sections of the urban Sikh elite in Delhi, Bombay, and Calcutta where he had visited and preached on several occasions.[16] The Akhand Kirtani Jatha also demanded strict action against the Nirankaris. In order to assuage inflamed Sikh sentiments, Badal's government temporarily banned entry of Nirankari leader Gurbachan Singh into the state and also banned publication of the Nirankaris' main newspaper. The Sikh political spectrum after the Nirankari–Sikh clash looked like the following (Table 3.1):

Table 3.1
Sikh Political Spectrum (Mid-1978)

Moderates	*Radicals*	*Extremists*
Akali Dal[1]	Tohra[1]	Bhindranwale/ Damdami Taksal
Badal[1]	Talwandi[1]	Akhand Kirtani Jatha

Source: Author.
Note: [1] Akali Dal and its leaders.

RESURRECTION OF THE ANANDPUR SAHIB RESOLUTION BY SIKH "RADICALS"

The growing power of "the radicals" within the Akali Dal was evident at the 1978 annual All-India Akali Conference held in Ludhiana in late-October. During this conference, the Akali Dal resurrected an important document called the Anandpur Sahib Resolution (ASR). The ASR was a manifesto of the Akali Dal's ideology and goals approved earlier in October 1973 at Anandpur Sahib—the birthplace of the Khalsa and a place of great emotional significance for the Sikhs.[17] The version of the ASR passed in 1973 stated that the Shiromani Akali Dal was "the very embodiment of the hopes and aspirations of the Sikhs" and, thus, "fully entitled to its representation".[18] It described the foremost purpose of the Akali Dal as being the "[p]reservation and keeping alive the concept of distinct and sovereign identity of the Panth and building up of appropriate conditions in which the national sentiments and aspirations of the Sikh Panth will find full expression."[19] To achieve this goal, the ASR asked for the creation of "an autonomous region in the north of India" where

Sikh interests would be a part of official state policy. Yet, the ASR clearly stated that this "autonomous Sikh region" would be "an integral part of the Union of India."[20] A number of specific demands were also outlined in the text.

The general postulates found in the original 1973 version of ASR were reformulated into 12 sub-resolutions (or demands) during the 1978 convention.[21] The specific political, economic, and social demands contained in the sub-resolutions of the 1978 document included the following: the massive decentralization of power from the center to the states, the merger of Chandigarh and Punjabi-speaking areas into Punjab, giving control of the Bhakra-Nangal Dam headworks to Punjab, a more "just" redistribution of river waters flowing through the state, giving Punjabi second-language status in other north indian states, the creation of a larger airport at Amritsar and a stock exchange in Ludhiana, direct relaying of *gurbani* (Sikh scriptures or religious hymns) from the Golden Temple, maintaining the policy of merit-based army recruitment, more economic facilities for scheduled castes, and various changes in tax laws to benefit Sikh women.[22] In many ways, the ASR was a "catch-all" document designed to please various segments of Sikh society and maintain support for the Akali Dal in Punjab.

The Janata central government supported, in principle, the demand for decentralization, but it refused to accept the ASR or any concept of a separate "Sikh homeland."[23] In fact, the Janata Party and most other national Indian parties considered the ASR to be a potentially secessionist document that could threaten the unity of India because it called for the center to have powers relating only to foreign relations, defense, currency, and general communications. For its part, the Akali Dal did not aggressively press the demands contained in the ASR because of its need to maintain the Akali–Janata alliance, but passage of the ASR at the October 1978 annual Akali conference was, nonetheless, an important affirmation of the perceived sovereignty of the Panth. It also demonstrated the increased power of "the radicals" within Sikh politics after the Nirankari–Sikh clash.

THE 1979 SGPC ELECTIONS AND THE EMERGENCE OF "EXTREMIST" SIKH GROUPS

A number of extremist and separatist Sikh groups emerged in Punjab shortly after the Nirankari–Sikh clash. Some of these were aided and abetted by elements within the Congress party, while others emerged independently. Regarding the former, senior Congress (I) leaders—including prime minister Indira Gandhi's son Sanjay Gandhi and his ally in Punjab, Giani Zail Singh—had wanted to use extremist Sikh groups to destabilize the Akali Dal and split its Sikh support base in their attempt to improve the Congress (I)'s electoral prospects in the state.[24] The 1978 Nirankari–Sikh clash gave the Congress (I) leaders a renewed opportunity to try to do so. The Congress (I) also encouraged dissident Akali leaders in Delhi to hold massive anti-Nirankari rallies in the capital to embarrass the Akali Dal when, at the time, it was trying to maintain the stability of its ruling coalition with the Janata party.

Two extremist Sikh groups supposedly aided or abetted by the Congress (I) were the Dal Khalsa and the Panth Khalsa. The Dal Khalsa was formed in Chandigarh in mid-1978 with the stated goal of "liberating" the Sikhs, who it claimed were only partially free in Hindu-majority India. The Dal Khalsa's initial activities included organizing seminars and conferences on the perceived plight of the Sikhs in India, including the one titled "Why Khalistan?"[25] Its membership was quite small and initially limited to mostly urban, educated Sikhs of non-Jat background. Many of the Dal Khalsa's leaders were, in fact, associated with various Congress (I) party leaders through either family or professional ties.[26] Another group supposedly patronized by the Congress (I) was the short-lived, loose extremist alliance called the Panth Khalsa. The Panth Khalsa coalesced to contest the SGPC general house elections scheduled for March 1979. Baba Santa Singh, the chief of the Buddha Dal order of *Nihangs*, was the chairman of this group's parliamentary board and Dr Jagjit Singh Chohan was its vice-chairman.[27] Dr Chohan was a former Akali politician who had been dismissed from the party in the early-1970s for advocating the creation of an independent Sikh state.[28]

Two other extremist groups which "emerged" after the Nirankari–Sikh clash were the Babbar Khalsa and the All-India Sikh Students Federation (AISSF). In contrast to the Dal Khalsa and Panth Khalsa, the Congress (I) did not have any direct role in the emergence of these two Sikh groups. The Babbar Khalsa took its inspiration from the Babbar Akalis, a small band of militant Khalsa Sikhs who had emerged from the larger Gurdwara Reform Movement during the 1920s and 1930s.[29] The immediate goal of the Babbar Khalsa was to avenge the deaths of the 13 Sikhs killed by Nirankaris during the Amritsar clash and strictly enforce the Akal Takht's anti-Nirankari *hukamnama*.[30] The Babbar Khalsa was actually closely linked to the Akhand Kirtani Jatha, a religious organization from which it drew its active recruits. Finally, the AISSF had been created by the Akali

Dal in 1943 as the party's student wing. The AISSF originally had four major objectives—to organize Sikh students and protect their interests, to inculcate Sikh students with the teachings of Sikhism, to raise the political consciousness of Sikh students, and help to create an environment where Sikh national aspirations could find full satisfaction.[31] Many senior Akali leaders were actually themselves former office-bearers of the AISSF, but the AISSF had never established a mass support base of its own independent of the Akali Dal. This began to change after the Nirankari–Sikh clash and the election of Bhai Amrik Singh, the son of former Damdami Taksal *jathedar* Kartar Singh and Bhindranwale's "blood-brother," to the post of AISSF president in July 1978. Under Amrik Singh, the AISSF started moving closer to the Damdami Taksal, and also began organizing independent of the Akali Dal.

Several of these extremist organizations contested against the Akali Dal in the March 1979 SGPC elections. These SGPC general house elections— the first in 13 years—were important to determine the relative strength of various Sikh leaders, organizations, and factions in Sikh politics in Punjab. The Panth Khalsa's manifesto for these elections consisted of four points—improving the administration of *gurdwaras*, restoring the independent authority of the Akal Takht, establishing "Khalsa Raj," and setting-up a Golden Temple radio station for relaying *kirtan* (devotional hymns) to Sikhs worldwide.[32] The Dal Khalsa, whose candidates were supported by the AISSF, stated that its goal was to establish an independent Sikh state and indicated that it would use the SGPC to approach the United Nations for this purpose. In support of the Dal Khalsa, the AISSF general secretary stated that the Akali Dal and SGPC had "for the last many years consigned the fate of the panth into the hands of leaders who subordinate panthic interests to selfish motives."[33] Lastly, Bhindranwale also put up his own candidates for these elections and contested largely on the Nirankari issue. Some of the non-Akali candidates had the support of the Dal Khalsa, Panth Khalsa, the AISSF, and Bhindranwale, whereas others were supported only by some (or one) of these extremist groups or leaders.

In these elections, the Akali Dal won 133 out of 140 elected seats and Bhindranwale's candidates won only four.[34] Those supported by the Panth Khalsa coalition won none. Akali Dal president Talwandi thanked God for his party's victory in these elections by saying "[w]e are indebted to the Almighty that our enemies and their agents within our folds stand fully exposed, isolated, and discarded."[35] The term "agents" referred to the Panth Khalsa, Dal Khalsa, and Bhindranwale, who were purportedly supported by elements within the Congress (I) party to challenge the Akalis' hold on the SGPC. While this challenge failed, the aggregate seat count in these elections hid some important political dynamics. For example, the Panth Khalsa and the Dal Khalsa combined to win 12.7 percent of the vote, and Independents—consisting mostly of Akali dissidents and also some of Bhindranwale's candidates—won 21.81 percent in general constituencies.[36] In reserved constituencies, the corresponding figures were 21.76 percent combined for Panth Khalsa and Dal Khalsa candidates, and 17.40 percent for Independents. Thus, while the Akali Dal was clearly the dominant group in Sikh politics, its control was neither complete nor uncontested. Bhindranwale, in particular, had developed significant pockets of support in the Majha as demonstrated by the victory of four of his candidates in the region out of a total of 18 seats.[37] The political power and influence of "the extremists," while still comparatively limited in contrast to the Akali Dal, was nonetheless evident and gradually growing in Sikh politics.

FALL OF THE AKALI GOVERNMENT IN PUNJAB AND THE TALWANDI–BADAL SPLIT IN SIKH POLITICS

The Janata central government began deteriorating in July 1979 when prime minister Morarji Desai lost his parliamentary majority as a result of factionalism both within his party and its ruling coalition. The Akali leadership was split in the inter-party tussle between Desai and dissident Janata leader Charan Singh. Badal supported Desai and his faction, which included the Jan Sangh. In contrast, Talwandi and Tohra wanted to align with Charan Singh, partly because of his promised support to them in any future intra-Akali power struggles.[38] The Akali Dal held a position of bargaining power within the central government with its bloc of nine MPs. Yet, unable to adopt a unified stand, the Akali Dal remained neutral in Desai's confidence vote in which Charan Singh emerged as the temporary victor with the support of the Congress (I).[39]

These political developments at the national level had important repercussions on politics in Punjab. In particular, it led to the disintegration of the Akali–Janata coalition in the state. This occurred when the five Janata ministers in Badal's cabinet—all belonging to the Hindu-nationalist Jan Sangh party—resigned from their posts in protest of the Akali Dal's unwillingness to back Desai in his vote of confidence. Thus, Talwandi and Tohra's support for Charan Singh in the center had cost Badal his alliance with the Jan Sangh and weakened his government. Nonetheless,

Badal's ministry remained in office because it still commanded a slight majority in the state assembly, but Akali factionalism had destroyed the Akali–Janata alliance in Punjab only two years after it had been forged. This left Badal potentially more vulnerable to challenges by "the radicals" within the "Sikh political system".

After the disintegration of the Akali–Janata coalition in Punjab, Akali leaders squabbled over which way the party would vote in Charan Singh's upcoming vote of confidence in the center. Talwandi eventually won this argument and, in a risky gamble, the Akali Dal's parliamentary delegation was ordered to support Charan Singh. For his part, Tohra dissented and, instead, cautiously recommended that Charan Singh be given the Akali Dal's full support but only after the vote, assuming that he won. Yet, this vote never took place because, in late-August, Charan Singh's government fell after the Congress (I) withdrew support, and fresh elections were scheduled for January 1980.[40] Thus, the Akali Dal's gamble—which was vigorously pushed by Talwandi over the objections of Badal—had proven costly for the party. Badal subsequently used this opportunity to reassert his power in Sikh politics.

After weeks of infighting between Badal and Talwandi, a potential split within the party was averted through the intervention of the *Panj Pyara*, including the *Jathedar* of the Akal Takht. Putting "the glory" and "unity" of the Panth at the forefront, the *Panj Pyara* issued a *hukamnama* in early-October 1979 creating a seven-member committee chaired by Harchand Singh Longowal for distributing party tickets and making electoral "adjustments" with other parties for the upcoming elections.[41] This arrangement was designed to maintain the status quo in Akali politics and temporarily forestall a split in the party. But, the fact that the committee consisted of four generally pro-Badal members and only three pro-Talwandi members demonstrated that Badal was slowly gaining the upper hand in his dispute over Talwandi.[42] For his part, Tohra strategically remained neutral, placing himself into a position of holding the balance of power between the two of them.

Parliamentary elections were held as scheduled in January 1980, and the Akali Dal and its allies were routed! The Congress (I) swept 12 of Punjab's 13 seats and the Akali Dal, which previously had nine seats, won only one.[43] At the national level, Mrs Gandhi's Congress (I) came into power with 353 seats, and the old Janata coalition and its offshoot under Charan Singh won only 73 seats combined.[44] Thus, the Akali Dal no longer had a "sympathetic" Janata-led government in power in New Delhi. Instead, its traditional nemesis, the Congress (I), was back in power. The Akali Dal also fared poorly in the Punjab state elections held in June 1980, partly as a result of the continued infighting between Talwandi and Badal. In these elections, the Congress (I) won 63 out of 117 seats, the Akali Dal won 37, and its allies won an additional 15 seats.[45] Thus, Badal's government was voted out of power, and the Congress (I) formed its first state ministry in Punjab after the Emergency with Darbara Singh as its chief minister. The Akali Dal, once again, was left in the opposition in both Chandigarh and New Delhi.

Once out of power at the state and national levels, the Akalis could pursue their intra-party feuds with increased vigor and vengeance. As a result, the power struggle between Talwandi and Badal intensified and reached a point of no return in late-July 1980, when the Talwandi faction declared that Longowal no longer had the authority to call himself "chairman" of the seven-member administrative committee because Talwandi was the actual president of the Akali Dal.[46] In response, Badal's supporters called for Talwandi's ouster and the holding of fresh elections for the presidency of the Akali Dal.

The political arithmetic between Talwandi and Badal swayed conclusively toward the latter's favor when Tohra announced his support for Longowal to be the next party president.[47] With Tohra's defection, Talwandi's fate was sealed! Tohra, who had previously leaned toward Talwandi, apparently recalculated that Badal's faction was gaining the upper hand in Sikh politics and, by throwing his support to Badal, he could ensure his re-election as SGPC president. As a result, Talwandi was formally expelled from his post and from the party in August 1980, and Longowal was formally elected to be the new Akali Dal president.[48] Thus, after over two years of constant infighting, the Akali Dal split into two separate parties—the Akali Dal (Longowal) supported by Badal and Tohra, and the Akali Dal (Talwandi).

Tension between the Akalis and the central government emerged almost immediately after the Akali Dal bifurcated. In the fall of 1980, both the factions or "parties" of the Akali Dal presented their lingering demands to Mrs Gandhi's central government. The Akali Dal (T) asked for full implementation of the ASR, the strict enforcement of the *hukamnama* against the Nirankaris, and the enactment of an all-India Gurdwara Act.[49] In fact, the Akali Dal (T) also threatened to launch a *morcha* (agitation) against the government if its demands were not met by Baisakhi day (13 April) of 1981. Not to be outdone, the Akali Dal (L) subsequently reaffirmed its desire for the "federalization" of the nation's Constitution, enactment of an all-India Gurdwara Act, the transfer of Chandigarh and the

Bhakra-Nangal dam head works to Punjab, and other religious demands.[50] In essence, the volatile process of competitive Akali radicalization against the central government had begun!

THE INCREASED INFLUENCE OF EXTREMISTS IN SIKH POLITICS

While the Akalis were busy infighting, the influence of Sikh extremist and separatist groups grew steadily in Sikh politics. The growing power of these groups was partially facilitated by the support of "radical" Akali politicians, including SGPC president Tohra, who attempted to increase their own power within Sikh politics since the party was out of office. For example, Tohra allowed Dr. Jagjit Singh Chohan's Akali Dal (Revolutionary) to install a radio transmitter to broadcast live *kirtan* from the Golden Temple without getting the required approval from the central government. Even though the transmitter could only transmit a few hundred yards, thousands of Sikhs flocked to the Golden Temple complex in Amritsar to witness this spectacle because its symbolic value was immense. [51] After all, it operated in open defiance of the central government's authority. Shortly thereafter, Dr Chohan's group openly called for the creation of Khalistan as a solution to the Sikhs' "plight" in India, and changed its name to the National Council of Khalistan.[52] Even though both the Akali Dal (T) and Akali Dal (L) disassociated themselves from the demand for Khalistan, they publicly supported the installation of a radio transmitter in the Golden Temple complex. The SGPC's willingness to allow Dr Chohan to install the radio transmitter in defiance of the central government's authority and the two main Akali Dal factions' support of it, demonstrated how extremist groups could influence the emerging Sikh political agenda and help mold the tenor of Sikh political discourse. These extremist groups were, in fact, potential allies for the Akali Dal against the Congress (I) central government and also for individual Akali leaders in their power struggles against each other.

The first act of political violence committed by Sikh extremists also occurred during this period when, in April 1980, suspected Sikh extremists/militants assassinated the Nirankari *guru*, Baba Gurbachan Singh, at his headquarters in New Delhi.[53] Government intelligence agencies suspected Bhindranwale's followers of committing this crime and rounded-up dozens of them. For their part, the Akalis refused to explicitly condemn Gurbachan Singh's assassination, but, instead, reserved their most vocal criticism for police and central intelligence agencies who they accused of harassing "innocent Sikhs" and Bhindranwale's supporters after the killing.[54] The Akalis' reluctance to condemn this act of violence, purportedly committed by Sikh extremists, was ominous of future political trends to come in Punjab.

By the end of 1980, the Sikh political spectrum looked like the one showed in Table 3.2:

Table 3.2
Sikh Political Spectrum (Late-1980)

Moderates	Radicals	Extremists/Militants	Separatists
Akali Dal (L)[1]	Akali Dal (T)[2]	Bhindranwale/ Damdami Taksal	Dal Khalsa
Longowal [1]	Talwandi[2]	Akhand Kirtani Jatha	National Council of Khalistan
Badal[1]	Tohra[1]		

Source: Author.
Notes: [1] Akali Dal (Longowal) and its leaders.
  [2] Akali Dal (Talwandi) and its leader.

The Akali Dal was not only out of power at both the state and national levels, but it was also split into two different factions or "parties"—one led by Longowal and supported by Tohra and Badal, and the other by Talwandi. Mrs Gandhi's Congress (I) was in power in both Chandigarh and New Delhi. Sikh extremist/militant groups had emerged in Punjab and were gradually gaining influence within the Sikh community. Sikh politics was, in fact, moving in an increasingly dangerous direction, and Punjab would get its first taste of both Hindu–Sikh communal violence and organized Sikh militancy in the upcoming year.

SUMMARY AND CONCLUSION

This chapter examined the "patterns of political leadership" facilitating the initial potential for conflict between segments of the Sikh community and the central Indian state. To explain, the Nirankari–Sikh clash of April 1978 catalyzed a number of changing dynamics within internal Sikh politics. In particular, it allowed Sikh "radicals" such as Tohra and Talwandi to challenge the leadership of the "moderate" Badal, and it also precipitated the emergence of "extremist" Sikh leaders and groups such as Bhindranwale, the Akhand Kirtani Jatha, the Dal Khalsa, and the National Council of Khalistan. Some, but not all, of these extremist groups were aided and abetted by the Congress (I) in its attempt to weaken the

Akali Dal in Punjab and ruin its cordial relationship with the ruling Janata party in the center.

At the beginning of this period, the relationship between the Akali Dal and the central government was generally "cooperative" because the Akalis were coalition partners in the Janata-led central government, and they were also in power along with their Janata (that is to say Jan Sangh) allies in Punjab. Yet, Akali–Center relations changed from being "cooperative" to becoming potentially "conflictual" when the Congress (I), a bitter foe of the Akali Dal, came into power in both New Delhi and Chandigarh in 1980. This occurred after the Janata government in the center fell, and the Akali–Janata coalition in Punjab disintegrated, partly due to internal Akali factionalism.

Intra-Akali power struggles intensified after the Congress (I) regained power in both New Delhi and Chandigarh. Once out of power, the Akalis no longer needed to remain moderate and unified in order to maintain the stability of their ruling coalition with the Janata. The intensified feud between Talwandi and Badal resulted in the Akali Dal splitting into two separate parties—the "radical" Akali Dal (Talwandi) and the "moderate" Akali Dal (Longowal). The "radical" Tohra played a pivotal role in tilting the balance of power within Sikh politics in favor of Badal over Talwandi in order to advance his own personal partisan interests.

Intensified factionalism within the Akali Dal prompted competing Akali leaders, especially "the radicals", to look toward "the extremists" as potential allies in future intra-party power struggles. Collectively, the Akali Dal also began aligning with "the extremists" in order to enhance its power vis-à-vis the Congress (I) central government. Thus, "the extremists'" power and influence in Sikh politics began to increase after the Akalis went out of power, the Congress (I) came into office, and fractionalized Akali leaders began to engage in the process of competitive "ethnic-outbidding." These "patterns of political leadership" would soon intensify and combine with others, leading to the onset of violence and the "Punjab crisis."

NOTES

1. For details, see Harbans Singh, ed., *The Encyclopaedia of Sikhism*, volume 3 (Patiala: Punjabi University, 1995), 234; and Sukhdev Singh, "Who are the Nirankaris," *The Tribune*, 15 April 1978, 6. Other sources states that the actual bifurcation occurred earlier in 1893. See Narendra Pal Singh, "Splitting The Sikhs," *India Today*, 16–31 July 1978, 27.
2. Sukhdev Singh, "Who are the Nirankaris," *The Tribune*, 15 April 1978, 6; and Roopa Singh, "The Sikhs: Ominous Signs," *India Today* 16–31 October 1978, 19.

3. The Khalsa "institution" of the *Panj Pyara* (Five Beloved) was started by the tenth Sikh guru, Gobind Singh, in 1699. It is composed of any five baptized (Khalsa) Sikhs who are collectively viewed as being the symbolic embodiment of the entire Sikh Panth for religious rituals and collective decision-making. For more details, see H. Singh, *The Encyclopaedia*, volume 3, 282–84.

4. Narendra Pal Singh, "Splitting The Sikhs," *India Today*, 16–31 July 1978, 27. The baptismal nectar given to those who wish to join the Khalsa fold is called *khanda ki amrit* which is sweetened water stirred with a double-edged sword and administered by other five baptized Sikhs.

5. Interview with close relative of Sant Bhindranwale and high-level member of the AISSF active from 1978 to the late-1980s, 26 November 2001. Hereafter referred to as "Interview with AISSF member and close relative of Bhindranwale previously cited, 26 November 2001."

6. This story was cited by militant Sikh leader Sant Jarnail Singh Bhindranwale. See Ranbir Singh Sandhu, *Speeches and Conversations of Sant Jarnail Singh Khalsa Bhindranwale* (Dublin, Ohio: Sikh Educational and Religious Foundation, 1999), 11–12.

7. Author's interview with senior Khalistani activist and leader, active in the militant movement since 1978, Fremont, California, USA, 19 November 2001. Hereafter referred to as "Interview with senior Khalistani leader and activist previously cited, 19 November 2001."

8. Author's interview with close associate of Sant Bhindranwale and militant organizer active from 1978 to 1990, Yuba City, California, USA, 22 November 2001. Hereafter referred to as "Interview with associate of Bhindranwale and militant organizer previously cited, 22 November 2001."

9. The Akhand Kirtani Jatha was a small religious organization devoted to its own brand of Khalsa Sikhism. For a quick background of the Akand Kirtani Jatha refer to D.P. Sharma, *The Punjab Story: Decade of Turmoil* (New Delhi: APH Publishing Corporation, 1985), 52–55.

10. Narendra Pal Singh, "Splitting The Sikhs," *India Today*, 16–31 July 1978, 27. For a list of all *hukamnamas* issued from the Akal Takht from 1606 to 1978, see Harjinder Singh Dilgeer, *The Akal Takht* (Jullundur: Punjabi Book Company, 1980), 102–103.

11. Staff Correspondent, "Hukamnama for Social Boycott Of Nirankaris," *The Tribune*, 11 June 1978, 1 and 14.

12. D.R. Ahuja, "Mammoth Protest March by Sikhs," *The Tribune*, 15 May 1978, 10.

13. Correspondents, "Hukamnama an Internal Affair, Says Talwandi", *The Tribune*, 13 June 1978, 1; and Staff Correspondent, "Hukamnama is 'Above Law,'" *The Tribune*, 14 June 1978, 1 and 10.

14. Ibid.: 10.

15. Sukhdev Singh, "Akalis Keen to Contain Bhindranwale," *The Tribune*, 23 August 1978, 1; Correspondent, "Bhindranwale to Work for Panthic Unity," 25 August 1978, 6; and Staff Correspondent, "Bhindranwale in Fighting Mood," 17 September 1978, 1.

16. Interview with senior Khalistani leader and activist previously cited, 19 November 2001.

17. A text of the original 1973 version of the ASR is found in H. Singh, *The Encyclopaedia*, volume 1, 134–37.

18. Ibid.: 135.

19. Ibid.

20. Ibid.: 134.

21. J.S. Grewal, *The Sikhs of the Punjab* (New York: Cambridge University Press, 1990), 214. The text of the 1978 version of the ASR is found in H. Singh, *The Encyclopaedia*, volume 1, 137–41; and Government of India, *White Paper on the Punjab Agitation* (New Delhi: Government of India Press, 1984), 67–90.

22. Ibid.

23. Correspondent, "No Rift with Dal, Says Janata Chief," *The Tribune*, 30 October 1978, 1 and 7.

24. Evidence of the Congress (I) patronage of Sikh extremist and separatist groups is provided by Kuldip Nayar and Khushwant Singh in *Tragedy of Punjab* (New Delhi: Vision Books, 1984), 30–34; and Mark Tully and Satish Jacob, *Amritsar: Mrs. Gandhi's Last Battle* (New Delhi: Rupa and Company, 1985), 57–61.

25. Gur Rattan Pal Singh, *The Illustrated History of the Sikhs, 1947–78* (Chandigarh: Akal Printmatics, 1979), 335; and Interview with senior Khalistani leader and activist previously cited, 19 November 2001.

26. Sangat Singh, *The Sikhs in History* (New Delhi: Uncommon Books, 1996), 367; and Interview with senior Khalistani leader and activist previously cited, 19 November 2001.

27. Tribune Reporters, "Panth Khalsa's 4-Point Plank," *The Tribune*, 10 March 1979, 1. The Nihangs are an important sub-sect of Khalsa Sikhs who consider themselves as being remnants of Guru Gobind Singh's Sikh armies. Nihangs have historically been bifurcated into two main orders—the Buddha Dal (the Old Army) and the Taurna Dal (the Young Army)— in addition to local *deras* (religious shrines and encampments).

28. For Dr Jagjit Singh Chohan's background, see G.R.P. Singh, *The Illustrated History*, 279 and *The Tribune* (online edition), 28 June 2001.

29. Tully and Jacob, *Amritsar*, 110; and Interview with senior Khalistani leader and activist previously cited, 19 November 2001.

30. Author's interview with Babbar Khalsa member and close relative of Sukdev Singh Babbar, San Jose, California, USA, 29 July 1994.

31. G.R.P. Singh, *The Illustrated History*, 46.

32. Tribune Reporters, "Panth Khalsa's 4-Point Plank," *The Tribune*, 10 March 1979, 1.

33. Ibid.: 14.

34. Staff Correspondent, "Akalis Make Clean Sweep of S.G.P.C. Poll," *The Tribune*, 2 April 1979, 1.

35. Ibid.: 12.

36. Calculated from Surinder S. Suri and Narinder Dogra, "A Study of the SGPC Elections, March 1979," in *Political Dynamics and Crisis in Punjab*, eds, Paul Wallace and Surendra Chopra (Amritsar: Guru Nanak Dev University Press, 1988), 131.

37. Ibid.: 128 and 132.

38. D.R. Ahuja, "Janata Ministers in Punjab resign," *The Tribune*, 20 August 1979, 12.

39. Tribune Bureau, "Akali Stand Vindicated," *The Tribune*, 27 July 1979, 1.

40. D.R. Ahuja, "Janata Ministers in Punjab Resign," *The Tribune*, 20 August 1979, 1.

41. A copy of the *hukamnama* in the Gurmukhi script is contained in Dilgeer, *The Akal Takht*, 88–89.

42. "Punjab: Priestly Intervention," *India Today*, 16–31 October 1979, 51.

43. Tribune Bureau, "Punjab Poll Results," *The Tribune*, 8 January 1980, 1.

44. U.N.I and P.T.I., "Congress (I) Prepares To Take Over," *The Tribune*, 10 January 1980, 1.

45. Kuldeep Kaur, *Akali Dal in Punjab Politics: Splits and Mergers* (New Delhi: Deep and Deep Publications, 1999), 68.

46. Staff Correspondent, "Talwandi Men Throw Down Gauntlet," *The Tribune*, 27 July 1980, 1.
47. Staff Correspondent, "Tohra Supports Longowal," *The Tribune*, 14 August 1980, 1.
48. Staff Correspondent, "Talwandi's expulsion ratified: Sant Elected Akali Chief," *The Tribune*, 21 August 1980, 1.
49. Staff Correspondent, "Akali Clash Averted," *The Tribune*, 20 August 1980, 1. The proposed All-India Gurdwara Act would have expanded the SGPC's jurisdiction over all of the historical Sikh shrines in India.
50. Staff Correspondent, "Talwandi's expulsion ratified: Sant Elected Akali Chief," *The Tribune*, 21 August 1980, 1.
51. Staff Correspondent, "Radio Golden Temple," *The Tribune*, 11 November 1979, 1.
52. Staff Correspondent, "'Khalistan' proclaimed," *The Tribune*, 17 June 1980, 1.
53. "Baba Assassination: In Cold Blood," *India Today*, 1–15 May 1980, 15.
54. Tribune Bureau, "Protest March by Sikhs," *The Tribune*, 21 July 1980, 1.

4

Emergence of Ethnonationalist
Violence (1981–1983)

DARBARA SINGH–ZAIL SINGH FEUD AND THE CONGRESS PARTY'S CONTRIBUTION TO THE "KHALISTAN ISSUE"

The Congress (I) had come to power in the center in January 1980 after the disintegration of the Janata coalition. It had also been voted into power in Punjab in June 1980 shortly after the break-up of the Akali–Janata alliance and the intensification of Akali factionalism. Yet, all was not well within the Congress (I) party in Punjab in 1981. An internecine factional struggle had erupted between Darbara Singh, the chief minister of Punjab, and Giani Zail Singh, the Union home minister. Both Congress (I) leaders were close to prime minister Indira Gandhi, but they were also bitter personal rivals who saw the other as a threat to his own power base within the party. In particular, Zail Singh, who had been Punjab's chief minister in the early-1970s, wanted to maintain his own independent support base in Punjab in case the Congress (I) eventually lost power in the center. About half of the 63 Congress (I) legislators in Punjab were supporters of Darbara Singh and the other half were considered to be Zail Singh loyalists.[1] This made their intra-party rivalry particularly intense. Darbara Singh refused to induct even a single Zail Singh loyalist into his cabinet, and, for his part, Zail Singh repeatedly visited Punjab and held public meetings with legislators loyal to him without inviting those close to Darbara Singh.[2]

Zail Singh also began using extremist Sikh groups, who he had earlier patronized, and his powerful position as Union home minister to try to undermine Darbara Singh in Punjab. This became evident during the March 1981 All-India Sikh Educational Conference sponsored by the traditionally conservative Chief Khalsa Diwan in Chandigarh. The keynote speaker of this conference was Ganga Singh Dhillon, a naturalized American citizen and prominent businessman. In his speech to the gathering, Dhillon expounded his theory that Sikhs were a "separate nation," and asked that they be given "associate membership" in the United Nations as had been granted to other groups, including the Palestinians and Native Americans.[3] The press immediately reported that Dhillon had openly called for the creation of Khalistan—a charge that both the Chief Khalsa Diwan and Dhillon adamantly denied.[4] Nonetheless, Dal Khalsa activists used the conference to distribute "Khalistan" passports, stamps, and currency to the attendees.[5] The fact that this conference received unusually extensive press coverage raised suspicions that Zail Singh had used his political connections in Chandigarh to ensure that the conference be well-covered by the media. Dhillon, in fact, admitted to having met with Zail Singh earlier that same week.[6]

Shortly after this conference, Dal Khalsa activists took out a march during the annual Holla Mohalla celebrations at Anandpur Sahib and raised pro-Khalistan, anti-India slogans.[7] Much like the educational conference earlier, this event too hit national news headlines, demonstrating that the "Khalistan issue" had resurfaced in Punjab's political discourse. The fact that Dal Khalsa activists were not arrested, once again, raised well-found suspicions that they had the tacit support of elements within the Congress (I), namely, Union home minister Zail Singh. One senior official in the Punjab secretariat summed-up the situation by saying that "[o]bviously, Zail Singh wanted to use the issue to try and dislodge Darbara Singh."[8] Supporting Sikh extremist groups also allowed the Congress (I) to try to weaken the Akali Dal by either undermining its ethnic credentials within the Sikh community or by splitting its support base in Punjab. Thus, by early-1981, Sikh extremists had become pawns in the political rivalry both between competing Congress (I) leaders, and also between the Congress (I) and the Akali Dal.

THE ANTI-TOBACCO AGITATION AND METEORIC RISE OF ALL-INDIA SIKH STUDENTS FEDERATION (AISSF)

An important religious issue emerged in May 1981 that galvanized the Sikh community and forced the Akalis to support the demands put forth by extremist Sikh groups, including those pampered by the Congress (I). The focal point for this issue was the Sikh holy city of Amritsar which houses Sikhdom's holiest shrine, the Golden Temple.[9] In May 1981, activists of the All-India Sikh Students Federation (AISSF), the Dal Khalsa, and the National Council of Khalistan resurrected the demand that the sale of tobacco be banned in Amritsar because the use of tobacco is considered taboo for Sikhs. This demand had originally been proposed by the Akali Dal in 1977 during celebrations commemorating the 400th founding anniversary of the city.[10]

This demand—resurrected primarily by the AISSF—was communally sensitive because almost all the tobacco users and merchants in the city, as the case with most of Punjab, were Hindu. Sikhs claimed that the religious sentiments of Hindus had been honored by declaring Hardwar, Kashi, and Mathura "holy cities," and that certain products had been banned near Hindu holy shrines in them.[11] For its part, the Government of Punjab agreed with the AISSF demand in principle, but pleaded that it could not constitutionally enforce such a ban. The AISSF subsequently began forcibly preventing merchants in Amritsar from selling cigarettes, thus causing communal tension in the city. Akali Dal (L) president, Harchand Singh Longowal, raised the stakes in this controversy by publicly expressing his support for the AISSF's demand.[12] After all, how could the Akali Dal not support a demand which it had itself raised only four years earlier?

In late-May 1981, thousands of Hindus took out a massive march, protesting the AISSF's demand to ban tobacco and the Dal Khalsa's demand for Khalistan.[13] To make their point clear, many carried sticks capped with lighted cigarette packets as the procession marched through Amritsar's bazaars. The processionists also yelled provocative slogans against Sikhs and beat up Sikh bystanders in their route. In response to this massive Hindu march, Sikhs led by Bhindranwale, the AISSF, Dal Khalsa, and National Council of Khalistan planned a counter march to highlight their own grievances. Bhindranwale's support for this proposed march was understandable because AISSF president Bhai Amrik Singh was his "blood-brother" and the son of the Damdami Taksal's previous *jathedar*, Sant Kartar Singh. Thus, the Damdami Taksal and the AISSF had become closely linked through both personal and institutional ties by 1981.

Over 20,000 people participated in the Sikh protest in Amritsar, supporting the AISSF demand. Many of the processionists raised pro-Khalistan slogans, thus giving a secessionist edge to the march.[14] While no major Akali leader participated in the protest, Longowal publicly expressed his party's support for the AISSF demand to declare Amritsar a "holy city." After the march, Hindu–Sikh clashes erupted in Amritsar, forcing the government to institute special laws banning non-religious processions in the state. Communal tension subsided only after the government agreed to form a panel to determine the modalities for eventually granting "holy city" status to Amritsar.

The anti-tobacco agitation had several important political ramifications. First, it sparked the first Hindu–Sikh communal violence in Punjab since the *Punjabi Suba* movement over 15 years earlier. Second, this agitation led to the meteoric rise of the AISSF as an important player within Sikh politics. The AISSF previously had only a small active membership in Punjab, but Sikh students and youth began "flocking" to the Federation after the anti-tobacco agitation and its active membership rose rapidly.[15] Third, the anti-tobacco agitation compelled the Akali Dal to openly support a demand put forth by an extremist Sikh organization—the AISSF. Thus, the Akali Dal became, in many ways, wedded to the AISSF and Bhindranwale through its support for the anti-tobacco agitation in Amritsar. Lastly, as a result of the anti-tobacco agitation, the Akali Dal realized that it could use Sikh extremist groups as potentially effective allies to help mobilize Sikhs against the Congress (I) central government when and if it became necessary. After all, Bhindranwale and the AISSF had proven their ability to effectively mobilize the rural Sikh population in the Majha region around an emotive ethnic issue on short notice.

THE CENTRAL STATE'S INTERFERENCE IN "INTERNAL SIKH AFFAIRS" AND AKALI PROTESTS IN DELHI

Political competition between the Congress (I) and the Akali Dal had become increasingly intense after the Akalis had gone out of power in June 1980. It became even more intense in early-1981 when Mrs Gandhi's Congress (I) central government took several steps to try to weaken the Akali Dal—its main electoral competitor in Punjab. First, the Congress (I) attempted to break the Akali Dal and SGPC's traditional dominance over important Sikh political institutions by unilaterally amending parts of the 1925 Sikh Gurdwaras Act. This was done to ensure that the Akali factions in Delhi supported by the Congress (I) could more readily control the powerful Delhi Sikh Gurdwaras Management Committee (DSGMC).[16]

The Akali Dal expressed its extreme displeasure, describing this as being direct governmental "interference" in "internal Sikh affairs." Second, elements within the Congress (I) government allegedly facilitated the kidnapping of several pro-Akali Dal (L) members of the DSGMC to prevent them from voting and electing a candidate loyal to their party.[17] As a result, the pro-Congress (I) *jathedar* Santokh Singh was elected to be president of the DSGMC by a razor-thin margin. Third, the Union Home Ministry under Zail Singh stripped the SGPC of its historical privilege of sending *jathas* (bands) of Sikh pilgrims to visit Sikh shrines in Pakistan, and entrusted this duty to the government-appointed Deputy Commissioner of Amritsar and the DSGMC.

This governmental "interference" in "internal Sikh affairs" set-off alarm bells within the Akali Dal, which feared the continued erosion of its power and authority by the Congress (I) central government. Longowal responded by announcing that the Akali Dal (L) would launch a *morcha* against Mrs Gandhi's central government if his party's lingering demands were not met by late-August 1981. The Akali Dal (L) presented the government with a list of 45 demands and grievances listed under four separate categories—religious, political, economic, and social.[18] The Akali Dal's religious grievances included the government's "interference" in Delhi's *gurdwaras*, its failure to name a train for the Golden Temple, its delay in granting Amritsar "holy city" status, not permitting the installation of a radio transmitter at the Golden Temple, the usurping of the SGPC's authority to send pilgrims to Pakistan, and not enacting an All-India Gurdwara Act.[19] The political demands and grievances were the government's rejection of the ASR, its supposed violation of assurances given to Sikhs for an "autonomous region," the exclusion of Chandigarh and other Punjabi-speaking areas from Punjab, and issues relating to the distribution of river waters. The economic issues generally dealt with the center's unwillingness to further industrialize and develop Punjab, and the low procurement prices for agricultural products.

Mrs Gandhi refused to negotiate on these issues, and the Akali Dal (L) subsequently launched its threatened *morcha* on 7 September 1981. On this day, an estimated 100,000 Sikhs held a massive protest march in New Delhi under the leadership of the Akali Dal (L).[20] Before courting arrest, senior Akali leaders—including Tohra, Longowal, and Badal—gave the central government one last warning to accept the party's demands or face a renewed agitation in the coming months. Four Akali workers were also shot and killed by the Haryana police at Madhuban while trying to proceed to Delhi for the protest. With these deaths, the proverbial

"Sikh cause" gained its first set of "martyrs" in this confrontation with Mrs Gandhi's Congress (I) central government, and many more would soon come. The confrontation between the Akali Dal and the central government had begun!

LALA JAGAT NARAIN'S ASSASSINATION AND THE METEORIC RISE OF SANT JARNAIL SINGH BHINDRANWALE

On September 10, 1981 suspected Sikh extremists gunned down Lala Jagat Narain, a major Hindu leader in Punjab since Independence and a former MP.[21] This was the second assassination of an important leader committed by Sikh extremists—the first being the killing of Nirankari *guru*, Baba Gurbachan Singh, in April 1980. Narain was the owner and managing editor of Punjab's largest circulating newspaper group, the *Hind Samachar* group, and had been a long-time critic of the Akali Dal.[22] He had angered Sikhs by regularly publishing excerpts from Nirankari religious texts *Avtar Bani* and *Yug Pursh* in his newspapers. He had also given crucial testimony in support of Nirankari leader Baba Gurbachan Singh during his murder trial for the killing of 13 Sikhs in the Nirankari–Sikh clash of 1978.[23] Thus, Narain was a prime target for assassination by Sikh extremists. Narain's killing had important implications on the dynamics of internal Akali politics and the Akali Dal's confrontation with the central government.

Bhindranwale was immediately implicated in Narain's assassination and warrants were issued for his arrest. A large police party was dispatched from Punjab to arrest Bhindranwale from Chando Kalan in Haryana where he had been preaching, but, when the police party arrived at Chando Kalan, they found that Bhindranwale had fled. To the dismay of the Punjab police, he had apparently reached the safety of his *gurdwara* in Mehta Chowk over 200 miles away in Punjab. Infuriated policemen subsequently went on a rampage at Chando Kalan, burning two buses belonging to the Damdami Taksal and roughing-up Bhindranwale's followers. Several copies of the *Guru Granth Sahib* (the Sikh holy text and "living guru") were also burned in those buses, as were irreplaceable transcripts of both Bhindranwale and his predecessor's sermons. It was later surmised that Bhindranwale had been tipped-off by Zail Singh's men about his impending arrest and had been escorted back to Punjab by Dal Khalsa activists.[24] After all, Bhindranwale was a potentially valuable asset for Zail Singh in trying to undermine his intra-party rival, Darbara Singh.

Nonetheless, Bhindranwale would never forgive the government for the police's excesses at Chando Kalan. He would later declare:

> If the [Sikh] Nation is awake today, it is because of the martyrdom of Siri Guru Granth Sahib. September 14 [1981] marks the awakening of this Nation…if the volumes had not been set on fire, I am prepared to say with confidence that we could not have achieved such an awakening.[25]

Thus, by the fall of 1981, the perceived interests of the Akali Dal, the AISSF, and Bhindranwale had converged against the Congress (I) government. The Akali Dal was smarting over the usurping of its powers and the government's "interference" in "internal Sikh affairs," the AISSF was peeved at the government's continued unwillingness to accede "holy city" status to Amritsar, and Bhindranwale was infuriated at the government for the "sacrilege" committed at Chando Kalan. In fact, it was probably at this point that Bhindranwale turned against Giani Zail Singh and other senior Congress (I) leaders with whom he had been previously associated through his religious activities.

After the incident at Chando Kalan, Bhindranwale announced that he would offer himself for arrest on October 20 outside his *gurdwara* at Mehta Chowk.[26] He made this announcement after getting the Akali Dal's public support. On the eve of his planned surrender, over 75,000 Sikhs descended on Bhindranwale's headquarters about 40 kilometers away from Amritsar. At this gathering, major Akali leaders—including Longowal, Tohra, and Talwandi—gave emotional speeches proclaiming Bhindranwale's innocence and highlighting the treatment meted out to the Sikhs by the central government.[27] Bhindranwale made a particularly electrifying speech in which he chastised Akali leaders for their petty personal squabbles, and stated that the Sikh flag would one day fly above the Red Fort in Delhi if they could unite.[28] After his speech, Bhindranwale courted arrest, and agitated Sikhs subsequently clashed with the police and paramilitary forces resulting in the death of 18 protestors. Thus, the "Sikh cause" got another dosing of "martyr's blood" at Mehta Chowk in October 1981.

Sikh extremists responded to Bhindranwale's arrest in a quick and forceful manner. In the first events of their kind, a goods train was derailed by an act of sabotage in Punjab, there were a series of bomb blasts and shoot-outs throughout the state, and an Indian Airlines plane was hijacked by Dal Khalsa activists. For its part, the Akali Dal threatened to launch a civil disobedience campaign if the government did not unconditionally release Bhindranwale and accept its other demands by mid-October.[29] A few days before the Akalis' deadline, Bhindranwale was indeed released from police custody to the surprise of many. The official explanation given for his release was the lack of evidence against him, but another reason may have been Zail Singh's personal intervention as Union home minister. After all, Zail Singh had publicly proclaimed Bhindranwale's innocence in an address to Parliament only a few days earlier.[30]

Upon his release, a huge crowd of boisterous supporters, including SGPC president Tohra, greeted Bhindranwale at the jail's gate. Bhindranwale explained his amorphous goals and motivations to the congregation by saying:

> [H]e who unites people under the saffron *Nishaan Sahib* (Sikh religious flag), he who resolutely supports the *Panth*...is given the name "extremist." The Government has said this. I am the kind of extremist I have just described to you. I appeal to you that if you are in agreement...to support the claiming of justice for the spilt blood of the martyrs, if you are such extremists then...raise your arms...I am one.[31]

One source described the spectacle of Bhindranwale's arrest and the subsequent release as being "the most effective personality buildup Punjab has seen in recent times. In one stroke, Sant Jarnail Singh Bhindranwale... became a household name."[32] As a result of his meteoric rise, Bhindranwale also became an effective ally for both the Akali Dal and the Congress (I) as well as for elements within both the parties. For the Akali Dal, he became a potentially effective ally in helping mobilize Sikhs against the Congress (I) central government. For the Congress (I), Bhindranwale became an even more valuable tool in trying to divide the Akali Dal's Sikh support base in Punjab. In addition, Zail Singh could use him to try to embarrass and destabilize Darbara Singh's state government and to further his own personal political interests. Bhindranwale also became a valuable tool and ally for "the radicals" in Sikh politics—namely, Tohra and Talwandi—to use against the "moderate" Longowal and Badal in their intra-party struggles.

Thus, by the end of September 1981, the emerging Punjab "problem" had become a national issue and a political "crisis" in India. Within a period of four weeks, the Akali Dal had launched its *morcha* against the central government, 22 Sikhs had been killed by the police, Punjab's major Hindu leader had been assassinated, several acts of sabotage and political violence had been committed, and the moderate Akali Dal had aligned itself with the quickly rising extremist/militant leader, Sant Jarnail

Singh Bhindranwale. *India Today* described the quickly developing situation in Punjab by writing "[n]o one is sure of the exact moment when the smoldering saga of the Sikhs took a turn for the worse, but for over a month now the battle being waged in Punjab has been both bloody and bitter."[33] It appeared that only a political settlement between the Akali Dal and Mrs Gandhi's central government could prevent further escalation of this emerging "crisis" and more bloodshed in Punjab.

FIRST THREE ROUNDS OF AKALI–CENTER NEGOTIATIONS AND THE AKALI DAL'S UNSUCCESSFUL "NEHAR ROKO" MORCHA

After Bhindranwale's release, Akali leaders met with Mrs Gandhi to discuss their grievances. Mrs Gandhi chastised the Akalis for supporting Bhindranwale during his arrest, and the Akalis retorted by telling Mrs Gandhi that the Congress (I) had been supporting him for over four years to undermine their party in Punjab.[34] Nonetheless, Mrs Gandhi agreed to hold additional talks in the coming weeks and, in return, the Akali Dal agreed to temporarily postpone its agitation. For their part, Bhindranwale and the AISSF tried to convince Akali leaders not to negotiate with the center until those guilty of the police "excesses" at Chando Kalan and Mehta Chowk were punished, but the Akalis proceeded with their talks with the government regardless. After all, the Akalis knew that they eventually had to face the Punjab electorate, and thus could not afford to be held "prisoner" by Bhindranwale and his amorphous revivalist goals.

The Akalis' agenda for upcoming talks with the government consisted of a revised list of only 15 demands of which one—the unconditional release of Bhindranwale—had been met. The other demands included judicial inquiries into police actions at Chando Kalan and Mehta Chowk, holding fresh elections for the DSGMC, restoration of the SGPC's right to send pilgrims to *gurdwaras* in Pakistan, permission for Sikhs to wear *kirpans* (ceremonial daggers or swords) on domestic and international flights, the enactment of an All-India Gurdwara Act, granting Amritsar "holy city" status, installing a radio transmitter at the Golden Temple, naming a train after the Golden Temple, consider implementing the ASR, the merger of Chandigarh and Punjabi-speaking areas into the Punjab, handing over control of the Bhakra dam to Punjab and the re-distribution of river waters, and granting second language status for Punjabi in states bordering Punjab.[35]

Progress was made on the Akali Dal's religious demands, but those demands involving inter-state disputes (that is, the distribution of river waters, the status of Chandigarh, and the inclusion of Punjabi-speaking areas into Punjab) proved more contentious.[36] Nonetheless, the talks between the Akalis and the government were described as being "cordial" and the prospects for an amicable settlement were not a far-fetched possibility. Shortly after this first round of official talks, "secret" negotiations between Rajiv Gandhi and the Akali Dal also ensued. Rajiv apparently suggested to the Akalis that they form a coalition government with the Congress (I) in Punjab. The Akalis responded by pointing out that this would essentially mean handing over leadership of the Sikh community to more extremist elements in Sikh politics.[37] In contrast, the Akalis suggested that they be allowed to form the government and that the Congress (I) support them from the outside. Rajiv rejected this proposal because it would essentially mean losing Hindu support in Punjab to the BJP. Thus, both parties wanted the return of "normalcy" to Punjab, but neither was willing to potentially give-up a portion of their party's support base in the state to do so. *The Tribune* described this predicament by writing, "In view of all this, the Government and the Akalis seem to be set on a collision course in spite of their desires to the contrary."[38]

The Akalis held another round of negotiations with Mrs Gandhi in November, but no compromise could be reached. The Akalis, once again, postponed their *morcha* to give time for "behind-the-scenes" talks to hammer-out a comprehensive solution, but the prospects of this happening were shattered when Mrs Gandhi unexpectedly and unilaterally announced the redistribution of Ravi–Beas river waters without consulting the Akali Dal. Under the new formula, the central government slightly raised Punjab's share of river waters, but the lion's share still went to Rajasthan, a Hindu-majority state.[39] Mrs Gandhi's announcement also mandated the construction of the Sutlej–Yamana Link Canal (SYL) to divert water from Punjab to Haryana—another Hindu-majority state—to meet its growing irrigation needs. This unilateral decision shocked the Akalis, who had postponed their *morcha* several times to allow a bilateral compromise to be reached. Mrs Gandhi appeared to be testing the Akalis' will.

Nonetheless, the Akali Dal reluctantly entered into a third round of talks with the government in April 1982, but these negotiations quickly broke down after Mrs Gandhi refused to reconsider the revised river waters allocation that she had unilaterally formulated.[40] As a result, the Akalis left the talks humiliated, and they subsequently announced that they would resume their *morcha* (agitation) which, at the time, had been suspended for over six months. In particular, the Akali Dal announced that it would try to prevent the government from digging the SYL, which had been mandated in Mrs Gandhi's unilateral Beas–Ravi river waters accord.

The Akali Dal's *nehar roko morcha* (block the canal agitation) began in late-April, when about a thousand activists of the Akali Dal (L) attempted to block the digging of the SYL canal near the village of Kapuri in the Patiala District.[41] To the Akalis' chagrin, this agitation was unable to maintain a steady stream of volunteers to sustain it. Thus, the *nehar roko morcha*, which was based on a single economic issue, become a huge embarrassment to the Akali Dal. Yet, as had been the case with the anti-tobacco agitation a year earlier, emotional ethnic issues would soon emerge that would unite the various Sikh groups and provide a basis for effective mobilization on a communal, as opposed to economic, grounds.

EMERGING PANTHIC UNITY: ACTS OF RELIGIOUS "DESECRATION" AND THE KILLING OF "AMRITDHARI" SIKHS BY THE POLICE

In the spring and summer of 1982, several Sikh *gurdwaras* and religious texts were desecrated by Hindu communalists, and a number of *amritdhari* (baptized) Sikhs were killed by the Punjab police in extrajudicial "encounters." These incidents brought all Sikh leaders and factions together in a show of ethnic solidarity. This process began when Dal Khalsa activists placed two severed cow heads outside a Hindu temple in Amritsar, protesting the government's failure to grant "holy" status to the city.[42] This act outraged the Hindus, who revere the cow as being a sacred animal that, like a mother, nurtures life and thus should not be slaughtered or eaten. This "desecration" of a Hindu temple sparked Hindu–Sikh violence throughout Punjab, and the counter desecration of Sikh shrines. For example, Hindu communalists placed cigarettes in the Akal Takht and in a number of *gurdwaras* in Delhi in early-May 1982.[43] A few weeks later, several volumes of the *Guru Granth Sahib* were also found partially burned in different parts of Punjab.[44] All Sikh leaders and factions united in response to these acts of "desecration," and took-out huge protest marches in both Punjab and Delhi. The size of these processions, which dwarfed the Akali Dal's protests at Kapuri, demonstrated that ethnic issues would better mobilize Sikhs than exclusively economic ones.

In mid-July 1982, Zail Singh left the powerful post of Union Home Minister to become President of India, a highly-esteemed but less powerful position. Zail Singh's departure from the Union Home Ministry, which oversees law enforcement, allowed Punjab's Chief Minister Darbara Singh to confront Sikh extremism with an iron fist without interference from his rival in the central government, who had previously pampered and shielded extremist Sikh elements for his own partisan reasons. As a result, the use of torture and "faked encounters" by the Punjab police—in which a suspect is eliminated while in custody but is officially reported to have been killed in an armed confrontation—escalated dramatically through the summer of 1982.[45]

The Akali Dal (L), Akali Dal (T), AISSF, and Bhindranwale all condemned these "faked encounters" and referred to their victims, often *amritdhari* (baptized) Sikhs, as being "martyrs." Bhindranwale, in fact, swore to avenge the deaths of these "martyrs".[46] Recalling the condition of one victim of police torture, Bhindranwale exclaimed:

> The day that Bhai Kulwant Singh was cremated, I was present there in the village. When his body was bathed, there was no part of his body—not a single one—which was not broken...Heated rods were put through his body. His skull at the forehead, at this spot, was burnt with heated rods...[The police] hung him upside down. The weight of bricks was tied to him to cause additional pull.[47]

In fact, Bhindranwale's men began a campaign of selectively assassinating police officers suspected of torturing Sikhs in the summer of 1982. This bloody and brutal "mini-war" between Bhindranwale's followers and the Punjab police, which involved an escalating cycle of killing and counter-killings, would continue unmitigated for the next several years.

The Akalis, for their part, attended the last rites ceremonies of these victims of state violence and presented their families with *siropa*s (robes of honor) for their sons' "sacrifices." Even though the Akalis did not support the violent tactics of the extremists, they could not afford to remain silent while *amritdhari* Sikhs were being killed by the police under a Congress (I) state government. Thus, the "desecration" of Sikh *gurdwara*s and the extra-judicial killing of *amritdhari* Sikhs brought the Akalis and Bhindranwale closer together in defense of their religion and co-religionists in a way that mere economic issues could not do before. This would prove to be an effective, but ultimately dangerous, nexus.

LAUNCHING OF THE AKALI DAL'S MASSIVE "DHARAM YUDH" *MORCHA* AGAINST THE CENTRAL GOVERNMENT

A near complete Panthic unity was forged in late-summer 1982. A day after Zail Singh left the Home Ministry to become President of India, Bhindranwale's closest associate—AISSF president Bhai Amrik Singh—was arrested in connection with an attack on a senior Nirankari leader.[48]

Amrik Singh's arrest was pivotal in bringing about Panthic unity. Fearing his own arrest, Bhindranwale quickly shifted from his headquarters at Mehta Chowk into the Golden Temple complex—the center of Sikhdom whose "sanctity" the police historically avoided violating by never entering in an official capacity. From here, Bhindranwale announced that he would launch a *morcha* for Bhai Amrik Singh's release. This *morcha* started a few days later and, to both the government and Akalis' surprise, attracted significant popular support including Sikh peasants flowing in from the Majha countryside to participate. Chief minister Darbara Singh's sudden and overzealous pursuit of Bhindranwale's followers, including "excesses" on *amritdharis*, had caused deep resentment within the Sikh community and appeared to have backfired, giving Sikh nationalists an emotive issue around which to mobilize the community.

For its part, the Akali Dal tried to capitalize on this sentiment by supporting Bhindranwale and also demanding Bhai Amrik Singh's immediate release.[49] Supporting Bhindranwale was a strategically wise move for the Akalis. After all, Mrs Gandhi had simply refused to negotiate with them earlier in April and their *nehar roko morcha* had failed to evoke a significant popular response. Thus, Longowal and the Akalis felt that they needed Bhindranwale to help re-energize the party's agitation against the central government. For this reason, the Akali Dal (L) shifted its *morcha* from the village of Kapuri in the Patiala district to the Golden Temple complex in Amritsar—the heart of Sikhdom.[50] Longowal subsequently announced that his party's new *morcha* would be for Bhai Amrik Singh's release and for the attainment of the original 45 demands presented to Mrs Gandhi in September 1981. Thus, the Akali Dal planned to piggyback on Bhindranwale's existing *morcha* to launch their own reinvigorated *Dharam Yudh* (religious war or war of righteousness) agitation.

The Akalis' open proclamation of support for Amrik Singh's release was sufficient for Bhindranwale, who agreed to discontinue his own agitation and join the Akali Dal (L)'s planned *Dharam Yudh morcha* in the larger interests of the Panth. Talwandi also agreed to discontinue his party's miniscule "*desh* Punjab" agitation in Delhi, and join the *Dharam Yudh morcha* initiated by the Akali Dal (L) and Bhindranwale.[51] Thus, the new *Dharam Yudh morcha* began on 4 August 1982 when over 1,000 Akalis led by former chief minister, Parkash Singh Badal, courted arrest in Amritsar.[52] The Akali Dal announced that dozens of party activists would court arrest every day, calculating that they could overflow Punjab's jails within a matter of months and force Mrs Gandhi to negotiate more on their terms. The "Sikh political spectrum" at this critical moment in mid-1982 looked like the following (Table 4.1):

Table 4.1
Sikh Political Spectrum (Mid-1982)

Moderates	Radicals	Extremists/Militants	Separatists
Akali Dal (L)[1]	Akali Dal (T)[2]	Bhindranwale[3]	Dal Khalsa
Longowal[1]	Talwandi[2]	AISSF[3]	National Council
Badal[1]	Tohra[1]	Akhand Kirtani	of Khalistan
		Jatha	

Source: Author.
Notes: [1] Akali Dal (Longowal) and its leaders.
       [2] Akali Dal (Talwandi) and its leader.
       [3] Bhindranwale and AISSF closely linked.

Thus, relative unity between all major Sikh leaders and factions in Punjab had been forged in mid-summer of 1982. Battle lines were drawn between large segments of the Sikh community on one side, and the Congress (I) state and central governments on the other. This portended more violence to come in an allegorically rich symbolic battle between the Sikh Panth and the Delhi *Durbar* (central government).

FAILURE OF FOURTH ROUND OF TALKS AND THE HUMILIATION OF SIKHS DURING THE ASIAN GAMES

The launching of the *Dharam Yudh morcha* was followed by acts of political violence committed by Sikh extremists. These included the hijacking of two Indian Airlines flights and the attempted assassination of chief minister Darbara Singh. By the end of September 1982, nearly 20,000 Akalis had courted arrest throughout Punjab and the state's jails, designed for only 7,000 detainees, were overflowing.[53] The Akali Dal had, beyond expectations, proven its ability to mobilize the Sikh community with its new, and unified, *Dharam Yudh morcha*. The Punjab government had estimated that less than 10,000 people would ever court arrest, but the number of Akali detainees reached nearly 25,000 by early-October.[54] This was a surprisingly large number considering that the *morcha* was only two months old and that Punjab was one of India's smallest states. In contrast, only about 60,000 people had ever courted arrest nationally during the "Quit India" movement launched by Mahatma Gandhi during the struggle for Independence from British rule.[55]

The escalating momentum of the *Dharam Yudh morcha*, including protest marches by sympathetic Sikhs in Delhi, prompted Mrs Gandhi to order the release of all 25,000 Akali workers in mid-October in an attempt to restart talks with the Akalis. Longowal responded to this overture by calling for a brief "cooling off" period. The Akalis appeared to have forced the central government back to the negotiation table! Mrs Gandhi took advantage of this interlude in the agitation to send her emissary, former defense minister Swaran Singh, to discuss the prospects of talks with Longowal, Badal, and Tohra inside the Golden Temple complex. Accompanied by the Akalis, Swaran Singh also met with Bhindranwale, but Bhindranwale rebuffed Mrs Gandhi's emissary after he divulged that he had come to only lay the groundwork for talks but that no concessions had been granted.[56] Bhindranwale, who one source described as being "the single most important Akali leader" at the time, immediately announced that nothing short of the full implementation of the ASR was acceptable to the Panth, thus putting the Akalis in a difficult situation.[57] Nonetheless, the Akalis took the risk of alienating Bhindranwale and agreed to enter into formal negotiations with the central government.

A marathon of talks between the Akalis and Mrs Gandhi's representatives began on October 29. During these negotiations, several "package deals" were discussed, altered, and discussed again. A compromise settlement was eventually reached which included the release of Bhindranwale's associates, the relaying of *kirtan* from the Golden Temple via an existing All-India Radio transmitter, giving Chandigarh to Punjab, appointing a commission to examine all other territorial issues, settling the river waters dispute through the Supreme Court, and creating an all-party group to look into the ASR and other issues of center–state relations.[58] Mrs Gandhi accepted this settlement through her negotiating team, but, when it was presented to Parliament the following day, parts of the original agreement had been unilaterally altered.[59] Mrs Gandhi had apparently reneged on the agreement overnight under pressure from the Congress (I) chief ministers of Haryana and Rajasthan, two Hindu-majority states bordering Punjab.

This left the Akalis, who were planning on announcing victory in their *Dharam Yudh morcha* the following day, dismayed and outraged. They had no alternative except to radicalize further after this perceived betrayal of trust. Longowal responded a few days later by dropping a virtual bombshell when he announced that the Akali Dal would disrupt the upcoming Asian Games in New Delhi by sending *jathas* to court arrest in the capital starting in mid-November.[60] This announcement shocked

Mrs Gandhi and the rest of India for whom hosting the Asian Games in front of the international media was a source of great national pride. In an attempt to forestall disruption of the Asian Games, Mrs Gandhi instructed both Amarinder Singh, a Congress (I) MP and former scion of the Patiala state, and Farooq Abdullah, the chief minister of Jammu and Kashmir, to approach the Akalis for last-ditch negotiations.

Hectic negotiations ensued, and a compromise settlement similar to the one reached only a few weeks earlier was once again formulated and approved by both the Akalis and Mrs Gandhi.[61] But, as had been the case earlier, Mrs Gandhi once again backed out of the agreement at the last minute.[62] Haryana chief minister Bhajan Lal had apparently managed to convince Mrs Gandhi that it was unwise to announce the transfer of Chandigarh to Punjab without concurrently announcing what areas of Punjab would go to Haryana. The Akalis, who were expecting an announcement of the settlement the following morning, stood humiliated yet again and subsequently vowed to flood Delhi with protestors to highlight the perceived "plight" of Sikhs in India. The stage was set for an apparent physical confrontation between Akali activists and the government in Delhi in front of the world media.

A week before the Asian Games, Bhajan Lal sealed the border between Punjab and Haryana, and turned it into a virtual "militarized zone" as he had promised Mrs Gandhi. All Sikhs traveling from Punjab to Delhi, including those legitimately doing so to attend the Asian Games, were searched and often humiliated at scores of checkpoints set up by the Haryana police. Those searched included sitting Sikh MPs and retired senior defense force personnel.[63] Others were forced to return back to Punjab. In contrast, no Hindus were stopped or searched while traveling through Haryana. Bhajan Lal's security measures proved effective as the Akalis could muster only a few small and scattered protests in Delhi, but the psychological and symbolic impact of the discriminatory treatment meted out to Sikhs, including non-Akalis, during the Asian Games was immediate and would be long-lasting.

Many Sikhs previously unsympathetic to both the Akali *morcha* and Bhindranwale began actively sympathizing with them after the Asian Games, having experienced humiliation by the government first hand. This strengthened the power of "the extremists" in Sikh politics, and compelled the Akalis to radicalize even further. Akali leader Jagdev Singh Talwandi summed up the situation by saying, "We realise that we are our own prisoners…But we are left with no alternative but to repeat these [radical] slogans."[64] After the Asian Games, an exasperated Longowal announced that a convention of Sikh ex-servicemen would be held in Amritsar in late-December to discuss the Sikhs' "plight" in India. This convention, with its immense symbolic value, promised to bring together Sikhs who had served in the Indian Army to publicize the growing level of Sikh discontent with Mrs Gandhi and her central government.

Far beyond the expectations of both the Akali Dal and the government, about 10,000 retired officers and *jawans* (soldiers) attended the convention. They included at least five ex-generals and 1,000 former officers, including about 170 over the rank of colonel.[65] Five other retired Sikh generals sent messages of support. Amongst those attending the convention was retired Major General Shubeg Singh, a hero of the 1971 Indo-Pakistani War, who had subsequently been dismissed from the Army on charges of corruption. Even though he was later exonerated of these charges in a civil court, he had lost his pension because he was dismissed without a court marshal before officially retiring.[66] Shubeg Singh had also been humiliated by the Haryana police when going to Delhi for the Asian Games, and subsequently agreed to become Bhindranwale's informal military advisor. The possibility of armed revolt against India was briefly discussed at this convention, but it was quickly dismissed as being unadvisable or impractical.[67] Nonetheless, the convention passed a resolution supporting the Akali Dal's *Dharam Yudh morcha* and its goals.

Mrs Gandhi and her intelligence agencies took serious note of the Akali Dal's ex-servicemen's convention and, before the end of 1982, the government quickly announced it would hold a fresh round of talks with the Akali Dal during the first week of January 1983. By this time 40,000 Akalis had courted arrest, and Punjab was in the midst of intense political ferment on the part of its majority Sikh population. Furthermore, the Akalis had succeeded in mobilizing the Sikh community in Punjab after the forging of unity, Sikh "radicals" and "extremists" continued to gain increased stature and influence in Sikh politics, and political violence had become endemic in the state. An escalation of these trends appeared imminent absent a compromise solution to the "Punjab problem" between the Sikh leadership and Mrs Gandhi's central government.

SUMMARY AND CONCLUSION

During the period under examination in this chapter, three "patterns of political leadership" combined to facilitate the emergence of the "Punjab crisis." First, intra-Congress (I) competition between Union home minister Zail Singh and Punjab chief minister Darbara Singh—two bitter personal rivals—contributed to the rise of Sikh extremism. This happened when Zail Singh actively supported and protected Sikh extremist groups and leaders such as the Dal Khalsa and Bhindranwale in his attempt to undermine Darbara Singh and forward his own personal political interests. As a result, Sikh "extremists" strengthened and gained increased stature within the community, instead of being quickly suppressed and marginalized before becoming too influential in Sikh politics.

Second, the increasingly intense and unprincipled competition between the Akali Dal and Congress (I)—which had come into power at both the center and state levels—also contributed to the emergence of the "Punjab crisis." In particular, Mrs Gandhi's central government tried to weaken the Akali Dal—the Congress (I)'s main electoral rival in Punjab—by usurping its traditional dominance over Sikh institutions, and by patronizing extremist Sikh groups in its effort to either divide or undermine the traditional Akali leadership's support base in Punjab. In response to the Congress (I)'s interference in "internal Sikh affairs" and its political challenge, the Akali Dal launched a *morcha* against the central government for the attainment of its lingering political, economic, and religious demands. Sikh "extremists," such as the AISSF and Bhindranwale, became important allies of the Akali Dal. After all, they had gained significant influence within the Sikh community by raising symbolically-salient ethnic demands which the Akali Dal had been compelled to support. In essence, the Akali Dal needed "the extremists" to help mobilize the Sikh community against the central government in its *Dharam Yudh morcha*. Ironically, Bhindranwale was also an obstacle to compromise, thus demonstrating his complex and paradoxical relationship with both the Akalis and the Congress (I) central government.

Third, intra-party competition within the Akali Dal between its various leaders and factions also contributed to the emergence of the "Punjab crisis." To explain, Akali "radicals" such as Tohra and Talwandi continued to use Sikh "extremist" groups and leaders, especially Bhindranwale, to their advantage in individual and factional struggles with "the moderates" including Badal and Longowal. For their part, even "the moderates" were, in many ways, wedded to "the extremists" as a result of the Congress (I)'s challenge to the Akali Dal and thus could not readily divorce themselves from them, especially considering "the extremists'" importance in helping mobilize Sikhs against the central government. As a result, "the extremists" became even more powerful and important within Sikh politics.

In short, the culmination of these "patterns of political leadership"—the intra-party competition between ruling Congress (I) leaders, the unprincipled political competition and conflict between the Akali Dal and Congress (I), and intra-party factionalism between individual leaders within the Akali Dal—combined to facilitate the emergence of Sikh extremism and the "Punjab crisis." The "extremist" Bhindranwale became an important tool and/or ally for almost every actor in the emerging "Punjab crisis": Zail Singh used Bhindranwale to try to undermine his Congress (I) intra-party rival Darbara Singh; the Akali Dal used him to build and maintain Sikh support in its confrontation with the Congress (I) central government; the Congress (I) used Bhindranwale to try to split the Akali Dal's support base in Punjab; and the Sikh "radicals" used him in their internal factional struggles with "the moderates." In the absence of a negotiated settlement between the Akali Dal and Mrs Gandhi's central government, the "Punjab crisis" appeared headed for a dangerous and violent escalation.

NOTES

1. "Punjab: Singhs Fall Out," *India Today*, 1–15 August 1980, 23.
2. Satindra Singh, "Swaran Singh on a 'peace mission,'" *The Tribune*, 5 November 1980, 1.
3. P.D. Mohindra, "C.M.'s 'no' to Sikh leader," *The Tribune*, 18 March 1981, 1.
4. For example, see "Punjab: A Bizarre Demand," *India Today*, 1–15 May 1981, 37.
5. Ibid.
6. For example, see P.D. Mohindra, "Separatist elements: Punjab to Invoke Security Act," *The Tribune*, 9 April 1981, 1.
7. Sukhdev Singh, "Parade by armed Separatists," *The Tribune*, 21 March 1981, 1.
8. "Punjab: A Bizzare Demand," *India Today*, 1–15 May 1981, 37. Dal Khalsa leaders would, in fact, later admit that they had been indirectly supported by Zail Singh. See Satindra Singh, "Cong (I) leaders 'helped' Harsimran Singh," *The Tribune*, 28 January 1982, 1.
9. Harbans Singh, ed., *The Encyclopaedia of Sikhism*, volume 1 (Patiala: Punjabi University, 1995), 108.
10. Author's interview with senior Khalistani activist and leader active in the militant movement since 1978, Fremont, California, USA, 19 November 2001. Hereafter referred to as "Interview with senior Khalistani leader and activist previously cited, 19 November 2001."
11. See text of Sant Bhindranwale's speech translated in Ranbir Singh Sandhu, *Struggle for Justice: Speeches and Conversations of Sant Jarnail Singh Bhindranwale* (Dublin, Ohio: Sikh Educational and Religious Foundation, 1999), 67.
12. Staff Correspondent, "Longowal re-elected Dal (L) President," *The Tribune*, 18 May 1981, 1.
13. Dalbir Singh, "Procession by Hindus," *The Tribune*, 30 May 1981, 1 and Om Gupta, "Amritsar: A Slow-burning Fuse," *India Today*, 1–15 July 1981, 29.

14. P.D. Mohindra and Dalbir Singh, "Minor incidents in anti-tobacco march," *The Tribune*, 1 June 1981, 1.
15. Author's interview with close relative of Sant Bhindranwale and high-level member of the AISSF active from 1978 to the late-1980s, Sacramento, California, USA, 26 November 2001. Hereafter referred to as "Interview with AISSF member and relative of Bhindranwale previously cited, 26 November 2001."
16. See Jitinder Kaur, *The Politics of Sikhs: A Study of Delhi Sikh Gurdwara Management Committee* (New Delhi: National Book Organization, 1986), 147–51.
17. See Tribune Bureau, "No support to 'Khalistan': Badal," *The Tribune*, 4 June 1981, 1 and 14.
18. The complete list of these 45 demands is available in the Government of India, *White Paper on the Punjab Agitation* (New Delhi: Government of India Press, 1984), 61–63.
19. Ibid.
20. For a description of the march see Satindra Singh, "Confrontation feared: 30,000 Akalis Reach Delhi," *The Tribune*, 7 September 1981, 1 and Tribune Bureau, "2,000 Akalis Court Arrest: Tohra, Longowal, Badal also held." *The Tribune*, 8 September 1981, 1.
21. K.S. Chawla, "Lala Jagat Narain Shot Dead," *The Tribune*, 10 September 1981, 1.
22. For figures on the circulation of various newspapers in Punjab, see Harnik Deol, *Religion and Nationalism in India: The Case of the Punjab* (London: Routledge, 2000), 153.
23. For an excerpt of Lala Jagat Narain's testimony in Gurbachan Singh Nirankari's case, see Gurmit Singh, *History of Sikhs Struggles*, volume 2 (New Delhi: Atlantic Publishers, 1991), 200–05.
24. Mark Tully and Satish Jacob, *Amritsar: Mrs. Gandhi's Last Battle* (New Delhi: Rupa and Company, 1985), 67–68.
25. Sandhu, *Struggle for Justice*, 274.
26. Staff Correspondent, "Sant's Surrender Offer," *The Tribune*, 17 September 1981, 1.
27. According to Tully and Jacob, the pro-Congress (I) *jathedar* Santokh Singh of Delhi, a Zail Singh loyalist, also personally proclaimed Bhindranwale's innocence to Mrs Gandhi. Refer to Tully and Jacob, *Amritsar*, 70–71.
28. Interview with senior Khalistani leader and activist previously cited, 19 November 2001.
29. Correspondent, "Civil Disobedience Threat by Dal (L)," *The Tribune*, 28 September 1981, 1.
30. P.C. Alexander, *Through the Corridors of Power: An Insider's Story* (New Delhi: Harper-Collins, 2004), 241.
31. Sandhu, *Struggle for Justice*, 93–94.
32. Sreekant Khandekar, "Punjab: A Closing of Ranks," *India Today*, 15 October 1981, 44.
33. Sunil Sethi and Prabhu Chawla, "Punjab: Tinderbox of Religion and Politics," *India Today*, 31 October 1981, 32.
34. Kuldip Nayar and Khushwant Singh, *Tragedy of Punjab* (New Delhi: Vision Books, 1984), 44.
35. For the full text of these demands, refer to Government of India, *White Paper*, 64–65.
36. Satindra Singh, "Ominous silence on Rao-Akali meeting," *The Tribune*, 24 October 1981, 1. Also see Prabhu Chawla, "Punjab: Talks and Terror," *India Today*, 15 November 1981, 31 and 33 for a more detailed description of the talks.
37. Tribune Bureau, "Rajiv-Akali (L) Secret Talks," *The Tribune*, 1 November 1981, 1.
38. Ibid.

39. U.N.I., "Accord on Ravi-Beas waters," *The Tribune*, 1 January 1982, 1; and Sangat Singh, *The Sikhs in History* (New Delhi: Uncommon Books, 1996), 383.

40. Nayar and K. Singh, *Tragedy of Punjab*, 48–49.

41. *The Tribune*, 25 April 1982, 1.

42. *The Tribune*, 27 April 1982, 1.

43. *The Tribune*, 5 May 1982, 1.

44. Nayar and K. Singh, *Tragedy of Punjab*, 54.

45. Darbara Singh, in fact, admitted to have ordered "faked encounters." See Tully and Jacob, *Amritsar*, 105–06.

46. Dalbir Singh, "Sikhs to observe protest day," *The Tribune*, 13 June 1982, 12.

47. Sandhu, *Struggle for Justice*, 155.

48. Jatinder Sharma, "Bhindranwale Launches Morcha," *The Tribune*, 20 July 1982, 1.

49. Jatinder Sharma, "Longowal has talks with Bhindranwale," *The Tribune*, 23 July 1982, 1.

50. Jatinder Sharma, "Morcha venue to be shifted," *The Tribune*, 27 July 1982, 1 and 12.

51. Staff Correspondent, "Dal (T) to participate in Amritsar morcha," *The Tribune*, 9 September 1982, 1.

52. Jatinder Sharma, "Morcha peaceful: 1,100 held," *The Tribune*, 5 August 1982, 1.

53. Gobind Thukral, "Punjab: All Together Now," *India Today*, 15 October 1982, 35.

54. Satindra Singh, "C.W.C. (I) ignores Punjab," *The Tribune*, 11 October 1982, 1.

55. Ibid.

56. Satindra Singh, "5-Man Panel Set Up: Centre-Akali Dal contact begins," *The Tribune*, 25 October 1982, 1. For details of earlier "secret" discussions, see "Sikh Militancy: Bracing For a Showdown," *India Today*, 15 November 1982, 76.

57. Ibid., 72; and Sukhdev Singh and Jatinder Sharma, "Akali Strategy on November 4," *The Tribune*, 21 October 1982, 1.

58. Nayar and K. Singh, *Tragedy of Punjab*, 61–63.

59. Ibid.

60. Sukhdev Singh and Jatinder Sharma, "Akalis Plan to Disrupt Asiad," *The Tribune*, 5 November 1982, 1.

61. D.R. Ahuja, "Oral understanding vs. draft accord," *The Tribune*, 20 November 1982, 1; and Jatinder Sharma, "Hectic Bid To End Deadlock," *The Tribune*, 21 November 1982, 1.

62. Nayar and K. Singh, *Tragedy of Punjab*, 64–65; and S. Singh, *The Sikhs*, 387. For an insider's account of these negotiations, see Alexander, *Through the Corridors*, 256–59.

63. See Tully and Jacob, *Amritsar*, 86–87; and Nayar and K. Singh, *Tragedy of Punjab*, 66.

64. Prabhu Chawla and Gobind Thukral, "Punjab: Too Many Cooks," *India Today*, 31 December 1982, 29.

65. Tully and Jacob, *Amritsar*, 88; and Sukhdev Singh and Jatinder Sharma, "Ex-Servicemen Back Akalis," *The Tribune*, 24 December 1982, 1.

66. Tully and Jacob, *Amritsar*, 126.

67. Ibid., 88–89 and 126.

5

Agitation, Ethnic Insurgency, and the Road to Operation Bluestar (1983–1984)

Failure of the Fifth Round of Akali–Center Talks

The beginning of 1983 saw initial glimmers of hope that the "Punjab crisis" may be resolved through negotiation and compromise. After all, the Akali Dal had convincingly proven its ability to mobilize the Sikh population of Punjab with its *Dharam Yudh morcha*, and Mrs Gandhi appeared willing to negotiate after the Akali Dal's successful ex-servicemen's convention held in December 1982. Thus, the Akalis and Mrs Gandhi's Congress (I) central government entered into a series of talks in the months of January and February of 1983 which included leaders of national opposition parties as demanded by the Akali Dal.[1]

These talks were initially heralded as being potentially "ground breaking," but they eventually broke down much like many of the previous rounds of negotiations. The major obstacles, once again, were inter-state disputes, especially the issue of Chandigarh. In essence, the Congress (I) chief ministers of Haryana and Rajasthan—two Hindu-majority states bordering Punjab—were unwilling to accept the terms being offered by the Akalis, and the Akalis were unwilling to moderate their demands any further. Mrs Gandhi, whose party had lost state assembly elections in two key South Indian states only a few weeks earlier, was reluctant to pressure her Congress (I) chief ministers to accept the Akalis' terms.[2]

Thus, 18 months of direct and indirect negotiations between the Akali Dal and Mrs Gandhi had failed to resolve the "Punjab crisis." This left the Akalis with little choice except to resume their *Dharam Yudh morcha*.

By this time, the Akali Dal estimated that 82,000 volunteers had courted arrest, making their agitation the largest non-violent movement in either colonial or independent India.[3] After the failure of these talks, all Akali state legislators and MPs publicly tendered their resignations in Chandigarh and New Delhi, respectively, in a symbolically-rich act of protest to express their discontent against the Delhi *Durbar* (central government).[4]

Instead of re-entering into negotiations with the Akali Dal, Mrs Gandhi tried to undermine the Akalis' *morcha* by unilaterally acceding to some of their religious demands. In late-February, she addressed a congregation assembled by a pro-Congress (I) Sikh faction in New Delhi. During this gathering, Mrs Gandhi announced that the government had accepted three of the Akalis' religious demands—the removal of tobacco, liquor, and meat shops from the vicinity around the Golden Temple; the transmission of *kirtan* from the Golden Temple via an existing All-India Radio station; and permission for Sikhs to carry nine-inch *kirpan*s on domestic flights.[5] But, these concessions were not sufficient for the Akalis for two reasons. First, the Akali Dal needed a "package settlement" including concessions on their territorial, economic, and political demands involving inter-state disputes to call-off their *morcha* without losing Sikh support to more "extreme" Sikh elements. Second, the Akalis were also irked by the fact that Mrs Gandhi did not grant these "concessions" directly to them, but rather announced them at a function sponsored by a pro-Congress (I) Sikh faction in Delhi. For her part, Mrs Gandhi could not concede too much directly to the Akalis, calculating that this would increase the likelihood of the Akali Dal winning future state assembly elections in Punjab. She also feared losing support in key north indian states bordering Punjab with large Hindu majorities. Thus, both Mrs Gandhi and the Akalis apparently wanted the return of "normalcy" to Punjab, but neither could agree on how to do so without undermining their perceived political interests.

The failure of Akali–center talks and Mrs Gandhi's unilateral "award" to the Sikhs without consulting the Akali Dal strengthened "the extremists" in Sikh politics. For example, Sant Jarnail Singh Bhindranwale publicly hardened his stance regarding the goals of the *morcha* by explicitly demanding the full implementation of the ASR after these events.[6] The hardening of Bhindranwale's attitude was also partially the byproduct of his continuing "mini-war" with the Punjab police. Bhindranwale continued to threaten police officers "who have drank Sikh blood" with dire consequences, and his hit-men escalated their campaign of selective assassinations against them.[7] Nonetheless, the Akali Dal continued to coexist with Bhindranwale. After all, with his growing popularity and superb rhetorical skills, he was an asset for the Akalis in helping mobilize the Sikh community against the government as long he did not openly challenge their leadership. Yet, ironically, he was also an obstacle for compromise, thus leaving him in a paradoxical relationship with the Akalis.

THE "RASTA ROKO" AGITATION AND DEPUTY INSPECTOR GENERAL AVTAR SINGH ATWAL'S ASSASSINATION

In the heated political atmosphere of spring of 1983, Harchand Singh Longowal announced that the next phase of the *Dharam Yudh* agitation would consist of a *rasta roko morcha* (block the traffic agitation) during which Akali volunteers would attempt to stop all vehicular traffic in Punjab. The Akali Dal hoped that another demonstration of popular Sikh support for its cause would make Mrs Gandhi realize the seriousness of the political conflict brewing in Punjab and compel her to compromise more earnestly. On 4 April vehicular traffic came to a virtual standstill as tens of thousands of Akali workers blocked roads throughout Punjab. When the police tried to arrest the demonstrators, they resisted explaining that they had been instructed to block the roads by their leaders, not court arrest. As a result, pitched battles between Akali workers and security forces ensued throughout Punjab in which more than 40 Akalis were killed and scores of others seriously wounded. This took the number of Sikhs "martyred" since the beginning of the *Dharam Yudh morcha* to over 150.[8]

Violence during the *rasta roko morcha* was largely unexpected, and it left senior Akali leaders shocked at the deaths of their party's workers. As a result, the Akalis publicly moved even closer to "the extremists." For example, a distraught Longowal exclaimed:

> I want to tell Mrs Gandhi that our patience is getting exhausted. She should stop playing with fire in Punjab…Let her test. If we can die at the hands of the police chanting *sat nam wahe guru* [translated "God is the truth and the greatest teacher"], we can die like the soldiers we are. Once the cup of patience is full, it will be difficult for me to hold the people [in check].[9]

The wedge between Hindus and Sikhs in Punjab, even in the rural areas, was also becoming more discernable in the spring of 1983, but Mrs Gandhi still refused to relent. For its part, the Akali Dal had few alternatives except to radicalize even further as it had been doing for nearly two years. As a part of this process, Longowal announced the creation of a 100,000-strong force of *sirjiware* (do or die squads) to be amassed from Punjab's villages who would be prepared to sacrifice everything for the party's program.[10] It was clear that Longowal was prepared, at least publicly, to ride the tide of rising radicalism but, at the same time, "behind-the-scenes" talks were also underway with the central government. After all, the moderate Akalis desperately needed a compromise settlement from Mrs Gandhi to end their *morcha* and avoid losing further Sikh support to "the radicals" and "extremists." They were, in essence, stuck in a difficult predicament.

An important incident occurred in late-April which was quite possibly linked to the "secret" talks underway between the Akali Dal and the government at the time. On April 25, a senior police officer, Deputy Inspector General (DIG) Avtar Singh Atwal, was gunned down outside of the Golden Temple complex.[11] It was initially assumed that Bhindranwale's men had killed Atwal because he had planned several police operations against suspected Sikh extremists. Yet, both the Akali Dal and Bhindranwale immediately condemned Atwal's murder. Bhindranwale, in fact, described it as being "the handiwork of the Government to malign Sikhs" and a pretext to raid the Golden Temple complex.[12] Credible reports soon surfaced that painted a much more complicated picture of the dynamics behind Atwal's murder.[13]

Atwal had apparently gone to the Golden Temple complex along with other senior Sikh security officers at the behest of the central government to hold "secret" talks with the Akalis and Bhindranwale. These negotiations had included the possibility of forming an Akali–Congress (I) coalition with Parkash Singh Badal as chief minister, but they never reached fruition due to Atwal's murder.[14] Within this context, Atwal may have been killed by either Sikh extremists to wreck any potential compromise with "the moderates," or, alternatively, by a section of the Congress (I) leadership in Punjab—namely, the Darbara Singh faction—for the same reason. The first explanation seemed to be more plausible, but the latter was not far-fetched either because there were indications that Mrs Gandhi was considering replacing Darbara Singh from his position as chief minister of Punjab.[15] After Atwal's assassination, Mrs Gandhi could no longer afford to sack Darbara Singh who had been emphatically and publicly pleading for permission to raid the residential portion of the Golden Temple complex to arrest Bhindranwale and his men for months, but to no avail.

Either way, the nation stood shocked at the assassination of a senior police officer just outside the Sikhs' holiest shrine. For its part, the central government demanded that the SGPC hand over Atwal's suspected killers and other wanted men taking shelter in the Golden Temple complex, but, predictably, the Akalis flatly refused to do so. After all, they were wedded to Bhindranwale and had too much to potentially lose by prematurely divorcing themselves from "the extremists," especially in the absence of a negotiated settlement from Mrs Gandhi. By this time, the Akali *morcha* was almost a year old, and the communal situation in Punjab had steadily eroded with Hindu–Sikh clashes becoming increasingly frequent throughout the state.

CHANGING DYNAMICS WITHIN THE "DHARAM YUDH" *MORCHA* AND THE WEAKENING OF PANTHIC UNITY

In the summer of 1983, "the extremists" gained increased influence in the *Dharam Yudh morcha*, and Panthic unity, which had been forged a year earlier, began to weaken. This process began when AISSF president Bhai Amrik Singh, who had been arrested a year earlier for supposedly conspiring to assassinate a top Nirankari leader, was acquitted of these charges and released from jail. Bhai Amrik Singh's release considerably strengthened Bhindranwale's power in Sikh politics and within the *Dharam Yudh morcha*. After all, this had been Bhindranwale's exclusive demand for originally launching his *morcha* a year earlier. In addition, Amrik Singh's release gave increased momentum to the AISSF, which quickly replaced the leftist-oriented Punjab Students Union (PSU) as the dominant student organization in Punjab's universities and colleges. In fact, the AISSF's membership rose from less than 10,000 in the late-1970s to well over 100,000 by summer 1983 under the leadership of Bhai Amrik Singh and its highly articulate general secretary, Harminder Singh Sandhu.[16] In addition to the Akali Dal, the AISSF and its cadres were the backbone of the agitation.

Amrik Singh's release raised the speculation that Bhindranwale might abandon the Akalis and their *morcha* since his main demand had apparently been met, but Bhindranwale quickly put this speculation to rest by announcing that he would continue to support the *Dharam Yudh morcha* until the ASR was conceded in the wider interests of the Panth.[17] After all, he was an ideological purist and, by this time, an estimated 150,000 Akali volunteers had courted arrest and over 150 had been "martyred" in the year-old agitation.[18]

After Amrik Singh's release, the reinvigorated Bhindranwale and "extremists" began to aggressively assert themselves in Sikh politics and within the *morcha* program. As a result, the first signs of overt tension between "the moderates," "the radicals," and "the extremists" began to be seen in late-summer 1983. Several events precipitated this emerging schism. First, Bhindranwale made a particularly provocative statement in mid-August when he threatened to slaughter 5,000 Hindus if his seminary's bus, which had been illegally impounded by the police, was not released within 24 hours. Bhindranwale later retracted this statement, but such a provocative and communally-sensitive utterance embarrassed the Akalis, who eventually had to contest elections in Punjab's secular political system which also included Hindus.[19] Second, Bhindranwale organized a conference of "clean-hearted Sikhs," including intellectuals, in Amritsar without consulting Longowal.[20] This was seen by the "moderate" Akalis as being an open challenge to their leadership. Third, the "radical" Talwandi broke ranks with the Akali Dal (Longowal) in late-summer 1983 after criticizing Longowal for his "weak policies and mishandling" of the agitation by supposedly not giving it any "concrete shape."[21] Lastly, the AISSF openly criticized the Akalis for "secularising Panthic politics to help realise [their] mundane, personal ambitions" during its annual convention held in September.[22] This statement perturbed Longowal and "the moderates" who had counted on the AISSF's unequivocal support in the *morcha* program to help mobilize the community. Thus, the "Panthic unity" forged a year earlier for the *Dharam Yudh morcha* was beginning to unravel in the fall of 1983.

The civil administration in Punjab was also paralyzed by this time because of the continuing Akali agitation, communal clashes, and rapidly escalating political violence committed by Sikh extremists. At this point, even Longowal warned that heightened Sikh frustrations would inevitably lead to the creation of Khalistan if a compromise settlement for the "Punjab crisis" was not found soon. Longowal's sheer frustration was evident when he proclaimed, "The *morcha* has become a play without an end, its performers trapped on a stage whose wings are sealed."[23] The "moderate" Akali leaders were, in essence, trapped by Mrs Gandhi's unwillingness to compromise on one side, and by Sikh "radicals" and "extremists" favoring escalation against New Delhi on the other. Longowal and "the moderates" were losing control of the Sikh political agenda, and their authority and power in Sikh politics were quickly eroding in favor of "the radicals" and "extremists."

"MASSACRE" OF HINDUS AND THE IMPOSITION OF "PRESIDENT'S RULE" ON PUNJAB

Sikh extremists had previously directed their violence toward Nirankaris, police officers accused of committing "atrocities," and politicians considered to be "anti-Sikh." But, this changed on 6 October 1983. On this day, suspected Sikh extremists hijacked a bus in the Kapurthala district in Punjab, singled out Hindu passengers, and shot six of them dead.[24] The abandoned bus was later found in Amritsar near the Golden Temple complex. This overtly communal killing shocked and angered the nation, and jolted the central government into action. Mrs Gandhi reacted by immediately sacking Darbara Singh's government, declaring Punjab to be a "disturbed area," and imposing direct President's Rule over the state. More than 4,000 suspected Sikh extremists and their sympathizers were also rounded up in security operations throughout Punjab.[25] Mrs Gandhi had finally acted in an aggressive manner against Sikh extremists, calculating that the indiscriminate killing of Hindus in Punjab would cost her valuable political support in Hindu-majority states in north india if she failed to do so.

The Akalis strongly condemned this "massacre," but also expressed concern about the government's security operations in Punjab, characterizing them as being "brutality on the Sikhs" and comparing them with the actions of the Mughals.[26] They suspected foul-play in the "massacre," pointing out that the perpetrators of this crime probably enjoyed "the blessings" of the government because they were able to drive the bus from the Kapurthala district all the way to Amritsar without being stopped.[27] Bhindranwale also condemned this killing, but questioned why the central government reacted so quickly to the killing of only 6 Hindus when nearly 200 Sikhs had died at the hands of the Punjab police during the *Dharam Yudh morcha*?[28]

Reacting to national public outrage over this "massacre," Longowal and Akal Takht *jathedar* Kirpal Singh agreed to entertain the government and opposition parties' requests to have the Akal Takht issue a *hukamnama* against such killings. Sikh "radicals"—including Tohra and Talwandi—and "the extremists" objected to this request, questioning whether the *hukamnama* would also be binding on the government and its security forces or only on Sikhs?[29] As a result, Longowal and "the moderates" eventually refused the government's request for a religious edict against violence. This refusal demonstrated that "the radicals" and "the extremists" had gained increased influence over the *morcha* program and Sikh politics by the fall of 1983.

DISINTEGRATION OF BHINDRANWALE–LONGOWAL UNITY AND FORTIFICATION OF THE GOLDEN TEMPLE COMPLEX

Numerous "extremist" and "militant" groups had been residing uneasily with each other inside the Golden Temple complex, along with the Akali Dal, since the beginning of the *Dharam Yudh morcha* in the summer of 1982.

These included Bhindranwale's followers, the AISSF, the Babbar Khalsa, and the National Council of Khalistan. Two events occurred in late-1983 that contributed to Bhindranwale's eventual falling-out with the "moderate" Akalis, including Longowal. First, Ranjit Singh—the main accused in the April 1980 assassination of Nirankari leader Baba Gurbachan Singh—was arrested by security agencies in New Delhi in late-November. The circumstances around Ranjit Singh's arrest were unclear, but Bhindranwale and the AISSF accused the Akalis of either convincing Ranjit Singh, who had fallen out with Bhindranwale, to surrender or actually betraying him to the government.[30] Bhindranwale began to suspect that elements within the Akali Dal were negotiating for his arrest as well. As a result, Bhindranwale's men began constructing observation posts and bunkers overlooking the Golden Temple complex, fearing a possible raid by the security forces. Longowal denied any involvement in Ranjit Singh's arrest and asked the SGPC to stop Bhindranwale's men from fortifying the Golden Temple complex, arguing that this would actually instigate an armed response by the government. But, Tohra refused to act. After all, he still needed Bhindranwale as potential ally in future intra-party battles with Longowal and Badal. Retired Sikh military officers subsequently began giving arms training to Sikh youth loyal to Bhindranwale inside the Golden Temple complex.[31] "Militant" Sikhs under Bhindranwale, it appeared, were preparing for battle in open defiance of both the Akali Dal and the central government's authority by late-1983!

The second incident that contributed to Bhindranwale's initial break-up with Longowal involved near-violent hostility between Bhindranwale's men and the Babbar Khalsa. The Babbar Khalsa, which had been formed after the 1978 Sikh–Nirankari clash, had been aggressively implementing the Akal Takht's *hukamnama* against the Nirankaris, often through violent means. Its leader, Sukhdev Singh, had in fact admitted to killing over 35 Nirankaris throughout Punjab and had complained that Bhindranwale's men were getting credit for these actions instead of his organization.[32] Sukhdev Singh had initially been close to Bhindranwale but the two had fallen out for personal reasons.[33] In mid-December, armed Babbar Khalsa activists confronted Bhindranwale's men and ordered them to vacate rooms in the residential portion of the Golden Temple complex. Bhindranwale frantically sent messages to Longowal asking him to intervene in the situation but a disgruntled Longowal refused to act, hoping that the Babbar Khalsa's challenge would compel Bhindranwale to leave the temple complex. Instead, Bhindranwale and his men quickly vacated the Guru Nanak Niwas, which lies outside of the walled portion of the

Golden Temple complex, and unexpectedly moved into rooms near the Akal Takht. Longowal, once again, appealed to SGPC president Tohra to act, but he refused to do so.

This move effectively pre-empted prospects of government security forces simply raiding the residential portion of the complex to arrest Bhindranwale. If Mrs Gandhi wanted to get Bhindranwale, she would now have to send security forces into the central portion of the Golden Temple complex which housed several sacred Sikh shrines. This act would be considered "sacrilege" by most Sikhs in Punjab and would likely invite a violent response.

After Ranjit Singh's arrest and the averted clash with the Babbar Khalsa, Bhindranwale stopped addressing Akali *jathas* going to court arrest in the *Dharam Yudh morcha* and, instead, began openly criticizing Akali leaders of being interested only in winning political office.[34] For his part, Longowal responded by calling Bhindranwale a Congress (I) agent, a traitor to the Panth, and a bandit. Thus, Panthic unity—which had been carefully crafted for the *Dharam Yudh morcha*—was quickly shattering, and potentially violent battle lines between various Sikh factions were being drawn within the Golden Temple complex in the winter of 1983.

THE BHINDRANWALE–LONGOWAL SPLIT, LAST DITCH NEGOTIATIONS, AND HINDU–SIKH COMMUNAL VIOLENCE IN NORTH INDIA

After these events within the Golden Temple complex, the "moderate" Akalis finally tried to part ways with Bhindranwale, but they could not successfully do so for several reasons. First, the Akalis still did not have a compromise settlement from Mrs Gandhi to call-off their agitation and avoid losing Sikh support to "the extremists." Second, while not addressing Akali *jathas* going to court arrest, Bhindranwale still continued to support the goals of the *Dharam Yudh morcha*, explaining that its success was a matter of honor for the entire Sikh Panth and not for any particular party or leader.[35] Thus, Bhindranwale strategically refused to disassociate himself from the Akalis' cause even though the Akalis, especially "the moderates," may have wanted him to do so. Finally, Akali "radicals" such as Tohra and Talwandi were reluctant to completely separate from Bhindranwale for their own partisan reasons, thus making his divorce from the Akalis incomplete. Bhindranwale had, in fact, built-up a Robin Hood-type image and was gaining increased popular support, especially amongst the Sikh youth, throughout Punjab.

In an attempt to counteract Bhindranwale's growing popularity, the Akalis formulated a new issue to try to solidify their ethnic credentials within the Sikh community and retain their dwindling support base. On January 26, 1984 (the anniversary of India's Republic Day), Longowal announced a "revolutionary" phase of the *morcha* which was to include the Akali Dal's threat to burn copies of the Indian Constitution—which is forbidden under Indian law—unless the government amended its Article 25 to re-define Sikhism as being a distinctly different religion from Hinduism.[36] To the Akalis' chagrin, large sections of the Sikh community scoffed at this idea, questioning whether this was, in any way, a "revolutionary" plan of action. As a result, Bhindranwale's popularity within the community continued to grow. While continuing their agitation, the Akalis also concurrently entered into "secret" pre-negotiation talks with the government through Rajiv Gandhi, calculating that negotiations at this point could potentially be more fruitful than they had been in the past since they had tried to separate from Bhindranwale and his brand of extremism a month earlier.

These secret, "behind-the-scenes" talks bore fruit when, in early-February 1984, the central government formally invited the Akali Dal to join in tripartite talks on the "Punjab tangle." This development renewed hope that the "Punjab crisis" may be solved through compromise, but, in reality, these talks were doomed even before they began! On the eve of the proposed talks, the Punjab Hindu Suraksha Samiti, a militant Hindu organization that had emerged in response to the Akali *morcha*, announced its plans for a *bandh* to be held in Punjab and most parts of north India to protest the arrest of its leader.[37] While the tripartite talks were underway in New Delhi, violence erupted in Punjab and Haryana after Sikhs refused to observe the Hindu Suraksha Samiti's call for a *bandh*. Punjab's four largest cities were quickly put under a total curfew to contain the communal violence, and paramilitary forces were rushed into parts of Haryana. As a result of this violence, the tripartite talks were temporarily adjourned, but, in reality, they would never again resume!

Shortly thereafter, communal violence re-erupted in Haryana in which over a dozen of Sikhs were killed, property belonging to Sikhs looted, and several *gurdwaras* torched. In response to this renewed violence, the Akali Dal was compelled to boycott the talks as a public show of solidarity with their co-religionists. In reality, it was suspected that Haryana chief minister Bhajan Lal had purposely orchestrated this violence to scuttle any prospects for renewed negotiations between the Akali Dal and Mrs Gandhi's central government. Only a week earlier, he had ruled out any concessions to the *Akalis* by stating, "[N]ow our tolerance has reached the limit."[38] For his part, Bhindranwale swore revenge for the "excesses" committed against Sikhs in Haryana, and, through mid and late-February, suspected Sikh militants killed more than 20 Hindus—many of them belonging to militant Hindu organizations—throughout Punjab.[39] In the end, the communal death toll in Punjab and Haryana for the last week of February stood at over 60, making it the worst week of Hindu–Sikh violence in memory and threatening a Partition-like situation in north India.

As the violent month of February ended, the Akali Dal made good on its threat to desecrate copies of Article 25 of the Constitution when senior Akali leaders—including Badal, Tohra, and Barnala—publicly tore copies of the article along with hundreds of their supporters and subsequently courted arrest. Yet, this symbolic act of protest did not achieve its desired effect of weaning Sikhs away from Bhindranwale and back to the Akali Dal. After all, the Akalis' tactics seemed anemic in contrast to Bhindranwale who had been backing up his words with deeds such as avenging the deaths of Sikhs killed in Haryana. Thus, the month of February, which had began with a mood of optimism with the breaking of ranks between Bhindranwale and the Akali "moderates," ended with the worst Hindu–Sikh communal violence in India's history. Punjab appeared to be at a communal boiling point in the spring of 1984!

BHINDRANWALE'S USURPING OF THE AKALIS' COMMUNITY LEADERSHIP AND EMERGENCE OF ETHNIC INSURGENCY IN PUNJAB

In March 1984, the central government finally acted in a concerted way to try to control the emerging Sikh ethnonationalist insurgency in Punjab. It took several concrete steps to this effect. First, the central government banned the AISSF and arrested hundreds of its members.[40] Second, it also belatedly tried to strengthen Longowal and bolster his ethnic credentials within the Sikh community by charging him with "sedition." Third, the government tried to empower "the moderates" by agreeing to have discussions with the Akali Dal's legal advisors on the issue of altering Article 25 of the Constitution.[41] While the Akalis vocally hailed this announcement as a "major victory," Bhindranwale refused to accept it as being even a "concession," explaining that "discussions" were not a substitute for formal written settlements.[42] Sikh extremists also intensified their military activities in spring-1984 with several spectacular, high-profile assassinations of "anti-Sikh" politicians in Punjab and New Delhi.[43] For the first time, Hindu families also began to migrate from border villages in the Majha region to Hindu-majority cities in the state or out of Punjab altogether, fearing the wrath of emboldened Sikh extremists in their locales.[44]

Around this time, several pivotal events took place within the Golden Temple complex that completely destroyed Bhindranwale's already extensively damaged relationship with Longowal and the Akalis. In mid-April 1984, Surinder Singh Sodhi—Bhindranwale's chief bodyguard and "right-hand" man—was shot and killed outside the Golden Temple complex by assassins supposedly hired by Gurcharan Singh, the Akali Dal (L)'s general secretary. The same assassins had also apparently attempted to kill Bhindranwale only a few days before, but had backed out at the last second.[45] Sodhi's death and the alleged Akali involvement infuriated Bhindranwale, who declared, "They (the Akalis) killed our young man. They severed my right arm...I know what role that lion, that son of his mother, played in seeking vengeance for the martyrs."[46] Bhindranwale vowed to avenge Sodhi's murder and, referring to Gurcharan Singh and possibly even to Longowal, indicated that those leaders who had conspired in Sodhi's death would also be held accountable after the *morcha* was over. A day later, all three of Sodhi's assassins were tracked down and hacked to pieces by Bhindranwale's men. In an ironic move, Longowal desperately turned to the Babbar Khalsa, an openly secessionist and violent group which had broken ranks with Bhindranwale, for armed protection. Yet, even after Sodhi's killing, Bhindranwale continued to support the *Dharam Yudh morcha* explaining that the honor of the entire Sikh Panth, and not only the Akali Dal, was at stake in its success.[47] Besides this, Bhindranwale's relationship with the Akalis was essentially over! At this point in the spring of 1984, the Sikh political spectrum looked like the following (Table 5.1).

Shortly after Sodhi's killing, Longowal called a meeting of his party's leaders to assess the status of the *morcha* and rally support for his leadership now that his break with Bhindranwale was complete. But, instead of re-consolidating his leadership, this meeting resulted in a major shift of power within Sikh politics when over 40 SGPC members and 130 Akali leaders, including former legislators, revolted against Longowal's leadership and, in a dramatic move, publicly swore their allegiance to Bhindranwale in front of the Akal Takht.[48] These and continuing defections set-off alarm bells within the Akali Dal and Mrs Gandhi's central government.

Table 5.1
Sikh Political Spectrum (Early-1984)

Moderates	Radicals	Extremists/Militants	Separatists
Akali Dal (L)[1]	Akali Dal (T)[2]	Bhindranwale[3]	Dal Khalsa[5]
Longowal[1]	Talwandi[2]	AISSF[3]	National Council of Khalistan[5]
Badal[1]	Tohra[1]	Akhand Kirtani Jatha[4]	
		Babbar Khalsa[4]	

Source: Author.
Notes: [1] Akali Dal (Longowal) and its leaders.
[2] Akali Dal (Talwandi) and its leader.
[3] Bhindranwale and AISSF closely linked.
[4] The AKJ and Babbar Khalsa closely linked and supportive of the Akali Dal (L).
[5] The Dal Khalsa and National Council of Khalistan supportive of Bhindranwale and the AISSF.

Bhindranwale had apparently become the most powerful Sikh leader in Punjab, eclipsing even the traditional Akali leadership!

At this point, the Akali Dal's interests began converging with those of Mrs Gandhi in the need to somehow "neutralize" Bhindranwale. After all, for the Akalis, Bhindranwale had usurped their traditional role as the premier source of Sikh leadership in Punjab. For Mrs Gandhi, Bhindranwale had become a threat to the Congress (I) party and also possibly to the very unity of India. While Bhindranwale never explicitly demanded Khalistan, many of the "extremist" groups aligned with him openly did so. Bhindranwale's usual response to the issue of Khalistan was as follows:

> Brothers, I don't oppose it nor do I support it. We are silent. However, one thing is definite, if this time the Queen of India (referring to Mrs Gandhi) does give it to us, we shall certainly take it. We won't reject it. We shall not repeat the mistake of 1947. As yet we do not ask for it…[W]e like to live in India. Indira should tell us whether she wants to keep us or not.[49]

By leaving this decision to Mrs Gandhi, Bhindranwale seemed to be implying that either she concede to the ASR or that the Sikhs would have no choice except to demand a sovereign Sikh state. Since Mrs Gandhi had no intention of implementing the ASR, she feared that it was only a matter of time before Bhindranwale would begin openly demanding the creation of Khalistan. Mrs Gandhi also feared the loss of Hindu electoral support throughout India unless she acted forcefully against the Sikh extremists. Thus, Mrs Gandhi's interests and those of the Akali Dal in relation to Bhindranwale had finally converged. He had become their enemy in common, and a Sikh ethnic insurgency was underway in Punjab.

In a near last-ditch attempt to prevent a military solution to the "Bhindranwale problem," the central government released senior Akali leaders who had been jailed for tearing copies of the Constitution a few months earlier, and the two sides entered into "secret" negotiations in the middle of May. The Akalis sought at least one major concession from Mrs Gandhi to call-off their *morcha* since a "package settlement" appeared to be an impossibility. In this attempt, a compromise "settlement" on the issue of Chandigarh was reached under which Mrs Gandhi assured the Akalis that a "neutral" commission would grant Chandigarh to Punjab in exchange for the city of Abohar, not the entire Abohar and Fazilka *thesils* as originally demanded by Haryana.[50] The possibility of forming an Akali–Congress coalition in Punjab was also discussed. The only remaining obstacle to this agreement was Bhindranwale.

The government and Akalis adopted a "carrot-and-stick" approach in trying to convince Bhindranwale to support this agreement. High-level Akali and Congress (I) intermediaries met with Bhindranwale to try to convince him to leave the Golden Temple complex and continue his purely religious activities in exchange for immunity from any criminal prosecution.[51] Concurrently, Akali leaders pressured the High Priests to issue a *hukamnama* banning the firing of guns within the Golden Temple complex and ordering that all political killings in Punjab stop.[52] In response to the "carrot," Bhindranwale simply refused to quit the *morcha* or leave the Golden Temple complex without the government's full acceptance of the ASR. Bhindranwale also quickly disposed of the "stick" by warning the High Priests that he would approach the *sangat* (congregation) to have them removed from their posts for being overtly inclined toward the Akali Dal if they attempted to issue such a *hukamnama*. This was not an empty threat as Bhindranwale had built up a legend-like image within the Sikh community in Punjab, and he commanded hundreds of armed followers within the Golden Temple complex.

Undeterred, the Akalis continued to try to convince Bhindranwale to accept the compromise settlement on Chandigarh by trying to reason with him. Tohra accepted this task because he was closer to Bhindranwale than any other Akali leader. Tohra also desired Bhindranwale's support to become the next chief minister of Punjab over Badal in case an Akali–Congress coalition emerged after any potential compromise between the Akali Dal and Mrs Gandhi.[53] Yet, Bhindranwale flatly refused to accept the single-issue settlement on Chandigarh as being sufficient to end the *Dharam Yudh morcha*. After Bhindranwale's refusal, Tohra met with Punjab's governor, who is appointed by the central government, to apprise him of Bhindranwale's intransigence. It is likely that at this point the Akali leadership began actively co-operating with the government to make the option of neutralizing Bhindranwale through military means more viable.[54]

In a desperate, last-ditch attempt to reconsolidate his eroded position as the premier Sikh leader, Longowal announced in late-May 1984 that the Akali Dal would launch a "non-cooperation" movement consisting of the total blockage of foodgrains leaving Punjab and the refusal to pay all forms of tax revenue to the central government.[55] He also promised to further intensify this "non-cooperation" movement into a "total non-cooperation" movement if Mrs Gandhi refused to accede to his party's demands. For her part, Mrs Gandhi expressed concern that inevitable bloodshed would occur throughout north India if Akali workers attempted to block trains containing foodgrains from leaving Punjab for food deficit parts of India. In lieu of the *Akalis* unilaterally calling off their *morcha* or Mrs Gandhi conceded to their demands, the only option seemingly left for "neutralizing" Bhindranwale appeared to be a military one. The proverbial "day of reckoning" had apparently arrived after years of political violence!

THE INDIAN ARMY'S ASSAULT ON THE GOLDEN TEMPLE COMPLEX

On 1 June 1984, there was a major exchange of gunfire between government security forces and Sikh militants holed up within the Golden Temple complex, resulting in several deaths. Two days later, the Indian Army moved into Punjab, took over military positions around the Golden Temple complex, and imposed a complete curfew on the entire state. At the time, the temple complex was filled with Sikh pilgrims coming to observe the martyrdom anniversary of the fifth Sikh guru, Arjun Dev, and Akali volunteers preparing to launch their "non-co-operation" movement against the government.

Mrs Gandhi and the Akalis made one final attempt to avoid having the Army enter the Golden Temple complex to arrest Bhindranwale. When the curfew in Amritsar was briefly lifted on the morning of 4 June 1984, Tohra gingerly walked out from the SGPC office and across the Golden Temple complex to the Akal Takht.[56] There he tried to convince Bhindranwale to quit the Golden Temple complex, arguing that armed resistance against the Army would be futile and it would lead to the temple complex being damaged. Bhindranwale adamantly refused to do so, and Tohra subsequently scampered across the temple complex into the relative safety of the Akali Dal headquarters on the other side. Shortly thereafter, paramilitary and Army forces began "softening-up" operations in preparation for their full-scale assault on the Golden Temple complex later that night. It is likely that the Akali leadership had, at this point, authorized Mrs Gandhi to raid the Golden Temple complex to arrest Bhindranwale.[57]

A "shoot-on-sight" curfew was subsequently imposed on all of Punjab and the state was completely sealed. Journalist Mark Tully described the scene of being escorted out of Amritsar that day by writing:

> Every alley had been sealed off by troops…As the sun rose I saw a spectacle I had never expected—the Grand Trunk road empty. During the five and a half hours it took us to drive to the border I did not see a single civilian vehicle, not even a bullock cart. The shops in the villages we passed through were closed…[t]he only trains I saw were troop trains…Punjab was cut off from the rest of the world.[58]

That night, the Indian Army launched its full-scale assault (code-named "Operation Bluestar") on Bhindranwale and his followers holed up in the Golden Temple complex. The Indian Army simultaneously entered 37 other Sikh *gurdwaras* in Punjab as well to flush out armed Sikh extremists.[59] In short, a military operation expected to take only a few hours instead turned into a fierce and bloody battle between highly-motivated Sikh extremists and the Indian Army, lasting three days and nights. The estimated death toll resulting from Operation Bluestar ranged from the hundreds to the thousands.[60] Bhindranwale, Bhai Amrik Singh, and retired Major General Shubeg Singh lay dead. The only member of Bhindranwale's "inner circle" to survive the military operation was AISSF general secretary Harminder Singh Sandhu who was arrested. Longowal and Tohra, who had publicly stated that they would sacrifice their lives in defense of the Golden Temple, were either arrested or surrendered to the security forces inside the temple complex. Other Akali leaders, including Barnala and Badal, were arrested in the coming days from different parts of Punjab. The entire Golden Temple complex suffered damage and the Akal Takht, the symbolic seat of spiritual and temporal authority for the Sikhs, stood nearly destroyed.

In response to Operation Bluestar, Sikh villagers throughout Punjab defied the curfew and attempted to rush to Amritsar. They were stopped by Army personnel, tanks, and even helicopters and hundreds of them were killed. In the subsequent Operation Woodrose, the Army fanned out into the villages of rural Punjab and arrested thousands of suspected Sikh extremists. The arrests were particularly massive in the Majha region where hundreds of terrified Sikh youth crossed over into Pakistan to avoid detention and possible abuse. Yet, Operation Bluestar and Operation Woodrose were not successful in quelling extremist violence in Punjab. Violence and sabotage continued as Sikh villagers and extremists engaged the Army and other government security forces in continued armed resistance, resulting in a daily death toll throughout the state.

Shortly after Operation Bluestar, at least 2,000 Sikh soldiers mutinied and attempted to dash to Amritsar to "liberate" the Golden Temple complex in the first ever large-scale mutiny in the Indian Army since Independence.[61] Most of the deserters were either arrested or killed in battles with loyalist Indian troops. Prominent Sikhs throughout India resigned their government positions or returned honors given to them by the government, and Sikhs in New Delhi rioted and clashed with the police resulting in dozens of deaths. Operation Bluestar also affected Sikh diaspora as there were demonstrations, often violent, at Indian embassies and consulates throughout the world. In essence, Punjab had hit international news headlines in a sudden and violent way!

Mrs Gandhi had succeeded in physically eliminating Bhindranwale with Operation Bluestar but, in the process, she had alienated large sections of the Sikh community in India and throughout the world. For many Sikhs, Bhindranwale became a "martyr" overnight who died "defending" the Sikhs' holiest shrine and the dignity of the Sikh Panth. Mrs Gandhi had ended one problem—Bhindranwale—but had created another—the basis for an overtly separatist Sikh ethnonationalist movement for the creation of Khalistan. Punjab was at a political crossroads surrounded by frightening uncertainty.

SUMMARY AND CONCLUSION

During the period in question in this chapter, Sikh "extremists" became dominant within Sikh politics and an ethnic insurgency emerged in Punjab. Several continuing "patterns of political leadership" contributed to this precipitous escalation of the emerging conflict in the state. First, the Akali Dal and Mrs Gandhi's Congress (I) central government were unable to negotiate a settlement to the "Punjab crisis." Mrs Gandhi avoided compromising too much with the Akalis, fearing the loss of support in key

Hindu-majority states bordering Punjab. For its part, the Akali Dal could not compromise too much with Mrs Gandhi without losing Sikh support to "the extremists." Second, disunity within the ruling Congress (I) also prevented a settlement to the "Punjab crisis." In particular, Haryana chief minister Bhajan Lal vigorously guarded the perceived interests of his state which bordered Punjab and, on multiple occasions, convinced Mrs Gandhi to scuttle comprehensive settlements with the Akalis at the last minute. This further undermined the Akalis' stature within the Sikh community and strengthened "the extremists." Third, intra-party factionalism within the Akali Dal contributed to the escalation of the "Punjab crisis" and the strengthening of "the extremists" as well. In particular, Sikh "radicals" such as Tohra and Talwandi initially continued to pander to Bhindranwale and "the extremists" in order to keep them as potential allies in their power struggles with "the moderates," including Longowal and Badal. Thus, the "Punjab crisis" lingered and, in fact, escalated as a result of these continuing "patterns of political leadership."

Yet, the relationship between the Akalis and "the extremists," and between the Akali Dal and Mrs Gandhi's Congress (I) government, transformed in a fundamental way during the course of this period. Regarding the former, the Akali Dal and Bhindranwale had been in a tenuous but largely mutually-symbiotic relationship since the beginning of the *Dharam Yudh morcha*. But, by the spring of 1984, Bhindranwale had usurped the Akalis' traditional position as the premier source of Sikh leadership in Punjab, thus turning the Akalis (both "moderates" and "radicals" alike) against him.

Not only did the Akalis become antithetical to Bhindranwale, but Mrs Gandhi also began to perceive the need to act aggressively against "the extremists" to avoid losing precious Hindu support in north India. She also began fearing that Bhindranwale would eventually start demanding a sovereign Sikh state (Khalistan) and threaten the very unity of India. Thus, the Akali Dal and Mrs Gandhi's interests in "neutralizing" Bhindranwale and "the extremists" converged by the spring of 1984.

For these reasons, Mrs Gandhi ordered the Indian Army to raid the Golden Temple complex in June 1984 in Operation Bluestar. This operation was "successful" in eliminating Bhindranwale, but it also embittered and alienated Sikhs throughout India. Mrs Gandhi and the Akalis had apparently "solved" one problem—Bhindranwale—but they had also potentially created another one—the basis for a separatist ethno-nationalist insurgency in Punjab. It remained to be seen what "patterns of political leadership" would emerge after Operation Bluestar and in which direction—escalation or de-escalation—these would take the political crisis and conflict in Punjab?

NOTES

1. For contrasting accounts of these talks see P.C. Alexander, *Through the Corridors of Power: An Insider's Story* (Harper Collins Publisher, 2004), 263–68; and Gurdarshan Singh Dhillon, *Truth About Punjab: SGPC White Paper* (Amritsar: Shiromani Gurdwara Parbandhak Committee, 1996), 216–18.

2. U.N.I., "Poll Setback to Congress (I)," *The Tribune*, 7 January 1983, 1.

3. See Tribune Bureau, "Plea for Talks Ignored: Akali M.P.'s Quit Parliament," *The Tribune*, 22 February 1983, 1.

4. See P.D. Mohindra, "35 Akali M.L.A.s and 4 Akali M.P.s Resign," *The Tribune*, 28 January 1983, 1 and 12.

5. Satindra Singh, "P.M. Accepts 3 Akali Demands," *The Tribune*, 28 February 1983, 1 and 14.

6. For example, see Ranbir Singh Sandhu, *Struggle for Justice: Speeches and Conversations of Sant Jarnail Singh Bhindranwale* (Dublin, Ohio: Sikh Educational and Religious Foundation, 1999), 59.

7. Ibid.: 54.

8. Sunil Sethi, Gobind Thukral, and Prabhu Chawla, "Punjab: Rising Extremism," *India Today*, 30 April 1983, 16.

9. Ibid.: 18.

10. Jatinder Sharma, "31,500 Dal Men Take Oath Of Sacrifice," *The Tribune*, 15 April 1983, 1.

11. For a more details, see Gobind Thukral, "Punjab: Murder Most Foul," *India Today*, 15 May 1983, 19 and 20; and Jatinder Sharma, "D.I.G. Shot Near Golden Temple," *The Tribune*, 26 April 1983, 1.

12. Gobind Thukral, "Punjab: Murder Most Foul," *India Today*, 15 May 1983, 19.

13. For example, see Sunil Sethi and Gobind Thukral, "Atwal Murder: A New Twist," *India Today*, 31 May 1983, 18–19.

14. Mark Tully and Satish Jacob, *Amritsar: Mrs. Gandhi's Last Battle* (New Delhi: Rupa and Company, 1985), 99.

15. See Sangat Singh, *The Sikhs in History* (New Delhi: Uncommon Books, 1996), 390. Also refer to Satindra Singh and D.R. Ahuja, "Dissidents seek C.M.'s ouster," *The Tribune*, 26 April 1983, 1.

16. Hamish Teleford, "The Political Economy of Punjab: Creating Space for Sikh Militancy," *Asian Survey* 32, no.11 (1992): 982.

17. See text of Bhindranwale's speech in Sandhu, *Struggle for Justice*, 229–30.

18. Staff Correspondent, "Longowal warns Centre," *The Tribune*, 29 August 1983, 1.

19. See Man Singh Deora, *Akali Agitation to Operation Bluestar*, volume 1 (New Delhi: Anmol Publications, 1991), 157–58.

20. P.T.I. and U.N.I., "Sants heading for showdown," *The Tribune*, 22 August 1983, 1.

21. P.T.I. and U.N.I., "Talwandi assails Dal leadership," *The Tribune*, 5 September 1983, 1.

22. Satindra Singh, "Bhindranwale's men plan another meeting," *The Tribune*, 10 September 1983, 14.

23. Satindra Singh, "Punjab: An inside view-I," *The Tribune*, 4 October 1983, 3.

24. D.N. Chaturvedi and Karam Singh Ahluwalia, "Terrorists Hijack Bus, Gun Down 6," *The Tribune*, 7 October 1983, 1.

25. Tribune Reporters, "Over 4,250 held in Punjab," *The Tribune*, 11 November 1983, 1.

26. Shekhar Gupta and Gobind Thukral, "Punjab: Defying Solution," *India Today*, 15 November 1983, 12.

27. Some sources have suggested that the central government's intelligence agencies may have been responsible for these killings. For example see Gurmit Singh, *History of Sikh Struggles* volume 2 (New Delhi: Atlantic Publishers, 1991), 316–23.

28. Sandhu, *Struggle for Justice*, 291.

29. Shekhar Gupta, "Punjab: A State of Fear,"*India Today*, 15 December 1983, 20.

30. P.D. Mohindra, "Did Ranjit Singh surrender?" *The Tribune*, 26 November 1983, 1; Deora, *Akali Agitation*, 223; and author's interview with senior Khalistani activist and leader active in the militant movement since 1978, Fremont, California, USA, 19 November 2001. Hereafter referred to as "Interview with senior Khalistani leader and activist previously cited, 19 November 2001."

31. See Shekhar Gupta, "Punjab: Fortress for the Faith," *India Today*, 31 December 1983, 36–40.

32. Ibid., 36; and U.N.I., "Babbars admit killing 35," *The Tribune*, 21 December 1983, 1 and 8.

33. Tully and Jacob, *Amritsar*, 60; and Interview with Babbar Khalsa member and close relative of Sukhdev Singh Babbar, 29 July 1994.

34. See text of Bhindranwale's speech in Sandhu, *Struggle for Justice*, 325 and 341–43.

35. For example, see Ibid., 359.

36. Shekhar Gupta and Gobind Thukral, "Punjab: The Sparring Sants," *India Today*, 15 February 1984, 8. Article 25 of the Indian Constitution concerns the right to religious freedom. "Explanation II" of the Article reads, "In sub-clause (b) or clause (2), the reference to Hindus shall be construed as including a reference to persons professing the Sikh, Jaina, or Buddhist religion, and the reference to Hindu religious institutions shall be construed accordingly." Excerpted from Government of India, *White Paper on the Punjab Agitation* (New Delhi: Government of India Press, 1984), 20. Thus, it is a matter of interpretation whether this Article classifies Sikhs under the category or rubric of Hindus or if it clearly states that Sikhism is a different religion.

37. Tribune Bureau, "Bandh today: Security tightened," *The Tribune*, 14 February 1984, 1; and S. Singh, *The Sikhs*, 391.

38. Y.P. Gupta, "Bhajan Lal rules out concessions to Punjab," *The Tribune*, 9 March 1984, 1.

39. Tribune Reporters, "8 Shot in Amritsar," *The Tribune*, 23 February 1984., 1; Tribune Bureau, "Six More Killed in Punjab," *The Tribune*, 26 February 1984, 1.

40. P.P.S. Gill, "A.I.S.S.F. to adopt new plan on April 13," *The Tribune*, 11 April 1984, 14.

41. Deora, *Akali Agitation*, 448.

42. Sandhu, *Struggle for Justice*, 424–25.

43. For details, see Tully and Jacob, *Amritsar*, 122–24.

44. Shekhar Gupta, "Punjab: The Spread of Terrorism," *India Today*, 30 April 1984, 9.

45. Shekhar Gupta, "Extremists: Temple Intrigue," *India Today*, 15 May 1984, 30–31.

46. Sandhu, *Struggle for Justice*, 451.

47. Ibid.

48. U.N.I., "Akali leaders back Bhindranwale: Revolt Against Longowal," *The Tribune*, 28 April 1984, 1.

49. Sandhu, *Struggle for Justice*, 73–74.

50. Tully and Jacob, *Amritsar*, 138–39.
51. Sukhdev Singh, "Bid to 'neutralise' Bhindranwale," *The Tribune*, 7 May 1984, 1.
52. Tully and Jacob, *Amritsar*, 134–35.
53. Ibid.: 138–39.
54. Ibid.: 139.
55. P.P.S. Gill, "Non-cooperation from June 3: Dal Announces New Plan," *The Tribune*, 24 May 1984, 1.
56. See Tully and Jacob, *Amritsar*, 149.
57. Ibid.
58. Ibid.: 152.
59. For detailed accounts see Ibid., 155–217; and Shekhar Gupta, "Crackdown in Punjab: Operation Bluestar," *India Today*, 30 June 1984, 8–21.
60. The government's official *White Paper* describes the casualty toll as follows: 83 soldiers killed, 249 soldiers injured, 493 Sikhs killed, and 86 Sikhs injured. Government of India, *White Paper*, 169. In contrast, *India Today* calculated the casualty toll to be about 1,000 "extremists" killed and over 200 army personnel killed. *India Today*, 30 June 1984, 17. Journalist Kuldip Nayar cites Rajiv Gandhi as admitting that nearly 700 soldiers were killed. Quoted in Tully and Jacob, *Amritsar*, 183.
61. For details, see Shekhar Gupta, "Crackdown in Punjab: Operation Bluestar," *India Today*, 30 June 1984, 18.

PART III

The Sustenance of the Sikh Ethnonationalist Movement (1984–1992)

6

Failed Political Compromises and
Re-marginalization of Sikh
Moderates (1984–1986)

Political Role of the "Head Priests" and the Congress (I)'s Attempt to "Capture" Sikh Institutions

A "surface calm" prevailed in Punjab after Operation Bluestar. *Indian Express* described the atmosphere as follows:

> A deep anguish pervades in the countryside. People say they have been humiliated but at the same time express their helplessness. They simply do not know how to react. For the time being they have come to terms with the situation. Every villager this reporter talked to...expressed strong views... [they] do not know whom to look to.[1]

Operation Bluestar stunned the Sikh community, and large segments of it—from rural peasants to the urban elite—felt humiliated. Sikh civil servants, government officials, army officers, and police officers throughout India resigned from their positions as acts of protest. Operation Bluestar was successful in eliminating Jarnail Singh Bhindranwale and the bulk of his extremist followers inside the Golden Temple complex, but it did not solve the "Punjab crisis." After all, the Akali Dal still did not have a negotiated settlement from Mrs Gandhi to declare victory in its *morcha* and end its confrontation with the central government.

New problems also emerged for the Akali Dal as a result of Operation Bluestar. First, large segments of the Sikh community were alienated from the party. After all, its senior leaders had apparently "surrendered" to the Indian Army instead of fighting to the end in "defense" of the Golden Temple as they had repeatedly proclaimed that they would do. Instead, this was left to Bhindranwale and his followers who became "martyrs." Second, all senior Akali leaders were put behind bars after Operation Bluestar, resulting in vacuum of leadership within the Sikh community. Lastly, the central government was in complete control of the Golden Temple complex which housed the Sikhs' holiest shrine, and both the Akali Dal and SGPC headquarters. This was a symbolic affront to both the Akali Dal and the Sikh community in Punjab.

Shortly after Operation Bluestar, the imprisoned Akali Dal president Harchand Singh Longowal asked Akal Takht *jathedar*, Kirpal Singh, and the five *Singh Sahiban*s (Head Priests) to lead the Sikh Panth in this period of crisis.[2] This was a strategic move on the part of Longowal. After all, the Akal Takht *jathedar* and most of the other Head Priests were loyal to "the moderates," and their stewardship would prevent factionalism between the second-rung party leadership. Longowal also knew that Mrs Gandhi would be reluctant to arrest the Head Priests and provoke additional Sikh backlash because they were respected religious personalities with no official or direct political roles. For their part, the Head Priests initially played a delicate balancing act by criticizing Operation Bluestar on the one hand, while also concurrently co-operating with the government to prevent further bloodshed by calling for Hindu–Sikh amity. The "Sikh political spectrum" immediately after Operation Bluestar looked like the following (Table 6.1):

By eliminating Bhindranwale, Mrs Gandhi created a "window of opportunity" through which concessions to the Akali Dal could pass, but the Akalis could not afford to compromise with the central government

Table 6.1
Sikh Political Spectrum (Mid-1984)

Moderates	Radicals	Extremists	Militants/Separatists
Head Priests[1]	-----------[3]	-----------[4]	Unorganized individuals
Akali Dal (L)[2]			

Source: Author.
Notes: [1] Acting, collective leadership supported by the Akali Dal (L).
     [2] Longowal and Badal in jail; Akali Dal (L) led by second-rung leadership.
     [3] Tohra and Talwandi in jail.
     [4] All dead, arrested, or effectively underground.

only days after its army had raided the Sikhs' holiest shrine and killed hundreds, if not thousands, of their co-religionists. Negotiating with Mrs Gandhi was actually on the backburner for the Akalis; instead, their most immediate concern was the withdrawal of government troops from the Golden Temple complex. This issue gained even more pertinence for the Akali Dal when the central government announced plans to unilaterally repair and rebuild parts of the Golden Temple complex damaged or destroyed in Operation Bluestar. This would be an affront to Sikh religious sensibilities and their sense of self-pride because, since the mid-1920s, the SGPC had actually organized all *kar sewa* (voluntary community service) to maintain and repair historical Sikh shrines in Punjab. For her part, Mrs Gandhi had serious reservations about handing the Golden Temple complex over to the SGPC before all repairs were complete. The central government feared that the SGPC and Akali Dal would keep the damaged Golden Temple complex and Akal Takht as permanent and lasting monuments to the Indian state's "invasion" of the Sikhs' holiest shrine. This was not a viable option for the Congress (I) party, which relied on a degree of Sikh support to remain politically competitive in Punjab.

About a month after Operation Bluestar, the Head Priests and Akali Dal tried to launch a *morcha* to "liberate" the Golden Temple complex, but it received only a miniscule popular response for several reasons. The government had enacted strict security measures, the second-rung Akali leaders lacked sufficient political stature to mobilize party activists, and large sections of the Sikh community were disillusioned with the party. After seeing the lack of Sikh response to the Akalis' *morcha*, the central government began quickly cleaning up and rebuilding the Golden Temple complex. It used Baba Santa Singh, the chief of the Buddha Dal order of *Nihang*s, to give the government-sponsored *kar sewa* a façade of legitimacy. Santa Singh and his followers proudly posed for media pictures holding various tools and implements, but paid day laborers and artisans did the actual work of rebuilding. The Head Priests responded to this "transgression" by issuing a *hukamnama* (religious edict) declaring Santa Singh to be *tankhaiya* (guilty of religious misconduct), and shortly thereafter excommunicated him and others from the Sikh Panth for participating in the government-sponsored "*kar sewa*".[3]

Instead of entering into negotiations with the Akalis after Operation Bluestar, Mrs Gandhi brazenly chose to try to control the future direction of Sikh politics by challenging the Akali Dal for its Sikh support base, its hold on the SGPC, and its power to select the Head Priests. In this attempt, the central government authorized Santa Singh to convene a *Sarbat*

Khalsa (a collective meeting of the Sikh Panth) to be held in Amritsar on 11 August 1984. The purpose of this *Sarbat Khalsa* was not to prevent Sikh holy places from becoming hotbeds of political activity, but rather to "to turn these shrines into hotbeds of politics, not of the Akali variety but of the Congress (I) variety".[4] Santa Singh, in fact, admitted that the goal was to have non-Akali groups in control of both the SGPC and *jathedari* of the Akal Takht.[5] In essence, Mrs Gandhi was trying to undermine the Akalis instead of negotiating with them.

On the eve of the *Sarbat Khalsa,* the government used public transportation to bring people to Amritsar for the convention, but only about 30,000 showed up.[6] A large portion of these were non-Sikhs from outside of Punjab associated with the Congress (I) party, who were brought to the convention under heavy security escort. Several prominent Sikh religious figures, who the government advertised would attend the convention, refused to do so after the Head Priests issued an appeal for Sikhs to boycott the so-called *Sarbat Khalsa*. Nonetheless, several *gurmatas* (collective decisions taken by the *Sarbat Khalsa*) were passed at this convention, including one asking the central government to rescind or amend the 1925 Sikh Gurdwara Act in order to break the dominance of the SGPC in Sikh politics.[7] Yet, aside from Santa Singh, no major Sikh political or religious leader from Punjab appeared ready to endorse these *gurmatas*. Thus, the government-sponsored *Sarbat Khalsa* flopped in terms of effectively challenging the Akali Dal and SGPC's dominance over Sikh politics. Instead, it actually proved to be counterproductive for the Congress (I) because it shored up sagging Sikh support for the Akali Dal, as most Sikhs viewed the Congress (I)'s brazen attempt to "capture" Sikh institutions as being overt "interference" in the Sikhs' internal affairs and a purely partisan move by the central government.

The failure of this government-sponsored *Sarbat Khalsa* emboldened the Head Priests, and they subsequently summoned an "All-World Sikh Convention" to be held during the first week of September at Gurdwara Shaheedan in Amritsar. This convention promised to be the first mass assembly of Sikhs after Operation Bluestar and a test of the Head Priests' stature within the Sikh community in comparison to the Congress (I). The government tried desperately to prevent Sikhs from attending this convention, but they flocked to it anyhow in spite of the government's strict preventative security measures and rainy weather. Conservative estimates put the congregation between 50,000 and 75,000, thus at least doubling the number of people who had attended the government-sponsored *Sarbat Khalsa* about three weeks earlier.[8]

During the convention, the Head Priests criticized the central government, and compared it to 18th century Mughal rule during which the Golden Temple complex had also been "desecrated" and *amritdhari* Sikhs targeted for persecution. The *sangat* (congregation) at the "All-World Sikh Convention" passed ten resolutions, including one declaring both President Zail Singh and union minister for Parliamentary Affairs Buta Singh to be *tankhaiya*.[9] The most important resolution was one authorizing the Head Priests to lead a "massive march" of a million Sikhs to "liberate" the Golden Temple complex if it was not handed over to the SGPC by 1 October 1984. The High Priests strategically used heated ethnic rhetoric during this convention, but they did not openly declare their support for either violence or separatism. This was not surprising because the central government was sending "secret" feelers to jailed Akali leaders at the time, including Longowal, to re-enter negotiations to try to solve the "Punjab problem".[10]

The "All-World Sikh Convention" was a major success for the SGPC and Akali Dal, but events during the meet illustrated that Sikh extremism was not dead as the central government and Akali Dal had hoped. For example, batches of agitated Sikh youth shouted pro-Bhindranwale slogans during the convention and demanded a more aggressive response to the government's storming of the Golden Temple complex than the Head Priests were willing to support. In addition, Sikh extremists continued to commit acts of political violence throughout Punjab during the period after Operation Bluestar. In fact, armed encounters between Sikh extremists and Indian security forces, and the killing of Hindus and suspected government sympathizers by extremists were an almost daily occurrence. In a particularly spectacular act of protest, AISSF activists internationalized their sense of grievance by hijacking two domestic air flights in the summer of 1984. Operation Bluestar appeared to have aggravated Sikh discontent and alienation instead of ameliorating or quelling it.

RETURN OF THE GOLDEN TEMPLE TO THE SGPC

By the fall of 1984, it became apparent that Mrs Gandhi and the Congress (I) had failed to either wean Sikhs away from the Akali Dal, or capture important Sikh political institutions as they had desired. Without doing either of these, Mrs Gandhi simply could not have the Army continue to occupy the Golden Temple complex for too long without further embittering Sikh sentiments. For this reason, the central government officially reopened the Golden Temple complex to the public in late-September after major repairs to it were complete. In exchange for regaining control of the temple complex, the SGPC agreed to ban the carrying of firearms in the complex and ensured that it would not be used for violent or secessionist activities. The Head Priests also exonerated President Zail Singh of any religious misconduct, in part, because he had played an instrumental role in convincing Mrs Gandhi to withdraw the Army from the temple complex.[11]

The Head Priests were certainly "moderates," but they were not "government stooges" as alleged by the extremists. For example, they refused to issue a *hukamnama* ordering Sikhs to eschew violence and disassociate themselves from "terrorists" in Punjab as demanded by the government. The Head Priests explained this refusal by saying that it was "the Government's business to handle law and order outside the temple complex[,]" not theirs.[12] The Head Priests also enumerated four conditions that were necessary to "heal the wounds" inflicted on the Sikh community—revoking the ban on the AISSF, the unconditional release of all AISSF and Akali detainees, an end to arresting Sikh youth in "false cases," and compensation for families of those killed in the Army's various security operations. This demonstrated that the "Punjab problem" would not be resolved until some sort of settlement was reached between the Akali Dal and Mrs Gandhi's government. After all, the Akali Dal simply could not end its "confrontation" with the Congress (I) central government without getting some concessions, especially after such a traumatic event like Operation Bluestar. For this reason, Mrs Gandhi continued to send "feelers" to detained Akali leaders to enter into talks. For their part, the Akalis began considering doing so since Bhindranwale was no longer alive to be an obstacle to compromise. Thus, the prospects for a potential "new beginning" in Punjab appeared to be emerging in the fall of 1984.

MRS GANDHI'S ASSASSINATION AND THE ANTI-SIKH POGROMS

The emerging "window of opportunity" for renewed Akali–center talks and a possible settlement to the "Punjab problem" slammed shut in late-October. On 31 October 1984, prime minister Indira Gandhi was gunned down at her official residence in New Delhi by two of her Sikh bodyguards in revenge for Operation Bluestar. The price that the Sikhs living outside of Punjab paid for this act of vengeance was enormous. Mrs Gandhi's assassination sparked a massive Hindu backlash against

Sikhs throughout India, especially in north India and Delhi.[13] For four days and nights, Hindu mobs engaged in murder, rape, looting, and arson in the worst communal violence in India since Partition. In many cities, especially in Delhi, the civil administration simply broke down partially due to the police's apathy or active participation with the marauding Hindu mobs.[14] These mobs were often instigated or led by local Congress (I) politicians, including sitting MPs, who provided them with liquor, weapons, and lists of Sikh homes in their constituencies. The deployment of the Army in Delhi and other Indian cities was delayed for four days, raising suspicions that the highest levels of the Congress (I) government deliberately refrained from ending the pogroms in order to teach the Sikhs "a lesson."[15]

While anti-Sikh violence raged in the rest of north India, Punjab remained relatively calm as over 80,000 military and paramilitary troops sealed the state and barred any traffic from either entering or leaving.[16] The Head Priests reacted to Mrs Gandhi's assassination by issuing a balanced statement condemning both Mrs Gandhi's assassination and also the wave of anti-Sikh violence that followed it.[17] Thus, the Head Priests continued to engage in a delicate balancing act of appeasing alienated Sikh sentiment without disassociating themselves from the national "mainstream." During this period of crisis, the Head Priests also acted as a stabilizing force in Sikh politics and controlled Akali factionalism to maintain the status quo in the party.[18] The anti-Sikh pogroms were the second traumatic event for the Sikh community in 1984—the first being Operation Bluestar.

THE ELECTION OF RAJIV GANDHI AS PRIME MINISTER AND HIS INITIAL CONCILIATORY STEPS TO SOLVE THE "PUNJAB CRISIS"

After Mrs Gandhi's assassination, her son Rajiv Gandhi was immediately chosen to be India's interim prime minister until fresh national elections could be held by year end. Rajiv chose to ride the wave of sympathy for his slain mother and played up the specter of Sikh "terrorism" to consolidate Hindu votes in India for these elections. He did so with great skill, claiming that only the Congress (I) could ensure the unity of India and thwart the evil designs of separatist forces in the country. In fact, the perceived "Sikh threat" to India's unity became a central theme in Rajiv and the Congress (I)'s election rallies.[19] But, Rajiv's attitude towards the Akalis and the "Punjab problem" began to change once it became evident that the Congress (I) was headed for an overwhelming victory. Toward the end of the election campaign, Rajiv actually began emphasizing the need to solve the "Punjab tangle" through negotiations and compromise.

As expected, the Congress (I) won the December 1984 parliamentary elections, but, beyond expectations, it did so by obtaining an unprecedented three-fourths majority in Parliament. After being sworn in as prime minister, Rajiv immediately announced the creation of a three-member panel of union cabinet ministers to take a fresh look into the Akali Dal's demands. The second-rung Akali leadership characterized Rajiv's actions as being positive steps, but indicated that absolutely no negotiations or compromises would be entertained until the party's senior leaders were "unconditionally" released from jail.[20] After all, none of these second-rung Akali leaders had sufficient political stature to reach a settlement with the government. For this reason, Rajiv decided to continue with "behind-the-scenes" parleys with the jailed senior Akali leaders through various intermediaries.

While Rajiv and the Akalis continued with their political maneuvering, Sikh alienation and frustration in Punjab was growing noticeably. *India Today* described this trend as follows:

> Blue (the traditional Akali color) is fast yielding to saffron [in Punjab]...Senior Punjab officials touring the state have recently been greeted by a sea of saffron turbans at public meetings and functions everywhere. Saffron is the colour signifying sacrifice and, in this case, defiance of Central authority.[21]

The Akalis tried to cater to this growing sense of Sikh resentment but without endorsing any forms of violence. In the first week of March 1985, the Akali Dal held a major political conference at Anandpur Sahib to announce a concrete plan of action to force the government to concede to its preconditions for talks. The second-rung Akali leaders made fiery speeches and gave the central government an ultimatum that their party would launch a new *morcha* within a month if their demands were not met. These demands included a judicial inquiry into the anti-Sikh riots, the release of all Sikhs arrested after Operation Bluestar, the release of Sikh deserters and their reinstatement into the Army, the withdrawal of "black laws" declaring Punjab to be a "disturbed area," the withdrawal of Army and paramilitary forces from Punjab, and lifting the ban on the AISSF.[22] After passing these resolutions, the Akali leaders quickly left the gathering and the stage was captured by extremists, including AISSF activists, who led the massive crowd in shouting pro-Bhindranwale and pro-Khalistan slogans. For the next several hours, the huge gathering listened to poets and *dhadis* (ballad singers) extolling the heroic deeds of

Sant Bhindranwale and Mrs Gandhi's assassins, Beant Singh and Satwant Singh. This indicated to the government that Sikh politics was moving in a more extremist direction and alienation was building in Punjab. Rajiv subsequently realized that something needed to be done to stymie the re-emergence of organized extremism in the state.

THE RELEASE OF SENIOR AKALI LEADERS AND THEIR COMPETITIVE RADICALISM TO WIN BACK SIKH SUPPORT

In mid-March 1985, the central government unexpectedly released select senior Akali leaders—including Longowal, Jagdev Singh Talwandi, and Surjit Singh Barnala—from jail.[23] The government, which had been talking to Longowal for months, wanted to prevent a shift in Sikh politics toward further extremism. By releasing Longowal, the government hoped that he would be able to consolidate Sikh support behind his "moderate" leadership and reach a compromise solution to the "Punjab problem." Upon his release, Longowal initially adopted a moderate tone, but it soon became apparent that this mild rhetoric was not having the desired effect of consolidating Sikh support behind his leadership. Both the central government and the Akali Dal were alarmed at the small, unenthusiastic crowds that he attracted after his release.[24]

In contrast, dissident Akali leader, Jagdev Singh Talwandi, came out of jail in a confrontational and fiery mood. As a result, he attracted huge and energetic Sikh crowds. Talwandi refused to compromise on the ASR and exclaimed:

Longowal and Tohra are people because of whom Sant Jarnail Singhji Khalsa Bhindranwale and his brave followers were riddled with bullets. These are the same leaders who used to say that if the Government entered the Golden Temple it will have to walk over their dead bodies. But when the crunch came they themselves jumped over the bodies of martyrs preferring the safety of army vehicles.[25]

Talwandi's success in attracting large crowds with his heated rhetoric forced Longowal to also veer toward an increasingly radical direction in his attempt to avoid becoming further marginalized within Sikh politics. As a part of this shift, Longowal visited Bhindranwale's elderly father, Baba Joginder Singh, at his native village of Rode to pay respects for his "martyred" son. He also began publicly referring to prime minister Rajiv Gandhi and President Zail Singh as being "the biggest enemies of the Sikhs," and eulogizing the great "sacrifices" made by Mrs Gandhi's assassins and the AISSF for the Sikh Panth.[26] One of Longowal's aides explained the rationale behind this strategy by saying:

> He can hardly afford to speak any other language for at least another six months. There is a vast storehouse of pent-up anger among the Sikhs. It is our strategy to let the community give vent to it through angry utterances and once passions show signs of cooling we can proceed towards conciliation.[27]

This fact was not lost on Rajiv Gandhi who allowed Longowal to spew radical rhetoric. This soon began having its desired effect as the crowds gathering to hear Longowal grew consistently larger. In addition, the central government also took other steps to strengthen the Sikh "moderates" and ameliorate Sikh discontent including lifting the ban on the AISSF, agreeing to a judicial inquiry into the anti-Sikh riots in Delhi (but not other parts of India), and releasing both Gurcharan Singh Tohra and Parkash Singh Badal as demanded by the Akali Dal.[28] Rajiv appeared to be laying the groundwork for finding a negotiated solution to the "Punjab problem" with the Akali Dal in the spring of 1985.

SIKH POLITICS IN A TAILSPIN: THE CREATION OF BABA JOGINDER SINGH'S "UNITED" AKALI DAL AND THE RE-EMERGENCE OF THE AISSF

After the release of all senior Akali leaders, Longowal's rhetoric began to change from being radical and confrontational to becoming more moderate and conciliatory. For example, in a meeting with senior opposition leaders in New Delhi, Longowal reaffirmed the Akali Dal's commitment to the unity and well-being of India. The central government reciprocated by expressing its desire to enter into negotiations on all outstanding issues. Yet, Longowal's earlier catering to extremist Sikh sentiments caught up with him in the first week of May when Baba Joginder Singh, father of the "martyr" Sant Jarnail Singh Bhindranwale, surprisingly announced that he had dissolved both the Akali Dal (Longowal) and Akali Dal (Talwandi) and had formed a new "united" Akali Dal under the leadership of a nine-member ad hoc committee which included Longowal, Talwandi, Tohra, and Badal.[29] The convenor of the "united" Akali Dal's ad hoc committee was to be former Indian Police Service officer Simranjeet Singh Mann who had resigned his post in protest of Operation Bluestar, gone underground, and had been arrested in December 1984 in connection with Mrs Gandhi's assassination.[30] Since Mann was in prison, Baba Joginder Singh conveniently nominated himself to be the acting convenor of the party.

Baba Joginder Singh justified his decision to create this "united" Akali Dal by explaining that it was necessary to forge unity in the Panth during this period of crisis. He legitimized his authority to undertake this move by producing a letter given to him by Longowal earlier in April in which Longowal agreed to abide by any decision taken by him in the wider interests of the Panth.[31] Talwandi had also signed a similar letter, but with an additional rider specifying that he would abide by any decision taken by the Baba as long as Longowal was not made the president of any new Akali party.

The creation of the "united" Akali Dal shocked the traditional Akali leadership, especially "the moderates." After all, Baba Joginder Singh had emerged from being a virtual unknown to becoming a potentially important leader virtually overnight with his decision to actively enter Sikh politics. The fact that his son had been "martyred" for the Sikh Panth gave the Baba an aura of respectability that few other Akali leaders could match individually. The "moderate" Akali leaders were put into a bind with the creation of the "united" Akali Dal because they could not afford to overtly show disrespect to the Baba. In a politically shrewd move, Longowal, Badal, and Tohra announced their resignations from their respective positions within the Akali Dal and SGPC, and agreed to follow the leadership of the new "united" Akali Dal as ordinary party members. Longowal explained by saying:

> We decided to resign our positions to help the Panth and the Akali Dal forge unity...By resigning, we have shown that we do not want to cling to our posts...Someone who would have been merely pulling our legs (trying to undermine us) is now there to guide and lead us. We accept him as our leader and let him show his worth. Baba Joginder Singh will have to shoulder responsibility.[32]

Yet, Longowal strategically left himself and the other traditional Akali leaders a path to eventually re-enter Sikh politics by saying, "Ours is a democratic party. The general house is supreme. Its directions will be carried out by everybody. Only the Akal Takht is above it."[33] The traditional Akali leaders, of course, had a majority in the general house of the Akali Dal and the Akal Takht *jathedar*, Kirpal Singh, was also their ally. Thus, the traditional Akali leadership showed respect to the Baba by accepting his decision, but they also carefully protected their own political interests.

In response, Baba Joginder Singh repeatedly met with Longowal, Tohra, and Badal in his attempt to convince them to join the "new" party's ad hoc committee, but they refused to do so. A frustrated Baba exclaimed:

Both Longowal and Talwandi had given me in writing that they would take whatever steps I thought best to bring unity in the panth at this critical and crucial hour and I decided to merge these two Dals and form a real Akali Dal, an organization of martyrs and not self-seekers. I included all major leaders in the committee...I have tried but with no success...God will grant us some sense.[34]

Baba Joginder Singh described the goals of the "united" Akali Dal as being *"Khalsa da bolbala. Khalsa di chardi kala.* (Glory to the Sikhs) ...Justice and peace in the country and the struggle for the acceptance of the Anandpur Sahib Resolution."[35] Thus, the party did not demand the creation of Khalistan but rather only increased regional autonomy for Punjab as specified in the ASR. The "united" Akali Dal also received support from the resurrected AISSF. Shortly after the creation of the "new" Akali party, detained AISSF president Bhai Manjit Singh and general secretary Harminder Singh Sandhu announced the formation of an ad hoc committee to lead the Federation while they were incarcerated. This committee was to be headed by its convenor, Harinder Singh Kahlon, who was instructed by Manjit Singh and Sandhu to work under the guidance of Baba Joginder Singh for the attainment of "Khalsa Raj" (Khalsa Rule).[36] Sikh politics was quickly becoming more complex with new actors entering into the fray.

In late-May, 23 out of 26 district *jathedars* of the Akali Dal (L) rejected the resignations of Longowal, Tohra, and Badal, and ordered them to resume their official party posts.[37] This vote effectively split the Akali Dal into two parties—the Akali Dal (L) supported by Longowal, Badal, Tohra, and Barnala, and the Akali Dal (United) supported by Baba Joginder Singh, Talwandi, and the AISSF. This Akali bifurcation occurred in the backdrop of resurgent Sikh political violence, including a series of deadly bomb blasts throughout north india which killed over one hundred people in May. These blasts were carried out by the regrouped Babbar Khalsa in retaliation for the anti-Sikh pogroms of November 1984.[38] Deadly clashes also occurred between Sikhs and Hindus in several cities in Punjab in early-summer 1985.[39] The changed "Sikh political spectrum" in mid-1985 looked like the following (Table 6.2).

SIGNING OF THE "PUNJAB ACCORD" AND THE ASSASSINATION OF SANT HARCHAND SINGH LONGOWAL

The Government of India provided the Akali Dal (L) with additional concessions in late-June 1985 in order to bolster its position in Sikh

Table 6.2
Sikh Political Spectrum (Mid-1985)

Moderates	Radicals	Extremists	Militants/Separatists
Akali Dal (L)[1]	Tohra[1]	Akali Dal (U)[2]	Babbar Khalsa
Longowal[1]	Talwandi[2]	Joginder Singh[2]	Unnamed gangs
Badal[1]		AISSF (Kahlon)[3]	

Source: Author.
Notes: [1] Akali Dal (L) and its leaders.
  [2] Akali Dal (U) and its leaders.
  [3] AISSF (Kahlon) linked to Akali Dal (U).

politics in comparison to the Akali Dal (U).[40] But, Rajiv subsequently ruled out any further concessions to the Akali Dal (L) until it agreed to enter into formal negotiations to find a comprehensive solution to the "Punjab problem." What occurred next surprised government officials, the media, and India's population alike. On 22 July 1985, it was announced that Longowal and Rajiv were engaged in one-on-one negotiations in New Delhi to hammer out a settlement to the "Punjab problem." Longowal was accompanied to the capital by only two of his closest lieutenants, Barnala and ex-finance minister Balwant Singh. Both Tohra and Badal were purposely excluded from these talks. Tohra was most likely left out because he was a "radical" and had been an obstacle to compromise in the past, and Badal was excluded because a number of his top loyalists had defected to the extremist Akali Dal (U), thus prompting concerns that he was "hedging his bets" within Sikh politics.

After only two days of talks, Rajiv and Longowal unexpectedly announced that a compromise, the Rajiv–Longowal Accord, had been reached. The memorandum of the Accord contained the following eight written points:

1. the transfer of Chandigarh to Punjab by 26 January 1986;
2. the transfer of specific Hindi-speaking areas from Punjab to Haryana which would be determined by a commission;
3. the binding adjudication of the river waters dispute between Punjab and Haryana within six months by a tribunal headed by a Supreme Court judge;
4. the completion of the Sutlej–Yumana Link (SYL) canal by 15 August 1986;
5. the consideration to formulate an All-India Sikh Gurdwara Act;
6. referring sections of the ASR dealing with center–state relations to a governmental commission;

7. expanding the jurisdiction of the commission of inquiry into the November anti-Sikhs riots to include Kanpur and Bokaro; and

8. having special courts adjudicate only cases of "waging war against the state" and hijacking, not any other political offences relating to Punjab.[41]

Most of India, including opposition parties and the media, were over-joyed over this Accord! But, in reality, the Accord was only a poten-tial breakthrough and not an iron-clad solution itself. In essence, it suffered from three major weaknesses. First, it lacked specificity. Many of its provisions were either contingent or they postponed resolution of contentious issues by referring them to various commissions for future settlement.[42] Second, many Sikhs felt that the Akali Dal had compromised too much on the ASR. While a majority of Sikhs in Punjab probably supported the Rajiv–Longowal Accord, a significant portion did not and perceived that Longowal had "sold-out" the Sikh Panth for his party's own narrow self-interests. For example, the Akali Dal (U) and AISSF stated that the accord was an agreement made by Longowal only in his "individual capacity," and represented an "atrocious betrayal" of the Sikhs on all major issues. In fact, the Akali Dal (U) threatened to conti-nue the *morcha* explaining that "[t]hese are the same men who swore in the sacred presence of the [*Guru Granth Sahib*] that they would not give up the morcha till the Anandpur Sahib Resolution was accepted."[43] Third, both Badal and Tohra, who were not privy to the negotiations adamantly refused to support the Accord. Both criticized Longowal for selling out on the ASR and for the accord's lack of specificity.

Thus, Longowal was not in an envious position with this Accord. After all, he needed to sell it to both his party and also to the wider Sikh community in Punjab in order for it to be effective. He got a chance to do so when Akali district *jathedars*, former MPs, and MLAs met at Anandpur Sahib in late-July to vote on the Accord. Both Badal and Tohra refused to support it, but a large majority of the other Akali delegates did approve it, thus allowing Longowal to declare "victory" in the *Dharam Yudh morcha* launched three years earlier. This was apparently a major victory for Longowal, but he alienated both Badal and Tohra in the process. In the attempt to accelerate the process of "normalization" in Punjab, Rajiv subsequently announced that both legislative assembly and parliamen-tary elections would be held in the state in late-September. The Akali Dal (L) had initially opposed holding elections until the Rajiv–Longowal Accord was fully implemented, but it eventually decided to participate and geared up for the polls. Both Badal and Tohra also subsequently fell into line and reluctantly agreed to support the Accord. After all, they did not want to be left marginalized within the party after these elections. Thus, supporting the Accord was a strategic decision on their part to protect their personal political interests.

Yet, an unexpected thing happened less than a month after the signing of the Punjab Accord. On August 20, Longowal was brutally gunned down by Sikh extremists while addressing a *gurdwara* congregation, apparently in retaliation for "selling-out" the Sikh *quam* (community or nation) by negotiating the Rajiv–Longowal Accord.[44] The entire nation was shocked at this assassination, and Longowal's funeral attracted tens of thousands of Sikh and Hindu mourners alike. Over 200,000 people, including leaders of all national political parties, attended Longowal's *bhog* (last rites) ceremony held 10 days later at his home village in Punjab.[45] Thus, Longowal became a "martyr" for the Akali Dal (L) much like Bhindranwale had become a "martyr" for "the extremists" earlier. In the wake of Longowal's assassination, district *jathedar*s of the Akali Dal (L) formally elected Barnala to be the acting president of the party, largely because he had been one of the only two senior Akali leaders who had accompanied Longowal to New Delhi during negotiations with Rajiv Gandhi. Thus, he best symbolized the Rajiv–Longowal Accord for the Akali Dal (L). Badal's name was not even proposed because he had initially opposed the Rajiv–Longowal Accord and many of his top loyalists had defected to the Akali Dal (U). Longowal's assassination portended emerging political cleavages within the Sikh politics.

THE 1985 STATE ASSEMBLY ELECTIONS AND THE FORMATION OF SURJIT SINGH BARNALA'S "MODERATE" AKALI GOVERNMENT IN PUNJAB

The September 1985 state assembly elections in Punjab took place under unprecedented security. The Akali Dal (L) campaigned on the basis of the Rajiv–Longowal Accord, arguing that a victory for the Akali Dal would be a victory for Punjab and Punjabis irrespective of religion. Surjit Singh Barnala declared, "All sections of people who are for peace and amity in the State will help us hold aloft the torch lit by Santji (referring to Longowal)."[46] The Akali Dal's election manifesto mildly criticized the Congress (I) for its policies and promised a general amnesty for all Sikhs arrested for political offenses against whom no serious charges were pending. Yet, it purposely avoided using heated ethnic rhetoric. The Congress (I) party's election plank was similar to that of the Akali Dal (L) in the sense that it also emphasized the Rajiv–Longowal Accord and the return of peace to Punjab, and avoided using confrontational language. This led to continual allegations, probably well-founded, that a "secret understanding" had been forged between the Congress (I) and the Akali Dal (L) in which the Congress (I) would purposely field weak candidates in order to allow the Akali Dal (L) to win and form the next state government in Punjab.[47] For their part, the Akali Dal (U) and AISSF decided to boycott the elections and, instead, hold meetings to "educate" the people on how the Accord was a "total sellout" of the Sikhs.[48]

The results of the elections were overwhelming. Voter turnout, 66.54 percent, was greater than the turnout in 1980, which had been 62.7 percent.[49] The Akali Dal (U) and AISSF's electoral boycott failed except in villages around Amritsar which had been worst affected by Operation Bluestar and Operation Woodrose. Out of 117 seats, the results were as follows: the Akal Dal (L) 73 seats, the Congress (I) 32 seats, the BJP 4 seats, the Janata Party 1 seat, the CPI 1 seat, Independents 4 seats, and 2 seats were countermanded.[50] Thus, the Congress (I)'s seat total was cut in half from 1980, and the Akali Dal won an unprecedented two-thirds majority. The popular vote, in contrast, was much closer with the Akali Dal (L) getting 38.5 percent in comparison to 26.9 percent in 1980 and the Congress (I) getting 37.7 percent in comparison in comparison to 45.2 percent in 1980.[51] In parliamentary voting, the Akali Dal (L) won seven seats and the Congress (I) won six.

His party's loss aside, Rajiv reconciled to the election results by proclaiming that "[t]he Congress (I) may have lost the electoral battle, but it has won the war for India's unity and integrity."[52] Rajiv was not necessarily more altruistic than his mother Indira Gandhi, but, instead, he could afford to let the Akalis win in Punjab because he commanded a huge majority in Parliament and felt that his position of power was secure.

The Akalis were now in power in Punjab, and Barnala became the chief minister of the state. After these elections, Tohra threw his support behind Barnala. In return, Barnala promised to support Tohra's re-election to the post of SGPC president. In order to avoid being further marginalized within the party, Badal also backed Barnala for the chief ministership. In return, Barnala offered Badal a cabinet position of his choice in the initial six-man ministry, but Badal refused this offer.[53] After all, Badal knew that Barnala's government had numerous and daunting obstacles to overcome, irrespective of the party's huge majority in the state assembly. For this reason, Badal strategically decided to take a "wait-and-see" approach instead of joining the government. Barnala's "moderate" Akali government was threatened from three sides. First, Barnala had to deliver on his election promises, including having the central government fully implement the Rajiv–Longowal Accord beginning with the scheduled transfer of Chandigarh to Punjab on 26 January 1986. Second, the Akali Dal (U) and AISSF continued to retain significant support within the Sikh community, and extremist violence had not been stomped out in Punjab. Third, Barnala's "allies" within the Akali Dal (L)—namely Badal and Tohra—were lurking in the background for an opportunity to undermine his government when, and if, the opportunity presented. Thus, Barnala's position of power, in reality, was not as secure as it appeared to be on face-value.

After coming into office, Barnala's government took several steps to ameliorate Sikh discontent including releasing hundreds of Sikh political detainees, providing jobs to victims of state repression, and starting to rehabilitate both Sikh army deserters and Sikh riot victims.[54] Barnala and his ministers, including Capt. Amarinder Singh, paid obeisance at the Golden Temple but refused to enter the government-built Akal Takht, thus publicly demonstrating their sense of resentment against Operation Bluestar.[55] In essence, Barnala tried to play a delicate balancing act by giving vent to continuing Sikh frustrations, while also trying to ameliorate the factors that were contributing to it. The "Sikh political spectrum" after the September 1985 elections looked like the following (Table 6.3):

Table 6.3
Sikh Political Spectrum (Late-1985)

Moderates	Radicals	Extremists	Militants/Separatists
Akali Dal (L)[1]	Tohra[1]	Akali Dal (U)[2]	Babbar Khalsa
Barnala[1]	Talwandi[2]	Joginder Singh[2]	Unnamed gangs
Badal[1]		AISSF (Kahlon)[3]	

Source: Author.
Notes: [1] Akali Dal (L) and its leaders.
        [2] Akali Dal (U) and its leaders.
        [3] AISSF (Kahlon) linked to Akali Dal (U).

THE REASSERTION OF "THE EXTREMISTS" IN SIKH POLITICS AND THEIR PRESSURE ON BARNALA'S "MODERATE" AKALI MINISTRY

Surjit Singh Barnala's Akali Dal (L) government had a tenuous "love–hate" relationship with the "extremist" Akali Dal (U) and the AISSF. Barnala's emissaries often met with Akali Dal (U) and AISSF representatives in an attempt to gain their support for the Rajiv–Longowal Accord and the Akali ministry. After all, the AISSF had made tremendous "sacrifices" for the Panth, and Baba Joginder Singh was the father of the great Sikh "martyr" Sant Jarnail Singh Bhindranwale. For their part, the Akali Dal (U) and AISSF publicly praised Barnala for his efforts regarding Sikh detainees and the rehabilitation of Sikh victims, but both organizations also called on Sikh youth to continue their "struggle to face the black deeds of the [central] Government and for unconditional release of all [remaining] detained Sikhs."[56]

Political violence committed by armed Sikh extremists also continued during this period, and the Punjab police raided the residential portion of the Golden Temple complex several times under instructions from the central government to arrest suspected militants. These "transgressions" harked back to Operation Bluestar, and soured the Barnala government's relationship with the Akali Dal (U), AISSF, and large sections of the Sikh community. Thus, Barnala was caught between the continuing demands of the Akali Dal (U) and AISSF on one side, and the unwillingness of Rajiv's Congress (I) central government to concede to them on the other.

The "extremists" had generally been united after Operation Bluestar, but initial indications of emerging fissures within their ranks began to be seen for the first time in late-fall of 1985. This occurred when Baba Joginder Singh refused to fund an AISSF convention planned to honor "Sikh martyrs" unless he was allowed to determine the convention's speakers. The AISSF apparently wanted to use the Baba as a figurehead for its movement, but he refused to play this role and, instead, wished for the AISSF to remain subservient to his party.[57] After Baba Joginder Singh's refusal, AISSF convenor Harinder Singh Kahlon turned to Baba Thakur Singh— the acting head of the Damdami Taksal—for support, who agreed to provide the necessary funding for the AISSF function.[58] Baba Joginder Singh resented this move by the AISSF because the Damdami Taksal was a potential competitor for his leadership of the extremist-wing of the "Sikh movement." Thus, a schism was gradually emerging within the ranks of "the extremists" with the Akali Dal (U) on one side, and the AISSF and the Damdami Taksal on the other.

In late-December 1985, a religious controversy emerged that would have major consequences on Sikh politics when SGPC president Tohra announced that a *kar sewa* for rebuilding the government-constructed Akal Takht would begin on 27 January 1986 (a day after the planned transfer of Chandigarh to Punjab).[59] A day after Tohra's announcement, the Damdami Taksal and AISSF held a joint *shaheedi samagam* (martyrs' ceremony) during which the families of 500 Sikh "martyrs" were honored, including the wife and two young sons of Sant Bhindranwale.[60] During this convention, a *gurmata* was passed by the congregation declaring that the *kar sewa* should be done under the auspices of the Damdami Taksal, not the SGPC, because the Taksal had made "supreme sacrifices" in protecting the sanctity of the Golden Temple and Akal Takht during Operation Bluestar. Thus, the political fault lines in Punjab were gradually becoming intra-Sikh ones over the future direction of the Panth and for dominance within the community.

THE CENTER'S NON-IMPLEMENTATION OF THE "PUNJAB ACCORD," AND MARGINALIZATION OF BARNALA AND "THE MODERATES"

In light of the apparent challenge posed by "the extremists," Barnala needed the central government to implement the first provision specified in the Punjab Accord—the transfer of Chandigarh to Punjab—as scheduled on 26 January 1986. But, serious complications emerged regarding this issue when the Mathew Commission proved unable to determine which Hindi-speaking areas of Punjab would go to Haryana in exchange for Chandigarh.[61] In lieu of a decision made by the Mathew Commission, Barnala and Haryana's Congress (I) chief minister Bhajan Lal also could not agree on mutually acceptable territorial adjustments for each state. For its part, Rajiv's central government was stuck between the two bickering chief ministers, each of whom wanted to protect his political support base in his respective state. At about this time, Rajiv's "honeymoon" in power as a national leader beyond criticism was also ending, and Hindu resentment against the central government for its inability to wipe out political violence in Punjab was growing throughout north India. Within this context, Bhajan Lal advised Rajiv not to undermine Haryana's interests and risk alienating Hindu voters throughout north India by unilaterally supporting Punjab's case. Thus, after a series of "terrorist" killings, Rajiv publicly warned Barnala to control Sikh extremism in his state or consider stepping-down from power. Shortly thereafter, Barnala, for the first time, openly accused the AISSF of trying to pull down his "Panthic Government" and ordered the arrest of hundreds of AISSF activists.[62] This sparked vocal accusations in the Sikh community that Barnala was acting as a proxy for the Delhi *Durbar* (central government).

The Mathew Commission finally presented its final report on 25 January 1986, which identified 83 Hindi-speaking villages and two towns in the Abohar and Fazilka *thesils* of Punjab which should go to Haryana in exchange for Chandigarh. But, another problem soon arose because these Hindi-speaking areas were not contiguous with Haryana, and Barnala refused to give up even a single Punjabi-speaking village as a matter of principle to form a corridor to the identified Hindu-speaking areas.[63] Central government authorities tried desperately to formulate some sort of compromise, but they were unsuccessful. Rajiv had no solution to offer, and the 26 January deadline passed without the transfer of Chandigarh to Punjab. Thus, the first phase of the much heralded solution to the "Punjab crisis"—Rajiv–Longowal Accord—appeared to be dead on arrival!

With this failure to implement the first phase of the Punjab Accord, the central government appeared to have squandered an important opportunity to strengthen Barnala's "moderate" Akali government and take a huge step toward finally solving the "Punjab crisis." Instead, the most intense and bitter battle over Sikh political institutions since the 1920s was about to begin between "the moderates" and "the extremists" within Sikh politics. Over eighteen months after Operation Bluestar, the "Punjab problem" remained unresolved and, in fact, seemed poised for a potential dangerous re-escalation at the beginning of 1986.

SUMMARY AND CONCLUSION

The years analyzed in this chapter represented a "transitory period" in which the "Punjab problem" could either escalate or de-escalate based on emerging "patterns of political leadership" after Operation Bluestar. After Mrs Gandhi's initial attempts to break the Akali Dal's dominance over traditional Sikh institutions failed, she began sending "feelers" to jailed Akali leaders to re-enter negotiations for settling the "Punjab problem." Yet, prospects for the return of "normalcy" to Punjab became shattered when Mrs Gandhi was assassinated by her Sikh bodyguards, and thousands of Sikhs were subsequently killed in anti-Sikh pogroms throughout north India.

The new Indian prime minister, Rajiv Gandhi, began seeking a solution to the "Punjab problem" after winning an unprecedented three-fourths majority in Parliament. Yet, his government faced a major obstacle in immediately compromising with the Akali Dal—namely, that the Akalis were internally divided. To explain, the "moderate" Longowal came out of jail in a conciliatory mood whereas the "radical" Talwandi came out in a defiant one, attracting huge crowds with his fiery uncompromising rhetoric. This forced Longowal to strategically radicalize in order to shore-up his own ethnic support base and avoid being undermined by Talwandi.

Yet, Longowal's attempt to strategically "outbid" Talwandi—which was initially tolerated by the government—also had unintended consequences. In essence, it helped foster the creation of the "extremist" Akali Dal (United) led by Bhindranwale's father, Baba Joginder Singh, and also the re-emergence of the "extremist" AISSF. Thus, the Akalis' internal divisions and their competitive "outbidding," once again, prevented effective compromise and helped foster the emergence of Sikh extremist groups.

In their subsequent attempt to forestall the ascendance of renewed extremism, Rajiv and Longowal signed the Punjab Accord as a compromise solution to the "Punjab problem." Shortly after signing the Accord, Longowal was assassinated by armed Sikh extremists for supposedly "selling-out" the Sikh *quam* (community). Barnala, who was Longowal's closest aide, was made president of the Akali Dal over either Badal or Tohra because both of them had initially refused to support the Punjab Accord. The "moderate" Barnala received a huge boost when the Akali Dal won the state assembly elections in Punjab in September 1985. Yet, Barnala's "moderate" government faced challenges from within Sikh politics, including from the reorganizing "extremists" and Barnala's comparatively more "radical" rivals within the Akali Dal; for example, Badal and Tohra.

The situation in Punjab reached a critical juncture in early-1986 when the first major provision of the Punjab Accord—the transfer of Chandigarh to Punjab—failed to be implemented. This occurred because both Barnala and Haryana's Congress (I) chief minister Bhajan Lal could not agree on which Hindi-speaking areas of Punjab should be transferred to Haryana in exchange for Chandigarh. Barnala refused to compromise too much with Bhajan Lal, for the fear of being criticized by "the extremists" and his more "radical" intra-party rivals, and Bhajan Lal vigorously guarded the perceived interests of Haryana. For his part, Rajiv was reluctant to act in a decisive way by dictating terms to his intra-party Congress (I) underling, Bhajan Lal, whose regional political support he desired in Hindu-majority states bordering Punjab.

The failure to implement the Punjab Accord severely weakened the "moderate" Barnala, and strengthened the largely united "extremists" and also "the radicals" within the Akali Dal. Thus, three "patterns of political leadership"—competitive "outbidding" and factionalism between the traditional Akali leadership, the relative unity within the ranks of "the extremists," and internal disunity amongst ruling Congress (I) state authorities—coalesced to stymie successful implementation of the Punjab Accord, and contributed to the initial resurgence of Sikh extremism in Punjab in the post-Bluestar period.

NOTES

1. Express News Service, "Surface calm in Punjab," *Indian Express*, 15 June 1984, 7.
2. The "Head Priests" at the time consisted of the *Jathedars* of the Akal Takht, Takht Sri Kesgarh Sahib, Takht Sri Damdama Sahib, and the Head *Granthis* of both the Golden Temple and the Akal Takht. Traditionally, the "institution" of Head Priests had consisted of the *Jathedars* of the Five Sikh Takhts which also includes Takht Sri Patna Sahib in Bihar and Takht Sri Hazoor Sahib in Maharashtra. These two shrines are over a thousand miles away from Amritsar, and their *Jathedars* are not always readily available for deliberation and decision-making. These two Takhts are also not under the control of the SGPC, and thus their *Jathedars* do not always sympathize with the religious interpretations and political compulsions of the other three *Jathedars*, the SGPC, or the Akali Dal in Punjab. For this reason, the SGPC has historically used the Head *Granthis* of both the Akal Takht and the Golden Temple to substitute for the *Jathedars* of Patna Sahib and Hazoor Sahib.
3. This is narrated by Kirpal Singh in Anurag Singh (translator and editor), *Giani Kirpal Singh's Eye-Witness Account of Operation Bluestar: Mighty Murderous Army Attack on the Golden Temple Complex* (Amritsar: B. Chattar Singh Jiwan Singh Publishers, 1999), 74–75.
4. Quoted in Gobind Thukral, "Punjab: Abortive Advances," *India Today*, 15 September 1984, 34.
5. Ibid.: 35.
6. Express News Service, "Sarbat Khalsa call to change Gurdwara Act: Meet excommunicates Tohra," *Indian Express*, 12 August 1984, 1.
7. Gobind Thukral, "Punjab: Abortive Advances," *India Today*, 15 September 1984, 34; and Express News Service, "Sarbat Khalsa call to change Gurdwara Act: Meet excommunicates Tohra," *Indian Express*, 12 August 1984, 1 and 7.
8. Sunil Sethi, "Punjab: Show of Strength," *India Today*, 30 September 1984, 23.
9. Express News Service, "Convention ultimatum for Army pull-out," *Indian Express*, 4 September 1984, 2. For a complete list of the ten resolutions passed by the congregation see A. Singh, *Giani Kirpal Singh's*, 130–35.
10. See G.S. Chawla, "Longowal against truck with extremists," *Indian Express*, 29 August 1984, 1.
11. Buta Singh would be excommunicated from the Panth in April 1985 after refusing to present himself before the Akal Takht. See A. Singh, *Giani Kirpal Singh's*, 215–17.
12. Prabhu Chawla, "Punjab: A Glimmer of Hope," *India Today*, 15 October 1984, 27.
13. For a detailed description of this violence, see Shekhar Gupta, Coomi Kapoor, Raju Santhanam, and Sunil Sethi, "The Violent Aftermath," *India Today*, 30 November 1984, 38–48; and *India Today*, 15 December 1984, 52–57.
14. Virginia Van Dyke, "The Anti-Sikh Riots of 1984 in Delhi: Politicians, Criminals, and the Discourse of Communalism," in *Riots and Pogroms*, ed. Paul R. Brass (London: MacMillian Press Limited, 1996), 210–13.
15. See Jaskaran Kaur, *Twenty Years of Impunity: The November 1984 Pogroms of Sikhs in India* (London: Nectar Publishing, 2004), 45–73.
16. Shekhar Gupta, Coomi Kapoor, Raju Santhanam, and Sunil Sethi, "Punjab & Haryana: Uneasy Calm," *India Today*, 30 November 1984, 47.
17. Shekhar Gupta, Coomi Kapoor, Raju Santhanam, and Sunil Sethi, "High Priests: Contortions," *India Today*, 30 November 1984, 46.

18. During this period, Badal tried to challenge Longowal's authority with possible support of the Congress (I) by opposing Tohra's re-election to the post of SGPC president. The Head Priests acted to quell this challenge and maintain the status quo in Sikh politics by backing Longowal and Tohra. For details see Ibid., 66–67; and A. Singh, *Giani Kirpal Singh's*, 183–85.

19. For an example of the Congress (I)'s playing on the fear of Sikh separatism, see paid election advertisement titled "Will The Country's Border Finally Be Moved To Your Doorstep" appearing in *Indian Express*, 27 November 1984, 8.

20. P.T.I., "Thekedar rules out talks unless Akali leaders are released," *Indian Express*, 20 December 1984, 1.

21. Ramindar Singh, "Punjab: A Dangerous Limbo," *India Today*, 15 March 1985, 28.

22. Shyam Khosla, "Akali ultimatum to Centre," *The Tribune*, 9 March 1985, 1.

23. Satindra Singh, "Sant's Terms for Talks," *The Tribune*, 12 March 1985, 1.

24. See A. Singh, *Giani Kirpal Singh's*, 214–15.

25. Shekhar Gupta and Gobind Thukral, "Punjab: Moving Cautiously," *India Today*, 15 April 1985, 8.

26. For examples, see Staff Correspondent, "'Khalistan' slogans at Sant's meeting," *The Tribune*, 4 April 1985, 1; U.N.I., "Sant raises pro-Bhindranwale slogans," *The Tribune*, 9 April 1985, 1; and Tribune Correspondent, "Sant's praise for assassin," *The Tribune*, 10 April 1985, 1.

27. Shekhar Gupta and Gobind Thukral, "Punjab: Moving Cautiously," *India Today*, 15 April 1985, 9.

28. Tribune Bureau, "Probe Into Delhi Riots Ordered; Ban on A.I.S.S.F. goes; more Akalis to be freed," *The Tribune*, 12 April 1985, 1.

29. U.N.I., "Dal Factions Dissolved," *The Tribune*, 2 May 1985, 1.

30. For an account of Mann's arrest and detention see Raju Santhanam, "The Assassination: The Silent Prisoner," *India Today*, 15 January 1985, 64–65.

31. Shekhar Gupta and Gobind Thukral, "The Punjab Crisis: The Return of Terrorism," *India Today*, 31 May 1985, 13; U.N.I. "Dal Factions Dissolved," *The Tribune*, 2 May 1985, 1; and Interview with a close relative of Sant Bhindranwale and high-level member of the AISSF active from 1978 to the late-1980's, 27 March 2002.

32. Gobind Thukral, "H.S. Longowal: 'I don't fear anything,'" *India Today*, 31 May 1985, 16.

33. Ibid.: 17.

34. Gobind Thukral, "Baba Joginder Singh: 'God will grant us sense," *India Today*, 15 June 1985, 19.

35. Ibid.

36. Staff Correspondent, "6-member panel to run A.I.S.S.F.," *The Tribune*, 10 May 1985, 1.

37. Ramindar Singh and Gobind Thukral, "Akali Dal: Feuding Factions," *India Today*, 15 June 1985, 18.

38. Shekhar Gupta and Gobind Thukral, "The Punjab Crisis: The Return of Terrorism," *India Today*, 31 May 1985 9.

39. For details see Gobind Thukral, "Hoshiarpur: Danger Signs," *India Today*, 30 June 1985, 15.

40. For details see P.P.S. Gill, "Detainees To Be Freed: PM for starting new chapter," *The Tribune*, 29 June 1985, 1.

41. Satindra Singh and D.R. Ahuja, "Chandigarh Goes to Punjab, Hindi Areas' Transfer by Jan 26: Accord at a Glance," *The Tribune*, 25 July 1985, 1. A complete text of the Rajiv-Longowal Accord is contained in Gurmit Singh, *History of Sikh Struggles*, volume 4 (New Delhi: Atlantic Publishers and Distributors, 1992), 113–15.

42. Press reports also suggested that there were also several unwritten parts of the Accord. For details, see Shekhar Gupta and Gobind Thukral, "Punjab: Breakthrough," *India Today*, 15 August 1985, 17 and 18.

43. Shekhar Gupta and Gobind Thukral, "Punjab: Breakthrough," *India Today*, 15 August 1985, 13.

44. Tribune Reporters, "Sant shot at, injured," *The Tribune*, 21 August 1985, 1.

45. A.S. Prashar, "Lakhs pay homage to Sant," *The Tribune*, 2 September 1985, 1.

46. P.D. Mohindra, "Poll manifesto: Akalis to project accord," *The Tribune*, 28 August 1985, 1.

47. Suman Dubey and Gobind Thukral, "Punjab: Election Under the Gun," *India Today*, 30 September 1985, 32.

48. P.P.S. Gill, "'United' Dal to boycott poll," *The Tribune*, 29 August 1985, 1.

49. Ashok Lahri, "Punjab Elections: Growing Polarisation," *India Today*, 30 September 1985, 35; and Ramindar Singh and Gobind Thukral, "Punjab Election: Verdict Against Extremism," *India Today*, 15 October 1985, 12.

50. Ibid.

51. Ashok Lahri, "Punjab Election: Growing Polarisation," *India Today*, 30 September 1985, 35; and Raminder Singh and Gobind Thukral, "Punjab Election: Verdict Against Extremism," *India Today*, 15 October 1985, 14.

52. U.N.I., "Cong (I)'s loss is India's gain: P.M.," *The Tribune*, 28 September 1985, 1.

53. A.S. Prashar, "6-man Akali Ministry sworn-in: Badal stays out," *The Tribune*, 30 September 1985, 1.

54. For examples, see Staff Correspondent, "Barnala reviews law and order," *The Tribune*, 22 October 1985, 1; Tribune Bureau, "8,000 youths to get jobs," *The Tribune*, 6 November 1985, 1; A.S. Prashar, "Rehabilitation of deserters begins," *The Tribune* 25 November 1985, 1; and Tribune Bureau, "Steps to help Sikh migrants," *The Tribune*, 12 December 1985, 1.

55. Staff Correspondent, "Police entry into temple not to be allowed: C.M.," *The Tribune*, 1 October 1985, 1.

56. Tribune Correspondent, "Sikh youths asked to 'continue struggle,'" *The Tribune*, 7 October 1985, 1.

57. Author's interview with senior Khalistani activist and leader active in the militant movement since 1978, Fremont, California, USA, 19 November 2001.

58. D.P. Sharma, *The Punjab Story: Decade of Turmoil* (New Delhi: APH Publishing, 1996), 91–92.

59. Tribune Correspondent, "Akal Takht 'kar seva' on Jan 27," *The Tribune*, 29 December 1985, 1.

60. P.P.S. Gill, "Controversy over Takht rebuilding," *The Tribune*, 30 December 1985, 1.

61. See Gobind Thukral, "Punjab & Haryana: Discord over the Accord," *India Today*, 15 January 1986, 21–23.

62. See A.S. Prashar, "Akali Dal mandate: Stern warning to AISSF activists," *The Tribune*, 7 January 1986, 1; Shyam Khosla, "AISSF hideouts raided: Stage set for confrontation," *The Tribune*, 8 January 1986, 1.

63. For details, see Sumit Mitra, Prabhu Chawla, and Gobind Thukral, "Punjab & Haryana: The Bungled Accord," *India Today*, 15 February 1986, 16–20.

7

Reorganization of the Militants and the Armed Struggle for Khalistan (1986–1988)

January 1986 "Sarbat Khalsa" and Formation of the Militant "Panthic Committee"

By early-1986, the Damdami Taksal had emerged as the primary nucleus around which Sikh extremists and loosely-knit "gangs" of armed militants rallied and organized for a possible renewed "Sikh struggle".[1] The families of Sikh "martyrs" lobbied the reinvigorated Taksal to give political direction to the Sikh *quam* (community or "nation") in place of the Akalis. In mid- and late-January 1986, the Damdami Taksal, AISSF, and the Akali Dal (United) took over the Golden Temple complex and prepared for the *kar sewa* (community service) to tear down the government-constructed Akal Takht and build a new one. These extremist organizations also announced that a *Sarbat Khalsa* (representative or symbolic meeting of the entire Sikh Panth) would be held at the Akal Takht on 26 January to discuss the political crisis facing the Panth and chart out a future course of action. By calling this *Sarbat Khalsa*, the "extremists" strategically harked back to the 18th century and resurrected a much-forgotten Sikh political institution that had been previously used to make collective decisions for the community.[2] This "capture" of the Golden Temple complex also symbolized a direct challenge to the authority and power of Barnala's ministry, the Akali Dal (Longowal), and SGPC.

On 26 January 1986 (India's Republic Day), tens of thousands of Sikhs thronged to the Golden Temple complex to attend the Damdami Taksal-sponsored *kar sewa* and *Sarbat Khalsa*. The SGPC had approved the rebuilding of the Akal Takht but had not authorized the Damdami Taksal to take the lead in the *kar sewa*. Thus, senior SGPC officials, including its president Gurcharan Singh Tohra, failed to show up for this convention as originally planned, fearing for their physical safety. As a result, the Damdami Taksal and "extremists" had exclusive control over the convention, and it became one of the most important political gatherings of the entire "Punjab crisis."

During this *Sarbat Khalsa*, the Damdami Taksal presented an eight-page *gurmata* (collective resolution) which the congregation "passed" with an overwhelming show of hands. This *gurmata* accused the Akali Dal and SGPC of having "connived" with the Government of India "to attack the Golden Temple," and characterized Barnala's government as being "subservient to the Centre and determined to please the Delhi Durbar (rulers in Delhi)."[3] It also declared that a "long-drawn struggle" against the government was necessary and justified because "the Sikhs are slaves in India and to get freedom is their basic right."[4]

This *gurmata* identified several steps for helping attain "freedom" for the Sikhs. First, it sacked and excommunicated two of the Head Priests, including Akal Takht *jathedar* Kirpal Singh, and replaced him with Bhindranwale's nephew, Jasbir Singh Rode. Gurdev Singh Koanke, another product of the Damdami Taksal seminary, was made acting *Jathedar* since Rode was being held in government custody. The three other Head Priests were directed to tender their resignations or force being sacked in the near future. Second, the *gurmata* dissolved the SGPC and created a five-member "Panthic Committee" in its place as the premier source of Sikh leadership to make all future religious and political decisions for the Panth under the guidance of the Akal Takht. The Panthic Committee consisted of Wassan Singh Zafferwal, Gurbachan Singh Manochahal, Dhanna Singh, Aroor Singh, and Gurdev Singh Usmanwala—all proclaimed offenders.[5] Third, the *gurmata* specified that a *Sarbat Khalsa* would be held twice every year—in April and November—to make collective decisions for the Sikh *quam*, including replacing members of the Panthic Committee, if necessary.

Thus, "the extremists" and re-organizing "militants" created a set of parallel political institutions with which to challenge and supercede the traditional Akali leadership found in the Akali Dal and SGPC. In essence, Sikh "extremists" and "militants" wanted to capture key Sikh political and religious institutions in order to gain increased authority over the Sikh community and also give their renewed "Sikh struggle" added legitimacy. The *Sarbat Khalsa* did not declare the creation of an independent Sikh state, but saffron-colored flags emblazoned with the words "Khalistan *zindabad* (long live)" were raised atop buildings in the Golden Temple complex in open defiance of central authority. The congregation also began demolishing the government-built Akal Takht. Thus, "the extremists'" grip on the temple complex was complete, and the traditional Akali leadership, including Barnala's "moderate" government, faced a serious intra-Sikh challenge to their authority and power.

Yet, the dramatic public events at the *Sarbat Khalsa* hid some important political dynamics occurring behind the scenes which involved "the extremists"—namely increased factionalism within their ranks. In essence, three main lines of cleavage emerged both within and between the various extremist organizations. First, a schism emerged between Manbir Singh Chaheru and Sukhdev Singh Sakhira—the chiefs of two of the largest "gangs" of armed Sikh militants. Chaheru was firmly committed to the creation of Khalistan, whereas Sakhira was willing to compromise on this issue if the government declared a general amnesty for all Sikh political prisoners.[6] As a concession to both Sakhira and Baba Joginder Singh, the Taksal and the Panthic Committee appointed Koanke to be the acting *Jathedar* of the Akal Takht until Rode was released from jail. Koanke was respected by all extremist organizations but, like both Sakhira and the Baba, he was not an avowed separatist. Sakhira would, in fact, be killed by Chaheru a few months later in inter-gang rivalry.

Second, AISSF convenor Harinder Singh Kahlon objected to the Damdami Taksal challenging Barnala's government and directly confronting the Indian state.[7] Instead, he advised first focusing on the *kar sewa* issue to build increased legitimacy within the Sikh community before directly challenging the central state. Kahlon was overruled by the armed "militants" who wanted an immediate political front group for their separatist cause, thus forcing the AISSF to reluctantly accept the Panthic Committee's authority. In essence, supporters of the Panthic Committee were committed separatists, whereas Kahlon and the AISSF were still willing to settle for the Anandpur Sahib Resolution (ASR) and "Khalsa Raj" (Sikh Rule) short of Khalistan.

Third, Akali Dal (U) leader Baba Joginder Singh objected to the dissolution of the SGPC and the creation of the Panthic Committee, which he accused of being given authority above the Akal Takht.[8] The Baba was actually not privy to the deliberations before the *Sarbat Khalsa* that specified the exact content of the *gurmata* and, thus, he walked-out of the convention as an act of protest when the *gurmata* was presented to the congregation without his knowledge. Baba Joginder Singh viewed both the Damdami Taksal and the Panthic Committee as being competitors to his leadership of the extremist-wing of the "Sikh movement." Being a life-long Akali worker, he also did not want to dissolve the Akali Dal and SGPC but, instead, only wanted to capture these esteemed Sikh institutions from "the moderates".[9] In order to placate the Baba, the Damdami Taksal agreed to appoint his jailed grandson, Jasbir Singh Rode, to the position of Akal Takht *jathedar.*

The January 1986 *Sarbat Khalsa* was an important, if not pivotal, event in the history of the "Punjab crisis." After all, it marked the resurgence of organized Sikh militancy for the first time after Operation Bluestar and represented an overt challenge to the authority and power of the traditional Akali leadership. Yet, it also exposed emerging faultlines within the ranks of "the extremists" and reorganizing "militants" which may eventually affect the trajectory of their ethnonationalist movement.

AKALI DAL (L)'S COUNTER *SARBAT KHALSA* AND INDUCTION OF THE RIBEIRO–RAY "LAW-AND-ORDER" TEAM INTO PUNJAB

The extremists' "capture" of the Golden Temple complex and their creation of parallel structures of political authority set off alarm bells in both Chandigarh and New Delhi. The Akali Dal (L), which was already reeling from the non-implementation of the Punjab Accord, responded by challenging the authenticity of the extremist-sponsored *Sarbat Khalsa.* It argued that the convention had only represented the views of the Damdami Taksal and other extremist organizations, and not that of the entire Sikh Panth because it was not fully "representative" as required by Sikh tradition.[10] To counter "the extremists," the traditional Akali leadership announced that another *Sarbat Khalsa* would be held under the guidance of the Akal Takht *jathedar* Kirpal Singh at Anandpur Sahib to discuss the "arbitrary decisions of certain people who violated the sanctity and traditions of the community."[11] The popular response to this counter *Sarbat Khalsa* organized by the Akali Dal (L), SGPC, and the High Priests was enormous and many times greater than the Damdami Taksal-sponsored *Sarbat Khalsa* held earlier in Amritsar. A *gurmata* was passed during this counter convention which authorized the Akali Dal and SGPC "to end the illegal interference in [the] Darbar Sahib and restore the Sikh traditions which have been usurped [by the extremists]."[12]

Thus, Barnala appeared to have won this battle of competing *Sarbat Khalsa* conventions, but several problems emerged during the Akali Dal (L)-sponsored *Sarbat Khalsa* that weakened Barnala's power in Sikh politics. First, Parkash Singh Badal publicly warned Barnala not to use force to vacate the Golden Temple complex as Mrs Gandhi had done during Operation Bluestar.[13] Second, Tohra resigned from his position as SGPC president without explanation. These were strategic moves by both Badal and Tohra who wanted to distance themselves from any possible police action against "the extremists" in Golden Temple complex. Barnala appeared to be in control of institutionalized Sikh politics but, in reality, his position was quite vulnerable. After all, the Punjab Accord had not been implemented, and his fellow Akalis and supposed allies—Badal and Tohra—were lying in wait for an opportunity to undermine his leadership and enhance their own political power. The "Sikh political spectrum" at this point looked like the following (Table 7.1):

Table 7.1
Sikh Political Spectrum (Early-1986)

Moderates	Radicals	Extremists	Militants/Separatists
Akali Dal (L)[1]	Tohra[1]	Akali Dal (U)[2]	Damdami Taksal[3]
Barnala[1]	Talwandi[2]	Joginder Singh[2]	Panthic Committee[3]
Badal[1]			AISSF (Kahlon)[3]
			Babbar Khalsa

Source: Author.
Notes: [1] Akali Dal (L) and its leaders.
[2] Akali Dal (U) and its leaders.
[3] Damdami Taksal, Panthic Committee, AISSF (Kahlon) united.

After the two competing *Sarbat Khalsa* conventions, there was a sharp upsurge in political and communal violence in Punjab which was described as being "the worst-ever violence since the traumatic days leading to Operation Bluestar."[14] Fifty-three people were killed in this violence during the last two weeks of March 1986, in comparison to only 82 in the five previous months of Barnala's rule combined.[15] The situation became so communally-volatile and widespread that seven cities in Punjab containing over one-tenth of the state's population were put under total curfew due to Hindu–Sikh clashes in late-March![16]

As the communal situation deteriorated in Punjab, Rajiv Gandhi and his central government publicly warned Barnala to control the spiraling cycle of violence and extremism in the state. In response, Barnala requested the services of distinguished police officer, Julio Francis Ribeiro, to become Director General of Police (DGP) in Punjab. Ribeiro had successfully tackled underworld mafia violence in Bombay and had also prevented large-scale communal disturbances while serving as police chief in

Gujarat.[17] The central government also inducted Siddhartha Shankar Ray into the post of Governor of Punjab. Ray had been chief minister of West Bengal in the 1970s and had been credited with crushing the Naxalite insurgency. The Ribeiro–Ray team symbolized a renewed "law-and-order" approach to the "Punjab problem," which the press colorfully termed as being a "bullet-for-bullet" policy for dealing with escalating Sikh extremism in Punjab.[18]

EMERGING BIFURCATION OF THE AISSF AND THE "EXTREMISTS"

Sikh extremism was on the rise in the spring of 1986, but all was not well within the ranks of "the extremists" whose relative unity broke apart in April, resulting in the emergence of two distinct blocs. This clear split—the first within "the extremists" in the post-Bluestar period—was precipitated by internal factionalism within the AISSF, and competition between the Damdami Taksal and the Akali Dal (U). To explain, AISSF convenor Kahlon had succeeded in making the AISSF the largest mass-based "extremist" organization in Punjab within a year of the central government lifting the ban on the organization. Kahlon's success sparked resentment with lower-level AISSF leaders, who complained to the organization's senior leadership jailed in Jodhpur that Kahlon was becoming too autocratic and that he may have been holding "secret negotiations" with the central government.[19] The jailed "Jodhpur leadership," consisting of AISSF president Manjit Singh (younger brother of the "martyred" previous AISSF president Bhai Amrik Singh) and general secretary Harminder Singh Sandhu (the only surviving member of Bhindranwale's "inner circle"), felt threatened by Kahlon's charismatic leadership and his close association with the Damdami Taksal. In fact, both Manjit Singh and Sandhu had earlier tried to prevent the Taksal from leading the post-Bluestar "extremist" movement by supporting Baba Joginder Singh and his Akali Dal (U) instead. For this reason, the Damdami Taksal had actually moved closer to the armed "militants" and the Panthic Committee, and away from the Akali Dal (U).

In mid-April 1986, Manjit Singh and Sandhu ordered the dissolution of the AISSF ad hoc committee led by Kahlon and ordered the creation of a new five-member "Presidium" to lead in its place. Kahlon refused to accept this decision arguing that he had the support of the Panthic Committee, which the January 1986 *Sarbat Khalsa* had "affirmed" to be the premier source of Sikh political leadership.[20] This caused a split within the AISSF with two factions emerging—the AISSF (Manjit) and the AISSF (Kahlon).[21] Thus, "the extremists" split into two competing blocs by the middle of April 1986 with the "militant" Damdami Taksal–Panthic Committee–AISSF (Kahlon) combine on one side and the "extremist" Akali Dal (U)–AISSF (Manjit) alliance on the other.

The "Declaration of Khalistan" and Operation Black Thunder

The split within the "extremists'" ranks resulted in a lower-than-expected turnout for the second "extremist/militant"-sponsored *Sarbat Khalsa* held on 13 April (Baisakhi day) 1986. The Panthic Committee had originally planned to use this *Sarbat Khalsa* to compel the acting Akal Takht *jathedar* Gurdev Singh Koanke to declare the creation of Khalistan, but Koanke—who was not an avowed separatist—refused to take such a dramatic step without the support of other Sikh groups, including the Akali Dal (U) and both factions of the AISSF.[22] Koanke's refusal to declare the creation of Khalistan prompted the chiefs of several armed militant "gangs" to refuse to "fight, kill, and die" any further unless the goal for which they were struggling was made publicly clear.[23] For its part, the Panthic Committee feared remaining overshadowed by the less militant but vastly more mass-based AISSF factions and Akali Dal (U) unless it did something spectacular to reinvigorate the "Sikh movement."

For these reasons, the Panthic Committee hastily arranged a press conference in the Golden Temple complex on 29 April 1986 at which it formally declared the creation of Khalistan in front of the world media.[24] India stood stunned at this declaration of Sikh independence! The ten-page "Declaration of Khalistan" appealed to all countries in the world and the United Nations to recognize the creation of a sovereign Sikh state. The Panthic Committee offered to start talks with the Government of India on all bi-lateral issues between India and Khalistan, and indicated that Khalistan wished to have "good relations" with all of its neighbors, including Hindu-majority India.[25] The declaration further urged India to voluntarily leave the "territory" of Khalistan or face certain "upheavals." The constitution of Khalistan, according to this declaration, would adhere to the Sikh concept of *sarbat ka bhalla* ("welfare for all") by which there would no discrimination in religious practice, but Sikhism would be the country's official religion.[26] The newly created Khalistan Commando Force (KCF) led by Manbir Singh Chaheru was declared to be the armed wing of the Khalistan movement and the nucleus of Khalistan's official defense forces.

Its immense symbolic value aside, the Panthic Committee did not make this declaration from a position of strength, but rather from a position of weakness as a desperate attempt to distinguish itself from other "extremist" organizations, to create a niche for the itself as the apex body for separatist Sikh "militants," and to please Pakistan and the Panthic Committee's supporters in the overseas Sikh diaspora. Thus, the "Declaration of Khalistan" was not only an overt act to achieve independence, but it served other purposes as well. Nonetheless, for the first time in the post-1984 period, a Sikh political organization had formally declared the creation of an independent Sikh state and launched an armed struggle that openly threatened the unity and territorial integrity of India. Not even Bhindranwale had been so bold in his stated goals in the days before Operation Bluestar!

The Panthic Committee's "Declaration of Khalistan" shocked political leaders in both Chandigarh and New Delhi alike. An enraged Rajiv Gandhi ordered Barnala to immediately raid the Golden Temple complex or resign from office. For his part, Barnala reluctantly agreed to Rajiv's demand to send security forces into the Golden Temple complex. The following day, National Security Guard (NSG) commandos and the Punjab police raided the Golden Temple complex, and arrested about 300 AISSF and Damdami Taksal activists, including Akal Takht *jathedar* Gurdev Singh Koanke without any resistance.[27] No known Sikh militant or member of the Panthic Committee was arrested because they had slipped out of the complex immediately after declaring the creation of Khalistan a day earlier. The national press and all major political parties praised Barnala for his "firmness" against the militants, but he would soon pay a steep political price for supposedly "desecrating" the Golden Temple complex on behest of the *Delhi Durbar* (central government).

BIFURCATION OF THE "TRADITIONAL AKALI LEADERSHIP," AND BADAL AND TOHRA'S METAMORPHOSIS INTO BECOMING NEAR "EXTREMISTS"

Immediately after Operation Black Thunder, prominent members of Barnala's cabinet—including Capt. Amarinder Singh—resigned from their posts, and both Badal and Tohra resigned from the Akali Dal (L)'s working committee in protest of this "desecration" of the Golden Temple complex. These leaders explained the rationale behind their resignations by issuing a joint statement stating that "[t]he action has not only desecrated the shrine and violated the glorious traditions of the Panth but [has] also put a black spot on the history of the Akali Dal."[28] Badal and Tohra had, in fact, been lying in wait for months for an opportunity to challenge and hopefully undermine Barnala, and Operation Black Thunder gave them this chance.

For his part, Barnala defended Operation Black Thunder by explaining that he had only implemented the *gurmata* passed by the Akali Dal (L)-sponsored *Sarbat Khalsa* authorizing the government "to end the illegal interference in the Darbar Sahib" by "whatever means" necessary.[29] This explanation aside, 27 Akali legislators broke from the Akali Dal (L) and formed a new party under the leadership of Badal, Tohra, and Capt. Amarinder Singh called the Akali Dal (Badal).[30] Thus, the traditional Akali leadership was openly split, and, as a result, Barnala's government was reduced to a minority in the state legislative assembly with only 48 seats in a house of 117.[31] It had to rely on 32 Congress (I) and four BJP legislators to remain in power. An increasing number of Sikhs also began perceiving Barnala as an ineffective leader who selfishly catered to the *Delhi Durbar* in order to protect his own *gaddi* (position of power). This was not an enviable position for a party and government claiming to represent "Sikh interests" in Punjab.

After the Panthic Committee's "Declaration of Khalistan" and the formal split within the Akali Dal, the KCF began vigorously implementing a strategy of killing Hindus in order to prompt their migration out of Punjab. This proved increasingly successful as hundreds of Hindu families from rural and semi-rural areas of the Majha region left for the relative safety of Hindu-majority cities such as Amritsar, or out of Punjab altogether for Hindu-majority states and Delhi.[32] As a result, Sikh militants publicly declared areas of the Amritsar and Gurdaspur districts to be "liberated areas" of Khalistan in which the civil administration could not operate. Songs urging Sikh youth to take up arms against the Indian state were played in buses, during fairs, in Sikh-owned homes and shops, and even from loudspeakers atop village *gurdwaras* in open defiance of central authority in areas throughout Punjab.[33]

Dissident Akalis both played on and exacerbated this growing sense of Sikh resentment and alienation. For example, Tohra shed his traditional blue turban (the symbolic color of the Akalis) and began wearing a saffron one symbolizing martyrdom and defiance of central authority. Tohra likened Barnala's government to the Mughals, eulogized Mrs Gandhi's assassins, and lauded Bhindranwale for his great sacrifices for the Sikh Panth.[34] Even Badal, once the most moderate of all Akali leaders, shifted to using openly extremist rhetoric. He attended the *bhog* (last rites) ceremonies of slain Sikh militants and declared:

Barnala is a traitor. He is a tyrant worse than the Mughals. Even Mrs Gandhi's despotic regime pales before his misdeeds. At the behest of the Centre, he is finishing the Sikh youth and attacking Sikh holy shrines. Neither God nor the Sikhs shall pardon him...I shall go to each Sikh youth's house killed by the security forces and visit Sikhs detained in jail.[35]

Badal and Tohra even selected imprisoned Akali Dal (U) convenor, Simranjeet Singh Mann, to be the Akali Dal (B) nominee for the vacant Rajya Sabha seat from Punjab.[36]

This was a strategic use of symbolism and rhetoric by Badal and Tohra. Ideologically, they were actually closer to "the moderates" than to either "the extremists" or "the militants," but they felt the need to use heated ethnic rhetoric to differentiate them from Barnala and to try to displace him from power. Political pragmatism, not ideology or statesmanship, appeared to dictate action within Akali politics.

By the summer of 1986, the configuration of Sikh politics looked like the following (Table 7.2):

Table 7.2
Sikh Political Spectrum (Mid-1986)

Moderates	Radicals	Extremists	Militants/Separatists
Akali Dal (L)[1]	Akali Dal (B)[2]	Akali Dal (U)[3]	Damdami Taksal[4]
Barnala[1]	Badal[2]	Joginder Singh[3]	Panthic Committee[4]
	Tohra[2]	AISSF (Manjit)[3]	KCF[4]
	Talwandi[3]		AISSF (Kahlon)[4]
			Babbar Khalsa

Source: Author.
Notes: [1] Akali Dal (Longowal) and its leaders.
   [2] Akali Dal (Badal) and its leaders.
   [3] Akali Dal (United)–AISSF (Manjit) combine demanding "Khalsa Raj".
   [4] Damdami Taksal-Panthic Committee-KCF-AISSF (Kahlon) combine demanding Khalistan.

The armed separatist movement for Khalistan was being led by the "militant" Panthic Committee and the KCF. Both the Damdami Taksal and the AISSF (Kahlon) provided the Panthic Committee with institutionalized political support, but neither openly endorsed the demand for Khalistan or the use of violence. The Akali Dal (U) and the AISSF (Manjit) represented the "extremist" wing of Sikh politics and continued to demand full implementation of the ASR and the release of all Sikh detainees. "Radical" Akali dissidents led by Badal and Tohra catered to the alienated mood of the Sikh community with their inflammatory rhetoric, but their main goal was to oust Barnala from the powerful positions of Akali Dal president and chief minister of Punjab. Barnala's Akali Dal (L) was on the most "moderate" end of Sikh politics. By this time, the Punjab Accord was effectively dead and an armed Sikh separatist insurgency demanding an independent Sikh state was in full swing in Punjab.

"Secret" Center–Extremist Talks and the Growing Rift between "the Extremists" and "the Militants"

In early-summer of 1986, the security forces' anti-insurgency operations succeeded in eliminating several top militants and arresting many others. The most prominent of those arrested was the "extremist" AISSF leader Harinder Singh Kahlon. Kahlon's arrest came shortly after Rajiv expressed his willingness to negotiate with any Sikh group whose demands were within the framework of the Indian Constitution and were not openly separatist.[37] This raised speculation that Kahlon had been detained so that the government could initiate dialog with him in order to help find a solution to the "Punjab crisis." Both the Akali Dal (L) and Akali Dal (B) contributed to this speculation by indicating their willingness to act as intermediaries for such talks if they could help bring peace and stability to Punjab.[38] These speculations proved true when, in mid-July 1986, the other major AISSF faction—the AISSF (Manjit)—openly admitted that its senior leaders, Manjit Singh and Harminder Singh Sandhu, had been holding "secret" talks with the government along with Kahlon to help find a solution to the "Punjab problem".[39] After all, Manjit Singh, Sandhu, or Kahlon were not overt separatists.

This public admission that "secret" talks were being held between the "extremist" AISSF leaders and the government pointed to two important dynamics. First, it showed that the central government accepted the reality that "the extremists" carried significant power within Sikh politics and had substantial support within the Sikh community, and that negotiations with them was one possible route to solving the "Punjab crisis." Second, the Akalis ("moderates" and "radicals" alike) also accepted the growing power of "the extremists" and tried to retain their own sense of political utility by offering to act as intermediaries for talks between the central government and "the extremists." Interestingly, the growing power of "the extremists" also alarmed "the militants," who feared being isolated and their separatist cause doomed if "the extremists" reached a compromise settlement with the central government short of Khalistan. For this reason, the KCF massacred over a dozen Hindus on a bus on July 25 in an attempt to sabotage the "extremist"–center talks and also demonstrate "the militants'" centrality in Punjab's energing political scenario.[40] The massacre of innocent Hindus strengthened the government's resolve to neutralize the "militant" Panthic Committee and the KCF, partially because both were obstacles to possible settlement with "the extremists." For this reason, the security forces renewed their anti-insurgency operations, which eventually resulted in the arrest of KCF chief, Manbir Singh Chaheru.[41] A section of "the militants" blamed "the extremists" for Chaheru's arrest, thus causing further tension between the two broad ideological groupings within the "Sikh movement."

The vacuum of leadership in the "extremist" AISSF (Kahlon) after Kahlon's arrest provided "the militants" with an opportunity to "capture" this organization, which commanded a huge mass-based network of support but had never openly endorsed the "Declaration of Khalistan." For this reason, the "militant" Damdami Taksal and Panthic Committee quickly organized an AISSF (Kahlon) meeting which removed Kahlon from the AISSF convenorship and replaced him with Gurjit Singh.[42] Gurjit Singh was Bhindranwale's nephew-in-law and an open supporter of Khalistan. Thus, he was an appropriate choice for this position for "the militants." With the appointment of Gurjit Singh as the new AISSF convenor, the AISSF (Kahlon) became known as the AISSF (Gurjit). The "militant" Damdami Taksal and the Panthic Committee immediately recognized the AISSF (Gurjit); whereas the "extremist" Akali Dal (U) continued to support the AISSF (Manjit). The former grouping demanded the creation of Khalistan through an armed struggle; whereas the latter demanded "Khalsa Raj" as envisioned in the ASR. Thus, a clear schism between "the extremists" and "the militants" had taken more definitive form by the early-fall of 1986.

This competition between the "militant" AISSF (Gurjit) and the "extremist" AISSF (Manjit), in turn, precipitated internal fissures within the ranks of the armed militants. During the November 1986 *Sarbat Khalsa*, "the militants" removed Aroor Singh from the Panthic Committee for allegedly initiating contacts with the government. This was not surprising because Aroor Singh had been close to Sukhdev Singh Sakhira—a prominent Sikh militant who had demanded increased autonomy for Punjab but not necessarily Khalistan.[43] Aroor Singh refused to accept his "removal" from the Panthic Committee, and, in response, formed a new armed organization called the Khalistan Liberation Force (KLF) which integrated several smaller militant "gangs," including Avtar Singh

Brahma's "Tat Khalsa." The KLF ushered in its creation by slaughtering 24 Hindus in a bus massacre in what was, at the time, the largest single killing by Sikh militants to date.[44] After its creation, the KLF immediately expressed loyalty to the "extremist" AISSF (Manjit) and the Akali Dal (U). In contrast, the KCF remained loyal to the openly separatist and "militant" Panthic Committee, Damdami Taksal, and AISSF (Gurjit). The other major armed militant group, the Babbar Khalsa, continued to operate independently. Thus, competition between "the extremists" and "the militants," as well as internal factionalism within the ranks the armed "militants," emerged by fall of 1986. The "Sikh political spectrum" in late-1986 looked like the following (Table 7.3).

Table 7.3
Sikh Political Spectrum (Late-1986)

Moderates	Radicals	Extremists	Militants/Separatists
Akali Dal (L)[1]	Akali Dal (B)[2]	Akali Dal (U)[3]	Damdami Taksal[4]
Barnala[1]	Badal[2]	Joginder Singh[3]	Panthic Committee[4]
	Tohra[2]	AISSF (Manjit)[3]	KCF[4]
	Talwandi[3]		AISSF (Gurjit)[4]
			KLF[5]
			Babbar Khalsa

Source: Author.
Notes: [1] Akali Dal (Longowal) and its leader.
        [2] Akali Dal (Badal) and its leaders.
        [3] Akali Dal (United)–AISSF (Manjit) combine demanding "Khalsa Raj".
        [4] Damdami Taksal-Panthic Committee-KCF-AISSF (Gurjit) combine demanding Khalistan.
        [5] KLF supportive of "the extremists," and demanding either "Khalsa Raj" or Khalistan.

THE "RADICAL" AKALI DAL (B)'S CAPTURE OF THE SGPC AND DISMISSAL OF THE "MODERATE" HEAD PRIESTS

While "the militants" were fractionalizing, well-wishers of the "traditional Akali leadership" coordinated with the Head Priests to try to forge Akali unity which had disintegrated after Operation Black Thunder. The Head Priests appealed to all traditional Akali leaders and factions "to sink their personal differences and rise above their narrow selfish interests to forge [Panthic] unity" during this "period of crisis."[45] For several months, the Head Priests tried to broker a unity deal between the Akali Dal (L) and Akali Dal (B), but without success.[46] The main sticking point was that Barnala was willing to give up either his position as chief minister or his position as party president, but not both as demanded by Badal, Tohra, and Capt. Amarinder Singh. An exasperated Akal Takht *Jathedar* Kirpal Singh eventually expressed his frustration by admitting, "We (the Head Priests) could not understand their (the Akalis') murky politics to date."[47] Another Head Priest added by saying, "The greed for the *kursi* (seat of political power) among the Akali leaders is frightening."[48] Thus, their efforts to forge Akali unity failed.

Since Akali unity could not be forged, the stage was set for a show-down between the Akali Dal (L) and Akali Dal (B) in the all-important SGPC presidential elections which would determine which Akali party or faction was dominant in Sikh politics. This contest promised to be close and the votes of "minor" factions within the SGPC general house—which had last been elected in 1979—could tip the balance in favor of one side or the other. For this reason, Badal sought and eventually received the support of Baba Joginder Singh's Akali Dal (U), which also included the Talwandi faction. As a result, the Akali Dal (B) candidate, Gurcharan Singh Tohra, won by a small margin, thus making the Akali Dal (B) the clearly dominant Akali faction within the Sikh community.[49] As a result of these elections, the "Sikh political system" was split with the Akali Dal (L) controlling the legislative and organizational wings, and the Akali Dal (B) controlling the temple wing.

Fearing a renewed challenge to his ministry after the SGPC presidential elections, Barnala quickly ordered Badal and Tohra to be arrested under the National Security Act (NSA) for supposedly aiding and abetting terrorism.[50] Unfortunately for Barnala, this was not sufficient to ward-off the Akali Dal (B)'s challenge to his leadership. On December 24, the SGPC executive committee accepted the "resignation" of Akal Takht *Jathedar* Kirpal Singh, sacked the Head Priest of the Golden Temple, and indicated that the other three Head Priests would also be replaced soon.[51] These moves were, in part, the Akali Dal (B)'s pay-back to Baba Joginder Singh and Talwandi for supporting its candidate in the SGPC presidential elections. Thus, it appeared that the Sikh "radicals" and "extremists" were quickly uniting and consolidating their power within Sikh politics, whereas the "moderate" Akali Dal (L) was a slowly "sinking ship." The "radicals" and "extremists" were finding common ground with "the militants" as well in their opposition to "the moderates." A shocking "radical-extremist-militant" alliance appeared to be emerging in Sikh politics by the end of 1986.

"RADICAL–EXTREMIST–MILITANT" ALLIANCE IN SIKH POLITICS AND THE SELECTION OF DARSHAN SINGH RAGI AS AKAL TAKHT *JATHEDAR*

The Akali Dal (B)-led SGPC selected Darshan Singh Ragi to be the acting *jathedar* of the Akal Takht in December 1986. Ragi was chosen for this post in part because he was acceptable to and respected by "the radicals," "the extremists," and "the militants" alike. The dissident traditional Akali leaders, who had strategically radicalized, saw him as being "an urban moderate Sikh and a well-known *ragi* (singer) of the *gurbani* (spiritual hymns) with a non-violent and soft personality."[52] After all, Ragi was not an avowed separatist, but he did often allude to the need for a "Sikh homeland" in his sermons. Thus, he could be used by the "radical" Akali Dal (B) to cater to alienated Sikh sentiment without openly supporting separatism or violence. The "extremists" and "militants" also supported Ragi because he had spent over a year in prison for singing hymns and giving sermons critical of the Indian government and lauding Sant Bhindranwale for his "gallant defense" of the Golden Temple complex. The "militants" knew that Ragi could be a powerful ally in their war against the Indian state if he could be swayed to openly support the creation of Khalistan. Thus, "the militants" were also willing, if not eager, to back Ragi.

In essence, Darshan Singh Ragi's coronation was a part of a "secret" understanding between "the radicals," "the extremists," and "the militants" to have a common Akal Takht *jathedar*.[53] The fact that the Akali Dal (B) entered into this arrangement with "the extremists" and "the militants" demonstrated their increased power and importance in Sikh politics. The Akali Dal (B) was apparently willing to ride the wave of extremism as long as the Akal Takht *jathedar* could coalesce the support of other major Sikh groups against Barnala and the "moderate" Akali Dal (L). The central government, in reality, was not totally averse to Ragi either, and wanted to see in what direction he would take Sikh politics. In particular, the government hoped that Ragi could win "the militants'" confidence and possibly convince them to accept a settlement short of Khalistan. For his part, Ragi accepted the position of Akal Takht *jathedar* "in order to protect the *quam* from direct [internal] conflicts and [unpleasant] situations...[and to serve] as a neutral link or common person [between various Sikh factions]."[54]

The "militants" formally endorsed the appointment of five new Head Priests, including Ragi, at the *Sarbat Khalsa* convention held in late-January 1987. During this gathering, they also reaffirmed that the Sikh nation's goal was the achievement of Khalistan. *India Today* described this mammoth *Sarbat Khalsa* convention as follows:

> For the Sikh militants, it marked their political graduation. This showed not just in the large crowd of Sikh youths they attracted—in spite of widespread preventive arrests—to the fourth Damdami Taksal-supported Sarbat Khalsa at Amritsar's Golden Temple. More important, it was strongly backed—unlike the three earlier ones—by not only the Akali Dals led by Parkash Singh Badal and Jagdev Singh Talwandi, but also the Shiromani Gurdwara Prabandhak Committee (SGPC).[55]

Flags emblazoned with the slogan "Khalistan *zindabad* (long live)" were raised by militant Sikh youth during this convention and defiantly fluttered in the wind in open defiance of the *Delhi Durbar*. In a strange twist of fate, "the radicals," "the extremists," and "the militants" appeared to be united, and only the "moderate" Akali Dal (L) remained out of this alliance. Meanwhile, separatist and communal violence in Punjab continued to escalate.

DARSHAN SINGH RAGI'S FORMATION
OF THE "UNIFIED" AKALI DAL

Shortly after being made Akal Takht *jathedar* by the SGPC, Ragi stated that his primary goals were to work toward complete Sikh unity and help solve the community's problems. He explained by saying:

> I feel that unity of the Sikhs, not just Akali unity, will be a solution to all the present problems facing the Sikh community. I am trying to build up rapport with all the groups. I shall soon call all of them to discuss the modalities of unity...[T]he question before us is to see how far the leaders can make sacrifices.[56]

Ragi and the new Head Priests took their first step towards forging Panthic unity by ordering that the chiefs of all Akali parties submit their resignations by February 5 for the purpose of creating a new "unified" Akali Dal.[57] Both Amarinder Singh of the Akali Dal (B) and Baba Joginder Singh of the Akali Dal (U) offered to tender their resignations. After all, it was in their interests to accept the Head Priests' directive because their parties were out of power and they could expect to have favorable standing in any new set-up formulated by the Head Priests. In contrast, Barnala's power would inevitably be diluted in any new organizational set-up, but he could not simply disregard the Head Priests' directive. For this reason, the Akali Dal (L) chose a "middle-of-the-road" approach by sending a delegation to meet with the Head Priests to discuss how best to forge Akali unity without formally agreeing to abide by any of their decisions, but this meeting never took place. The Panthic Committee-led "militants" threatened to eliminate these "proteges of the Delhi durbar" if they dared enter the Golden Temple complex, and thus the Akali Dal (L) delegation could not meet Ragi.[58]

Nonetheless, Ragi and the Head Priests went ahead and announced the formation of a "unified" Akali Dal with imprisoned former IPS officer, Simranjeet Singh Mann, as its president. Since Mann was in prison, the Head Priests directed that a five-member Presidium consisting of Baba Joginder Singh, Parkash Singh Badal, Jagdev Singh Talwandi, Surjan Singh Thekedar (a Tohra loyalist), and Gejja Singh (a Damdami Taksal activist) would temporarily lead the party.[59] Thus, every major Akali leader and faction, except the Akali Dal (L), was represented in this Presidium. The Head Priests' also announced a new "Panthic program" which essentially reiterated most of the postulates and resolutions spelled out in the ASR. This included reaffirming that the Akali Dal's goal was to carve out a "geopolitical" environment that would reflect the "aspirations and sentiments of the Sikh people" and protect the "identity" of the Khalsa.[60] The Khalsa Panth was described as being an "independent and separate nation," but the Head Priests did not openly call for the creation of Khalistan.[61] In addition to these general propositions, the Head Priests' "Panthic policy" also contained several specific demands, including declaring Amritsar to be a "holy city," the release of Sikhs detainees, the rehabilitation of Sikh army deserters, a judicial enquiry into "faked encounters" used by the Punjab police, and the withdrawal of false cases against Sikh youth.[62] This "Panthic policy" was, in many ways, an attempt to appease the various constituent factions that had supported Ragi without directly offending any of them or the central government.

The Akali Dal (B), Akali Dal (U), and AISSF (Manjit) seemed largely satisfied with the Head Priests' announcement. In contrast, the Panthic Committee-led "militants" accepted the Head Priests' decision, but criticized their choice of leaders none of whom, according to the Panthic Committee, were "Panthic" or had made any personal sacrifices for the *quam* except Mann. The Panthic Committee also reiterated its support for an independent Sikh state by warning that any Sikh leader, including those of the "Unified Akali Dal," who compromised on anything short of outright independence, would meet the same fate as the "traitors" of the Panth had in the past.[63] The only Sikh group to reject the Head Priests' decision outright was the Akali Dal (L), but it was also careful not to attack the institutions of the Akal Takht, Head Priests, or the *hukamnama* directly. Instead, Barnala explained that these institutions had been captured by extremist and militant elements, and thus were not acting independently.[64] According to Barnala, the only other alternative to his "moderate" Akali government was *fauji raj* (army rule), during which security forces would act with even more impunity against Sikh youth in Punjab. The Head Priests nonetheless rejected Barnala's appeal for further consultations, declared him to be *tankhaiya*, and later excommunicated him for not tendering his resignation as directed by them.[65]

The changed "Sikh political spectrum" in early-1987 looked like the following (Table 7.4):

Table 7.4
Sikh Political Spectrum (Early-1987)

Moderates	Radicals	Extremists	Militants/Separatists
Akali Dal (L)[1]	UAD[2]	UAD[2]	Damdami Taksal[4]
Barnala[1]	Ragi[2]	Ragi[2]	Panthic Committee[4]
	Badal[2]	Joginder Singh[2]	KCF[4]
	Tohra[2]	AISSF (Manjit)[3]	AISSF (Gurjit)[4]
	Talwandi[2]		KLF[5]
			Babbar Khalsa[5]

Source: Author.
Notes: [1] Akali Dal (Longowal) and its leader.
[2] "Unified" Akali Dal, and its leaders and supporters.
[3] AISSF (Manjit) linked to "extremist" faction within UAD.
[4] Damdami Taksal-Panthic Committee-KCF-AISSF (Gurjit) combine demanding Khalistan.
[5] Babbar Khalsa and KLF supportive of "the extremists," and demanding either "Khalsa Raj" or Khalistan.

DARSHAN SINGH RAGI'S ROLE AS AN "INTERMEDIARY" FOR MILITANT–CENTER TALKS

In the early-spring of 1987, "the militants" implemented a "social reform program" which included banning the sale and consumption of alcohol, meat, and tobacco products in Punjab.[66] This program had three objectives: to dry up the biggest source of revenue for the state government which was the auction of liquors licenses and excise tax; to further build support in the rural areas, especially amongst women, for the movement; and to demonstrate that the militants' writ, not that of the government, ran in Punjab.[67] This "social reform program" was successful in shutting down the vast majority of shops selling these products in rural areas of Punjab. The intimidation and killing of shopkeepers supplying these products also resulted in the renewed migration of Hindus out of the state. Sikh "militants" had flexed their muscles, and they were increasingly in control of Punjab.

It had been expected in many quarters that Ragi would eventually act as an intermediary for talks between the center and "the militants." Initial indications of possible talks were seen in mid-February when "the militants" unilaterally called a brief cease-fire, and watered down their demands from the creation of Khalistan to demanding only "Khalsa Raj" as envisioned in the ASR.[68] Ragi had apparently succeeded in convincing them to try to seek a negotiated solution to the "Punjab problem" instead of steadfastly continuing with their bloody separatist struggle. Indirect talks between "the militants" and the central government began in April 1987 with Ragi and Sunil Dutt, a Rajya Sabha MP and a famous film actor turned peace activist, acting as "intermediaries". Dutt was also a close confidant of Rajiv Gandhi. In his meeting with the new Head Priests, Dutt agreed with Ragi's suggestion that the central government engage the Sikh youth in direct dialog instead of negotiating only with the Akalis. Dutt also met privately with armed militants inside the Golden Temple complex, who relayed their stories of torture and extrajudicial killings at the hands of the security forces to him. After this meeting, Dutt agreed to give his recommendations to Rajiv, including the need to negotiate directly with "the militants" and grant a general amnesty for Sikh youth in Punjab.[69]

Dutt's meeting with the Head Priests and "the militants" was followed-up by a visit to Amritsar by India's most prominent Jain religious leader, Acharya Sushil Muni, who was also a close confident of Rajiv Gandhi. Muni met with the Head Priests, leaders of the Taksal, AISSF (Gurjit) leaders, and the armed "militants" in the Golden Temple complex. After several days of meetings, Muni announced his conclusions that the central government would have to take four steps before peace could be restored in Punjab. These were unconditionally releasing all Sikh political detainees, granting general amnesty to the Sikh youth, rehabilitating all of the Sikh army deserters, and withdrawing paramilitary forces stationed in the state.[70] He agreed to take up these issues with Rajiv Gandhi in New Delhi, and it appeared that a potential breakthrough was possible after the press reported that Muni had received assurances from the Head Priests and all "militant" groups that they were willing to negotiate a settlement to the "Punjab problem" within the parameters of the Indian Constitution if the government declared a general amnesty for Sikh youth in Punjab.[71] But, an unexpected thing happened before any possible peace initiatives could solidify. On May 11, 1987 the central government suddenly, and unexpectedly, dismissed Surjit Singh Barnala's Akali Dal (L) government and declared President's Rule on Punjab without any public warning! Such a dramatic, and unexpected, political move by the central government at this sensitive juncture raised confusion and suspicion within the ranks of "the militants," and subsequently sank the possibility of substantive "militant"–center talks held through Ragi.

DISMISSAL OF BARNALA'S "MODERATE" AKALI DAL (L) GOVERNMENT AND IMPOSITION OF PRESIDENT'S RULE ON PUNJAB

The timing and suddenness of the imposition of President's Rule on Punjab stunned most political observers in India because, only a few days earlier, Rajiv had stated his personal support for having Barnala's government continue in office. The central government justified the dismissal of Barnala's government by explaining that political violence in Punjab had risen sharply and that the state government's writ no longer ran in over half of Punjab's 13 districts. But, this was only a convenient excuse. In reality, there were a number of other reasons for dismissing the Barnala government at this particular point in time.

First, dismissing Barnala's government was an attempt to appease Punjab's police chief, Julio Ribeiro, who had threatened to resign unless he was given complete control over police administration, including the power to post and transfer officers at will.[72] Ribeiro was frustrated at what he perceived to be political interference by Akali legislators in his prosecution of the war against militancy. Second, there were suspicions that Union home minister Buta Singh had sabotaged the talks between "the militants" and Shushil Muni for his own personal political reasons.[73] Ragi, in fact, admitted that Muni had been sent to Amritsar by "one section within the central government" and that "several faces working behind the curtains…ruined the outcome of the talks."[74] Third, Barnala's government may have been dismissed in order to consolidate Hindu support for the Congress (I) in north india. The Congress (I) had been badly mauled in state elections in West Bengal and Kerala in late-March, and state assembly elections for Haryana, a state which bordered Punjab, were coming up in mid-June. It was suspected that Rajiv wanted to attract support for his party in Haryana by appearing to be tough on Sikh extremism.[75] Lastly, the central government calculated that Barnala had lost his political relevance in Punjab. Instead, a new structure of power had emerged within Sikh politics with the loose "alliance" forged between the "Unified" Akali Dal, the Head Priests, the Damdami Taksal, the Panthic Committee, and the AISSF factions. Akal Takht *jathedar*, Darshan Singh Ragi, was also a more effective intermediary for talks between the government and "the militants" than the Akali Dal (L), thus making Barnala expendable. All of these reasons aside, the Indian government lost a very important thing with the ouster of the Akali Dal (L) government—namely, a popularly-elected, moderate Sikh buffer between itself and the alienated Sikh community.

The Unified Akali Dal (UAD), Head Priests, and "the militants" initially welcomed the dismissal of Barnala's government. The UAD hoped that the center would hold fresh elections in Punjab after ousting Barnala. "The militants," for their part, thought that the center would negotiate more seriously with them once Barnala's government was out of the political scene. But, these calculations proved to be incorrect. Instead of holding elections or renewed negotiations, the government ordered its security forces to launch aggressive new anti-insurgency operations, resulting in the arrests of many "extremists" and forcing "the militants" further underground. The experiment with political negotiations through Ragi appeared to be over, and the central government had apparently reverted back to President's Rule and a "law-and-order" approach to handling the "Punjab problem"!

An important development occurred within the ranks of the armed militants about the same time that President's Rule was imposed on Punjab. In late-April 1987, Gurbachan Singh Manochahal resigned from the Panthic Committee, citing personal differences with other Panthic Committee members and complaining that the Committee had "failed to function as a well-knit unit."[76] Manochahal's resignation was important because he subsequently created a new armed militant group called the Bhindranwale Tigers Force of Khalistan (BTFK). The BTFK thus joined the KCF, KLF, and Babbar Khalsa as being one of the four major armed militant groups in Punjab. The armed militants were slowly factionalizing even further, signaling potential problems to come for the Khalistan movement.

MILITANT–RAGI SPLIT AND RAGI'S "WITHDRAWAL" FROM SIKH POLITICS

Serious fissures emerged between Darshan Singh Ragi, and the "militant" Panthic Committee-AISSF (Gurjit)-KCF combine after the imposition of President's Rule. The "militants" suspected that Ragi and the "radical/extremist" UAD had reached a "secret understanding" with the central government by which the UAD would be allowed to form the next state government in Punjab whenever elections were held. These fears were precipitated by repeated calls by the UAD for fresh elections, and Ragi's continued communications with Acharya Sushil Muni.

As a result, the "militants" felt threatened, and they launched a two-pronged strategy to prevent further negotiations and any possible elections, which they knew would set back their goal of creating an independent Sikh state. First, they warned Ragi not to engage in any further dialogue with intermediaries of the central government until either a general amnesty was declared for Sikh political prisoners or until the government agreed to give the Sikhs an independent Khalistan. The Panthic Committee also began issuing press releases with the Akal Takht seal affixed to them without Ragi's approval. This was a direct challenge to Ragi's authority who threatened to resign if the other Head Priests, three of whom were nominated by "the militants," refused to admonish the Panthic Committee for its actions.[77] To Ragi's chagrin, the other Head Priests refused to take sides on this issue. Thus, by the middle of July, Ragi appeared to have fallen out with "the militants." Second, "the militants" also engaged in increased political violence to prevent any elections from being held. For example, the KCF slaughtered 70 bus passengers, all of them Hindus, in two separate attacks within a 24-hour period in early July.[78] This massacre was a part of a sharp increase in political violence after the imposition of President's Rule on Punjab.

In early-August 1987, Ragi made one last attempt to rally the disparate "radical," "extremist," and "militant" groups around his leadership as Akal Takht *jathedar* by calling a meeting of all major Sikh sects, and political and social organizations at the Golden Temple complex to discuss the future political direction of the Sikh Panth.[79] Those political organizations invited included the UAD, the AISSF (Manjit), the Damdami Taksal, the AISSF (Gurjit), the Panthic Committee, the KCF, the KLF, the Babbar Khalsa, and the BTFK. The Akali Dal (L) was not invited because its leaders had previously refused to accept the authority of the Akal Takht. The attendees at this meeting were generally divided into two broad camps in terms of goals and strategy. Ragi, the UAD, the AISSF (Manjit), and most other Sikh sects and organizations succeeded in passing a resolution stating that the Sikhs' political goal was the creation of an "area and political set-up in north india where Sikhs can experience the glow of freedom."[80] This was, in essence, demanding the implementation of the

ASR. In contrast, the Panthic Committee, the AISSF (Gurjit), the KCF, and the KLF made it clear that nothing short of Khalistan was acceptable to the Panth. In their first ever joint statement, the KCF and the KLF stated "The gun is the only answer…We have taken to the gun not as a hobby. It has been thrust upon us. The war will end with our victory. There is no other alternative."[81]

Ragi and representatives of the other Sikh organizations tried desperately to convince "the militants" to alter their line of thought. In this attempt, Ragi and other Sikh intellectuals praised "the militants" for the "sacrifices" they had made and credited them for bringing the central government to the negotiating table (a reference to the talks with Dutt and Muni). They also suggested that negotiations were required to extract concessions to end the conflict, but "the militants" refused to be swayed. Thus, the convention ended with a divide between those advocating the ASR and negotiations, and those supporting Khalistan through armed means. Ragi admitted that he had failed to unify the philosophy of *josh* (emotion or strength) with the philosophy of *hosh* (reason or intellect).[82] Shortly thereafter, the Panthic Committee officially rejected the resolution passed at this convention. In apparent reference to Ragi and "the extremists," the Panthic Committee warned "[t]hose Sikh leaders or committees that bank on votes" with "dire consequences" if they compromised with the government.[83] Ragi's alliance with "the militants" was essentially over.

Instead of risking a confrontation with "the militants," Ragi withdrew from the political scene in order to give "the militants" an opportunity to lead the Sikh Panth. He had preferred *gal* (talks) whereas the militants preferred the *goli* (bullet). After Ragi's "withdrawal" from politics, the other militant-appointed Head Priests further consolidated "the militants'" hold on Sikh politics by issuing an appeal to the entire Sikh *quam* directing it to lend its support to "the militants," who they characterized as sacrificing their lives for "freedom" and for breaking the "shackles of slavery" imposed on the Panth.[84]

In mid-fall of 1987, Sikh politics was divided along the following lines (Table 7.5):

The most "moderate" Sikh political group was the Akali Dal (L) led by Barnala. It demanded implementation of the Punjab Accord, but had lost most of its relevance in Punjab. The "radical" and "extremist" organizations rallied around Ragi and demanded full implementation of the ASR. The "radicals" consisted of the SGPC and the Badal faction within the UAD, and the "extremists" included the AISSF (Manjit) and the Baba faction within the UAD. The "militant" Babbar Khalsa and the

Table 7.5
Sikh Political Spectrum (Late-1987)

Moderates	Radicals	Extremists	Militants/Separatists
Akali Dal (L)[1]	UAD[2]	UAD[2]	four Head Priests[4]
Barnala[1]	Ragi[2]	Ragi[2]	Damdami Taksal[4]
	Badal[2]	Joginder Singh[2]	Panthic Committee[4]
	Tohra[2]	AISSF (Manjit)[3]	KCF[4]
	Talwandi[2]		BTFK[4]
			AISSF (Gurjit)[4]
			KLF[5]
			Babbar Khalsa[5]

Source: Author.
Notes: [1] Akali Dal (Longowal) and its leader.
  [2] "Unified" Akali Dal, and its leaders and supporters.
  [3] AISSF (Manjit) linked to "extremist" faction within UAD.
  [4] Damdami Taksal-Panthic Committee-KCF-BTFK-AISSF (Gurjit)-four Head Priests combine demanding Khalistan.
  [5] Babbar Khalsa and KLF supportive of "the extremists," and demanding either "Khalsa Raj" or Khalistan.

KLF accepted the authority of Akal Takht *jathedar* Darshan Singh Ragi and urged other militant groups to do the same. These two armed militant organizations demanded Khalistan, but they were also not opposed to negotiations or a settlement short of outright independence. At the most "militant" end of the Sikh political spectrum was the Damdami Taksal, Panthic Committee, AISSF (Gurjit), KCF and BTFK, all of whom were not willing to compromise for anything short of Khalistan. All Sikh groups ranging from "moderate" to "militant" had animosity toward the central government, but they were also deeply divided amongst themselves. Sikh politics had become exceedingly more complex within a year and half than ever before during the entire "Punjab crisis."

"Failure" of President's Rule in Punjab

By late 1987, the central government realized that President's Rule had failed to curb political violence in Punjab. The number of killings in the state, in fact, escalated dramatically in the last half of 1987 in comparison to the first half.[85] The militants had also proven their ability to replenish their ranks even after the arrests of thousands and the killing of hundreds of them.[86] The militants were not "on the run" as both Ray and Ribeiro had so often stated; instead, they appeared to be gaining strength. Yet, the central government was reassured by the fact that a major restructuring of political alignments had occurred within Sikh politics by the end of 1987. The year had begun with "the radicals," "the extremists," and "the militants" forming an "alliance" against "the moderates" and the central government. It ended with the "radical/extremist" UAD, SGPC, and Ragi still aligned with the "extremist" AISSF (Manjit), but their collective relationship with "the militants" (the Panthic Committee-AISSF (Gurjit)-KCF combine) was clearly broken. Thus, the government saw an opportunity to pursue a strategy of building up "the radicals" and/or "the extremists" in its attempt to either weaken or isolate "the militants," and try to negotiate a solution to the "Punjab problem" short of Khalistan. It remained to be seen if and how the government could do this, and whether it would succeed?

Summary and Conclusion

The years analyzed in this chapter saw a re-escalation of the "Punjab crisis," and the emergence of an overtly separatist Sikh ethnonationalist insurgency facilitated by several "patterns of political leadership". These included the formal bifurcation of the "traditional Akali leadership" and its competitive outbidding with a section of the Akalis aligning with "the extremists" and "the militants," relative "unity" within the ranks of both "the militants" and "the extremists", "the militants'" retention of a viable political front with "the extremists," and the lack of unity and coordination among governing central state elites.

At the beginning of this period, the regrouping militants created a set of parallel political institutions under the Panthic Committee to both coordinate their separatist movement and also challenge the traditional Akalis for community leadership. This occurred after divided state elites failed to implement the Punjab Accord, thus severely weakening the "moderate" Akalis. Barnala's "moderate" Akali government reacted to "the militants'" "Declaration of Khalistan" by ordering security forces to raid the Golden Temple complex. Instead of supporting Barnala, the other "traditional Akali leaders"—including Badal, Tohra, and Capt. Amarinder Singh—used this opportunity to try to undermine his government. In this attempt, they split from the "moderate" Akali Dal (L) and formed a separate political party, thus formally bifurcating the "traditional Akali leadership." These other traditional Akali leaders, collectively called "the radicals," subsequently employed heated ethnic rhetoric to shore up their Sikh support base and entered into a mutually-symbiotic alliance with "the extremists" and "the militants" to capture important Sikh political institutions from "the moderates." The disintegration of Akali unity and their subsequently competitive "ethnic outbidding" strengthened both "the extremists" and "the militants," and also contributed to the escalation and sustenance of the Sikh ethnonationalist insurgency. In contrast, a united "traditional Akali leadership" could have quite likely provided an effective bulwark against increased violence and militancy in Punjab.

The central government entered into indirect talks with "the militants" in the spring of 1987 through Darshan Singh Ragi—the Akal Takht *jathedar* supported by "the radicals," "the extremists," and "the militants" alike. These talks may have led to a compromise settlement to the "Punjab crisis," but they were cut short when the central government unexpectedly dismissed Barnala's "moderate" Akali government and imposed President's Rule on Punjab. The Buta Singh faction within the Congress (I) central government apparently convinced Rajiv Gandhi to dismiss Barnala for its own factional partisan interests. Rajiv also wanted to appear tough on Sikh extremism for upcoming state assembly elections in Haryana, and he needed to placate its Congress (I) chief minister Bhajan Lal. Thus, the lack of unity within the governing state elites also prevented a possible solution to the "Punjab crisis," and, in fact, indirectly facilitated escalating Sikh militancy.

During the period in question, "the militants" remained largely united organizationally and also retained a viable political front with "the extremists," although potential problems between the two groupings did begin to emerge. Regarding the latter, the "Declaration of Khalistan" illuminated an emerging ideological fissure within the Sikh ethnonationalist movement between "the extremists" who were willing to compromise short of an independent Sikh state if given "Khalsa Raj" as envisioned in the ASR, and "the militants" who were firmly committed to the creation of Khalistan through armed means. Nonetheless, this emerging schism within the Sikh ethnonationalist movement between "the extremists" and "the militants," and internal divisions within "the militants" themselves remained at their incipient stages. Thus, internal competition between various factions within the Sikh ethnonationalist movement did not become overly destructive during the years under examination in this chapter. The UAD (which consisted of the "radical" Akali Dal (B) and the "extremist" (Baba faction), the "extremist" AISSF (Manjit), and the "militant" AISSF (Gurjit) also continued to provide the Sikh ethnonationalist movement with an effective political front in Punjab, with widespread networks of popular Sikh support.

Thus, the "Punjab problem" escalated and a full-blown insurgency emerged during the years 1986 and 1987 facilitated, in part, by the culmination of several "patterns of political leadership". These included the formal bifurcation of the "traditional Akali leadership" and its competitive outbidding which included a section of this leadership aligning with "the extremists" and "the militants," relative "unity" within the ranks of both "the militants" and "the extremists," "the militants" retention of a viable political front with "the extremists," and the lack of unity and coordination among ruling state elites.

NOTES

1. Interview by the author with high-level militant closely associated with the Damdami Taksal and the original Panthic Committee, Sacramento, California, USA, 19 May 2002. Hereafter referred to as "Interview with militant associated with the Taksal and original Panthic Committee previously cited, 19 May 2002."

2. The institution of the *Sarbat Khalsa* was primarily used between 1723 and 1804 to make collective decisions for the community when Sikhs lacked a unifying political leader. For a concise theological and historical explanation of the origins of the "*Sarbat Khalsa*," see Harbans Singh, ed., *The Encyclopaedia of Sikhism*, volume 4 (Patiala: Punjabi University, 1995), 62–64. Also refer to J.S. Grewal, *The Sikhs of the Punjab* (Cambridge: Cambridge University Press, 1990), 92–94.

3. Staff Correspondent, "'Sarbat Khalsa' dissolves S.G.P.C.: Akal Takht chief 'sacked,'" *The Tribune*, 27 January 1986, 12. For a theological and historical discussion of a "*gurmata*," see Harbans Singh in *The Encyclopaedia*, volume 2, 152–55 and *The Encyclopaedia*, volume 4, 62–64; and also J.S. Grewal, *The Sikhs*, 92–94.

4. Staff Correspondent, "'Sarbat Khalsa' dissolves S.G.P.C.: Akal Takht chief 'sacked,'" *The Tribune*, 27 January 1986, 1 and 12.

5. Ibid.: 1. Most members of the Panthic Committee were either followers or associates of Sant Bhindranwale who had escaped from the Golden Temple complex shortly before Operation Bluestar.

6. For an exhaustive analysis of the behind-the-scenes sequence of events and factionalism that resulted in the inclusion of each one of the five members of the Panthic Committee, see D.P. Sharma, *The Punjab Story: Decade of Turmoil* (New Delhi: APH Publishing Corporation, 1996), 96–97 and 116–18.

7. Raminder Singh, "Punjab: Capture of the Temple," *India Today*, 15 February 1986, 15; and Interview with militant associated with the Taksal and original Panthic Committee previously cited.

8. Interview by the author with close relative of Sant Bhindranwale and high-level member of the AISSF active from 1978 to the late 1980s, Sacramento, California, USA,16 May 2002. Hereafter referred to as "Interview with AISSF member and close relative of Bhindranwale previously cited, 16 May 2002."

9. Interview by the author with senior AISSF leader and human rights activist involved in the "Sikh movement" since 1981, Sacramento, California, USA, 4 June 2002.

10. It is unclear whether a "*Sarbat Khalsa*" can be called by only the *jathedar* of the Akal Takht. For a discussion of this issue, see H. Singh, *The Encyclopaedia*, volume 1, 56–59; and vol. 4, 62–64.

11. Tribune Bureau, "Step to 'avoid bloodshed': 'Sarbat Khalsa' at Anandpur Sahib," *The Tribune*, 12 February 1986, 1.

12. Gobind Thukral, "Punjab: Avoiding a Showdown," *India Today*, 15 March 1986, 10. A translated text of entire *gurmata* is found in Anurag Singh (translator and editor), *Giani Kirpal Singh's Eye-Witness Account of Operation Bluestar: Mighty Murderous Army Attack on the Golden Temple Complex* (Amritsar: B. Chattar Singh Jiwan Singh Publishers, 1999), 267–71.

13. Gobind Thukral, "Punjab: Avoiding a Showdown," *India Today*, 15 March 1986, 10–11.

14. Suman Dubey and Gobind Thukral, "Punjab: Upsurge of Violence," *India Today*, 15 April 1986, 10.

15. Ibid.: 11.

16. Ibid.

17. A detailed account of Ribeiro's career in the IPS is contained in his autobiography, *Bullet for Bullet: My Life as a Police Officer* (New Delhi: Penguin Books, 1998).

18. For example, see Shekhar Gupta and Gobind Thukral, "Punjab Police: Ribeiro's Challenge," *India Today*, 30 April 1986, 32–35.

19. Interview with AISSF member and close relative of Bhindranwale previously cited, 16 May 2002.

20. P.P.S. Gill, "Kahlon faction revolts," *The Tribune*, 12 April 1986, 1.

21. The AISSF (Manjit) was also known as the AISSF (Presidium).

22. Sharma, *The Punjab Story*, 120; Interview with militant associated with the Taksal and original Panthic Committee previously cited, 19 May 2002; and Interview by the author with senior Khalistani activist and intellectual advisor involved in the militant movement since 1986, Fremont, California, USA, 7 May 2002. Hereafter referred to as "Interview with senior Khalistani activist and intellectual advisor previously cited, 7 May 2002."

23. Interview with militant associated with the Taksal and original Panthic Committee previously cited, 19 May 2002.

24. Raminder Singh and Gobind Thukral, "Punjab: Return to Uncertainty," *India Today*, 31 May 1986, 8; and P.P.S. Gill, "AISSF group declares 'Khalistan,'" *The Tribune*, 30 April 1986, 1 and 12. A full length English translation of this "Declaration of Khalistan" is found in Gurmit Singh, *History of Sikh Struggles*, volume 1 (New Delhi: Atlantic Publishers and Distributors, 1989), 532–40.

25. P.P.S. Gill, "AISSF group declares 'Khalistan,'" *The Tribune*, 30 April 1986, 12.

26. Ibid.

27. Shyam Khosla and P.P.S. Gill, "Police action successful: One killed in firing," *The Tribune*, 2 May 1986, 1 and 3.

28. A.S. Prashar, "Badal, Tohra leave Dal panel: Two Punjab Ministers quit," *The Tribune*, 3 May 1986, 1.

29. A.S. Prashar, "Dissidents not for CM's ouster," *The Tribune*, 5 May 1986, 1.

30. Shyam Khosla, "27 Dal (L) MLAs form new party: Government reduced to minority," *The Tribune*, 9 May 1986, 1.

31. P.P.S. Gill, "Rival Akali Dal groups clash," *The Tribune*, 12 May 1986, 1.

32. Gobind Thukral and Tavleen Singh, "Punjab: Migrants of Fear," *India Today*, 15 June 1986, 22.

33. Shekhar Gupta, "A State of Desolation," *India Today*, 15 July 1986, 13–14.

34. Gobind Thukral, "Akali Dal: Barnala's Bid," *India Today*, 15 June 1986, 24.

35. Gobind Thukral, "Punjab: Militant Poses," *India Today*, 31 July 1986, 15.

36. V.P. Prabhakar, "Dissidents to field Mann," *The Tribune*, 12 June 1986, 1.

37. Gobind Thukral, "Terrorism: Turning the Tide," *India Today*, 31 July 1986, 16.
38. See Shyam Khosla, "Barnala's offer to hold talks with youth," *The Tribune*, 7 July 1986, 1; Shekhar Gupta and Gobind Thukral, "Terrorists: The Political Nexus," *India Today*, 30 September 1986, 42–46; and Tribune Bureau, "Badal, Tohra offer help in talks," *The Tribune*, 15 July 1986, 1.
39. Prabhjot Singh, "Amnesty 'vital for peace,'" *The Tribune*, 15 July 1986, 7. For details, see Sharma, *The Punjab Story*, 128. The central government was apparently willing to create a government in Punjab with "the extremists" in power if Manjit Singh, Sandhu, and Kahlon agreed to publicly disavow militancy. Apparently the former two refused without first being released and assessing the situation in the field. Interview with AISSF member and close relative of Bhindranwale previously cited, 16 May 2002.
40. K.S. Chawla, "Terrorists gun down 15: Curfew in Muktsar," *The Tribune*, 26 July 1986, 1.
41. Tribune Bureau, "'Khalistan Commando Force chief' held," *The Tribune*, 10 August 1986, 1 and 6; and Tribune Bureau, "3 Muktsar killers nabbed," *The Tribune*, 13 August 1986, 1.
42. Tribune Correspondent, "New AISSF panel formed," *The Tribune*, 25 September 1986, 1 and 3; and Sharma, *The Punjab Story*, 128.
43. Ravi Sidhu, "Terrorism takes a new turn," *The Tribune*, 2 September 1986, 1 and 16; and Sharma, *The Punjab Story*, 135–136.
44. Tribune Bureau, "22 passengers shot," *The Tribune*, 1 December 1986, 1. For details of the creation of the KLF, see Sharma, *The Punjab Story*, 136.
45. The entire text of the Head Priests' appeal is found in A. Singh, *Giani Kirpal Singh's*, 287–88.
46. A detailed account of these efforts in found in Ibid., 285–305.
47. Ibid.: 301.
48. Gobind Thukral, "Punjab: Futile Moves," *India Today*, 30 November 1986, 26.
49. Tavleen Singh, "SGPC: Centre Stage," *India Today*, 31 December 1986, 14, and P.P.S. Gill, "Tohra elected," *The Tribune*, 1 December 1986, 1.
50. A.S. Prashar, "Badal and Tohra among 100 held: Charge of aiding terrorists," *The Tribune*, 3 December 1986, 1 and 5.
51. P.P.S. Gill, "Takht chief, Head Priest go," *The Tribune*, 25 December 1986, 1 and 3.
52. Electronic mail interview by the author with the personal assistant of a former Akal Takht *jathedar*, 14 May 2002 (questions submitted) and 17 May 2002 (response received). Hereafter referred to as "E-mail interview with assistant to former Akal Takht *jathedar* previously cited, 17 May 2002." For short discussion of Darshan Singh Ragi's background, see *India Today*, 28 February 1987, 14–15.
53. Interview by the author with militant associated with the Taksal and original Panthic Committee previously cited, Sacramento, California, USA, 19 May 2002.
54. E-mail interview with assistant to a former Akal Takht *jathedar* previously cited, 17 May 2002.
55. Gobind Thukral, "Punjab: Militants Win," *India Today*, 15 February 1987, 35.
56. P.P.S. Gill and K.S. Chawla, "Six questions to Darshan Singh: Sikh unity will end all problems," *The Tribune*, 14 January 1987, 5.
57. Staff Correspondent, "Takht tells Dal chiefs to quit," *The Tribune*, 4 February 1987, 1.
58. P.P.S. Gill, "'Panthic policy' framed: Mann made chief of new Dal," *The Tribune*, 6 February 1987, 7.
59. Ibid.
60. Ibid.

61. Ibid.
62. Ibid.
63. P.P.S. Gill, "Priests' new directive: Barnala faces 'action,'" *The Tribune*, 7 February 1987, 10.
64. Quoted in Raminder Singh, "S.S. Barnala: 'The alternative is *fauji raaj*,'" *India Today*, 28 February 1987, 13.
65. Staff Correspondent, "Barnala declared tankhaiya: Summoned to Takht on Feb 11," *The Tribune*, 10 February 1987, 1.
66. For a list and discussion of these "social reforms," see Tavleen Singh, "Punjab: New Terrorist Targets," *India Today*, 30 April 1987, 23.
67. Interview of senior Khalistani leader and activist previously cited, 19 November 2001.
68. Staff Correspondent, "AISSF leader says new Dal not 'Panthic.'" *The Tribune*, 27 February 1987, 1.
69. Staff Correspondent, "Sunil Dutt to report to Centre," *The Tribune*, 14 April 1987, 1.
70. Staff Correspondent, "Muni for release of detainees," *The Tribune*, 8 May 1987, 1.
71. Inderjit Badhwar, Prabhu Chawla, and Raminder Singh, "Punjab: A Risky Gambit", *India Today*, 31 May 1987, 19–20.
72. See Julio Ribeiro's interview in Tavleen Singh, "Julio Francis Ribeiro: 'No chance of success,'" *India Today*, 15 May 1987, 58–59.
73. Inderjit Badhwar, Prabhu Chawla, and Raminder Singh, "Punjab: A Risky Gambit," *India Today*, 31 May 1987, 14–23; Interview with assistant to a former Akal Takht *jathedar* previously cited, 17 May 2002. This explanation is also given by Sangat Singh in *The Sikhs in History*, (New Delhi: Uncommon Books, 1996), 460 and 464–66.
74. Interview with assistant to a former Akal Takht *jathedar* previously cited, 17 May 2002.
75. Inderjit Badhwar, Prabhu Chawla, and Raminder Singh, "Punjab: A Risky Gambit," *India Today*, 31 May 1987, 14–23.
76. Staff Correspondent, "Cracks in 'Panthic committee'," *The Tribune*, 30 April 1987, 1.
77. Raj Chengappa, "Punjab: Discouraging Start," *India Today*, 15 July 1987, 29.
78. Dilip Bobb, Inderjit Badhwar, Tavleen Singh, Shekar Gupta, and Ramesh Chandran, "The Spectre of Terrorism," *India Today*, 31 July 1987, 8–19; and A.S. Prashar, "Bus Massacre," *The Tribune*, 8 July 1987, 1.
79. Staff Correspondent, "Takht chief call convention on Aug 4," *The Tribune*, 16 July 1987, 1; and Staff Correspondent, "Takht chief warns Akali leaders," *The Tribune*, 24 July 1987, 1.
80. See P.P.S. Gill, "Convention seeks 'Sikh area'," *The Tribune*, 5 August 1987, 1.
81. Ibid.: 12.
82. E-mail interview with assistant to a former Akal Takht *jathedar* previously cited, 17 May 2002.
83. P.P.S. Gill, "Militant-priest rift widens," *The Tribune*, 7 August 1987, 1.
84. Vimukh Singh, "Punjab: Defiant Call," *India Today*, 30 September 1987, 42.
85. For details see Sharma, *The Punjab Story*, 171–72.
86. In 1987, 3,687 militants were arrested and 327 were killed in comparison to 1515 arrested and 78 killed in 1986. Ibid.

8

The Divided State and Electoral Victory of the Extremists (1988–1990)

RELEASE OF AKAL TAKHT *JATHEDAR* JASBIR SINGH RODE AND THE CENTER'S NEW "POLITICAL INITIATIVE"

By the beginning of 1988, "the militants" had gained increased influence in Sikh politics, and they were effectively molding the tenor of Sikh political discourse in Punjab. Instead of challenging "the militants," "Unified" Akali Dal (UAD) leaders, including Parkash Singh Badal, radicalized their own rhetoric to avoid losing Sikh support to "the extremists" and "the militants." This included issuing an official party resolution lauding "the militants" for giving a "befitting response" to the government and for "keeping alive the traditions, history, and ethos of the Sikh people" by taking "recourse to other (meaning 'armed') modes of resistance."[1] Both the central government and the radicalized Akali leadership knew that no solution to the "Punjab crisis" was possible without either the active support of "the militants," or without somehow isolating them. Neither of these was an easy task. It was also clear that President's Rule had failed to reduce levels of political violence in Punjab; in fact, they had steadily risen. For this reason, the central government devised a new "political initiative" to try to curb the rising tide of separatism in Punjab and hopefully solve the "Punjab problem."

As a part of this "political initiative," the government suddenly and unexpectedly released Jasbir Singh Rode in early-March 1988, after three years of detention, and also released three other Head Priests who had been arrested the previous year.[2] Rode had been appointed as *jathedar* of the Akal Takht by the Damdami Taksal-sponsored *Sarbat Khalsa* in January 1986, but others had assumed this position during his incarceration. Rode was also Sant Jarnail Singh Bhindranwale's nephew, and came from a "family of martyrs" which had lost over a dozen of its members, including his own father and brother, in various security operations, including Operation Bluestar.[3] After Operation Bluestar, Rode had organized and led the International Sikh Youth Federation (ISYF) in the United Kingdom, and had publicly met with Pakistani leader, Zia ul-Haq, to elicit support for "the Sikh struggle." This earned him the wrath of the Indian government, which pressured British authorities to deport him from the United Kingdom back to India. After being denied entry into several countries, Rode was turned over to India by the Philippine government when he landed in Manila. Rode had never been actively involved in politics in Punjab but he was thought to be more of an "extremist" than a "militant," being Baba Joginder Singh's grandson.

After their release, Rode and the other Head Priests were taken to Amritsar at their request aboard a special military plane. The "militants" holed up inside the Golden Temple complex gave Rode and the returning Head Priests a "warm welcome" by personally greeting them, firing bullets into the air, and raising pro-Khalistan slogans. The mainstream press described the militants' firing as being a "salute" or "honor guard," but Rode's entourage perceptively interpreted it more as being a symbolic warning to Rode and the Head Priests not to challenge their power. After all, "the militants" suspected that Rode may have had reached some sort of secret "understanding" or "deal" with the central government in return for his release from jail.[4]

For his part, Rode denied these allegations. He explained that he had been released after having refused to negotiate with the government without first being allowed to consult with "the militants" in the field. In his own defense, Rode admitted having met with government emissaries before his release, but he tried to dispel suspicions about being a "government agent" by saying:

> If it is possible for Rajiv [Gandhi] to talk to us sensibly, it is also possible for us to talk to him and his government. But there will be no sell-out of the Sikh community...The truth is that our release was entirely unconditional...I'll be the last person to sell out fellow Sikhs who've fought so valiantly and given the Government a battered face.[5]

These explanations aside, "the militants" adopted a "wait-and-see" approach toward Rode. They correctly assessed that Rode could be a powerful ally for their separatist cause if he openly supported the creation of Khalistan, but they also realized that he could undermine their struggle if he compromised with the government short of outright independence. The "radical" Badal faction within the UAD was also apprehensive about Rode's leadership because he and the "extremists" represented a potentially powerful force in Sikh politics which the central government could use to help solve the "Punjab crisis." For this reason, the "traditional Akali leadership"—including Badal and Tohra—feared being permanently sidelined if Rode's leadership succeeded. Thus, the "moderates," "radicals," and pro-Khalistan "militants" alike all had reasons to see the "Rode initiative" fail. Nonetheless, all of these Sikh factions had little choice except to accept Rode's leadership, at least for the time being. Thus, Jasbir Singh Rode was formally installed as the *jathedar* of the Akal Takht only a few days after his release in an elaborate ceremony attended by "militants," "extremists," and "radicals" alike.[6]

In reality, Rode was the centerpiece of the government's new "political initiative" on Punjab. The government had released him hoping that he could either unite the various "militant" organizations under his leadership and convince them to negotiate for a solution short of Khalistan, or he could unite most of them and gain the support of the Sikh public in order to isolate the "militant" groups which refused to negotiate. In the first scenario, Rode would become a leader for "the militants" or act as an "intermediary" between them and the government for talks. In the second scenario, Rode would become an alternative pole of power within Sikh politics with which to undermine "the militants" who refused to compromise short of outright independence. This was an ingenious, but risky, gambit by the government.

Rode's release had, in fact, come after careful deliberations within the central government, and between emissaries of the government and Baba Thakur Singh of the Damdami Taksal.[7] Interestingly, his release corresponded with an evolving shift within the ranks of "the militants". By early-1988, a "new" leadership was gaining strength within the "militant movement" under the guidance of Dr Sohan Singh, who had been one of the intellectuals behind the creation of the Panthic Committee two years earlier. Dr. Sohan Singh and his supporters emphasized the exclusive political goal of creating Khalistan instead of focusing on Sikh religious revivalism as the Damdami Taksal had done since the late-1970s. In essence, the Damdami Taksal was quickly becoming marginalized within the "militant movement," and, for this reason, it was slowly shifting away from "the militants" and toward "the extremists."[8]

Before his release, Rode and his emissaries had actually contacted many of "the militants'" leaders in the field to try to convince them to negotiate a settlement to the "Punjab problem" short of outright independence consisting of the creation of a semi-autonomous Sikh region within India.[9] After all, this was a demand that the government was willing to consider if it would help end the violence in Punjab. A section of "the militants"— including Baba Thakur Singh of the Damdami Taksal, Gurbachan Singh Manochahal of the BTFK, Gurjit Singh of the AISSF (Gurjit), the KLF, and select Panthic Committee members—had reluctantly agreed to consider a "package settlement" to end their insurgency.[10] This "package settlement" was proposed to include a temporary cease-fire, minor concessions to Punjab and the Sikhs, the release of Sikh political prisoners, and the granting of safe passage for "the militants" to hold official talks with the central government for a binding solution to the "Punjab problem."[11] This "pro-negotiation" section of "militants" hesitantly supported Rode's initiative but they were also very cautious, suspecting the central government's sincerity and fearing being accused by the other militants of undermining the struggle for Khalistan.

The grouping of "anti-negotiation" militants included Bhai Mokham Singh of the Damdami Taksal, Wassan Singh Zafferwal of the Panthic Committee, Dr Sohan Singh, and "General" Labh Singh of the KCF.[12] This "anti-negotiation" section of militants initially continued with their "wait-and-see" approach toward Rode, trying to assess in which direction he would take Sikh politics, but their relationship with Rode eventually soured for several reasons. First, Rode declared that the Sikhs' political goal was the achievement of *puran azadi* (complete freedom), but he refused to elaborate exactly what this meant.[13] This was insufficient for the "anti-negotiation" militants who wanted him to unequivocally support Khalistan. Second, Rode refused to hold a *Sarbat Khalsa* on Baisakhi day at the Golden Temple complex as requested by "the militants." Instead, he planned to hold a convention, but not a formal *Sarbat Khalsa*, at Damdama Sahib in the Malwa region for the purpose of discussing the future of the Sikh Panth. The "anti-negotiation" militants were concerned that Rode may use this gathering to try to overturn some of the decisions taken by previous *Sarbat Khalsa* conventions, including the one creating the Panthic Committee, which he characterized as having been "taken in anger."[14] Lastly, Rode announced that the AISSF (Gurjit) and AISSF (Manjit) had agreed to merge after nearly two years of bifurcation.[15] Co-opting the "militant" AISSF chief, Gurjit Singh, was a major victory for Rode and "the extremists." After all, the AISSF (Gurjit) was the Panthic Committee-led "militants'" primary source of institutionalized mass support in Punjab.

The Panthic Committee reacted to Rode's actions by issuing an official statement threatening "dire consequences" to those who initiated dialog with the central government short of Khalistan.[16] This was a thinly-veiled threat to Rode and "the extremists." The "anti-negotiation" militants had not formally broken with Rode, but their relationship with him was getting increasingly strained and possibly even antagonistic. Thus, it became apparent by mid-April that Rode had failed to unite all of the militant groups under his leadership. Yet, he still remained useful for the government if he could somehow isolate or undermine the "anti-negotiation" militants who refused to negotiate. Thus, the government's "Rode initiative" appeared to be faltering, but it certainly was not dead. The "Sikh political spectrum" after Rode's release looked like the following (Table 8.1):

Table 8.1
Sikh Political Spectrum (Early-1988)

Moderates	Radicals	Extremists	Militants/Separatists
Akali Dal (L)[1]	UAD[2]	Rode[2]	Panthic Committee[3]
Barnala[1]	Badal[2]	UAD[2]	KCF[3]
	Tohra[2]	Joginder Singh[2]	BTFK[3]
	Talwandi[2]	AISSF (Manjit)[2]	AISSF (Gurjit)[2]
		Damdami Taksal[2]	KLF[2]
			Babbar Khalsa[2]

Source: Author.
Notes: [1] Akali Dal (Longowal) and its leaders.
          [2] Groups and leaders accepting authority of Akal Takht *jathedar* Rode and his goal of "Khalsa Raj".
          [3] Panthic Committee-KCF-BTFK combine unequivocally demanding creation of Khalistan.

NEW DIMENSIONS OF "POLITICAL VIOLENCE" AND UNION HOME MINISTER BUTA SINGH'S ATTEMPTS TO UNDERMINE THE "RODE INITIATIVE"

Levels of political violence in Punjab rose dramatically in early-1988, with 750 people killed by "terrorists" in the first three-and-half months of the year.[17] Violence after Rode's release skyrocketed even further, with the killing of over a hundred people in the last two weeks of April alone.[18] In particular, there was a dramatic rise of killings in Sikh-dominated parts of the Majha region, including a series of massacres in which entire Sikh families were wiped out.[19] This violence was qualitatively different from earlier forms of violence in which the targets tended to be much more selective and largely Hindu. Several explanations emerged for these changed dynamics of "terrorist" violence in Punjab.

First, it was possible that the Panthic Committee and the "militant" leadership had simply lost control over their cadres with the mushrooming of local armed outfits and the influx of weapons from Pakistan. The number of "armed militants" estimated to be operating in Punjab increased from only a few hundred in 1987 to between 2,000 and 3,000 by the spring of 1988.[20] Second, it was also plausible that the "anti-negotiation" section of "militants" were trying to undermine the "Rode initiative" by committing mass killings. Third, it was suspected that some of these massacres were carried out by government-sponsored "killer gangs" consisting of criminals and former militants. These "killer gangs" had been used by the police in the past to both track down and kill bonafide Sikh militants, and also to try to discredit the "militant movement" by committing random acts of violence.[21] Senior Punjab police officers, in fact, admitted that some of these unconventional, anti-insurgency gangs had committed excessive crime outside of their allotted operational tasks.[22] Fourth, it was also possible that elements within the central government opposed to the "Rode initiative" were abetting this increased violence in order to undermine the peace efforts.

Regarding the latter, suspicions fell squarely on powerful Union home minister, Buta Singh. Rajiv Gandhi and his other senior advisors had undertaken the "Rode initiative" without initially consulting Buta Singh and, thereafter, against his wishes.[23] In contrast, senior Congress (I) politicians from Punjab, including former chief minister Darbara Singh and Punjab Congress (I) president Beant Singh, both supported Rajiv's "Rode initiative" to try to bring peace to Punjab.[24] Buta Singh, a *Mazhbi* (lower caste) Sikh considered Darbara Singh and Beant Singh (both higher-caste Jat Sikhs) to be potential competitors in Punjab's Congress (I) politics. Buta Singh calculated that undermining the "Rode initiative" would help weaken both Darbara Singh and Beant Singh, and also help him build an independent support base in Punjab to hopefully one day become chief minister of the state like Zail Singh, also a non-Jat, had become in the mid-1970s. Rode, in fact, pointed directly toward Buta Singh as being one of the "vested interests" who wanted to ruin his peace efforts.[25] Buta Singh had actually sabotaged similar peace efforts in the past, including the militant–government talks held through Darshan Singh Ragi a year earlier, and had also convinced Rajiv to dismiss the Barnala government in favor of President's Rule in May 1987.[26] This amounted to a proverbial case of one hand of the government not knowing or, in this case, purposely undermining what the other was trying to achieve. Thus, the faltering

"Rode peace initiative" faced obstacles from multiple sides in the spring of 1988, including from the "anti-negotiation" section of militants, the "traditional Akali leadership," and the Buta Singh faction within the central government.

OPERATION BLACK THUNDER II AND DEMISE OF THE "RODE INITIATIVE"

Jasbir Singh Rode continued his mission of trying to convince "the militants" to negotiate with the government through the spring of 1988. His efforts resulted in a continuous number of archaic splits, mergers, and repositioning of alliances both between and within the various "militant" organizations. Yet, Rode's efforts eventually failed when KCF chief Labh Singh refused to give up his insistence on the creation of Khalistan during meetings with both Rode and AISSF chief Gurjit Singh in early-May 1988. After these meetings, Labh Singh accused Rode and Gurjit Singh of "being purchased by the Government" and speaking the language of "forming a government [in Punjab]."[27] Shortly thereafter, the Panthic Committee formally and unequivocally disowned Gurjit Singh in an open public announcement. Thus, the split between Rode and the Panthic Committee was complete!

After the break-up with the Panthic Committee, both Rode and former Akal Takht *jathedar* Gurdev Singh Koanke, in consultation with the "pro-Rode" section of the central government, devised a plan to use "militants" loyal to them to physically oust cadres of the "anti-negotiation" militants holed up inside the Golden Temple complex.[28] But, before this plan could be implemented, fighting broke out on 9 May 1988 between militants inside the Golden Temple complex and the security forces surrounding it. It is unclear who fired the first shots, but tension around the temple complex had been building for weeks. The actual fighting began when a senior police officer was shot and wounded by Sikh militants when he tried to prevent them from erecting fortifications behind the Akal Takht. Several competing explanations emerged about the exact sequence of events, but well-founded suspicions fell on Rode's detractors who wanted to undermine his peace efforts.

First, one explanation was that Buta Singh's loyalists instigated the confrontation in order to undermine the "Rode initiative" and forward their patron's political interests. For example, observers around the Golden Temple complex had noticed so-called "militants," possibly government-sponsored "killer gangs," roaming around the temple complex in the presence of paramilitary forces challenging the militants holed up inside the temple complex to do battle.[29] Another source identified a security officer who was close to Buta Singh of purportedly firing shots into the air, which subsequently triggered the confrontation between the security forces and the militants.[30] Second, it was also hypothesized that the "anti-negotiation" section of militants, either acting alone or in concert with elements within the central government, instigated the confrontation in order to sink the "Rode initiative." Rode had, in fact, complained only a few days earlier that his efforts were being undermined by an alliance of both pro-Khalistan militants and Buta Singh's coterie within the government.[31] Whatever the exact catalyst, the armed battle between the militants holed up in the temple complex and Indian security forces effectively sank the "Rode peace initiative." The Rode "political initiative" was over!

Immediately after the initial exchange of gunfire, government security forces sealed off the old walled portion of Amritsar, and cut off all water and power supplies to the Golden Temple complex. National Security Guard (NSG) commandos laid siege to the area and adopted a "wait-and-kill" strategy in confronting the militants. The besieged militants refused to surrender and, over the next several days, NSG snipers picked off militants as they moved from room to room or tried to fetch water from the *sarovar* (holy water tank) surrounding the central shrine.[32] After nearly 10 days of blistering summer heat and no escape route, the surviving militants inside the Golden Temple complex meekly surrendered to the security forces. Thirty militants had been killed, about a hundred were arrested after surrendering, and four militants committed suicide to avoid arrest.[33] In contrast, the security forces suffered no fatalities, and, in fact, never actually set foot in the central portion of the Golden Temple complex. Thus, "Operation Black Thunder II" was a tactical military success, but it did little to help solve the political conflict in Punjab. After all, "the militants" continued to operate with impunity throughout the state and all Sikh political groups, including the Akalis, appeared antagonistic to the Delhi Durbar (central government) absent a negotiated political settlement.

BIFURCATION OF THE UNIFIED AKALI DAL INTO THE "EXTREMIST" UAD (MANN) AND THE "RADICAL" UAD (TALWANDI)

Operation Black Thunder II gave the "radicals"—who were basically the dissident "traditional Akali leaders" such as Badal and Tohra who had been sidelined by the central government in favor of Rode and "the extremists"—an opportunity to re-exert themselves in Sikh politics. In this attempt, the SGPC executive committee, which was controlled by "the radicals," sacked Rode and the other "extremist" Head Priests from their positions blaming them for Operation Black Thunder II.[34] This announcement shocked Rajiv Gandhi, who had counted on the "traditional Akali leadership" to help strengthen Rode for the purposes of solving the "Punjab crisis." But, the dissident "traditional Akali leadership" had its own political interests to protect; namely, the success of the "Rode initiative" would have permanently marginalized it in Sikh politics and given the reins of community leadership to "the extremists."

In a desperate and last-ditch attempt to salvage the "Rode initiative," the central government ordered the police to detain members of the SGPC executive committee to try to convince them to reverse their decision to dismiss Rode and the other "extremist" Head Priests.[35] When persuasion failed, members of the SGPC executive were threatened but to no avail. Thus, the central government subsequently resigned itself to arresting senior Akali leaders under the National Security Act (NSA) and shifting them to different prisons at the southern most tip of India to prevent them from colluding or exercising their authority any further.[36] Most of these leaders, including both Badal and Tohra, would remain in detention for the next 18 months.

Rode's dismissal by the Badal faction-controlled SGPC executive sparked an intense factional struggle within the UAD between the "radicals" and the "extremists" led by Baba Joginder Singh, the AISSF (Manjit), and the Damdami Taksal. Jailed UAD convenor, Simranjeet Singh Mann, tried to control this factionalism, but "the radicals" interpreted his moves as being partisan in favor of "the extremists."[37] After all, Mann was ideologically closer to Baba Joginder Singh and "the extremists" than to the "traditional Akali leadership."

After sacking Rode, the "radicals" moved quickly to consolidate their position within Sikh politics by choosing Darshan Singh Ragi to return as *jathedar* of the Akal Takht.[38] Ragi accepted this position but promised that he would not involve the Akal Takht in contentious political issues in order to maintain the dignity of the institution.[39] The "moderate" Akali Dal (L), which still had a plurality of seats in the SGPC general house, also backed Ragi to be Akal Takht *jathedar*, calculating that Ragi would be more likely than the "extremist"-supported Rode to pardon its leader, Surjit Singh Barnala, who had been excommunicated from the Panth in early-1987.[40] For their part, the Panthic Committee-led militants selected one of their own, Gurbachan Singh Monochahal, to be their Akal

Takht *jathedar* whereas "the extremists" continued to back Rode. Thus, competing Akal Takht *jathedars* emerged in Sikh politics after Operation Black Thunder II.

In August 1988, friction between the "radical" and "extremist" factions within the UAD came to a head when the UAD formally split into two separate parties—the "extremist" UAD (Mann) led by Baba Joginder Singh in Mann's absence and the "radical" UAD (Talwandi) containing the dissident "traditional Akali leadership" including Badal, Tohra, and Talwandi.[41] Before being arrested, Badal and Tohra had successfully convinced Talwandi to shift his loyalty back to the "traditional Akali leadership." Talwandi had agreed to do so, calculating that his political interests would be better served by aligning with his fellow "traditional Akali leaders" since the "Rode initiative" had faltered and "the extremists" stood humiliated. Thus, Operation Black Thunder II was a pivotal event that led to the dismissal of the Rode-led Head Priests and the bifurcation of the UAD into the "extremist" UAD (Mann) and the "radical" UAD (Talwandi).

BIFURCATION OF THE "MILITANT" MOVEMENT INTO THE "OLD" FIRST PANTHIC COMMITTEE AND THE "NEW" SECOND (DR SOHAN SINGH) PANTHIC COMMITTEE

Operation Black Thunder II did not crush the Sikh separatist insurgency, but it did have important effects on the broader militant movement. First, the issue-based distinction between the "pro-negotiation" militants and "anti-negotiation" militants, which had emerged shortly after Rode's coronation as Akal Takht *jathedar*, evaporated after Operation Black Thunder II when all militant groups disassociated themselves from Rode, blaming him for the military operation. Second, a "new" and more educated leadership asserted itself within the militant movement after Operation Black Thunder II in opposition to the traditional, "old," and largely uneducated leadership of Zafferwal and Manochahal, who had been active in armed militancy since before Operation Bluestar.

This "new" grouping of more educated militants was led by Dr Sohan Singh, the former Director of Health Services in Punjab who had been intellectually involved in the "militant movement" since the late-1970s when he headed a discussion group supporting the Akal Takht's *hukamnama* against the Nirankaris and also the "Sikhs-are-a-nation" theory.[42] Dr Sohan Singh was an ardent separatist concerned primarily with the political goal of creating an independent Sikh state as opposed to also focusing on Sikh religious revivalism like many of the "old," uneducated militants. He had remained an intellectual advisor and important "behind-the-scenes" player within the "militant movement" for years, and, in fact, had been central in forming the Panthic Committee and drafting the "Declaration of Khalistan" in 1986. After Operation Black Thunder II, Dr Sohan Singh took advantage of the "humiliation" suffered by the armed militants to openly come to the forefront of the movement.

In mid-June 1988, senior members of the AISSF (Gurjit) met at the request of Dr Sohan Singh to chose a replacement for Gurjit Singh, who had mysteriously disappeared after Operation Black Thunder II.[43] This conclave selected Daljeet Singh Bittu, a postgraduate student in veterinary medicine, to be the new AISSF convenor. Thus, the AISSF (Gurjit) became the AISSF (Bittu).[44] The AISSF (Bittu) subsequently disassociated itself from the Damdami Taksal, describing it as being "a purely religious body," and also stated its discord with certain members of the Panthic Committee, especially Manochahal, whose "criminalized" lieutenants it held responsible for Operation Black Thunder II.[45]

The "old, uneducated" grouping of militants under Manochahal and Zafferwal responded to the creation of the AISSF (Bittu) by forming a AISSF faction of their own under the convenorship of Gurnam Singh Bundala and Gurnam Singh Buttar.[46] Thus, the AISSF (Gurjit) actually became reconstituted into two competing factions—the AISSF (Bittu) linked to the "new" emerging militant leadership of Dr Sohan Singh and the AISSF (Bundala/Buttar) under the "old, uneducated" militant leadership. The third AISSF faction—the AISSF (Manjit)—remained closely allied with "the extremists," including Rode and the UAD (Mann).

Dr Sohan Singh and the newly-created AISSF (Bittu) also tried to include the KLF and the Babbar Khalsa—two organizations that had never accepted the authority of the Panthic Committee—into its new emerging alliance of militants. The Babbar Khalsa and especially the KLF had previously remained close to "the extremists." Yet, after Operation Black Thunder II, both of these armed organizations began moving away from "the extremists" and toward the new grouping of "militants" associated with Dr Sohan Singh. The Babbar Khalsa, in fact, disassociated itself from Rode immediately after Operation Black Thunder II. The KLF's shift away from "the extremists" to becoming unequivocally devoted to the creation of a sovereign Sikh state emanated from a change in its leadership after its chief, Avtar Singh Brahma, was killed in a "police encounter" in the summer of 1988.[47] With Brahma's death, the KLF's tradition of being an armed organization willing to negotiate short of Khalistan was broken. In contrast to Brahma, his second-in-command, Gurjant Singh Budhsinghwala, was more closely associated with the batch of "new" hardcore separatists led by Dr Sohan Singh and Daljeet Singh Bittu.

These emerging divisions within the "militant movement" crystallized into definitive organization form in November 1988 when Bittu announced the formation of a new, separate Panthic Committee under the direction of Dr Sohan Singh.[48] He justified this split by explaining that a new organizational set-up was necessary to reinvigorate the Khalistan movement after the "humiliation" suffered during Operation Black Thunder II. The most powerful armed "militant" organization, the KCF, also split into two factions after the death of its chief "General" Labh Singh who was killed in a police encounter and the formal bifurcation of the Panthic Committee.[49]

Thus, the overall militant movement became bifurcated into two broad groupings by the fall of 1988. One "militant" grouping was being led by the "old" (First) Panthic Committee under Manochahal and Zafferwal, and included the AISSF (Bundala/Buttar), KCF (Rajasthani) under Gujrant Singh Rajasthani, and the BTFK. This grouping was supported by the Damdami Taksal. The "new" Second (Dr Sohan Singh) Panthic Committee included the AISSF (Bittu), KCF (Sultanwind) under Kanwarjit Singh Sultanwind, the KLF, and the Babbar Khalsa.[50] As a result of this restructuring, "the extremists" were left, for the first time in the post-Bluestar period, without a formal armed wing. The "Sikh political spectrum" looked like the following (Table 8.2):

There was a dramatic spurt of militant violence in Punjab after the bifurcation of the Panthic Committee, with each militant outfit and grouping trying to establish its dominance over the others by proving its firepower.[51] The death toll for 1988 was as follows: 1,839 "civilians" killed; 110 security men killed; 373 militants killed; and 3,882 militants arrested.[52] Thus, the total death toll for 1988 was 2,322 almost doubling the toll for 1987 (1,238). For the first time during the "Punjab problem," more Sikhs than Hindus were killed by "the militants." Out of the 1,949 total civilian and security force casualties, 1,044 were Sikhs, and 905 were Hindus.[53]

Thus, Operation Black Thunder II did not crush Sikh militancy in Punjab but it did result in the splintering of individual armed organizations, the bifurcation of the overall "militant movement" into two broad alliance-based groupings each led by a separate Panthic Committee, and a significant restructuring of organizational loyalties within the movement. In essence, the insurgency continued, but "the militants"

Table 8.2
Sikh Political Spectrum (Late-1988)

Moderates	Radicals	Extremists	Militants/Separatists
AD (L)[1]	UAD (T)[2]	UAD (M)[3]	First Panthic Committee[4]
Barnala[1]	Ragi	Rode[3]	BTFK[4]
	Badal[2]	Joginder Singh[3]	KCF (Rajasthani)[4]
	Tohra[2]	AISSF (Manjit)[3]	AISSF (Bundala/Buttar)[4]
	Talwandi[2]	Damdami Taksal[3]	Second Panthic Committee (Dr. Sohan Singh)[5]
			AISSF (Bittu)[5]
			KCF (Sultanwind)[5]
			KLF[5]
			Babbar Khalsa[5]

Source: Author.

Notes: [1] Akali Dal (Longowal) and its leader; demanding implementation of Rajiv-Longowal Accord through non-violent means.

[2] United Akali Dal (Talwandi) and its leaders; demanding implementation of the (ASR) through non-violent means.

[3] "The extremists" generally united behind United Akali Dal (Mann) demanding implementation of (ASR) or "Khalsa Raj" through either non-violent or violent means.

[4] First Panthic Committee-led militants demanding Khalistan through violent means.

[5] Second Panthic Committee-led militants demanding Khalistan through violent means.

were getting increasingly fractionalized and, in a potentially significant development, "the extremists" had lost their formal association with any of the armed "militant" groups for the first time in the post-Bluestar period. The ideological and organizational schism between "the extremists" and "militants" was widening.

RAJIV GANDHI'S "HALF-HEARTED" ATTEMPT TO SOLVE THE "PUNJAB CRISIS" BY GRANTING CONCESSIONS

By early-1989, it was becoming a distinct possibility that the Congress (I) might lose its parliamentary majority in upcoming national elections scheduled for later that year. Rajiv Gandhi had come to power in December 1984 with an unprecedented three-fourths majority in parliament after his mother's assassination, but the Congress(I)'s support base had eroded steadily over the years. Several of India's major opposition political parties had combined in late-1988 to form a new and more powerful Janata Dal under the leadership of dismissed defense minister V.P. Singh. Since then, the Congress (I) had lost a string of important state assembly elections.[54] In addition to issues such as corruption, the revitalized Janata-led opposition also criticized the Congress (I) central government for not making sufficient efforts to ameliorate Sikh discontent in Punjab and solving the "Punjab tangle."

In response to this barrage of criticism, Rajiv Gandhi announced a series of "political concessions" for the Sikhs and Punjab in March 1989. These concessions included the release all "Jodhpur detainees" charged under the National Security Act (NSA) except 86 of them whose cases were to be referred to regular civilian courts in Punjab, the relaxation of several parts of the NSA allowing for preventative detention, and a promise to prosecute more culprits in connection with the 1984 anti-Sikh riots.[55] These "political concessions" were loudly and euphorically applauded by both the government and opposition parties in New Delhi, but the Sikh response was much more subdued.[56] After all, piecemeal concessions did not represent a comprehensive settlement on the political, economic, and territorial demands for which large sections of the Sikh community had been agitating since 1982.

In essence, Rajiv's "half-hearted" granting of concessions failed to evoke the desired Sikh response. In fact, the prevailing trend in Sikh politics became apparent in spring of 1989 when "the moderates" dared not put-up a stage at the traditional Sikh festival of *Holla Mohalla* at Anandpur Sahib. Furthermore, the "radical" UAD (T)'s stage was taken over by the "extremists" and "militants," who criticized the "traditional Akali leadership" and openly demanded "Khalsa Raj" and Khalistan, respectively, during the convention.[57] These developments prompted Rajiv to change his rhetoric from being conciliatory to becoming more confrontational, and he subsequently began campaigning for the upcoming parliamentary elections by once again playing on the "nation-is-in-danger" theme. Punjab governor S.S. Ray admitted that a solution to the "Punjab problem" ultimately had to be a political one, but that no such settlement could be negotiated until after the parliamentary elections were held at the end of the year.[58] The Congress (I) position in the center, after all, was too weak for any bold initiative on Punjab. The upcoming national parliamentary elections appeared to be critical for the future of Punjab.

RETURN OF AISSF (MANJIT) LEADERS TO PUNJAB AND THE GROWING STRENGTH OF "THE EXTREMISTS"

The Sikh ethnonationalist movement showed no signs of slowing down through early- and mid-1989 despite sustained security operations. The movement, in fact, gained momentum after Satwant Singh, one of Mrs Gandhi's assassins, and an alleged co-conspirator, Kehar Singh, were executed in January 1989. Government security forces had only marginal control over rural areas of Punjab, especially in the Amritsar and Gurdaspur districts, where militant-sympathizers openly collected taxes for Khalistan at public gatherings. Police excesses in the name of fighting "terrorism" contributed to public sympathy for the militants and continued to alienate Sikhs from the government. The depth of Sikh discontent was evident by the fact that the funeral ceremonies of slain Sikh militants attracted huge crowds, often numbering over one hundred thousand. In short, the "Punjab crisis" was not getting any better; it was getting worse.

Rajiv's "political concessions" granted to Punjab and the Sikhs in March 1989, while not effective in ameliorating Sikh alienation and mitigating the insurgency, did have an important indirect effect on the "Punjab problem." In particular, the decision to try those "Jodhpur detainees" not released outright in normal civilian courts in Punjab allowed several top "extremist" leaders to return to the state to await trial. These included AISSF (Manjit) president, Bhai Manjit Singh, and its general secretary, Harminder Singh Sandhu. Both Manjit Singh and Sandhu's transfer to jails in Punjab allowed them to periodically meet with journalists and hold in-mass meetings with their supporters during visitation days. Sandhu defined his organization's goal as wanting to unite with the Damdami Taksal and form a political party "aimed at safeguarding Sikh interests and attaining an independent sovereign State."[59] This appeared to be a demand for Khalistan, but there were significant differences between the "extremist" Sandhu and "the militants." First, Sandhu did not openly endorse an armed struggle for the creation of an independent sovereign state. Second, he was not opposed to holding negotiations with the central government for a solution short of Khalistan. For this reason, he explicitly avoided using the word "Khalistan," but rather amorphously stated that attaining this "separate geographical area" for the Sikhs would require drastic constitutional and geographical changes.[60] Sandhu, in fact, admitted to having been taken to New Delhi along with Manjit Singh to negotiate a solution to the "Punjab problem" on four different occasions during their incarceration, but added that they had "refused to sign on the dotted line and sell our conscience."[61]

For its part, the government was not opposed to letting Manjit Singh and Sandhu speak to the press and use "inflammatory" language in order to build up their stature within the Sikh community. Even though Sandhu was a tough bargainer, the government realized that the "extremist" AISSF

(Manjit) was one source of Sikh political leadership that could possibly siphon-off support from "the militants" and help find a solution to the "Punjab problem" short of Khalistan. In contrast, the "traditional Akali leadership"—both "moderate" and "radical" alike—had lost its credibility with large sections of the Sikh community and appeared to have become peripheral to solving the "Punjab problem." The central government was, in fact, engaging Manjit Singh and Sandhu in talks, along with Simranjeet Singh Mann, about how possibly to resolve the "Punjab problem."[62]

The "extremist" AISSF (Manjit)'s power and influence grew rapidly through 1989. Several factors and events, in addition to the return of its senior leaders to Punjab, contributed to this process. First, the Damdami Taksal broke with the "militant" First Panthic Committee in May 1989, and squarely aligned itself with "the extremists," including the AISSF (Manjit).[63] Second, the AISSF (Manjit) received a boost to its credibility when it called for a Punjab *bandh* on June 30, protesting the escalated use of police torture and demanding the release of Mann from custody. Both the "moderate" Akali Dal (L) and "radical" UAD (T) piggy-backed in supporting this *bandh*, and it was a huge success as Punjab came to a virtual standstill.[64] Third, Manjit Singh was released from jail in late-July after a court dismissed the government's case against him.[65] After five years of incarceration, Manjit Singh toured parts of Punjab along with the Damdami Taksal chief Baba Thakur Singh and attracted huge crowds, thus revitalizing the AISSF rank-and-file throughout the state. Fourth, the AISSF (Manjit)'s power was enhanced when, in mid-September, the "militant" AISSF (Bundala) disassociated itself from the First Panthic Committee and shifted its support to the "extremist" AISSF (Manjit).[66]

Thus, "the extremists" and "the militants" were largely in control of the tenor of Sikh politics in fall of 1989. It was uncertain whether Rajiv's Congress (I) central government would allow Punjab to participate in the upcoming parliamentary elections, considering the deteriorating "law-and-order" situation in the state. But, in reality, the Congress (I) did have a political incentive to allow elections in Punjab. To explain, these national elections were expected to be very close and, considering the Congress (I)'s deteriorating support base in India and the growing popularity of the opposition united around V.P. Singh, Rajiv Gandhi knew that his party would need every possible seat it could win to gain a majority in parliament. In Punjab, the Akalis were divided into three parties—the "moderate" Akali Dal (Longowal), the "radical" UAD (Talwandi), and the "extremist" UAD (Mann). Rajiv calculated that these divisions within the Akalis' rank would split the Sikh vote, thus allowing the Congress (I) to win most of the parliamentary seats in the state. For this purely self-interested reason, Rajiv's central government decided to allow Punjab to participate in the parliamentary elections, even though this decision was publicly justified by stating that holding polls in the state would help solve the "Punjab problem."

LANDSLIDE VICTORY OF SIMRANJEET SINGH MANN AND "THE EXTREMISTS" IN THE 1989 PARLIAMENTARY ELECTIONS IN PUNJAB

A semi-chaotic situation emerged in Sikh politics after the government announced that parliamentary elections would, indeed, be held in Punjab. The three Akali parties tried for weeks to forge "unity" in order to give a direct "one-to-one" fight to the Congress (I), but failed to do so because they could not agree on a mutually suitable adjustment of seats. They could only agree on three things—the need to oppose the Congress (I), the decision to field Mann from the Tarn Taran constituency, and to field Bimal Kaur Khalsa (the widow of one of Mrs Gandhi's assassins) from the Ropar constituency. Thus, the Akalis went into the parliamentary elections largely divided. This, according to most political observers, virtually ensured a Congress (I) victory in most of Punjab's 13 parliamentary constituencies.

The polling in Punjab was held on November 25, and its results surprised almost all political observers and the nation alike! The "extremists" had shockingly dominated these elections with the UAD (Mann) winning six out of seven seats it contested and "extremist/militant" independents supported by the UAD (Mann) winning another two. In contrast, the Congress (I) won only two seats, the BSP one, the Janata Dal one, and one seat was won by a dissident Janata candidate contesting as an independent.[67] The "moderate" Akali Dal (L) and the "radical" UAD (T) were routed and won no seats. *The Tribune*, which before the elections had described the UAD (M) as being a "marginal force" in electoral politics, re-characterized it after these elections as being "a hurricane which had risen on the political firmament of Punjab."[68] The huge margins of victory for the UAD (M) candidates, including Mann's record-setting performance, clearly demonstrated the high levels of support "the extremists" had within the state's Sikh population.[69] This was previously only suspected, but it was now proven!

UAD (M) victors included Simranjeet Singh Mann (a jailed former IPS officer arrested in connection with Mrs Gandhi's assassination), Bimal

Kaur Khalsa (the widow of one of Mrs Gandhi's assassins), Rajdev Singh (a prominent human rights lawyer close to the Rode family), Baba Sucha Singh (the father of one of Mrs Gandhi's assassins), Jagdev Singh Khudian (a staunch supporter of Simranjeet Singh Mann), and Rajinder Kaur Bulara (the widow of a university professor allegedly killed by security forces in a "faked encounter").[70] In addition to these official UAD (M) candidates, two independents supported by the UAD (M) also won—Dhian Singh Mand (whose three brothers had been members of the KCF and had been killed by Indian security forces) and Attinderpal Singh Bhopal (a jailed former AISSF leader). Thus, all of the UAD (M) victors and the two independents were individuals closely associated with "extremist" and "militant" wings of the Sikh ethnonationalist movement in Punjab.

Several factors helped explain "the extremists'" landslide victory. First, the "moderate" Akali Dal (L) and the "radical" UAD (T) were not united for these elections, thus prompting many Sikhs to possibly cast a "negative vote" against the "traditional Akali leadership" and its "selfish and dithering politics."[71] Second, the UAD (T)'s most prominent leader and star campaigner, Parkash Singh Badal, was in detention in south India. Third, the lower-caste Bahajan Samaj Party (BSP) actively contested parliamentary elections in Punjab for the first time and siphoned-off potential Congress (I) votes in several electoral constituencies.[72] Fourth, and most importantly, the AISSF (Manjit)'s support for the UAD (Mann) was instrumental in energizing the party's election campaign and dampening those of other political parties. AISSF (Manjit) activists mobilized the Sikh population of Punjab in support of the UAD (M), helped UAD (M) candidates financially sustain their campaigns, and intimidated the workers of other political parties to the point that Congress (I) candidates rarely ventured into rural areas of the state.[73] In essence, the UAD (M) relied on the AISSF (Manjit)'s well-developed organizational networks throughout Punjab because the party lacked a formal grassroots infrastructure of its own.

Yet, contrary to popular misconceptions, the UAD (Mann)'s electoral victory in Punjab was not a clear referendum in support of Khalistan. After all, the party's candidates represented the "extremist" wing of the Sikh ethnonationalist movement but not necessarily its most "militant" or separatist wing. None of the UAD (M) candidates campaigned on an "anti-Hindu" platform but had rather stressed the need for Hindu–Sikh amity, while concurrently criticizing the policies of the government and the actions of its security forces. Mann had, in fact, repeatedly stated his willingness to work for a negotiated settlement to the Punjab crisis "within the framework of the Indian Constitution."[74] Instead of being a referendum in support of Khalistan, the UAD (M)'s landslide victory was actually a vote against the Congress (I), against the "traditional Akali leadership" found in the Akali Dal (L) and UAD (T), and against human rights abuses committed by Indian security forces. The UAD (M) victory was also a vote of sympathy for those who had made immense personal "sacrifices" for the Panth and the "Sikh cause." Yet, while not an avowed separatist or militant, Mann still carried significant respect with "the militants." After all, he had resigned his senior police post after Operation Bluestar, and had spent five years in government detention during which time he had been severely tortured and kept in solitary confinement.

Nationally, the number of parliamentary seats won by the Congress (I) dropped to only 194 from 397 in 1984. A coalition government under V.P. Singh called the "National Front" came into power with 142 seats from the Janata Dal, 88 from the BJP, 32 from the CPM, 11 from the CPI, and the rest from mostly regional political parties.[75] In Punjab, Simranjeet Singh Mann was clearly "the man of the hour." He could either use his stature to try to bring "the militants" to the negotiation table for a compromise short of an independent Sikh state, or he could help provide dangerous legitimacy to their secessionist cause by openly supporting the creation of Khalistan. It remained to be seen whether Mann could consolidate his power within the morass of Sikh politics and in which direction he would try to take Sikh politics? It also remained to be seen how V.P. Singh's National Front government, which consisted of an ideologically diverse conglomeration of parties, would approach handling the "Punjab problem?" The trajectory of the "Punjab problem" would largely depend on the answers to these questions. Punjab was, once again, at an important political crossroads after the November 1989 parliamentary elections.

SUMMARY AND CONCLUSION

The period analyzed in this chapter saw the sustenance of the Sikh ethnonationalist insurgency propelled by several continuing "patterns of political leadership," although new patterns also began emerging which could eventually have a destructive effect on the movement. First, disunity amongst ruling state elites continued to undermine attempts to solve the "Punjab problem" through "political initiatives." To explain, Rajiv Gandhi had realized by early-1988 that the "law-and-order" approach to solving the "Punjab problem" had failed. For this reason, he ordered the release of jailed Akal Takht *jathedar*, the "extremist" Jasbir Singh Rode, as a part of a new "political initiative" on Punjab. Rajiv hoped that Rode could either rally "the militants" around his leadership and convince them to accept a solution short of Khalistan, or divide them and isolate those who refused to compromise. Yet, the "Rode initiative" was undermined before it had a chance to play itself out. In particular, the Buta Singh faction within the central government, in possible connivance with other forces antithetical to the "Rode initiative," helped instigate an armed clash between militants inside the Golden Temple complex and Indian security forces for its own partisan political reasons. The subsequent Operation Black Thunder II effectively sank the "Rode initiative" and ruined the prospects of securing a solution to the "Punjab crisis" through his leadership. Thus, disunity between the governing state elites continued to undermine solving the "Punjab problem" through "political initiatives" and contributed to the sustenance of Sikh militancy.

Second, the "traditional Akali leadership" remained internally-divided during this period between Talwandi in the "extremist" Baba faction of the UAD, the "radical" Badal faction of the UAD (including Tohra and Capt. Amarinder Singh), and the "moderate" Akali Dal (L) led by Barnala. Each one of these parties (or factions) engaged in heated ethnic rhetoric against the central government. A small step in forging increased Akali unity was taken after Operation Black Thunder II when the Badal faction of the UAD attempted to break away from "the extremists," who it feared would permanently marginalize the "traditional Akali leadership" in Sikh politics. In particular, the Badal faction of the UAD dismissed the Rode-led Head Priests and bifurcated from its parent organization. Talwandi also defected from "the extremists" and joined his fellow "traditional Akali leaders" in forming the UAD (Talwandi/Badal), but complete Akali unity could not be forged because the Akali Dal (L) remained a separate and competing political entity. Thus, continued factionalism within the "traditional Akali leadership" and its competitive radicalism against the government provided a fillip, both indirect and direct, to militancy in Punjab. In contrast, "the extremists" remained internally-united during this period, which helped them widely expand their support base to the detriment of the divided "traditional Akali leadership." The "extremists," in fact, won the November 1989 parliamentary elections in a spectacular way, thus demonstrating strong and increasing popular support for the Sikh ethnonationalist movement.

Third, "the militants" remained generally united during the initial part of this period. In fact, internal competition between them was relatively minimal. Yet, this began to change after Operation Black Thunder II when "the militant movement" bifurcated into the "old," uneducated militants under the (First) Panthic Committee led by Manochahal and Zafferwal, and the "new," educated militants under the Second (Dr Sohan Singh) Panthic Committee led by Dr Sohan Singh and Daljeet Singh Bittu. The fractionalization of the "militant movement" after Operation Black Thunder II involved not only its bifurcation into two distinct blocs of militants, but also the mushrooming of armed organizations with clear organizational schisms and competition between them. Yet, the destructive effects of this bifurcation and increased factionalism on the Sikh ethnonationalist insurgency were only in their incipient stages.

Fourth, "the militants" continued to maintain a viable, but increasingly informal, political front with "the extremists" during this period. For example, "the militants," who officially boycotted the November 1989 elections, nonetheless informally supported the "extremist" AISSF (Manjit) and UAD (Mann) candidates in these polls, partially in the hopes of using them to increase the legitimacy of their separatist cause after the election. Yet, the previously close and formal organizational relationship between "the militants" and "the extremists" began to loosen in important ways during these years. In particular, "the militants" lost a formal institutionalized political front, except for their own internal AISSF (Bittu) and AISSF (Bundala/Buttar), shortly after Operation Black Thunder II. The emerging organizational bifurcation between "the militants" and "the extremists" was exacerbated when the KLF and the Babbar Khalsa aligned themselves squarely with the "militant" Second (Dr Sohan Singh) Panthic Committee after Operation Black Thunder II, thus robbing "the extremists" of an armed wing for the first time during the post-Bluestar period. In short, "the militants" and "the extremists" continued to maintain a close, mutually-symbiotic (but increasingly informal) relationship during this period, but they were becoming organizationally bifurcated in a qualitatively new emerging "pattern of political leadership."

Thus, continued incoherence between ruling state elites, disunity and competition between the "traditional Akali leaders," "the extremists'" complete internal unity, the lack of intense competition amongst "the militants," and the "militants" retention of an effective (but increasingly informal) political front with "the extremists" combined to help to sustain the Sikh ethnonationalist insurgency during the period analyzed in this chapter. Yet, as noted here, important changes were occurring within the Sikh ethnonationalist movement—including increased factionalism within "the militants", and an emerging formal schism between "the militants" and "the extremists"—that could ultimately affect the course of the Sikh ethnonationalist insurgency.

NOTES

1. Shyam Khosla, "Militants embarrass UAD leaders," *The Tribune*, 1 January 1988, 1; and Vipul Mudgal, "Punjab: Moving Apart," *India Today*, 15 March 1988, 26.
2. Staff Correspondent, "Freed priests seek 'puran azadi,'" *The Tribune*, 6 March 1988, 1. In addition to Rode and three other Head Priests, the previous militant-appointed Akal Takht *jathedar*, Gurdev Singh Koanke, and other Sikhs were also released.
3. Interview by the author with close relative of Sant Bhindranwale and high-level member of the AISSF, active from 1978 to the late-1980's, Sacramento, California, USA, 24 July 2002. Hereafter referred to as "Interview with AISSF member and close relative of Bhindranwale previously cited, 24 July 2002."
4. Interview by the author with senior Khalistani activist and intellectual advisor involved in the militant movement since 1986, Fremont, California, USA, 15 July 2002. Hereafter referred to as "Interview with senior Khalistani activist and intellectual advisor previously cited, 15 July 2002."
5. Shekhar Gupta, "Jasbir Singh Rode: 'It is up to Rajiv now'," *India Today*, 31 March 1988, 15.
6. See Ibid.; and Staff Correspondent, "Shrines not to be misused: Rode," *The Tribune*, 10 March 1988, 1.
7. "Rajiv Gandhi Trying to Initiate Dialogue with Freedom Fighters through Acharya Muni," *World Sikh News*, 19 February 1988, 1; Shekhar Gupta and Vipul Mudgal, "Punjab: A Risky Move," *India Today*, 31 March 1988, 11; and Maloy Krishna Dhar, *Bitter Harvest: A Saga of the Punjab* (Delhi: Ajanta Publications, 1996), 55–57. The latter is an invaluable novel written by a senior intelligence officer who served in Punjab during the years 1987 and 1988. I cite those accounts from his novel for which I have cross-referenced sources (either secondary or primary) or accounts which make intuitive sense in the sequence of events I have constructed through other primary or secondary source material.
8. The senior leadership of the Damdami Taksal was actually internally "divided" between its acting *jathedar* Baba Thakur Singh, who was closer to "the extremists," and its spokesman Bhai Mokham Singh, who was closely associated with "the militants." Tribune Bureau, "More militant leaders freed," *The Tribune*, 28 March 1988, 1.
9. Interview with AISSF member and close relative of Bhindranwale previously cited, 24 July 2002.
10. For details, see Maloy Krishna Dhar, *Open Secrets: India's Intelligence Unveiled* (New Delhi: Manas Publications, 2005), 329–32.
11. Ibid.: 331–32.
12. Ibid.: 332.
13. Shekhar Gupta and Vipul Mudgal, "Punjab: A Risky Move," *India Today*, 31 March 1988, 12.
14. Staff Correspondent, "Takht chief to meet militants," *The Tribune*, 7 March 1988, 1.
15. Shyam Khosla, "Unified AISSF formed," *The Tribune*, 14 April 1988, 1.
16. See Tribune Correspondent, "Talks only on 'Khalistan,'" *The Tribune*, 12 April 1988, 1; and Inderjit Badhwar and Vipul Mudgal, "Punjab: A Time of Reckoning," *India Today*, 30 April 1988, 37.
17. Ibid.
18. Ibid., 35.

19. For selective examples see Tribune Bureau, "34 massacred in Punjab: 18 of family killed in Amritsar district," *The Tribune*, 2 April 1988, 1; and U.N.I., "17 more killed in Punjab," *The Tribune*, 3 April 1988, 1.

20. Inderjit Badhwar and Vipul Mudgal, "Punjab: A Time of Reckoning," *India Today*, 30 April 1988, 36.

21. For an in-depth discussion of this phenomenon see Vipul Mudgal, "Punjab: The Underground Army," *India Today*, 15 September 1988, 42–44; and Julio Ribeiro, *Bullet for Bullet: My Life as a Police Officer* (New Delhi: Penguin Books, 1998), 348–54.

22. Ribeiro, *Bullet for Bullet*, 349.

23. See Sangat Singh, *The Sikhs in History* (New Delhi: Uncommon Books, 1996), 467 and Dhar, *Open Secrets*, 321–344 for details.

24. Dhar, *Bitter Harvest*, 46–52, 270–73.

25. See Shyam Khosla and Sarabjit Singh, "Gov't agents 'extort' money," *The Tribune*, 30 March 1988, 1; and Staff Correspondent, "Militants to meet shortly," *The Tribune*, 5 April 1988, 12.

26. Inderjit Badhwar, Prabhu Chawla, Raminder Singh, "Punjab: A Risk Gambit," *India Today*, 31 May 1987, 19; and Electronic-mail interview by the author with the personal assistant of a former Akal Takht *jathedar*, 17 May 2002. Hereafter cited as "E-mail interview with assistant to a former Akal Takht *jathedar* previously cited, 17 May 2002. Buta Singh's role is also outlined in S. Singh, *The Sikhs*, 460 and 464–66; and Dhar, *Bitter Harvest*, 48.

27. Staff Correspondent, "Takht chief under fire," *The Tribune*, 5 May 1988, 1 and 16; and "Panthic Committee Disowns Gurjit Singh," *World Sikh News*, 13 May 1988, 21.

28. See Dhar, *Bitter Harvest*, 289–95; and Dhar, *Open Secrets*, 337–43.

29. See Tribune Correspondent, "Tension in Golden Temple," *The Tribune*, 30 April 1988, 1.

30. See Dhar, *Bitter Harvest*, 296–97.

31. Ibid.

32. For a day-by-day description of Operation Black Thunder II see D. P. Sharma, *The Punjab Story: Decade of Turmoil* (New Delhi: APH Publishing, 1996), 198–206; Shekhar Gupta, "Punjab: The Battle Escalates," *India Today*, 31 May 1988, 12–16; and Shekhar Gupta and Vipul Mudgal, "Operation Black Thunder: A Dramatic Success," *India Today*, 15 June 1988, 36–48.

33. Sharma, *The Punjab Story*, 203–04.

34. Staff Correspondent, "SGPC sacks head priests," *The Tribune*, 31 May 1988, 1.

35. For details see Staff Correspondent, "SGPC quiet, DC denies sack," *The Tribune*, 1 June 1988, 1; and Vipul Mudgal, "Punjab: Sudden Turn," *India Today*, 30 June 1988, 26.

36. Tribune Bureau, "Badal detained under NSA," *The Tribune*, 30 May 1988, 1.

37. For details, see Tribune Bureau, "Mann expands UAD presidium," *The Tribune*, 6 August 1988, 1 and 3.

38. P.P.S. Gill, "Darshan Singh back as Takht chief," *The Tribune*, 14 August 1988, 1.

39. "Ragi Denies Entering into a Deal with Government," *World Sikh News*, 9 September 1988, 1. Also see interview with Professor Darshan Singh in K.S. Chawla, "Darshan Singh: 'Gurmit sidhant only solution,'" *The Tribune*, 18 August 1988, 1.

40. The Akali Dal (L) was estimated to have the loyalty of about 50 to 55 of the surviving 125 members of the SGPC general house. It had been last elected in 1979. H.S. Bhanwer, "UAD faction loses majority in SGPC," *The Tribune*, 30 August 1988, 5. Ragi would, in fact, readmit Barnala into the Sikh Panth several months later.

41. Tribune Bureau, "UAD splits into two: Talwandi elected President," *The Tribune*, 26 August 1988, 1.

42. Joyce Pettigrew, *The Sikhs of the Punjab: Unheard Voices of State and Guerilla Violence* (London: Zed Books, 1995), 48.

43. It was suspected that Gurjit Singh had either been arrested by the government or had been killed by the "anti-negotiation" militants. For details, see "Whereabouts of Gurjit Singh Not Known", *World Sikh News*, 3 June 1988, 29; Tribune Correspondent, "Panthic panel assails Gurjit Singh", *The Tribune*, 14 June 1988, 5; and A.S. Prashar, "Where is Gurjit Singh?" *The Tribune*, 21 May 1988, 6.

44. "Panthic Committee Appoints Manochahal as Akal Takht Chief," *World Sikh News*, 24 June 1988, 1.

45. Ibid., 24.

46. Sharma, *The Punjab Story*, 211; and *World Sikh News*, 11 November 1988, 9.

47. See Staff Correspondent, "Terrorists trying to regroup themselves," *The Tribune*, 25 June 1988, 1; and Staff Correspondent, "Brahma's death confirmed," *The Tribune*, 22 August 1988, 1.

48. P.T.I. and U.N.I., "25 killed in Batala bomb blasts," *The Tribune*, 5 November 1988, 3; and Sharma, *The Punjab Story*, 211.

49. See Tribune Bureau, "'KCF' chief Sukha Sipahi shot," *The Tribune*, 13 July 1988; and Vipul Mudgal, "Punjab: Fighting the Phoenix," *India Today*, 15 August 1988, 32.

50. Prabhjot Singh, "3 militant groups, AISSF 'unite'," *The Tribune*, 4 November 1988, 3; and Sharma, *The Punjab Story*, 211.

51. See P.T.I. and U.N.I., "25 killed in Batala bomb blasts: curfew clamped," *The Tribune*, 4 November 1988, 1.

52. Figures taken from Paul Wallace, "Political Violence and Terrorism in India: The Crisis of Identity," in *Terrorism in Context*, ed. Martha Crenshaw (University Park: The Pennsylvania State University Press, 1995), 354.

53. K.P.S. Gill, "Endgame in Punjab: 1988–1993," *Faultlines* 1, no. 1 (May 1999), 54.

54. Moses Manoharan (Reuters), "Congress I Party Revolts against Rajiv Gandhi after T.N. Defeat," *World Sikh News*, 31 January 1989, 1.

55. See Inderjit Badhwar and Vipul Mudgal, "Punjab: Encouraging Signals," *India Today*, 31 March 1989, 14–15; and Tribune Bureau, "Political Package: Many Jodhpur detainees to be freed," *The Tribune*, 4 March 1989, 1.

56. See Inderjit Badhwar and Vipul Mudgal, "Punjab: Encouraging Signals," *India Today*, 31 March 1989, 17.

57. "Massive Turnout at Hola Mohala: Conference Re-endorses Khalistan" *World Sikh News*, 31 March 1989, 1.

58. Harish Gupta, "Ray rules out political solution," *The Tribune*, 27 April 1989, 1.

59. Tribune Bureau, "Taksal, AISSF to form party," *The Tribune*, 23 April 1989, 1.

60. Ibid.

61· Ibid.

62. For details see Kuldip Nayar, "Secret talks on Punjab," *The Tribune*, 4 June 1989, 1.

63. Ramesh Vinayak, "Row over Taksal leadership," *The Tribune*, 14 May 1989, 1.

64. See P.T.I., "Punjab bandh today: AISSF activists, Akalis held," *The Tribune*, 30 June 1989, 1; and Tribune Bureau, "Near total bandh in Punjab," *The Tribune*, 1 July 1989, 1.

65. Staff Writer, "Bhai Manjit Singh Released: Given a Warm Welcome," *World Sikh News*, 4 August 1989, 1.

66. Staff Correspondent, "Manochahal 'misguiding' Sikhs," *The Tribune*, 11 September 1989, 1.

67. "Detailed poll results: Punjab," *The Tribune*, 29 November 1989, 4; Paul Wallace, "The Regionalization of Indian Electoral Politics 1989–90: Punjab and Haryana," in *India Votes: Alliance Politics and Minority Governments in the Ninth and Tenth General Elections*, eds Harold A. Gould and Sumit Ganguly, (Boulder: Westview Press, 1993), 144–48; and Gurharpal Singh, "The Punjab Problem in the 1990's: A Post-1984 Assessment," *The Journal of Commonwealth and Comparative Politics* 39, no.2 (July 1991), 182.

68. See "Akali Unity: Still a Mirage," *The Tribune*, 23 October 1989, 3 and "The Verdict in Punjab," *The Tribune*, 29 November 1989, 8, respectively.

69. Simranjeet Singh Mann received 527,707 out of a total 591,883 valid votes. "Detailed poll results: Punjab," *The Tribune*, 19 October 1989, 4. This was the largest margin of victory ever for a parliamentary candidate in Punjab.

70. A.S. Prashar, "UAD (M) wins six seats," *The Tribune*, 29 November 1989, 1 and 14.

71. Kanwar Sandhu, "Punjab: Rebels' Win," *India Today*, 15 December 1989, 36; and Wallace, "The Regionalization," 146–47.

72. Ibid., 146.

73. For a detailed description see A.S. Prashar, "Militants queer the pitch," *The Tribune*, 21 November 1989, 1 and 11.

74. See interview with Simranjeet Singh Mann in Kamaljeet Rattan, "Simranjeet Singh Mann: "I am against all killings," *India Today*, 30 April 1989, 40–41.

75. Wallace, "The Regionalization," 157.

9

Escalating Factionalism and Internecine Violence within the Separatist Movement (1990–1992)

SIMRANJEET SINGH MANN'S RELEASE FROM PRISON AND V.P. SINGH'S "NEW BEGINNING" FOR PUNJAB

The political scenario at the end of 1989 and the beginning of 1990 offered a flicker of hope for solving the "Punjab problem." V.P. Singh's "National Front" was the first non-Congress government in power in the center since the Janata government of 1977. Furthermore, the Akalis did not have any lingering animosity toward the parties that constituted the National Front as they did with the Congress (I). The National Front parties, after all, were not electoral competitors to the Akalis in Punjab as was the Congress (I). In early-December, outgoing Congress (I) prime minister Rajiv Gandhi released all Akali leaders from jail including Parkash Singh Badal and Gurcharan Singh Tohra, and also withdrew conspiracy cases against Simranjeet Singh Mann and AISSF (Manjit) leader Harminder Singh Sandhu. This, according to Rajiv and Punjab governor S.S. Ray, was necessary to help restore peace in Punjab. Ray further justified Mann's release by saying that Mann was regarded "as the only leader by the vast majority of Sikhs."[1] Thus, the Congress (I) appeared to have changed some of its views on the "Punjab crisis" after failing to get a parliamentary majority in the November 1989 elections. But, these public explanations aside, there were also purely partisan reasons for releasing Mann and Sandhu. In particular, the Congress (I) may have been trying to make it more difficult for the incoming National Front government to solve the "Punjab crisis" by releasing these controversial Sikh leaders and making the political dynamics in Sikh politics even more competitive.

Immediately upon his release from prison, Mann rushed to the Golden Temple complex in Amritsar where he and thousands of his supporters paid their respects to the Sikhs' holiest shrine. During this visit, Mann declared that his main goal was to fulfill Sant Jarnail Singh Bhindranwale's dream of "breaking the shackles of slavery of the Sikhs" by having the Anandpur Sahib Resolution (ASR) fully implemented.[2] The ASR, according to him, was not an "anti-national" document and nor was it outside the framework of the Indian Constitution. Thus, Mann did not publicly demand the creation Khalistan, but nor did he explicitly oppose it. Mann also stated his preference to use non-violent, constitutional means to achieve the Sikhs' goal, but he refrained from criticizing the use of force—"the militants'" preferred strategy.[3] These were pragmatic statements on the part of Mann who wanted to remain flexible in terms goals and tactics in order to avoid potentially alienating any party involved in the "Punjab problem."

Prime minister V.P. Singh also added to the anticipation that this may be a potential "new beginning" for Punjab by visiting the Golden Temple a few days after coming into office. The new prime minister explained the rationale behind his visit by saying:

> We have come on a pilgrimage to offer prayers and seek blessings to overcome all hurdles and give a healing touch to the hurt psyche of the people [of Punjab]...a new era has begun. We shall win the hearts of the people with love and not with bayonets.[4]

V.P. Singh did not offer any immediate political solutions, but his visit demonstrated, at least symbolically, an apparent change in the center's attitude toward the "Punjab problem" away from a policy of confrontation and toward one of reconciliation.

In late-1989, the "Sikh political spectrum" looked like the following (Table 9.1):

The "traditional Akali leadership" consisted of the "moderate" Akali Dal (Longowal) led by Surjit Singh Barnala, and the "radical" Akali Dal (Talwandi) led by Talwandi, Tohra, and Badal. The "traditional Akali leadership" had become marginalized in Sikh politics after the November 1989 parliamentary elections, in which Akali Dal (L) candidates received only 1.16 percent of the vote and Akali Dal (T) candidates 5.45 percent.[5] This was in sharp contrast to 38.82 percent won by "extremist"-supported

Table 9.1
Sikh Political Spectrum (Late-1989)

Moderates	Radicals	Extremists[3]	Militants/Separatists
AD (L)[1]	UAD (T)[2]	UAD (M)[4]	First Panthic Committee[6]
Barnala[1]	Badal[2]	Mann[4]	BTFK[6]
	Tohra[2]	Joginder Singh[4]	KCF (Rajasthani)[6]
	Talwandi[2]	Damdami Taksal	Second Panthic Committee
		AISSF (Manjit)[5]	(Dr. Sohan Singh)[7]
		Manjit Singh[5]	AISSF (Bittu)[7]
		H.S. Sandhu[5]	KCF (Panjwar)7
			KLF[7]
			Babbar Khalsa[7]

Source: Author.

Notes: [1] Akali Dal (Longowal) and its leader; demanding implementation of Rajiv-Longowal Accord through non-violent means.

[2] Unified Akali Dal (Talwandi) and its leaders; demanding implementation of the (ASR) through non-violent means.

[3] "Extremists" generally united behind United Akali Dal (Mann); demanding implementation of (ASR) or "Khalsa Raj" through either non-violent or violent means.

[4] Unified Akali Dal (Mann) and its leaders.

[5] AISSF (Manjit) and its leaders.

[6] First Panthic Committee-led militants demanding Khalistan through violent means.

[7] Second Panthic Committee-led militants demanding Khalistan through violent means.

candidates. The "moderates" continued to demand implementation of the Rajiv–Longowal Accord, and "the radicals" demanded the implementation of the ASR. Both were committed to peaceful and electoral means, and thus did not support the use of violence.

The "extremists" consisted of a loose coalition of leaders and groups rallying around Simranjeet Singh Mann and his party. They included the Akali Dal (Mann), Baba Joginder Singh, Jasbir Singh Rode, and the AISSF (Manjit) led by Manjit Singh and Harminder Singh Sandhu. The "extremists" stated goal was the establishment of "Khalsa Raj," which was usually interpreted as being semi-autonomy for Punjab within the Indian Union. The "extremists" did not support or oppose the creation of Khalistan, nor did they openly advocate or oppose the use of violence. The "extremists" were, in many ways, a "wild card" in Sikh politics in that they were important for the central government in trying to find a solution to the "Punjab crisis" short of Khalistan, but they also were important for "the militants" in order to provide added legitimacy to their separatist cause.

At the most extreme end of Sikh politics were "the militants." The "militants" were divided into two main groupings—the First Panthic Committee-led militants and the Second (Dr. Sohan Singh) Panthic Committee-led militants. The First Panthic Committee was led by Gurbachan Singh Manochahal and Wassan Singh Zafferwal, and included the BTKF and the KCF (Rajasthani) armed groups. The Second (Dr. Sohan Singh) Panthic Committee included the AISSF (Bittu), the KCF (Panjwar), the KLF, and the Babbar Khalsa.[6] Both groupings of "militants" advocated the creation of an independent Sikh state through armed struggle.

CROSS PRESSURES ON MANN'S LEADERSHIP FROM WITHIN SIKH POLITICS

Visits to the Golden Temple by Simranjeet Singh Mann and V.P. Singh created anticipation that the "Punjab problem" world possibly be solved through negotiations, but, this initial euphoria aside, both leaders faced significant obstacles from within their respective spheres of politics. To explain, the largest "party" in V.P. Singh's National Front government was the Janata Dal, which itself was a conglomeration of various political parties. The National Front government was also supported from "the outside" by the Bharatiya Janata Party (BJP) and the Communist parties.[7] The Hindu-nationalist BJP was adamant about preventing further decentralization of the Indian Union as demanded by the Akali Dal, and the Communists were vehemently opposed to granting any concessions to ethnic-based political parties. V.P. Singh's government was also vulnerable because the Congress (I) commanded a plurality of seats in parliament and was waiting for an opportunity to undermine it. Thus, V.P. Singh was limited in his ability to compromise with the Akalis and other Sikh groups.

Mann was also in a precarious position within Sikh politics even though his party, and independents supported by it, had won of eight of Punjab's 13 parliamentary seats. Mann faced cross-pressures from five different sources within Sikh politics—the AISSF (Manjit), Harminder Singh Sandhu, his party's own members of parliament (MPs), the "traditional Akali leadership," and "the militants." Regarding the first, Mann was largely dependent on the AISSF (Manjit) for institutionalized networks of support because the Akali Dal (Mann) lacked a solid organizational infrastructure of its own. Cadres of the revitalized AISSF (Manjit) had, in fact, been instrumental for "the extremists'" electoral success in the November 1989 elections. Thus, the AISSF (Manjit) was a powerful "pressure group" on or within the Akali Dal (Mann) political party.

Second, AISSF (Manjit) general secretary Harminder Singh Sandhu, who had been released from prison after over five years of incarceration, acted as a potential competitor to Mann's leadership.Upon his release, the highly articulate Sandhu declared that the victory of Akali Dal (Mann) candidates represented only a "phase and not a [final] destination" for the Sikhs.[8] Instead, he stated that the "ultimate goal" of the Sikhs was the creation of an independent Sikh state. It is unclear why Sandhu so unequivocally emphasized the need for "an independent Sikh state" after his release; after all, he had previously been willing to settle for a solution short of outright independence. Sandhu may have been a "government agent" working for either a section of the central government or for the Congress (I) to undermine Mann and V.P. Singh's peace efforts. Many militant groups had, in fact, suspected Sandhu of being a "government agent" for years. Alternatively, he may have simply been trying to compete with Mann and Manjit Singh for leadership of the extremist-wing of the "Sikh movement." Sandhu never openly opposed Mann, but his statements certainly caused a significant irritation for him and his party.

Third, Mann also faced significant pressure from some of his party's own MPs, many of whom carried "celebrity like" status of their own and thus were not beholden to Mann for their electoral victories. In this respect, Mann was largely a symbolic figurehead for his party MPs. For example, Dhian Singh Mand refused to take the oath of office unless he was allowed to enter the parliament building with his full-length *kirpan* (sword)—a Sikh religious symbol. In contrast, four other Akali Dal (M) MPs took the oath of office immediately after the elections, but Mann postponed doing so in order to show solidarity with Mand and the principled stand that he and others had taken.[9] This prevented Mann from officially becoming a MP and from being allowed to speak on the parliament floor. The newly-elected Akali Dal (M) MPs also consistently bickered amongst themselves, causing Mann significant frustration in his attempt to build a "unified" political party.[10]

A fourth source of pressure on Mann was the "traditional Akali leadership" found in the "moderate" Akali Dal (L) and the "radical" Akali Dal (B), which was not willing to be permanently sidelined by "the extremists" in Sikh politics.[11] The Akali Dal (L) and Akali Dal (B)'s performance in the parliamentary elections had been dismal, but they still dominated the SGPC general house which had last been elected over a decade earlier. The "traditional Akali leaders," in fact, waited patiently for a chance to undermine or challenge Mann's leadership when, and if, the opportunity presented.

A final source of pressure on Mann were "the militants." The "militants" knew that Mann could give their separatist cause immense political legitimacy if he and his party publicly supported Khalistan. In fact, "the militants" had termed the election results as being "a referendum on Khalistan" which, according to them, proved that "behind the Khalistan struggle, there are not only a handful of militants but the whole Khalsa Panth."[12] But, "the militants" also knew that Mann could conceivably undermine their struggle if he compromised with the government for a solution short of outright independence. In this respect, Mann was a potential competitor to "the militants" at the most extreme or militant end of the "Sikh political spectrum." The "militants," in fact, had a history of withdrawing support from "extremist" leaders—such as Jasbir Singh Rode and Darshan Singh Ragi, earlier—who refused to explicitly support their separatist cause.

Thus, the cross-pressures and challenges facing Mann from within Sikh politics were immense, even though his "party" had received an apparent "electoral mandate" to lead the *Sikh Panth*. In essence, Mann was the single most dominant Sikh leader in Punjab, but his continued power depended largely on his ability to maintain "party unity", and to either influence "the militants" or extract significant concessions from the central government. Neither of these was an easy task. Mann was quite "strong" in one sense, but very "weak" in another

MANN'S INFORMAL TALKS WITH PRIME MINISTER V.P. SINGH AND HIS ATTEMPT TO CONVINCE "THE MILITANTS" TO NEGOTIATE

V.P. Singh followed up on his visit to Amritsar by holding an "all-party meeting" in New Delhi envisioned to help restart the peace process in Punjab. This "all-party meeting" was attended by all of India's major political parties except the Akali Dal (M) and the Akali Dal (B). These two parties stated that the meeting would not be useful unless the conditions for holding talks were made more "amicable" by ending "faked police encounters," releasing Sikhs jailed on "trumped-up charges," rehabilitating all Sikh soldiers who deserted after Operation Bluestar, punishing those guilty of the November 1984 anti-Sikh riots, and dismantling the "repressive police machinery" in Punjab.[13] After the "all-party meeting," the National Front government also held an "all-party rally" in Punjab. V.P. Singh tried desperately to convince Mann to participate in this rally by, in part, releasing over a thousand Sikh youth detained in Punjab, but these concessions were insufficient for Mann who also demanded the scheduling of state assembly elections in Punjab.[14] The Akali Dal (M) calculated that it could win a majority of seats in the state legislative assembly and form the government in Punjab if elections were held, but V.P. Singh refused to concede this demand. He feared that "the extremists" would pass an official resolution either announcing semi-autonomy for Punjab or the creation of Khalistan if they ever came to power in Chandigarh.

Thus, Mann did not attend the "all-party rally," but he did secretly meet with V.P. Singh and other national leaders in New Delhi for discussions.[15] After these "secret" discussions, Mann decided to act more aggressively to try to solve the "Punjab crisis," calculating that he had to deliver on Sikh expectations placed upon him or that his personal luster would quickly wear-off thus making him just another Akali politician mired in the factionalism of Sikh politics. For this reason, he took an "all-or-nothing" gamble in early-January 1990 when he publicly assured the government that he could persuade "the militants" to come to the negotiation table to find a solution short of Khalistan if, in return, the government could offer "the militants" a truce and guarantee their safe passage for talks.[16] Mann had put his reputation "on the line!"

A few days later, Mann and the government got "the militants'" response, but it was not what they wanted. The AISSF (Bittu) released a statement describing Mann's assertion that he could persuade "the militants" to negotiate for a settlement short of Khalistan as being a "figment" of his imagination.[17] The AISSF (Bittu), which was a part of the Second (Dr Sohan Singh) Panthic Committee-led militants, stated that "the militants" would never accept a leader "who has faith in the Indian Constitution even if he has made some sacrifices…[And] the militants will never allow any person to sabotage the 'Sikh struggle.'"[18] This statement demonstrated, for the first time, that Mann clearly lacked enough influence with "the militants" to have them settle short of outright independence. As a result, Mann stood severely weakened and the Mann "peace initiative"—much like the Ragi "initiative" and Rode "initiative" before it—appeared to be crumbling only about two months after it had begun!

HARMINDER SINGH SANDHU'S ASSASSINATION AND SUBSEQUENT RECONFIGURATION OF "EXTREMIST"–"MILITANT" ALLIANCES

The electoral success of Simranjeet Singh Mann and "the extremists" in the November 1989 elections demoralized security forces in Punjab and prompted them to take a more conservative approach in fighting militancy. In particular, they feared being prosecuted for human rights violations and extra-judicial killings if "the extremists" ever came into power in Punjab which, at the time, appeared to be a distinct possibility if state assembly elections were held. As a result, there was a decrease in the number of militants killed by security forces and a sharp increase in the number of security force personnel killed by the militants in late-1989.[19] The insurgency, in essence, was escalating after the November 1989 parliamentary elections.

An event occurred in late-January 1990 that had important effects on the organizational evolution of the Sikh ethnonationalist movement. Harminder Singh Sandhu, the general secretary of the "extremist" AISSF (Manjit), was assassinated by "militants" associated with the Second (Dr Sohan Singh) Panthic Committee on January 23.[20] The Second Panthic Committee explained its reason for killing Sandhu by writing:

> Mr. Harminder Singh Sandhu was planted by government agencies and was authorized to make any statement to win the support and sympathy of Sikhs so that at an opportune moment he could destroy the strength of militant organizations…By removing Mr. Sandhu from the political scene, [we] have failed the conspiracy in its initial stage.[21]

Sikh militants had, in fact, suspected Sandhu of being a "government agent" for years ever since he had surrendered to Indian security forces during Operation Bluestar instead of courting "martyrdom" like all others in Sant Bhindranwale's "inner circle."[22] Sandhu was also an exceptionally articulate individual who was considered by "the militants" to be a potential competitor in leading the "Sikh movement." The fact that he was an "extremist" and not an avowed "militant" made him even more dangerous for "the militants" because he could potentially undermine their separatist struggle by reaching a compromise with the government short of Khalistan. Thus, "the militants" killed Sandhu for a variety of personal, ideological, and tactical reasons.

Sandhu's assassination was important in the wider political context because it catalyzed a split within the powerful AISSF (Manjit). A section of its leadership led by Amarjit Singh Chawla and Rajinder Singh Mehta, two senior AISSF leaders close to Harminder Singh Sandhu since before Operation Bluestar, accused Manjit Singh of being involved in Sandhu's murder.[23] Manjit Singh's suspected involvement was not surprising because the highly-articulate Sandhu had dramatically eclipsed the comparatively soft-spoken Manjit Singh in media attention since his release from jail.[24] These federation dissidents formed a new AISSF faction called the AISSF (Mehta/Chawla) in late-February 1990, splitting the powerful AISSF (Manjit).[25] Thus, "the extremists," who had been largely united for nearly six years since after Operation Bluestar, were becoming formally fractionalized.

Another important development, but one not directly linked to Sandhu's assassination, occurred within the "militant movement" in the spring of 1990. In late-April 1990, Manochahal and Zafferwal of the First Panthic Committee fell-out over the distribution of arms to their lieutenants in the field. [26] This prompted Manochahal to leave the First Panthic Committee and form his own separate Third Panthic Committee. This also led to a split within Manochahal's BTFK when his senior lieutenant, Sukhwinder Singh Sangha, broke from the mainstream BTFK and briefly allied with Zafferwal before creating his own armed group, the BTFK (Sangha), which he subsequently aligned with the Second (Dr Sohan Singh) Panthic Committee.[27] These splits increased tension between "militants" aligned with the First, Second and Third Panthic Committees, respectively, and resulted in the deaths of about two-thirds of the known militants in the Majha region in the first half of 1990 due to fratricidal warfare.[28] The "militants" were more fractionalized by the spring of 1990 than at any other point during the entire "Punjab crisis," and were also beginning to aggressively compete with each other, often violently. This would have serious implications for the trajectory of the Sikh ethnonationalist movement into the future.

Thus, the Sikh political spectrum in the middle of 1990 looked like the following (Table 9.2):

At the most moderate end was the Akali Dal (Longowal) led by Barnala and, after his departure to be governor of Tamil Nadu, Tota Singh. The "radicals" consisted of the other "traditional Akali leaders" within the Akali Dal (Badal), including Badal and Tohra. Thus, the "traditional Akali leadership" was bifurcated between the Akali Dal (L) and the Akali Dal (B). The "extremists" consisted of the Akali Dal (Mann), AISSF (Manjit), SSF (Mehta/Chawla), and the Damdami Taksal. The SSF (Mehta/Chawla) had broken-off from the AISSF (Manjit), and the relationship between the Akali Dal (Mann) and the AISSF (Manjit) had become strained because of the competition between the Baba Joginder Singh and Manjit Singh factions within the party. Mann, in essence, had only marginal control over his party and its MPs. The Damdami Taksal tried desperately to prevent "the extremists" from splintering, but its efforts were largely unsuccessful as "the extremists" became internally fractionalized for the first time in the entire post-Bluestar period.

Table 9.2
Sikh Political Spectrum (Mid-1990)

Moderates	Radicals	Extremists[3]	Militants/Separatists[5]
AD (L)[1]	AD (Badal)[2]	AD (Mann)[4]	First Panthic Committee[6]
	Tohra[2]	AISSF (Manjit)	KCF (Zafferwal)[6]
	Talwandi[2]	Damdami Taksal	Second Panthic Committee
		SSF (Mehta/Chawla)	(Dr. Sohan Singh)[7]
			SSF (Bittu)[7]
			KCF (Panjwar)[7]
			KLF[7]
			Babbar Khalsa[7]
			BTFK (Sangha)[7]
			Third Panthic Committee[8]
			BTFK (Manochahal)[8]
			KCF (Rajasthani)[8]

Source: Author.

Notes: [1] Atkali Dal (Longowal) demanding implementation of Rajiv-Longowal Accord through non-violent means.
[2] Akali Dal (Badal) and its leaders demanding implementation of the (ASR) through non-violent means.
[3] "Extremists" only marginally united; AISSF (Manjit) and SSF (Mehta/Chawla) bitter rivals, only Damdami Taksal excercises some authority over all "extremist" groups; "extremists" demanding implementation of (ASR) or "Khalsa Raj" through either non-violent or violent means.
[4] Akali Dal (Mann) internally divided between Baba and Manjit factions, and between various MP's.
[5] "Militants" divided into First, Second, and Third Panthic Committee-led groupings.
[6] First (Zafferwal) Panthic Committee-led militants demanding Khalistan through violent means.
[7] Second (Dr Sohan Singh) Panthic Committee-led militants demanding Khalistan through violent means.
[8] Third (Manochahal) Panthic Committee-led militants demanding Khalistan through violent means.

The "militants" were divided into three major groupings, each loyal to a separate Panthic Committee. The First Panthic Committee was led by Wassan Singh Zafferwal and included the KCF (Zafferwal). The most powerful grouping was the Second (Dr Sohan Singh) Panthic Committee which included the SSF (Bittu), KCF (Panjwar), KLF, Babbar Khalsa, and BTFK (Sangha). The Third Panthic Committee was led by Gurbachan Singh Manochahal and included the BTFK (Manochahal) and KCF (Rajasthani). In an important transformation within Sikh politics, disunity within "the extremists'" ranks allowed "the militants" to collectively gain increasing power in and control over Sikh politics, even though they too were increasingly fractionalized. The intensity of the Sikh separatist movement was escalating, but it was also becoming more decentralized, fractionalized, and chaotic than ever before.

"THE MILITANTS'" INCREASED CONTROL OVER THE AKALIS AND THEIR GROWING INFLUENCE OVER PUNJAB'S GOVERNMENTAL INSTITUTIONS

It was hoped that Mann and V.P. Singh could reach a compromise settlement to the "Punjab problem," but this hope proved to be misplaced. Mann lacked sufficient influence with or authority over "the militants" to convince them to compromise short of Khalistan, and V.P. Singh had to rely on the BJP and Communist parties for the survival of his government. In the absence of a negotiated settlement to the "Punjab problem," the "militants" began exerting increased control over the Akalis through mid-1990. For their part, the Akalis had little choice except to dramatically radicalize their own rhetoric to try to appease the increasingly powerful "militants."

This process escalated when the "militants" tried to assassinate SGPC president Gurcharan Singh Tohra in May 1990. He survived the assassination attempt, but was seriously wounded. The "militants'" message to the Akalis was clear—either support the separatist cause or risk being killed. Immediately after this attempted assassination, the "radicals," including Badal, once again began publicly eulogizing Sikh militants slain by Indian security forces as being "martyrs" who had given their lives for the Sikh *quam*. For his part, Tohra tried to appease militant sentiment by having the SGPC executive committee appoint Bhai Ranjit Singh, the prime accused in the 1980 assassination of the Nirankari *guru*, to be Akal Takht *jathedar*.[29] Ranjit Singh, who was lodged in jail awaiting trial for murder, was a "hero" to many Sikhs. Appointing him to the position of Akal Takht *jathedar* allowed the "traditional Akali leaders" to more effectively insulate themselves from criticism from "the militants" and also possibly enhance their support base at the expense of "the extremists." This move by the Akali Dal (B) temporarily forestalled further attacks against its leaders, but it also moved Sikh politics in a more extremist or militant direction.

The "militants" also exerted their influence over Mann. In mid-August 1990, the Second (Dr Sohan Singh) Panthic Committee released a press statement criticizing Mann's continual demand for state assembly elections and self-determination for the Sikhs within the framework of the Indian

Constitution. The Second Panthic Committee described Mann's strategy as being nothing more than a ploy to gain political power. It stated:

> It is not difficult to understand even for a common man that the party (referring to the Akali Dal-Mann) is making militant statements as a part of its tactics. This strategy has suited its leaders very well because on the one hand, it has kept the militants pleased or silent, and on the other it is putting pressure on the Centre to organize elections in Punjab so as to capture power with impunity by sharing it with the militants. The party is mysteriously silent as to what would happen to the militants or the future of the Sikhs after this?[30]

This message from the Second (Dr Sohan Singh) Panthic Committee had an immediate effect on the Akali Dal (Mann), which quickly announced that it would boycott any future state assembly elections in Punjab unless they were held under the auspices of the United Nations.[31] Several senior Akali Dal (B) leaders, including Tohra, responded to this "warning" by suggesting that "the militants" be allowed to take over the reins of community leadership for the Sikhs because they, referring to the "traditional Akali leadership," no longer had anything to offer the Sikh youth.[32] Thus, "the militants" were essentially molding the tenor of Sikh politics in Punjab in summer 1990, and the Akalis strategically tried to appease them without becoming outright separatists themselves. The Akalis also wanted to avoid getting further marginalized within the Sikh community as the ethnonationalist movement escalated.

This trend of appeasing "the militants" continued through fall of 1990 when the Akalis held a major political conference at Anandpur Sahib to discuss the future of the Sikh Panth in India. This convention also included representatives of the various AISSF factions and Panthic Committees. Two important decisions were reached at this conclave. First, the convention passed a resolution calling for the unanimous selection of SGPC office-bearers in upcoming SGPC presidential elections to help pave the way for forging complete "Panthic unity." Baldev Singh Sibia, a long-time Akali activist and legal advisor, was chosen to be the new "consensus" SGPC president.[33] Second, the meeting also passed a resolution supporting "the militants" which read, in part:

> The Sikhs will [now] have to think how to break the shackles of slavery, how to confront the rulers of India who violated all democratic norms...The Sikh quam feels that now there is no alternative but to extend all cooperation to the youth who are fighting for the freedom of the Sikh nation.[34]

Thus, all Akali factions—including the "moderate" Akali Dal (L)—were moving closer to "the militants," who were gaining increased control over Sikh politics. Yet, while passing this resolution in support of "the militants," the Akalis strategically stopped short of explicitly demanding the creation of Khalistan. The "militants" had become dominant in Sikh politics, but they were not fully hegemonic. For its part, V.P. Singh's National Front government seemed to have no additional "packages" or "initiatives" left for solving the "Punjab problem." Instead, the government was forced to rely on military means to try to control the Sikh separatist insurgency.

During the fall of 1990, "the militants" also effectively exerted their influence over governmental institutions in Punjab. The most powerful grouping of "militants," the Second (Dr. Sohan Singh) Panthic Committee-led "militants," issued a "code of conduct" for the press which directed journalists in the state to stop calling those struggling for the creation of Khalistan in pejorative terms as being "terrorists" but instead to start referring to them as "militants."[35] This code also ordered government-run television and radio in the state to telecast its programming in Punjabi instead of Hindi. Most newspapers caved in to the militants' demands overnight. The government-run television and radio also fell into line after the Second (Dr Sohan Singh) Panthic Committee-led militants assassinated several of their key personnel.[36] The "militants" had proved their power to both the Akalis and the government by the fall of 1990; they, not the Akalis or the government, were the most powerful force in Punjab!

FALL OF V.P. SINGH'S CENTRAL GOVERNMENT AND FORMATION OF CHANDRA SHEKHAR'S GOVERNMENT

The political scenario in the center changed in the fall of 1990. V.P. Singh's government faced nation-wide protests by the non-Scheduled Caste population of India for deciding to implement the Mandal Commission report. This report extended state benefits, including the reservation of seats in educational institutions, for the Backward Caste population in addition to those castes already categorized as "Scheduled Castes." These nation-wide protests and agitations threatened to split the National Front.

V.P. Singh's government also became embroiled in another controversy when the Hindu-nationalist BJP, which had been supporting the National Front from "the outside," threatened to demolish the Babri Masjid mosque in the city of Ayodhya. According to Hindu nationalists, this mosque had been built in the 16th century over a Hindu temple commemorating the place where the Hindu god, Rama, is believed to have been born. In late-October, the BJP withdrew support for V.P. Singh's government after the prime minister ordered the arrest of BJP president, Lal Krishna Advani, who tried to lead a huge march to "liberate" the disputed shrine in Ayodhya.[37]

The BJP's withdrawal of support allowed dissidents within the Janata Dal—which was the single largest party within the National Front government—to challenge V.P. Singh, thus splitting the party and causing V.P. Singh to lose his parliamentary majority.[38] The Congress (I) could not form a government by itself or with its allies because it had only a plurality, not majority, of seats. Instead, the Congress (I) decided to back Janata Dal dissidents led by Chandra Shekhar and allow him to form the next government in the center with Congress (I) support from "the outside."[39] Thus, a new non-Congress government came into power in November 1990.

The year 1990 ended as the bloodiest yet of the entire "Punjab crisis" with 3,787 people killed including 1,961 civilians, 506 security officers, and 1,320 militants.[40] In addition, 3,787 militants were arrested. The increased violence prompted the central government to launch Operation Rakshak in which the Army was inducted into the border districts of Punjab to assist police and paramilitary forces in tackling insurgency.[41] V.P. Singh had failed to resolve the "Punjab problem," and it remained to be seen if Chandra Shekhar would fair any better.

CHANDRA SHEKHAR'S OFFER OF "UNCONDITIONAL" TALKS WITH "THE MILITANTS" AND THE FALL OF HIS CENTRAL GOVERNMENT

Shortly after forming his government, prime minister Chandra Shekhar expressed an urgent desire to enter into negotiations with Sikh representatives to find a solution to the vexing "Punjab problem." In fact, he went dramatically further than any previous prime minister by offering to amend the Indian Constitution and negotiate directly with "the militants" without any preconditions if these steps would help find a lasting solution to the "Punjab problem" short of outright secession.[42] Shekhar had always been sympathetic to the demands of the Akali Dal and other regional parties, and he had been one of the few Indian leaders who had vocally criticized the central government for launching Operation

Bluestar in 1984. With the offer of talks, the proverbial ball was in the Sikh leadership's court.

All Akali factions met in late-December 1990 to discuss Shekhar's proposal, and they subsequently authorized Mann to hold talks with the central government.[43] The Akalis decided to press the government to recognize the Sikhs' right to "self-determination" which, they argued, was within the framework of the Indian Constitution. They also pandered to "the militants" by congratulating them for successfully enforcing the use of the Punjabi language in the media and government offices, and also assured them ("the militants") that they would not enter into formal negotiations or accept any settlement without first taking them into confidence.[44] After all, "the militants'" support was needed to forge a binding solution to the Punjab problem, and they also controlled the guns that could be trained on the Akali leaders! Thus, the Akalis pragmatically deferred to "the militants" regarding whether to enter into formal talks or not.

For their part, "the militants" reacted cautiously to Shekhar's proposal. The Second (Dr Sohan Singh) Panthic Committee agreed to enter into formal talks only if the government conceded to several pre-conditions, including that the agenda of the talks be put "into writing," the talks be held either at the Akal Takht or at United Nations offices in New York or Geneva, the Government of India allow safe passage for "the militants'" representatives for talks, and that the talks be held in full-view of the international media.[45] They also demanded the removal of Indian troops from the Northeast where other movements of "national liberation" were underway and the release of several Sikh militants from Indian prisons. Thus, "the militants" were willing to negotiate, but they put forth pre-conditions that any central government of India would find difficult to concede. This was especially the case with Chandra Shekhar's government which was quite "weak" since it relied on the "outside" support of the Congress (I) to remain in power.

Nonetheless, the Second (Dr Sohan Singh) Panthic Committee's response did not preclude the Akalis from meeting with Shekhar. Thus, Simranjeet Singh Mann met with prime minister Chandra Shekhar on December 28 for their first and only public meeting, but Mann refused to formally negotiate with him. Instead, he simply presented Shekhar with a memorandum approved by all major Akali factions outlining their view on the "Punjab problem" which read in part:

> The Sikhs, who opted for the Indian Union are today demanding the right to self-determination…[the Sikhs] are not prepared to accept any political

system which does not concede the right to self-determination while youths, we call them militants, are shedding their blood daily for a sovereign Sikh state…These are the hard realities we must face to find a correct solution. As militants are an important component in the situation, a formal invitation for talks must also be extended to them.[46]

This memorandum was designed to appease "the militants" by demanding Sikh "self-determination" and suggesting that Shekhar formally invite "the militants" for discussions. Yet, the Akalis also avoided explicitly demanding the creation of Khalistan. Mann very adroitly described the dilemma faced by individuals trying to mediate between the Sikh Panth and the government by saying, "If they don't fulfil the Panth's wishes, they are finished in the Panth's eyes. And if a mediator pleads the Panth's cause [too aggressively], he is written off by the government."[47] This was a classic "catch-22" situation for the Akalis, but they played their cards well given the situation. After Mann's meeting with Shekhar, the onus was on Shekhar's government to formally invite "the militants" for talks and on "the militants" whether to either accept or reject this invitation if it was forthcoming. Thus, the Akalis strategically absolved themselves from any responsibility whether these talks took place or not.

Shortly after this series of events, the leaders of the "moderate" Akali Dal (Longowal) and "radical" Akali Dal (Badal) agreed to merge their organizations under the leadership of Simranjeet Singh Mann.[48] All major Akali leaders agreed that the unified Akali Dal (Mann)'s goal would be to achieve "self-determination" for the Sikhs, but once again they avoided explicitly demanding the creation of a separate Sikh state. The Second (Dr Sohan Singh) Panthic Committee expressed its displeasure at this move toward Akali "unity" by writing, "The difference between Mr. Mann and us is that while we are unequivocal on the issue of an independent and sovereign Khalistan, Mr. Mann takes a few steps towards Khalistan only to retrace them."[49] This was not surprising because none of the Akalis, including Mann, were avowed separatists.

Through early-1991, Shekhar continued to express his willingness to engage in talks with "the militants" without pre-conditions, but he also complained that the fractionalized nature of "the militants" made identifying potential negotiators and entering into negotiations with them exceeding difficult.[50] The "militants" themselves were internally-divided over whether to enter into negotiations with the government or not. For this reason, they avoided either formally accepting or rejecting Shekhar's offer. Nonetheless, secret "exploratory" talks between emissaries of "the militants" and the government did take place as precursors for possible formal negotiations. Shekhar gave few details about these "exploratory" talks, but disclosed that he had met with select leaders of political parties who had contacts with "the militants," groups in the "shadow region" between political parties and "the militants," and with emissaries from all three Panthic Committees including with "elements" within the Second (Dr Sohan Singh) Panthic Committee.[51] Kanwar Singh Dhami, the founder of the separatist but largely peaceful Akal Federation, acted as the main intermediary in arranging "safe passage" for "the militants" from Pakistan to India to meet with government officials.[52] During these "exploratory" talks, the "militants" pressed their demand that formal talks be held regarding the formation of Khalistan, but Shekhar categorically refused to accept outright secession as a point of negotiation.[53]

Yet, these "exploratory" talks were unexpectedly cut short before they could potentially bear fruit when Chandra Shekhar resigned from office largely due to friction with Rajiv Gandhi's Congress (I) party. Rajiv had apparently threatened to withdraw support for Shekhar's government and force a vote of no-confidence, which would have inevitably resulted in the fall of his government. In response, Shekhar pre-empted this vote and resigned from office himself, thus prompting the President of India to call for fresh elections to be held in May.[54] Yet, Shekhar made a vitally important decision after becoming "caretaker" prime minister when he decided to allow both state assembly and parliamentary elections to be held in Punjab, along with those scheduled for the rest of India in June 1991. This was in sharp contrast to previous prime ministers all of whom had refused to hold state assembly elections in Punjab under conditions of insurgency, fearing the formation of an "extremist"-led state ministry. Thus, prospects for negotiations appeared to be over, but elections loomed close in the horizon for Punjab.

THE SCHEDULED JUNE 1991 STATE ASSEMBLY AND PARLIAMENTARY ELECTIONS IN PUNJAB

Political parties in Punjab responded to the announcement of upcoming elections in different ways. The Congress (I) and the two communist parties (the CPI and CPM), fearing not being able to effectively campaign in Punjab's militancy-affected rural areas, decided to boycott the Punjab polls. In contrast, the BJP decided to capitalize on the Congress (I)'s decision to boycott by contesting the elections, focusing on the state's large Hindu vote. Its main competitors in the urban, Hindu-majority areas would be the two Janata Dal factions—one led by V.P. Singh and the other by Chandra Shekhar.

The announcement of upcoming polls in Punjab had immediate effects on internal Sikh politics. First, the Akali "unity" which had been forged in January quickly eroded. The "radicals" led by Badal began the process of fractionalization by revolting against Mann's leadership and reactivating the Akali Dal (Badal).[55] Badal accused Mann of failing to provide effective leadership for the Sikhs and criticized him for not including any "traditional Akali leaders" in his party's parliamentary board. The Akali Dal (B), much like the Akali Dal (M), planned to contest the elections on the platform of "self-determination" for the Sikhs.[56] Second, the Akali Dal (Longowal), led by its acting president Kabul Singh and general secretary Capt. Kanwaljit Singh, also broke away from the Akali Dal (Mann) and reactivated itself, wanting to contest the elections on the issue of making India a more federalist system.[57] Third, the Rode faction within the Akali Dal (M) led by Baba Joginder Singh (Bhindranwale's father) and Captain Harcharan Singh Rode (Bhindranwale's elder brother) also rejected Mann's leadership, objecting to Mann's replacement of several local party leaders loyal to them. The Rode family would actually revitalize the Akali Dal (Baba) a few months later in July 1991.[58] Finally, Capt. Amarinder Singh of Patiala broke off from the Akali Dal (B) accusing Badal of not adequately consulting with the party's rank-and-file before issuing the party's election platform. He subsequently formed the Akali Dal (Panthic).[59] Amarinder Singh's "Akali Dal (Panthic)" was the second party in the electoral fray with the same name. The other was the Akali Dal (Panthic) led by former Akali Dal (Mann) MP, Rajdev Singh. All of these "parties" planned to contest the elections independently.

The AISSF (Manjit) also announced that it would participate in these polls. Manjit Singh explained this decision by stating that winning these elections would be an important stepping-stone for eventually securing "a home for the Sikhs," but he avoided elaborating on whether this entailed the creation of Khalistan.[60] In contrast, Manochahal, who supported the dual strategy of electoral and armed means for the "Sikh struggle," was more forthright by explaining, "Though we have no faith in the Indian Constitution, we are still in favor of participating in elections…If we get a majority and form a government we will pass a resolution for Khalistan."[61] Even the First (Zafferwal) Panthic Committee unofficially put up numerous candidates as "independents" in select state assembly constituencies in the Majha region.[62]

The pre-election scenario within Sikh politics before the scheduled 1991 polls contrasted significantly to that which existed before the 1989 parliamentary elections 18 months earlier. The biggest difference was that "the extremists" had been completely united in 1989, whereas now they were completely divided. Two issues prevented the most powerful "extremist" organizations—the Akali Dal (Mann) and AISSF (Manjit)—from uniting. First, the AISSF (Manjit) demanded at least 60 percent of seats for its candidates, but Mann refused to give more than 40 percent. Second, the AISSF (Manjit) refused to have an alliance with the Akali Dal (Mann) unless Mann expelled several second-rung party leaders who had previously been aligned with the "traditional Akali leadership."[63] For his part, Damdami Taksal chief Baba Thakur Singh tried desperately to negotiate an electoral alliance between the two organizations, but his efforts failed. Had they united, the AISSF (Manjit) and Akali Dal (Mann) would have probably constituted the most dominant electoral alliance in Punjab. Their unity may also have propelled other Sikh leaders to coalesce around them, but this was not to be. Instead of uniting, "the extremists" went into the scheduled June 1991 elections completely fractionalized, leading to predictions that the Sikh vote would be largely split between the AISSF (Manjit) and the Akali Dal (Mann).

The only Sikh grouping officially boycotting these elections was the Second (Dr Sohan Singh) Panthic Committee-led "militants," including the SSF (Bittu), KCF (Panjwar), KLF, BTFK (Chhandran), and Babbar Khalsa.[64] Yet, even this grouping was internally-divided about whether to participate or not. In particular, Dr Sohan Singh wanted to contest the elections in order to prove the Sikhs' support for Khalistan, but Daljeet Singh Bittu argued that doing so would violate the January 1986 *Sarbat Khalsa gurmata* refusing to recognize the Indian Constitution.[65] Bittu and the younger leadership eventually won the argument, and the Second Panthic Committee decided to officially boycott the polls. In fact, these "militants" tried to disrupt the campaigning by gunning down over two dozen candidates, most of them belonging to various "extremist" organizations which were contesting the elections.[66] Punjab was abuzz with frantic political activity, not to mention escalating militant violence, in late-spring 1991.

CANCELLATION OF THE SCHEDULED JUNE 1991 ELECTIONS IN PUNJAB

Congress (I) leader Rajiv Gandhi was assassinated on 21 May 1991 by a militant group demanding a separate Tamil homeland in Sri Lanka. Rajiv's assassination in South India prompted the Election Commission to postpone the first phase of the parliamentary elections in India for two weeks, but this did not officially affect the polls in Punjab which were scheduled for over a month later. Nonetheless, scheduled elections in Punjab never took place! In a bewildering move, the Election Commission unexpectedly cancelled the Punjab polls just 30 hours before voting was to begin. *India Today* described this cancellation as follows:

> On June 20, Punjab went to sleep with a relieved mind. The campaigning for the Lok Sabha and Vidhan Sabha polls, the bloodiest ever, had finally ended...But the biggest shock was yet to come. Next morning AIR and Doordarshan blared the news of poll postponement...The voting right in this case was snatched away not by the militants but by a constitutional instrument, the Election Commission.[67]

T.N. Seshan, the chairman of the Election Commission, publicly explained the rationale for canceling these polls by arguing that "fair and free elections" could not be held in Punjab because of existing conditions of insurgency. The Election Commission specifically pointed to the massacre of 74 train passengers, mostly Hindus, by the Second (Dr Sohan Singh) Panthic-led militants a few days before the polls to support its assertions.[68] Yet, this was only a convenient excuse.

In reality, these elections were cancelled because T.N. Seshan and the Election Commission "bent over backwards" to please the incoming Congress (I) central government under P.V. Narasimha Rao.[69] To explain, polling in the rest of India had been completed several weeks earlier. On the eve of the Punjab polls, it was becoming apparent that the Congress (I) had won a huge plurality of seats and that it, along with its allied parties, would most likely form the next government in the center. The Congress (I) was actually 28 seats short of an absolute majority alone and 10 short of a majority with its allies, but it was nonetheless invited to form the government because it also had the backing of several independents.[70] The incoming Congress (I) government under Narasimha Rao had apparently persuaded Seshan to cancel the Punjab polls. The Congress (I) had been boycotting elections in the state, and Rao calculated that winning at least 10 of Punjab's 13 parliamentary seats in a future election would give the Congress (I) and its loyal allies a clear majority in parliament. Thus, pure power considerations, not conditions in Punjab, prompted the cancellation of the scheduled June 1991 elections in the state. All other parties, except the Congress (I) and the Communists, expressed shock over this development.

In mid-1991, the "Sikh political spectrum" looked like the following (Table 9.3):

Table 9.3
Sikh Political Spectrum (Mid-1991)

Moderates	Radicals	Extremists[3]	Militants/Separatists[4]
AD (L)[1]	AD (Badal)[2]	AD (Mann)	First Panthic Committee[5]
	Tohra[2]	AISSF (Manjit)	KCF (Zafferwal)[5]
	Talwandi[2]	Akali Dal (Baba)	Second Panthic Committee
		Damdami Taksal	(Dr. Sohan Singh)[6]
		SSF (Mehta/Chawla)	SSF (Bittu)[6]
			KCF (Panjwar)[6]
			KLF[6]
			BTFK (Chhandra)[6]
			Third Panthic Committee[7]
			BTFK (Manochahal)[7]
			KCF (Rajasthani)[7]
			Babbar Khalsa[8]
			Akali Dal (Babbar)[8]

Source: Author.

Notes: [1] Akali Dal (Longowal); demanding full implementation of ASR through non-violent means.

[2] Akali Dal (Badal) and its leaders; demanding Sikh "self-determination" through non-violent means.

[3] "Extremists" totally divided; only Damdami Taksal exercises marginal authority over all "extremist" groups; "extremists" demanding Sikh "self-determination" through either non-violent or violent means.

[4] "Militants" divided into First, Second, and Third Panthic Committee-led groupings; Babbar Khalsa operates independently with Akali Dal (Babbar) as political front group.

[5] First (Zafferwal) Panthic Committee-led militants demanding Khalistan generally through violent means.

[6] Second (Dr. Sohan Singh) Panthic Committee-led militants demanding Khalistan through violent means.

[7] Third (Manochahal) Panthic Committee-led militants demanding Khalistan through both violent or electoral means.

[8] Babbar Khalsa-Akali Dal (Babbar) combine demanding Khalistan through violent means.

The "moderates" consisted of the Akali Dal (Longowal) and "the radicals" were contained in the Akali Dal (Badal). The Akali Dal (Panthic) led by Amarinder Singh was straddled somewhere between these two ideological groupings. The "extremists" included the Akali Dal (Mann), AISSF (Manjit), Akali Dal (Baba), SSF (Mehta/Chawla), and Damdami Taksal. These groups were largely fractionalized, but the Damdami Taksal tried to serve as a semi-authoritative institution trying to link them. The "militants" were divided into four groupings. First, the First (Zaffarwal)

Panthic Committee-led militants consisted of the KCF (Zafferwal). Second, the Second (Dr Sohan Singh) Panthic Committee was the most powerful militant grouping, and it included the SSF (Bittu), KCF (Panjwar), KLF, and BTFK (Chhandran). Third, the Third (Manochahal) Panthic Committee-led militants consisted of the BTFK (Manochahal) and KCF (Rajasthani). Lastly, the Babbar Khalsa, which had been expelled from the Second (Dr Sohan Singh) Panthic Committee in June 1991 for not accepting the Panthic Committee's authority, operated independently.[71] The Babbar Khalsa had also created its own miniscule political front organization called the Akali Dal (Babbar).Thus, both "the extremists" and "the militants," much like Sikh politics in general, were more divided in mid-summer 1991 than ever before during the entire "Punjab crisis." In fact, they were also competing against each other, often violently.

Panthic "Unity" under "the Militants" and the Central Government's New "Law-and-Order" Approach for Punjab

Cancellation of the June 1991 elections had immediate effects on Sikh politics. It prompted the highly-fractionalized Sikh political organizations, including the Akalis, to try to unite in order to form a common front against the Congress (I) central government. The cancellation of these polls also further increased the influence of "the militants," especially of the Second (Dr Sohan Singh) Panthic Committee, which had warned all Sikh political organizations not to participate in elections held under the Indian Constitution. The Second Panthic Committee's stand appeared to have been vindicated.

In August 1991, SGPC president Baldev Singh Sibia announced that a meeting of all Akali factions, Sikh religious bodies, federation groups, and militant outfits would be held to try to forge "Panthic unity" and chart the future course of the Sikh *quam*. Representatives of 36 Sikh religious and political organizations, including the Akalis, met at Anandpur Sahib on 1 September 1991 for this meeting.[72] *The Tribune* described the gathering as follows: "Never before [have] such a large number of Sikh organizations, including all factions of the Akali Dal and their youth wings, gotten together on one platform."[73]

The participants of this meeting agreed on a joint strategy to confront "police repression" by organizing sit-ins at police stations and holding mass rallies throughout the state. The "militants" also combined with hard-liners in other Sikh organizations and Akali factions to pass a unanimous resolution agreeing to boycott any future polls in Punjab.[74] This was a major victory for "the militants," but they were compelled to give a concession to the Akalis in order to get the unanimity required to pass this resolution. Capt. Amarinder Singh of the Akali Dal (Panthic) convinced the conclave to include a provision in the resolution making the decision to boycott elections binding for each Akali party only if their respective working committees approved it at the time. Thus, "the militants" got the Akalis' general agreement to boycott future polls, but the Akalis also left themselves a way open to contest if they desired to do so.

This conclave also had important reciprocal effects on internal Akali politics. The fact that Sibia gave "the militants" and other hardliners equal footing with the Akali Dal (Longowal) and Akali Dal (Badal) during this meeting angered the "traditional Akali leadership," which felt that Sibia was getting too close to "the militants." For this reason, the SGPC executive committee removed Sibia from his post and replaced him with Gurcharan Singh Tohra as the SGPC president.[75] Control over the SGPC was the Akali Dal (L) and Akali Dal (B)'s main source of authority, legitimacy, and power in Sikh politics because they had virtually no representation in national parliament unlike "the extremists." The SGPC was an institution they could hardly afford to lose in order to remain even marginally relevant in Sikh politics.

After coming to power in the center, Narasimha Rao's Congress (I) government declared that its top priority was to make the environment in Punjab more conducive for holding state elections. In mid-November 1991, the central government announced that both parliamentary and state assembly elections would be held in Punjab by the end of February 1992.[76] The Congress (I), along with its allies, was 10 seats short of an absolute majority in Parliament, and it calculated that it could sweep Punjab's 13 parliamentary seats since the Akalis were indicating that they would boycott. Thus, the Congress (I)'s rationale for holding elections in Punjab was largely partisan and self-centered.

Rao's central government implemented several new policies to help improve the deteriorating "law-and-order" situation in Punjab in preparation for the upcoming elections. First, it ordered the police and state administration to aggressively prevent Sikhs, including Akali leaders, from flocking to the *bhog* (last rites) ceremonies of slain Sikh militants which regularly attracted over 100,000 "mourners." Second, the new Congress (I) central government implemented a policy of forcibly preventing the Akalis from holding public rallies in Punjab except during traditional religious festivals. Third, the central government ordered K.P.S. Gill back to Punjab as the state's police chief for his second tenure in this position.[77] Gill was chosen, in part, because of his willingness to pursue anti-insurgency operations with little regard for bureaucratic and administrative protocol. He could also provide a public relations benefit for the government by having a tall, articulate, and handsome Jat Sikh pursuing anti-militant operations on behalf of the Indian government in Punjab. Lastly, the government inducted over 120,000 regular Army troops into the state in Operation Rakshak II to help improve the "law-and-order" situation in rural Punjab, especially in the Majha region.[78] These troops were deployed to bolster the approximately 160,000 police and paramilitary personnel already serving in Punjab, thus almost doubling the number of security forces in the state. In essence, the Congress (I) central government wanted desperately to prepare Punjab for elections by early-1992.

FEBRUARY 1992 ELECTIONS, AKALI BOYCOTT, AND FORMATION OF BEANT SINGH'S CONGRESS (I) GOVERNMENT IN PUNJAB

In mid-December 1991, the central government announced that the elections in Punjab would be held on 19 February 1992. As expected the Akali Dal (Mann), Akali Dal (Badal), Akali Dal (Baba), Akali Dal (Babbar), AISSF (Manjit), and SSF (Mehta/Chawla) all jointly announced that they would boycott these polls.[79] The leaders of these organizations had met about two weeks earlier after being warned by "the militants" to chalk out a common strategy for the boycott. Badal explained their rationale to boycott by saying:

> [Elections and President's Rule] are almost the same thing;…Moreover if elections are held what guarantee is there that they will not be a farce? We have warned the Centre that the hour of reckoning has come and it is no longer possible for treacherous Central leaders to cheat innocent Sikhs and mislead national and international opinion…My party is firm as a rock. It is the unanimous decision of the Panth to boycott the poll *tamasha* (drama or spectacle)… [W]e are men of steel.[80]

The Congress (I) central government responded to the Akalis' announcement to boycott and their plans to hold "anti-repression" rallies throughout the state by arresting all major "pro-boycott" Sikh leaders.

The only Akali faction which decided to participate in the elections was the "moderate" Akali Dal (Kabul) which had formed a few weeks earlier with the amalgamation of the Akali Dal (Longowal) led by Surjit Singh Barnala, Capt. Kanwaljit Singh and Kabul Singh, and the Akali Dal (Panthic) led by Capt. Amarinder Singh. The Akali Dal (Kabul) explained its decision to participate in these polls by arguing that boycotting would simply mean handing over power in the state to the Congress (I).[81] This, according to the Akali Dal (K), would invite even more governmental oppression of Sikhs. The Akali Dal (K) forged an alliance and made seat adjustments with the two Communist parties and the Janata Dal for these elections. In contrast, the Congress (I), BJP, and BSP planned to contest the elections individually. Electioneering was subdued and took place under unprecedented security with nearly 300,000 security personnel on duty in the state.[82]

The results of the state assembly elections were as follows: Congress (I) 87 seats, BSP 9, BJP 6, CPI 4, Akali Dal (K) 3, CPM 1, Janata Dal 1, independents and others 6.[83] As a result, the Congress (I) formed the state ministry in Punjab with an unprecedented three-fourths majority under the leadership of Beant Singh, the new chief minister of the state. The Congress (I) also won 12 out of 13 parliamentary seats, giving it and its allies a wafer-thin majority in the national parliament.[84] Yet, "the militants" and other Sikh organizations boycotting the polls successfully demonstrated their strength as well. Voter turnout in Punjab was only 23.9 percent, the lowest ever for the state, in comparison to 67.5 percent for the 1985 state assembly elections.[85] The turnout in Punjab's 70 rural, mostly Sikh-majority constituencies was particularly low at 15.1 percent in comparison to 68.8 percent for 1985.[86] There were also many polling stations in rural parts of the Majha and Malwa regions where not even a single vote was cast!

The Congress (I) had won the elections but the lack of Sikh participation made the legitimacy of Beant Singh's state government highly-questionable. *India Today* described the situation after the February 1992 elections as follows:

> The electoral process has been restored to Punjab; but the spirit of democracy is still at large. The Congress (I) has won the battle for the state legislature; but it may well have lost the war for the Sikh heart...if only turnout had not been so pathetic, with the Sikhs staying away in letter and spirit. This has...demonstrated once again the militant sway in the state.[87]

The question being asked in the beginning of 1992 was what effect, if any, would the formation of a Congress (I) state government in Punjab have on the Sikh separatist movement? The year 1991 ended as being the bloodiest one yet of the entire "Punjab crisis." A total of 4,768 people had been killed, including 2,094 civilians, 497 police and security personnel, and 2,177 militants.[88] In addition, 1,977 militants had been arrested. The "Punjab problem" had lingered on for close to a decade and had escalated precipitously through the late-1980s and early-1990s. Was there simply any way out of the "Punjab problem" and the increasingly bloody violence associated with it?

SUMMARY AND CONCLUSION

In many ways, the years examined in this chapter represent a critically important transitory period in the dynamics and trajectory of the Sikh ethnonationalist movement. During this period, the Sikh ethnonationalist movement continued and, in fact, escalated. But, a number of new "patterns of political leadership," many of which had begun in their incipient stages in earlier years, accelerated and began to gel in more definitive ways.

First, the biggest transformation was the almost complete fractionalization of "the extremists." The "extremists" had previously remained largely united. This factor had helped them sustain popular support for the Sikh ethnonationalist movement and contributed to their near sweep of the November 1989 parliamentary elections under the leadership of Simranjeet Singh Mann. Yet, immediately after this spectacular electoral victory, "the extremists" began fractionalizing and aggressively competing against each other. For example, Mann faced increased intra-party challenges and cross pressures from his party's own celebrity MPs, the Rode faction within his party, Harminder Singh Sandhu, and the AISSF (Manjit). Internal competition within "the extremists" also led to the bifurcation of the powerful AISSF (Manjit) and the emergence of the separate SSF (Mehta/Chawla) in early-1990. Factionalism within "the extremists" became so progressively intense that they went into the scheduled June 1991 elections totally divided, whereas having been completely united during the November 1989 elections, 18 months earlier. The total splintering of "the extremists" reduced the Sikh ethnonationalist movement's overall political efficacy, and allowed "the militants" to become collectively dominant over "the extremists" by mid-1991.

Second, "the militants" also became increasingly fractionalized and internally-competitive during this period. They had previously been bifurcated into two separate militant groupings led by the First and Second (Dr Sohan Singh) Panthic Committees, respectively. But, "the militants" split further in the spring of 1990 and three different Panthic Committees emerged—the First (Zafferwal) Panthic Committee, Second (Dr Sohan Singh) Panthic Committee, and Third (Manochahal) Panthic Committee. This split also led to the splintering of both the KCF and BTFK into separate factions loyal to the different Panthic Committees. In addition, the Babbar Khalsa operated independently. Thus, the armed "militant" wing of the Sikh ethnonationalist movement splintered with the mushrooming of organizations, and, in a qualitative transformation from the past, the various militant outfits also began engaging in violent internecine conflict with each other. Collectively, "the militants" became dominant in Sikh politics and the death toll in Punjab skyrocketed, but, at the same time, the movement was also degenerating into competitive violence between "militant" groups. In essence, the Sikh separatist movement was becoming more intense, but potentially less efficacious in many ways.

Third, "the militants" also began losing an effective political front in "the extremists" during the period under examination in this chapter. To explain, "the militants" and "the extremists" had remained closely linked during most of the post-Bluestar period, including on the eve of the November 1989 parliamentary elections when "the militants" informally, but actively, supported "the extremists." Yet, this changed after Mann tried to convince "the militants" to negotiate a solution short of Khalistan, and "the militants" refused to do so. The "militants" reacted to Mann's calls for negotiations by imposing their will over him and "the extremists," and by demanding that the Akalis unequivocally support their separatist cause. The "extremists" themselves were in a precarious position after the November 1989 elections because they had become internally-fractionalized, and, as a result, "the militants"—although also increasingly fractionalized themselves—became collectively dominant in Sikh politics. In essence, instead of having a mutually-symbiotic or cooperative relationship with "the extremists" as in the past, "the militants" began aggressively exerting control over them. This caused a divergence of interests between the two ideological groupings. In essence, "the gun" (that is, "the militants") became dominant over "politics" (for example, "the extremists"). The "extremists" had widespread, institutionalized networks of support within the Sikh community, and the widening schism between "the extremists" and "the militants" could potentially undermine the long-term sustainability of the Sikh ethnonationalist movement.

While the three changing "patterns of political leadership" described above could have potentially detrimental effects on the Sikh ethnonationalist movement, two other "patterns of political leadership" persisted from previous years which, both directly and indirectly, helped sustain the insurgency. First, governing state elites continued to be internally-divided, thus forestalling the formation and implementation of a coherent and effective policy on Punjab. To explain, V.P. Singh's National Front government relied on the support of the Communists and the BJP—political parties vehemently opposed to the Sikh ethnonationalists—to remain in power. This prevented V.P. Singh from offering substantive concessions to Mann which may have allowed him to undermine "the militants" or gain their support in helping resolve the "Punjab problem" through compromise. Similarly, Chandra Shekhar's Janata government—which was probably the most willing of all previous governments to offer major concessions to Sikh ethnonationalists—relied on the Congress (I) to remain in power in the center. This constrained Shekhar's range of action in relation to the "Punjab problem" and forestalled compromise with "the extremists" or "militants." Second, the "traditional Akali leadership" remained fractionalized and continued to pander to Sikh ethnonationalist sentiments. During this period, the "traditional Akali leadership" was divided between the "radical" faction led by Badal and Tohra, and "the moderates" led by Barnala. Talwandi fluctuated between aligning with his fellow "traditional Akali leaders," and floating his own party. Capt. Amarinder Singh formed his own party as well. For a period of time, the "traditional Akali leadership" also aligned squarely with Mann and "the extremists," and expressed support for "the militants." Thus, the fractionalization and competitive outbidding of the "traditional Akali leadership" also helped sustain Sikh discontent and separatism.

In essence, the Sikh ethnonationalist insurgency persisted in an escalated way during the period under examination in this chapter, partially sustained by continued disunity between governing state elites and internal factionalism within the "traditional Akali leadership." Yet, as described earlier, fundamental transformations were also taking place within the Sikh ethnonationalist movement, including the complete fractionalization of "the extremists," increasing factionalism and violent competition between "the militants," and "the militants'" loss of a viable political front in "the extremists" as the "gun" ("the militants") became dominant over "politics" ("the extremists"). The detrimental effects of these three changing "patterns of political leadership", if matured, would help undermine the movement in combination with other emerging "patterns of political leadership," would help undermine the movement.

NOTES

1. Kanwar Kandhu, "S.S. Ray: Acrimonious Departure,"*India Today*, 31 December 1989, 44.
2. Ramesh Vinayak, "Anandapur Proposal Only Solution: Mann," *The Tribune*, 4 December 1989, 1.
3. Ibid.
4. P.P.S. Gill and Ramesh Vinayak, "VP Promises New Era in Punjab," *The Tribune*, 8 December 1989, 1.
5. Tribune Bureau, "Badal, Tohra, Sandhu to be Freed," *The Tribune*, 1 December 1989, 1 and 14.
6. The KCF (Sultanwind) had been renamed the KCF (Panjwar) after Paramjit Singh Panjwar succeeded Kanwaljit Singh Sultanwind after the latter's death during a "police encounter" in October 1989.
7. The Congress (I) had 197 seats, the Janata Dal had 143 seats, the BJP 86 seats, and the Communist parties a total of 45 seats. Meenu Roy, *Elections 1998: A Continuity in Coalition* (New Delhi: National Publishing House, 1999), 25.
8. Staff Correspondent, "Sandhu Fred," *The Tribune*, 5 December 1989, 1; and Kanwar Sandhu, "Punjab: Flicker of Hope," *India Today*, 31 December 1989, 44.
9. The four Akali Dal (Mann) MP's who took the oath of office in late-December were Baba Sucha Singh, Rajinder Kaur Bulara, Rajdev Singh, and Jagdev Singh Khudian. P.T.I, "4 Dal (M) Members Sworn In," *The Tribune*, 22 December 1989, 1. Both Attinderpal Singh Bhopal and Bimal Kaur Khalsa would take the oath of office in the spring of 1990 in defiance of Simranjeet Singh Mann's personal orders.
10. The friction between the Rode family faction and the Manjit Singh faction within the Akali Dal (Mann) was particularly destructive for the party in 1990.
11. The Akali Dal (Talwandi) was renamed the Akali Dal (Badal) when Parkash Singh Badal was released from jail in early-December 1989 after about 18 months in detention.
12. Tribune Bureau, "PM Asked to Recognise 'Khalistan'," *The Tribune*, 14 December 1989, 4.
13. Ibid., 5.
14. Kanwar Sandhu, "Punjab: Seeking Solutions," *India Today*, 31 January 1990, 25.
15. Harish Gupta, "Mann-VP Secret Meeting in Delhi," *The Tribune*, 8 January 1990, 1.
16. Ramesh Vinayak, "I Can Persuade Militants: Mann," *The Tribune*, 7 January 1990, 1.
17. Staff Correspondent, " AISSF Challenges Mann's Claim," *The Tribune*, 13 January 1990, 1.
18. Ibid.
19. For exact figures, see Shyam Khosla, "Unprecedented Terror in Punjab," *The Tribune*, 5 January 1990, 1.
20. P.P.S. Gill, "Harminder Sandhu Shot Dead,"*The Tribune*, 25 January 1990, 1 and 14.
21. Tribune Bureau, " 'KCF', 'KLF' Claim Killing Sandhu," *The Tribune*, 26 January 1990, 3.
22. Interview by author with close relative of Sant Bhindranwale and high-level member of the AISSF active from 1978 to the late-1980s, 21 September 2002, Sacramento, California, USA. Hereafter cited as "Interview with AISSF member and close relative of Bhindranwale previously cited, 21 September 2002."Also, interview with senior Khalistani activist and leader active in the militant movement since 1978, 19 November 2001, Fremont, California, USA.

23. See Staff Correspondent, "AISSF Joint Secy Quits," *The Tribune*, 16 February 1990, 1 and 12, and Staff Correspondent, "3 AISSF Leaders Expelled," *The Tribune*, 18 February 1990, 1 and 16.

24. Interview with AISSF member and close relative of Bhindranwale previously cited, 21 September 2002.

25. K.S. Chawla, "Manjit Singh Removed," *The Tribune*, 22 February 1990, 1 and 16. After its formation, the All-India Sikh Students Federation (Mehta/Chawla) changed its name to the Sikh Students Federation (Mehta/Chawla) or SSF (Mehta/Chawla). This was to demonstrate its separatist ideology and unwillingness to be associated with India. This soon prompted the overtly separatist and militant AISSF (Bittu) become the SSF (Bittu).

26. For details see Joyce Pettigrew, *The Sikhs of the Punjab: Unheard Voices of State and Guerilla Violence* (London: Zed Books, 1995), 84–87.

27. U.N.I., "121 Terrorists Died in Inter-gang War," *The Tribune*, 1 June 1990, 3.

28. Ibid.

29. Staff Correspondent, "Ranjit Singh is New Akal Takht Chief," *The Tribune*, 10 June 1990, 1.

30. Tribune Bureau, "Mann Quits as Party Chief," *The Tribune*, 22 August 1990, 1.

31. Staff Correspondent, "Dal(M) to Boycott Poll," *The Tribune*, 30 August 1990, 1.

32. Ramesh Vinayak, "Tohra for Handing over Reins to Youth," *The Tribune*, 26 September 1990, 1.

33. Tohra agreed to this move, but only after being allowed to handpick the eleven members of the SGPC executive committee.

34. A.S. Prashar, "Conclave Held Despite Ban: Call for Unanimity in SGPC Poll," *The Tribune*, 26 November 1990, 1.

35. P.T.I., "Militants' Code for Press," *The Tribune*, 23 November 1990, 1.

36. For example, see Tribune Bureau, "City AIR Chief Shot Dead," *The Tribune*, 7 December 1990, 1; and Tribune Bureau, "Talib was Killed to Enforce Punjabi," *The Tribune*, 9 December 1990, 1.

37. Tribune Bureau, "Advani Held, BJP End Support: VP to Test Majority in House," *The Tribune*, 24 October 1990, 1.

38. Shyam Khosla, "JD Spilts," *The Tribune*, 6 November 1990, 1.

39. For details of this arrangement see Shyam Khosla, "Shekhar Sworn in PM, Devi Deputy," *The Tribune*, 11 November 1990, 1 and 16.

40. Paul Wallace, "Political Violence and Terrorism in India: The Crisis of Identity," in *Terrorism in Context*, ed. Martha Crenshaw (University Park, PA: Pennsylvania State University Press, 1995), 354.

41. For details of Operation Rakshak see Kanwar Sandhu, "Punjab: A Timely Reprieve," *India Today*, 15 March 1991, 65–68.

42. U.N.I., "Statute may be Changed on Punjab: PM," *The Tribune*, 23 December 1990, 1.

43. A.S. Prashar, "Mann Gets Go-ahead For Talks," *The Tribune*, 27 December 1990, 1 and 12.

44. Ibid., 12.

45. Tribune News Service, "Panthic Panel Welcomes Talks," *The Tribune*, 29 December 1990, 4.

46. U.N.I., "Mann's Memorandum to PM," *The Tribune*, 31 December 1990, 4.

47. U.N.I., "No Talks Minus Militants: Mann," *The Tribune*, 30 December 1990, 1.

48. Tribune News Service, "Akali Factions Merge," *The Tribune*, 12 January 1991, 1.
49. Tribune News Service, "Militants Move Away from Mann," *The Tribune*, 15 January 1991, 1.
50. K.S. Chawla, "Poll After Normalcy in Punjab: PM," *The Tribune*, 29 January 1991, 1.
51. P.T.I., "Centre Gauging Militants' Response," *The Tribune*, 17 April 1991, 1.
52. Ramesh Vinayak, "Centre Revives Link with Militants," *The Tribune*, 8 June 1991, 1; and Interview by the author with senior Khalistani activist and intellectual advisor involved in the militant movement since 1986, 21 September 2002, Fremont, California, USA. Hereafter referred to as "Interview with senior Khalistani activist and intellectual advisor previously cited, 21 September 2002."
53. Apparently, Dr Sohan Singh had favored holding these negotiations, but other leaders in the Second Panthic Committee-led grouping, including Daljeet Singh Bittu (SSF) disagreed. Interview with senior Khalistani activist and intellectual advisor previously cited, 21 September 2002.
54. C.M. Kumbhkarni, "Rajiv Vows to Avert Crisis," *The Tribune*, 8 March 1991, 1.
55. Tribune News Service, "Badal Revolts Against Mann," *The Tribune*, 24 April 1991, 1 and 12.
56. Ibid., 1.
57. Tribune News Service, "Dal (L) Also Breaks Away," *The Tribune*, 25 April 1991, 1.
58. K.S. Chawla, "Split in Dal (M) Widens," *The Tribune*, 12 May 1991, 1; and Tribune News Service, "Dal (Baba) to Launch Peaceful Stir," *The Tribune*, 15 July 1991, 1.
59. Tribune News Service, "Amarinder Floats Dal (Panthic)," *The Tribune*, 29 April 1991, 1.
60. Staff Correspondent, "Poll Step Towards Sikh Home: Manjit," *The Tribune*, 7 May 1991, 5.
61. See interview in Kanwar Sandhu, "Gurbachan Singh Manochal: 'We Will Not Budge An Inch'", *India Today*, 15 September 1991, 71.
62. Tribune News Service, "KCF (Z) Confidants to Contest Poll," *The Tribune*, 25 April 1991, 4.
63. Ramesh Vinayak, "AISSF(M)-Dal Talks Suffer Setback," *The Tribune*, 24 April 1991, 12.
64. The BTFK (Sangha) had changed its name to BTFK (Chhandran) after Rachpal Singh Chhandran replaced Sukhwinder Singh Sangha after his death in a police encounter in November 1990.
65. Ram Narayan Kumar, *The Sikh Unrest and the Indian State: Politics, Personalities, and Historical Perspective* (Delhi: Ajanta Publications, 1997), 281; and Interview with senior Khalistani activist and intellectual advisor previously cited, 21 September 2002.
66. Paul Wallace, "India's 1991 Elections: Regional Factors in Haryana and Punjab," in *India Votes: Alliance Politics and Minority Governments in the Ninth and Tenth General Elections*, eds Harold A. Gould and Sumit Ganguly (Boulder, CO: Westview Press, 1993), 410.
67. Kanwar Sandhu, "Punjab: Floundering Move," *India Today*, 15 July 1991, 32.
68. Ibid., 33.
69. Ibid.
70. For the final seat tally see Wallace, "India's 1991 Elections," 423.
71. For exact details on the Babbar Khalsa's expulsion from the Second (Dr Sohan Singh) Panthic Committee-led militants, see Tribune News Service, "Panthic Panel Parts Company with Babbars," *The Tribune*, 4 June 1991, 9.

72. For details see Prabhjot Singh, "Akalis to Boycott Elections," *The Tribune*, 2 September 1991, 5 and 12; and Prabhjot Singh, "Akalis Offer Their Arms for Twisting," *The Tribune*, 3 September 1991, 1 and 12.

73. Ibid., 12.

74. Prabhjot Singh, "Akalis to Boycott Elections," *The* Tribune, 3 September 1991, 5.

75. Tribune News Service, "Tohra is SGPC President," *The Tribune*, 13 November 1991, 1.

76. A.S. Prashar, "Forces to Seal Punjab," *The Tribune*, 16 November 1991, 1.

77. Shyam Khosla, "Gill Returns as DGP," *The Tribune*, 8 November 1991, 1. Gill had served as Punjab's Director General of Police (DGP) previously from April 1988 until December 1990.

78. Manoj Joshi, "Combating Terrorism in Punjab: Indian Democracy in Crisis," in *Rivalry and Revolution in South and East Asia*, ed. Partha Ghosh (Aldershot, UK: Ashgate Publishing, 1997), 198.

79. Tribune News Service, "Akalis to Boycott Poll," *The Tribune*, 17 January 1992, 1 and 16.

80. S.K. Pande, "Akali Voices," *Frontline*, 14 February 1992, 116.

81. K.S. Chawla, "Akali Dal (L) for Participation in Poll," *The Tribune*, 6 January 1992, 1.

82. Joshi, "Combating Terrorism," 198.

83. Tribune News Service, "Record Success for Cong in Punjab," *The Tribune*, 22 February 1992, 1.

84. P.T.I., "Cong May Manage Wafer-thin Majority," *The Tribune*, 22 February 1992, 1.

85. Yogendra Yadav, "Who Won in Punjab? Of the Real Contest," *Frontline*, 10 April 1992, 123.

86. Ibid. For a constituency-wise breakdown of turnout see Ibid.

87. Ramesh Vinayak and Harinder Baweja, "Punjab Elections: Accelerating Alienation," *India Today*, 15 March 1992, 20.

88. Wallace, "Political Violence," 354.

PART IV

The Demise of the Sikh Ethnonationalist Movement (1992–1997)

10

Crushing of the Violent Sikh Ethnonationalist Movement by the Unified State (1992–1993)

BEANT SINGH'S THREE-PRONGED STRATEGY TO "SOLVE" THE "PUNJAB PROBLEM"

In the spring of 1992, the "militants'" dictates ran throughout Punjab. Academic institutions and the state-run media had transitioned from using Hindi and English to using exclusively Punjabi; the government bureaucracy was paralyzed and confined itself to heavily-guarded offices in Chandigarh; and the people of Punjab were caught in a bloody war for physical control of the state between "the militants" and the Indian security forces. The "militants" had also exerted effective control over Sikh politics and the Sikh political agenda. Both "ideological" and "issue-based" unity had been forged between most Sikh political groups at the insistence of "the militants" on the eve of the scheduled elections in Punjab. The alliance of "six Panthic organizations"—which consisted of the Akali Dal (Badal), Akali Dal (Mann), Akali Dal (Baba), Akali Dal (Babbar), AISSF (Manjit), and SSF (Mehta/Chawla)—had joined together in support of "the militants" and their goal of "Sikh self-determination." They had collectively boycotted the February 1992 elections. Thus, the Panth, while still organizationally divided, appeared to be more "ideologically" united behind "the militants" and their goal of achieving Khalistan than any other point during the entire "Punjab crisis."

The Sikh political spectrum at this time looked like the following (Table 10.1):

Table 10.1
Sikh Political Spectrum (Early/Mid-1992)

Moderates	Radicals	Extremists	Militants/Separatists[4]
AD (Kabul)[1]	AD (Badal)[2]	AD (Mann)[2]	First Panthic Committee[5]
	Tohra[3]	AISSF (Manjit)[2]	KCF (Zafferwal)[5]
	AD (Talwandi)	Akali Dal (Baba)[2]	Second Panthic Committee
		SSF (Mehta/Chawla)[2]	(Dr. Sohan Singh)[6]
		Damdami Taksal	SSF (Bittu)[6]
			KCF (Panjwar)[6]
			KLF[6]
			BTFK (Chhandra)[6]
			Third Panthic Committee[7]
			BTFK (Manochahal)[7]
			Babbar Khalsa[8]
			Akali Dal (Babbar)[2/8]

Source: Author.

Notes: [1] Akali Dal (Kabul); previously called the Akali Dal (Longowal); demanding the decentralization of the Indian Union through non-violent means.

[2] Constituent members of the "six Panthic organizations" coalition; consisting of the AD (Badal), AD (Mann), AD (Manjit), AD (Baba), AD (Babbar), and SSF (Mehta/Chawla); united by "the militants"; supporting "the militants" and their violent struggle for the creation of Khalistan.

[3] Tohra also member of Akali Dal (Badal).

[4] "Militants" divided into First, Second, and Third Panthic Committee-led groupings; Babbar Khalsa operates independently with Akali Dal (Babbar) as political front group.

[5] First (Zafferwal) Panthic Committee-led militants demanding Khalistan generally through violent means.

[6] Second (Dr. Sohan Singh) Panthic Committee-led militants demanding Khalistan through violent means.

[7] Third (Manochahal) Panthic Committee-led militants demanding Khalistan through both violent means.

[8] Babbar Khalsa-Akali Dal (Babbar) combine demanding Khalistan through violent means.

At the most moderate end was the Akali Dal (Kabul), previously known as the Akali Dal (Longowal). This party was led by Kabul Singh, Surjit Singh Barnala, Capt. Amarinder Singh, and Capt. Kanwaljit Singh. Its basic demand was the increased decentralization of power within the Indian Union from the center to the states. The "radicals" consisted of the Akali Dal (Badal) and Akali Dal (Talwandi).[1] The Akali Dal (Badal), which included both Parkash Singh Badal and Gurcharan Singh Tohra, demanded "self-determination for the Sikhs." In contrast, the Akali Dal (Talwandi) demanded full implementation of the Anandpur Sahib Resolution (ASR), which it interpreted as also including the creation of a

"Sikh homeland." The "moderates" and "radicals" collectively comprised the "traditional Akali leadership."

The "extremists" included the Akali Dal (Mann), Akali Dal (Baba), AISSF (Manjit), SSF (Mehta/Chawla), and Damdami Taksal. None of these "extremist" organizations were formally linked to each other, although the Damdami Taksal tried to act as an umbrella organization for them. All of the "extremist" organizations demanded "self-determination for the Sikhs" preferably through peaceful means, although they did not openly disavow the use of violence either. In contrast to the "traditional Akali leadership," these "extremist" organizations had emerged during the post-Bluestar tumult in Sikh politics.

The "militants" were divided into four different groupings. The first grouping was the First (Zafferwal) Panthic Committee-led militants which included the KCF (Zafferwal). The second "militant" grouping was led by the Second (Dr Sohan Singh) Panthic Committee, and consisted of the SSF (Bittu), KCF (Panjwar), KLF, and BTFK (Chhandran). This was the most powerful grouping of militants in Punjab. The third grouping was the Third (Manochahal) Panthic Committee-led militants which included the armed BTFK (Manochahal). The fourth "militant" grouping was the Babbar Khalsa and its miniscule political wing, the Akali Dal (Babbar). All of "the militants" demanded the creation of an independent Sikh state—Khalistan—through an armed struggle.

After coming into power in the February 1992 elections, the Congress (I) chief minister of Punjab, Beant Singh, implemented a new strategy to try to solve the "Punjab problem" and hopefully end the Sikh ethnonationalist insurgency. This strategy included three elements—having the central government concede to the state's lingering demands, altering the political discourse in Punjab by regulating the Akalis' ability to propagate their views, and physically eliminating "the militants." The first element of this strategy quickly failed when Beant Singh and the chief minister of Haryana, Bhajan Lal, failed to resolve their lingering inter-state disputes, including the issues of Chandigarh and the sharing of river waters, after several weeks of negotiations.[2] For this reason, Beant Singh was forced to rely on the two other elements of his three-pronged strategy to try to solve the "Punjab problem."

The second prong of Beant Singh's strategy consisted of trying to control the Akalis, who he accused of exacerbating the "Punjab problem" by appeasing "the militants" and heightening the Sikhs' sense of alienation with their heated rhetoric. In essence, Beant Singh viewed the Akalis as being a part of the problem and not necessarily a part of the solution for Punjab. For this reason, his government strictly enforced a policy of not allowing the Akalis to hold public rallies, except at traditional religious festivals.[3] Beant Singh also began arresting Akali leaders, releasing them a few days later, and then re-arresting them again to make them appear impotent in comparison to his government. As a result, the Akalis found it more difficult to propagate their ethnonationalist views on behalf of "the militants."

The third part of Beant Singh's strategy was to try to eliminate "the militants" through concerted anti-insurgency operations. In this attempt, Beant Singh categorically ruled out holding any negotiations with pro-Khalistan groups and characterized the "Punjab problem" as being largely a "law-and-order" one as opposed to a "political" one.[4] He gave Punjab police chief K.P.S. Gill *carte blanche* power to confront militancy without interference from legislators or the state administration. This emboldened the Punjab police and security forces, who had previously feared being prosecuted for human rights violations if an "extremist" or "militant"-led government eventually came into power in Punjab. The "free hand" given to the security forces included the escalated use of torture, "faked police encounters," seizing the financial assets of families of militants, and arresting or killing the relatives of suspected Sikh militants in order to compel them to surrender. Gill justified the use of these extra-judicial methods by exclaiming, "If an officer has done something wrong, it is between him and his maker."[5] Beant Singh and K.P.S. Gill's virtually unrestricted "law-and-order" approach to Punjab also received the tacit support of Narasimha Rao's Congress (I) central government, which was securely in power in New Delhi after gaining additional parliamentary seats in the February 1992 elections in Punjab.

THE 1992 HOLLA MOHALLA FESTIVAL: THE AKALIS BECOME SEPARATISTS AND THE SIKHS' COMMON DEMAND FOR A "SOVEREIGN SIKH STATE"

The largely "united" Sikh leadership took a confrontational approach to Beant Singh's incoming Congress (I) government in Punjab. Akali Dal (B) general secretary Kuldeep Singh Wadala, who acted as party leader in the absence of Badal and Tohra both of whom were in jail, enunciated the Akalis' political views by saying, "The [election] boycott has united the Sikh masses as never before…All differences have been patched up. In this, everybody has cooperated—even the militants…We want real freedom…This is the idea we want to discuss with the Centre."[6] Thus, the Akalis edged even closer to "the militants." For their part, "the militants" wanted the "six Panthic organizations" to either unequivocally support the creation of an independent Sikh state, or to have them dissolve their respective organizations and amalgamate with them in the struggle to achieve Khalistan.

The "militants'" complete control over both Sikh politics and the Akalis became apparent during the annual Holla Mohalla festival held at Anandpur Sahib in mid-March 1992. During this massive gathering, the "six Panthic organizations" erected a joint stage with "the militants," and no other political party—including the Akali Dal (Kabul) or the Congress (I)—dared participate in the festival, fearing for their members' physical safety. The "six Panthic organizations" and "the militants" unanimously passed a resolution during this gathering unequivocally stating that their unified demand was the creation of an "independent Sikh state."[7] In this resolution, the "six Panthic organizations" also appealed to "the militants" to forge internal unity amongst themselves in order to strengthen their struggle and promised to act as a political "shield" for them against the government. Thus, for the first time during the entire "Punjab crisis," the Akalis (with the exception of "the moderates") openly demanded the creation of an "independent Sikh state" and agreed to support "the militants" in their armed struggle to achieve it.[8] The "ideological" unity between the "six Panthic organizations" and "the militants" appeared to be complete, and the Akalis seemed to be committed to the creation of Khalistan!

India Today described the prevailing situation after the Holla Mohalla festival by writing: "It's all in the open now. After years of ambivalence and ambiguity on enunciating their goal, six major Akali groups in Punjab have resolved to work for a sovereign Sikh state…in tandem with militants."[9] The only obstacle in forging complete unity between the "six Panthic organizations" and "the militants" remained the Akalis' unwillingness to dissolve their respective parties and organizationally amalgamate with "the militants." Nonetheless, "the militants'" separatist cause had openly and unequivocally received the Akalis' public backing in spring of 1992. The Akalis had become open separatists for the first time during the entire "Punjab crisis," and the insurgency was at its peak!

The Akali Dal (Badal) had been represented by its second-rung leadership—including Kuldeep Singh Wadala and Sukhdev Singh Dhindsa—at the Holla Mohalla festival because its senior leaders, including Badal and Tohra, were in jail. This raised hopes that these premier Akali leaders would possibly retract their party's support for the creation of Khalistan once released, but this did not happen. Instead, both Badal and Tohra openly endorsed the resolutions passed at the Holla Mohalla conference after coming out of jail.[10] For his part, Tohra exclaimed, "It is now Khalistan or nothing."[11] He further explained, "We are going into a struggle that will ultimately take us to a sovereign Sikh state, a state where we will be able to decide our own destiny...Our position is comparable to the PLO (Palestine Liberation Organization)."[12] Leaders of the "six Panthic organizations," including those of the Akali Dal (Badal), subsequently tried to meet with United Nations Secretary-General, Boutros Ghali, to present him with a memorandum demanding the creation of Khalistan, but they were arrested before being able to enter New Delhi to do so.[13]

The situation became so politically grim for the Indian state in the late-spring of 1992 that *panchayats* throughout Punjab began resigning in mass and, instead, Sikh villagers started creating Khalsa *panchayats* to act as parallel institutions of governance as directed by the Akali–"militant" alliance.[14] One source described the prevailing situation in Punjab at the time as being an "area of darkness" where "the militants' diktat (dictates) is now a living, breath-ing, and palpable fear which lies at every turn of the road and every hour of the day...Shuttered in steel and barricaded behind bulwarks, a sham of a government directs the course for the state's sinking ship."[15] At this juncture, the creation of Khalistan appeared to be eminent because the Panth was "united" for Khalistan, "the militants" collectively dominated large swaths of Punjab, and governmental institutions were quickly atrophying. Punjab seemed lost from the Indian Union!

Yet, this grim assessment hid important dynamics occurring within the Sikh ethnonationalist movement that could potentially help undermine it. First, the armed "militants" had become increasingly fractionalized, had mushroomed, and were fighting more against each other in internecine warfare than against the central state and its security forces.[16] Second, "the extremists" had become completely fractionalized, as opposed to being fully united only a few years earlier, and aggressively competed against each other for political dominance. This fractionalization split the loyalties of "the extremists'" extensive Sikh support base and reduced the long-term political efficacy of the ethnonationalist movement. Finally, "the gun" (that is, "the militants") had become dominant over "politics" (that is, "the extremists") instead of vice-versa or having a cooperative relationship as before. In many respects, "the extremists" were just as much hostages to "the militants" as were the "traditional Akali leaders" by the late-spring of 1992. Levels of violence associated with the Sikh ethnonationalist movement had skyrocketed, but a more intense yet fragmented movement was not necessarily as efficacious as a smaller, unified one in which "politics" controlled "the gun." The Sikh ethnonationalist movement was, in essence, potentially undermining itself. This did not necessarily translate into popular Sikh support for the Congress (I) government, but it did increase the general public's yearning for the return of "normalcy" to Punjab without the daily threats posed by either "the militants" or the Indian security forces, especially in the rural areas where a sense of lawlessness and near anarchy prevailed. In essence, "the militants" were at the height of their power in the spring of 1992, but their movement was also, in many ways, fragile as a result of these "patterns of political leadership" which had gotten progressively worse over time.

KILLING OF TOP MILITANT LEADERS AND "CONTAINMENT" OF SIKH MILITANCY IN PUNJAB

In the summer of 1992, Indian security forces scored a series of high-profile "successes" by unexpectedly tracking down and killing the chiefs of the BTFK (Chhandran), KLF, and Babbar Khalsa. The first top militant leader to fall was Rachhpal Singh Chhandran—chief of BTFK (Chhandran)—who was killed in mid-June.[17] Within a few days, eight of Chhandran's senior area commanders were also tracked down and eliminated. This was an important "success" for the security forces because the BTFK (Chhandran), which was linked to the Second (Dr Sohan Singh) Panthic Committee, had been one of the most powerful militant groups in rural parts of the Malwa region of Punjab.

Second, the security forces also succeeded in killing KLF chief Gurjant Singh Budhsinghwala, who carried a reward of 2.5 million rupees on his head, in late-July.[18] Budhsinghwala had led the KLF since the summer of 1988, and had been credited for both aligning the group to the Second (Dr Sohan Singh) Panthic Committee and also for making the KLF one of the most lethal and feared militant outfits in the state. Budhsinghwala was immediately replaced by Navroop Singh Dhotian, but the security forces quickly tracked down and eliminated Dhotian as well in an armed encounter in early-August.[19] Thus, the police succeeded in killing two successive KLF chiefs within a week of each other. The Second (Dr. Sohan Singh) Panthic Committee subsequently selected Dr Pritam Singh Sekhon to be the next KLF chief, but the KLF became a much weaker force after the death of its long-time leader, Gurjant Singh Budhsinghwala. In fact, the KLF would soon split with a section of its members forming their own splinter KLF outfit known as the "Engineer Group" independent of Sekhon.

The security forces scored their third major success by eliminating Babbar Khalsa chief Sukhdev Singh Babbar in mid-August.[20] Babbar carried a reward of 2.5 million rupees on his head and had been the longest-surviving Sikh militant in Punjab, tracing his involvement in the militant movement back to 1978 when he had originally formed the Babbar Khalsa. Sukhdev Singh Babbar's younger brother, Mehal Singh, and his chief lieutenant, Wadhawa Singh, quickly stepped in to lead the organization. While capable organizers, they lacked the personal charisma and aura of reputation attached to their predecessor. Thus, the security forces had successfully eliminated the top leaders of the BTFK (Chhandran), KLF, and Babbar Khalsa within two months of each other.

The police and security forces' "successes" in the summer of 1992 had several immediate effects on the militant movement. First, "the militants" were put into a state of fear, confusion, and suspicion after the killing of several of their top leaders because they could not ascertain who were the informers and moles within their ranks.[21] This confusion and suspicion sparked an escalating spiral of internecine bloodletting both within and between militant organizations in the summer of 1992, leading to the fratricide of entire networks of militants in the state. Second, the most powerful militant grouping—the Second (Dr Sohan Singh) Panthic Committee-led militants—became particularly weakened after the elimination of Chhandran and Budhsinghwala. Lastly, the militant groups found it increasingly difficult to attract new recruits into their ranks for the first time during the entire "Punjab crisis," thus progressively shrinking the number of active armed insurgents in the field.[22]

Regardless of these police "successes," a number of top militant leaders still remained at large and active in Punjab including KCF (Zafferwal) chief Wassan Singh Zafferwal, BTFK chief Gurbachan Singh Manochahal, KCF (Panjwar) chief Paramjit Singh Panjwar, SSF (Bittu) leader Daljeet Singh Bittu, and Second Panthic Committee chairman Dr Sohan Singh. In addition, the Babbar Khalsa remained largely intact under the leadership of Mehal Singh and Wadhawa Singh, and the KLF—while weakened overall—contained a deadly sub-unit called the "Engineer Group." Yet, the security environment in Punjab at the end of August 1992 showed signs of marked improvement. *India Today* described the improving situation as follows:

> Only three months ago, following the farcical Punjab elections, things had looked hopeless. But since then a concerted campaign mounted by the police and the army has seen the elimination of an unprecedented number of top-ranking militant leaders, and is restoring a modicum of confidence among

the common people. At least for the moment...The signs of an improved situation, like an unseasonable thaw, are suddenly discernable everywhere... the fear psychosis in the urban and rural areas [seems to be lessening].[23]

While militancy was not "crushed" by any means, "the militants" appeared to be organizationally and operationally crippled for the first time in the entire post-1984 period. Punjab police chief K.P.S. Gill hypothesized that militancy had been "contained," but it remained to be seen if "the militants" could bounce back from the security forces' "successes" against them.[24] After all, they had shown an uncanny ability to do so in the past.

September 1992 Municipal Committee Elections and the Akalis' Gradual Movement Away from "the Militants"

The "six Panthic organizations" alliance was in a peculiar situation in the summer of 1992 as the security forces scored numerous spectacular "successes" against "the militants." Its constituent members represented diverse ideologies, and had united largely under the influence (or compulsion) of "the militants." This "coalition" of "six Panthic organizations" ranged from a party closely aligned with "the militants" (the Akali Dal-Babbar) to four "extremist" groups (the Akali Dal-Mann, Akali Dal-Baba, Akali Dal-Manjit, and SSF-Mehta/Chawla) to a section of the "traditional Akali leadership" (the Akali Dal-Badal) that had radicalized largely for strategic reasons. The "moderate" Akali Dal (Kabul/Longowal) and recently-founded "radical" Akali Dal (Talwandi) remained outside of this alliance.

The security forces' "successes" gave the constituent members of the "six Panthic organizations" alliance a potential opportunity to break away from "the militants," but none of them were willing to do so in a quick and overt fashion. First, they were not sure whether the security forces' could sustain their onslaught against "the militants." After all, "the militants" had demonstrated a remarkable tenacity in bouncing back from such setbacks in the past. Second, each of the "six Panthic organizations" feared being characterized as being a "political opportunist" by the other organizations if it moderated its ideology too drastically. Third, the constituent members of the "six Panthic organizations" lacked salient issues—except for demanding "Sikh self-determination" and opposing the "repression of the Sikhs"—with which to effectively challenge the Congress (I) governments in both Chandigarh and New Delhi.

While none of the "six Panthic organizations" dared openly disassociate from "the militants," neither could they simply fail to react to the seemingly changing ground realities in Punjab. Beant Singh's Congress (I) government was, in fact, gaining increased public legitimacy as a result of the security forces' successful operations and the party's aggressive "mass contact program." The "moderate" Akali Dal (Kabul/Longowal) and the BJP also began "mass contact programs" of their own in the late-summer of 1992, causing the constituent members of the "six Panthic organizations" to fear being left behind in rallying public support in Punjab.[25] For this reason, each of the "six Panthic organizations" tried to "hedge their bets" by, on one hand, continuing to attend the *bhog* (last rites) ceremonies of victims of state repression in order to appease "the militants" while, on the other hand, also preparing to possibly re-enter electoral politics if the government resumed the "normal" political process.

Beant Singh, in fact, gave the Akalis an increased incentive to begin breaking away from "the militants" and re-enter electoral politics when he, in concert with Narasimha Rao's central government, announced that municipal and *panchayati* elections would be held in Punjab in September 1992 and early-1993, respectively. This proclamation caused a flurry of activity within the "six Panthic organizations" alliance, beginning with Badal publicly stating that his party was not unequivocally averse to contesting future elections depending on the prevailing political situation at the time.[26] While Badal did not announce his party's plan to contest this particular election, his apparent backtracking on his previous commitment to boycott elections held under the Indian Constitution nonetheless jolted "the militants," who counted on the Akalis' continued allegiance to help build and maintain popular support for their separatist cause. Shortly after Badal's proclamation, Manjit Singh of the "extremist" AISSF (Manjit) announced that he was forming a new political party called the Akali Dal (Manjit) because the existing Sikh political parties in Punjab had, according to him, "failed to deliver the goods and give any direction to the Sikh movement."[27] In reality, Manjit Singh feared being left behind in the electoral process once it resumed.

In early-September 1992, municipal elections were held in Punjab for the first time in 13 years. These elections involved only about 30 percent of the state's population because municipal committees existed only in the urban and semi-urban areas of Punjab, most of which tended to have large Hindu-majorities. Nonetheless, the municipal committee elections were vitally important for several reasons. First, voter turnout in these elections was over 70 percent, which tripled the turnout for the February 1992 state assembly elections. Second, even though the "six Panthic organizations" alliance did not officially participate in these elections, two of its constituent members (the Akali Dal-Badal and the Akali Dal-Mann) fielded "independent" candidates in some wards and backed select independents in others.[28] Thus, the two most powerful Akali factions (or parties) re-entered the electoral political process in Punjab, although unofficially, after boycotting the state assembly and parliamentary elections held only seven months earlier. This demonstrated that their commitment to "the militants" was wavering. Finally, the election results proved that the Akalis had not lost their electoral support base in Punjab to the Congress (I). After all, Congress (I) candidates won only about 33 percent of the seats, whereas "independents" won over 60 percent.[29] Akali-backed "independents" did particularly well in smaller municipalities surrounded by rural, Sikh-majority areas. Thus, the Akalis' strategy of "hedging their bets" by continuing with their heated ethnic rhetoric against the government on one hand, while concurrently "re-entering" the electoral political process on the other appeared to be working. In the fall of 1992, Akalis of all hues were moving away from "the militants," but in a cautious and calculated manner.

DISINTEGRATION OF THE "SIX PANTHIC ORGANIZATIONS" ALLIANCE AND THE SECURITY FORCES' CONTINUED SUCCESS AGAINST "THE MILITANTS"

The constituent members of the "six Panthic organizations" alliance continued their façade of "unity" through the fall of 1992, but indications began emerging that this "unity" was breaking apart. This became evident when "the extremists" refused to support the "radical" Tohra—who was aligned with the Akali Dal (Badal)—to be re-elected SGPC president, instead wanting to field their own "extremist" candidates. Tohra was nonetheless re-elected, but the relationship between "the extremists" and the dissident "traditional Akali leadership" found in the Akali Dal (Badal) appeared to have soured.[30] The Akali Dal (Badal) and Akali Dal (Mann) subsequently erected separate political stages at religious festivals in December 1992, and openly accused each other of sabotaging unity and betraying the Sikh Panth.[31] Thus, "unity" between the Akali Dal (Badal) and Akali Dal (Mann) essentially eroded. Shortly thereafter, "unity" between "the extremists" themselves also began to unravel after the Akali Dal (Baba), Akali Dal (Manjit), and SSF (Mehta/Chawla) started erecting separate stages themselves at religious festivals. Thus, the "six Panthic organizations" alliance, which had essentially been formed under the directive of "the militants" about a year earlier, effectively imploded by late-1992 and each of its constituent members began operating independently of each other.

In late-1992, Sikh politics was more fractionalized than ever before, and the Sikh political spectrum looked like the following (Table 10.2):

At the most "moderate" end was the Akali Dal (Longowal) led by Surjit Singh Barnala, Kabul Singh, and Capt. Kanwaljit Singh. This party demanded decentralization of the Indian Union. The "radicals" consisted of the Akali Dal (Badal) led by Badal and Tohra, and the Akali Dal (Talwandi). The Akali Dal (Badal) still officially demanded the creation of a "sovereign Sikh state", but its actions indicated that it was in the process of moderating its political ideology and demands. The Akali Dal (Talwandi) continued to demand full implementation of the ASR. These three parties collectively comprised the "traditional Akali leadership."

The "extremists"—who included the Akali Dal (Mann), Akali Dal (Baba), Akali Dal (Manjit), and SSF (Mehta/Chawla)—all demanded the creation of a "sovereign Sikh state." The Akali Dal (Mann) was clearly the most powerful of the "extremist" political parties. By the end of 1992, "the extremists" were totally fractionalized with the disintegration of the "six Panthic organizations" alliance and the Damdami Taksal's reversion back to being a purely religious, as opposed to a political, institution. Thus, "the extremists" lacked any overarching political authority to help them unite, and they actively competed against each other for political support within the Sikh community.

The "militants" appeared to be operationally ravaged by the security forces' successes against them in 1992, especially through the latter half of the year. They continued to be divided into four separate groupings. The First (Zafferwal) Panthic Committee-led "militants" consisted of only the KCF (Zafferwal), whose leader had fled to Pakistan. The Second (Dr Sohan Singh) Panthic Committee-led "militants" included the KCF (Panjwar), KLF, and SSF (Bittu). KCF leader, Paramjit Singh Panjwar, was permanently based in Pakistan; the KLF was bifurcated into a group led by Dr Pritam Singh Sekhon and the "Engineer Group" led by Navneet Singh Qadian; and SSF (Bittu) leader, Daljeet Singh Bittu, was in the process of going into hiding underground in Punjab. The Third (Manochahal)

Table 10.2
Sikh Political Spectrum (Late-1992)

Moderates	Radicals	Extremists[4]	Militants/Separatists[5]
AD (L)[1]	AD (Badal)[2]	AD (Mann)	First Panthic Committee[6]
	Tohra[2]	AD (Manjit)	KCF (Zafferwal)[6]
	AD (T)[3]	AD (Baba)	Second Panthic Committee
		SSF (Mehta/Chawla)	(Dr. Sohan Singh)[7]
			SSF (Bittu)[7]
			KCF (Panjwar)[7]
			KLF (Sekhon)[7]
			KLF (Engineer)[7]
			Third Panthic Committee[8]
			BTFK (Manochahal)[8]
			Babbar Khalsa[9]
			Akali Dal (Babbar)[9]

Source: Author.

Notes: [1] Akali Dal (Longowal) led by Surjit Singh Barnala, Kabul Singh, and Capt. Kanwaljit Singh; demanding the decentralization of the Indian Union through non-violent means.

[2] Akali Dal (Badal) officially demanding the creation of a "sovereign Sikh state" by non-violent means, but moderating its ideology/demands.

[3] Akali Dal (Talwandi) demanding the full implementation of the ASR.

[4] "Extremists" only very marginally united; demanding the creation of a "sovereign Sikh state" through either violent or non-violent means.

[5] "Militants" divided into First, Second, and Third Panthic Committee-led groupings; Babbar Khalsa operates independently with Akali Dal (Babbar) as political front group.

[6] First (Zafferwal) Panthic Committee-led militants demanding Khalistan through violent means.

[7] Second (Dr. Sohan Singh) Panthic Committee-led militants demanding Khalistan through violent means.

[8] Third (Manochahal) Panthic Committee-led militants demanding Khalistan through violent means.

[9] Babbar Khalsa-Akali Dal (Babbar) combine demanding Khalistan through violent means.

Panthic Committee-led "militants" included only the BTFK (Manochahal). The BTFK's operational effectiveness was severely limited and its leader, Gurbachan Singh Manochahal, was "on-the-run" in Punjab, trying to avoid being captured or killed. The fourth militant grouping consisted of the Babbar Khalsa and its miniscule "political-arm", the Akali Dal (Babbar). All four of these militant groupings continued to demand the creation of Khalistan through violent means, but "the militants" were no longer overtly dominant in Sikh politics as they had been earlier in the year. In fact, Akalis of all hues— "moderates," "radicals," and "extremists" alike—were breaking away from their influence and the militant movement appeared to be effectively "contained," but not necessarily "crushed," by the end of 1992.

The year 1992 had been a bloody one in Punjab. The total death toll was 1,266 civilians, 252 security force personnel, and 2,111 militants.[32] In addition, 3,629 militants had been arrested. There was strong evidence that the "law-and-order" situation in the state was on the mend as most of the killings by "the militants" had occurred in the first half of the year but had dramatically tapered off. In contrast, the number of "militants" killed by security forces had risen steadily through 1992.[33] A senior Punjab government officer described the overall trend in the state by saying, "Each month the situation is better than the previous month...success leads to further success."[34] The government's security forces appeared to have gained the upper hand over "the militants", and their political support base appeared to be quickly shrinking.

AKALI PARTICIPATION IN THE JANUARY 1993 PANCHAYATI ELECTIONS

The re-establishment of the "normal" democratic political process in Punjab continued through early-1993 as the government held *panchayati* elections to choose village councils for Punjab's nearly 12,000 villages after a gap of over 12 years.[35] These elections represented the last of a four-step process to re-establish the "normal" democratic political process in the state. The first and second steps had consisted of holding parliamentary and state assembly elections in February 1992. The third step was holding municipal committee elections for Punjab's urban areas in September 1992. This fourth step—the holding of *panchayati* elections—would help restore grassroots democracy and governance to the rural, mostly Sikh-majority areas of the state.

The Akalis had boycotted the February 1992 parliamentary and state assembly elections, but had unofficially participated in the September 1992 municipal elections by supporting or fielding "independent" candidates. In contrast, the Akalis—including both the Akali Dal (Badal) and Akali Dal (Mann)—decided to openly and officially contest the January 1993 *panchayati* election. After all, "the militants" appeared to be losing their war against the Indian state, and the Akalis knew that they eventually had to re-enter the electoral political process or risk being permanently marginalized by each other or the Congress (I) in Punjab. Yet, the Akalis conveniently justified their decision to participate in these polls by explaining that winning them would help advance the "Sikh struggle."[36]

The *panchayati* elections were held in mid-January 1993 as scheduled, and recorded an unexpected voter turnout of over 80 percent.[37] This was an impressive figure considering that the rural turnout for state assembly and parliamentary elections held less than a year earlier had been only about 15 percent. The results of the *panchayati* polls were as follows: approximately 36 percent of the 66,738 seats went to the Congress (I), 34 percent to the various Akali parties, 10 percent to the Communists, and the rest to "independents," BJP, and BSP.[38] The turnout and results of these elections pointed to several important political dynamics.

First, the high level of voter turnout demonstrated that "the militants'" influence and levels of popular support in the rural areas had eroded severely. Congress (I) chief minister Beant Singh explained by saying, "After the long spell of President's Rule, people wanted grassroots democracy... We gave them a chance and they responded overwhelmingly."[39] Second, the high turnout helped enhance the political legitimacy of Beant Singh's Congress (I) government in Punjab, which had been elected with only a small percentage of the eligible electorate in the state assembly elections in February 1992. Third, the election results showed that the Akalis still retained a strong rural support base in Punjab. In fact, it was hypothesized that the Akalis would have performed better in these elections if Beant Singh had not arrested their top leaders, thus preventing them from actively campaigning. The Akalis also accused the Congress (I) of widespread pollrigging. Fourth, the Akalis realized after these elections that their main adversary in Punjab was no longer "the militants," but rather the Congress (I). Yet, the Akalis were fractionalized into eight separate political "parties," thus reducing their overall competitiveness in electoral politics. After the January 1993 *panchayati* elections, it was hypothesized by many political observers that an intense battle between the various Akali factions for dominance within Sikh politics would begin once, and if, "the militants" were definitively "crushed" in Punjab.

THE APPARENT "CRUSHING" OF SIKH MILITANCY

The "militants" were in complete disarray in early-1993. The security forces' operations, especially during the last quarter of 1992, had rolled back entire networks of militants to the point that most of the armed organizations had become nearly dysfunctional in Punjab. In the words of one militant sympathizer, "These were dark days for us."[40] But, things would get even worse. In particular, the "law-and-order" situation in Punjab received a huge boost in late-February 1993 when the highly-touted and much-feared BTFK chief, Gurbachan Singh Manochahal, was killed by Indian security forces in an encounter near Tarn Taran.[41] Manochahal carried an official bounty of three million rupees on his head and had once commanded a force of over 500 militants in the Tarn Taran and Amritsar areas.[42] Yet, Manochahal's BTFK had become so weakened by early-1993 that, in the words of one senior police officer, he had been "moving from place to place with a bedroll flung on one shoulder and an assault rifle on the other" with only two of his followers, desperately trying to avoid arrest.[43] Manochahal's elimination was significant because he traced his involvement in Sikh militancy back to the pre-Bluestar days of Bhindranwale, and because he had previously built up a formidable militant force in the Majha region. With Manochahal's death, Punjab police chief K.P.S. Gill confidently and unequivocally proclaimed that "[w]e have won the battle [against militancy] in Punjab."[44] The Sikh separatist movement, at least in the eyes of the state and the media, appeared to have been "crushed"!

The prevailing social and economic climate in Punjab also appeared to have changed dramatically by the early-spring of 1993. *India Today* perceptively described this mood as follows:

> Punjab's descent into terror and chaos was gradual. Its recovery has been swift and dramatic. A year ago the state was given up as a lost cause because every single initiative which had taken place in the previous decade had been defeated by the militants' gunpower...But the state as well as Beant Singh, has managed to thwart the prophets of doom...The killing fields are back to being the granaries of the country...The state's highways are roaring with vehicular traffic and petrol pumps and dhabas (roadside cafes) are open to business till late in the night.[45]

Although the armed Sikh separatist insurgency appeared to have been crushed, political "normalcy" had not definitively returned to Punjab. This could not be achieved until the fractionalized "traditional Akali leadership" united, moderated its rhetoric and ideology, and established clear dominance over "the extremists" in Sikh politics. Unless this occurred, the re-escalation of insurgency and separatist violence in Punjab could not be realistically ruled-out. It remained to be seen if this would occur, or if this was only a brief interlude before a re-emerging violent storm.

SUMMARY AND CONCLUSION

The period under examination in this chapter began with "the militants" at the height of their power in Punjab and all major Sikh groups, including the Akalis, acquiescing to them in support of Khalistan, but it ended with "the militants" no longer in control of Sikh politics and the Akalis beginning to break free from their directives. Several "patterns of political leadership," many of which had began in earlier years, contributed to the "containment" and the potential "crushing" of the Sikh ethnonationalist insurgency by early-1993.

First, "the militants" had become highly-fractionalized and violently competed against each other, thus undermining their own movement. The multitude of the armed militant groups were divided into four major clusters—the First (Zafferwal) Panthic Committee-led militants, the Second (Dr Sohan Singh) Panthic Committee-led militants, the Third (Manochahal) Panthic Committee-led militants, and the Babbar Khalsa. The fractionalization of "the militants" may not have been detrimental to the movement had the various armed groups not begun engaging in intense internecine competition and violence. In essence, "the militants" began fighting more against each other for dominance within the separatist movement than against the central state and its security forces. Levels of anarchy resulting from this fratricidal warfare became so intense at the grassroots level that the rural population of Punjab yearned for a return to "normalcy." Furthermore, Sikh politicians previously supportive of "the militants" began reassessing their support for such a fractionalized and internally-competitive movement. The "militants'" internal fractionalization also contributed to the security forces' ability to "turn the tide" against militancy and start decimating their ranks in an escalating "snowball"-like fashion.

Second, "the militants" lost an effective "political front" for their separatist struggle in "the extremists" for two interrelated reasons—the fractionalization of "the extremists" and the dominance of "the gun" ("the militants") over "politics" ("the extremists"). To explain, "the extremists" had become completely fractionalized by 1992 into four competing organizations—the Akali Dal (Mann), AISSF (Manjit), Akali Dal (Baba), and SSF (Mehta/Chawla). These "extremist" organizations vied with each other for dominance within the political wing of the Sikh ethnonationalist movement in contrast to being almost completely united earlier. This divided the movement's extensive Sikh political support base and allowed the "traditional Akali leaders" to begin reasserting themselves in Sikh politics, thus reducing the movement's overall prospects for attaining success. The "gun" ("the militants") also became completely dominant over "politics" ("the extremists"), instead of vice-versa or having a mutually-symbiotic relationship as was the case in the past. In many respects, "the extremists" became just as much hostages to "the militants" as the "traditional Akali leadership" had become. For example, the "six Panthic organizations" alliance was one forged out of fear of "the militants" rather than voluntary cooperation with them. As the security forces began "turning the tide" against "the militants," "the extremists" began gradually breaking free of the militants and re-entering the "normal" democratic political process in order to compete with the "traditional Akali leadership." This robbed "the militants" of an effective political front with which to propagate their cause and retain an institutionalized political support base, thus weakening the separatist movement.

Third, a qualitatively new "pattern of political leadership"—namely, a shift in the relationship amongst ruling state elites—emerged during the period under examination in this chapter and contributed to the Indian state's ability to "contain" the Sikh separatist insurgency. To explain, during most of the "Punjab crisis," governing state elites had remained either internally-divided within the ruling party (that is, the Darbara Singh–Zail Singh feud, Bhajan Lal's intransigence to compromise and the dysfunctional Rajiv Gandhi–Buta Singh relationship), or divided within the ruling coalition (that is, V.P. Singh's reliance on the BJP and Communists to stay in power, and Chandra Shekhar's reliance on the Congress (I)). These divisions had forestalled the formulation and implementation of a coherent and effective approach to handling the "Punjab problem." This changed when Narasimha Rao's Congress (I) government consolidated its power in New Delhi after the February 1992 elections in Punjab, and the Congress (I) also came into power in the state under the leadership of Rao's close loyalist—Beant Singh. With the effective forging of unity amongst governing state elites, the Narasimha Rao-Beant Singh-K.P.S. Gill team was able to formulate and implement a coherent policy on Punjab consisting of limiting the Akalis' ability to inflame ethnic sentiments, physically eliminating "the militants" with a strict draconian "law-and-order" approach, and strategically holding a series of democratic elections designed to prompt Sikh political elites—including both "the extremists" and the "traditional Akali leadership"—to begin re-entering the "normal" democratic political process. This co-ordinated state action under the leadership of unified governing elites helped the government "turn the tide" against "the militants," and also contributed to Sikh political actors beginning to break away from "the militants" and start re-entering more "normal" modes of politics. This gradual defection further weakened the Sikh separatist movement in Punjab.

Due to the definitive culmination of these emerging "patterns of political leadership," the Sikh ethnonationalist insurgency was "contained" and apparently "crushed" by early-1993. These patterns included the fractionalization of "the militants," "the militants'" loss of an effective "political front" in the completely-fractionalized "extremists," and the effective forging of unity amongst ruling states elites. Yet, political "normalcy" had not definitively returned to Punjab and the re-escalation of armed Sikh militancy could not be realistically ruled out until the "traditional Akali leadership" united, moderated and fully re-entered the normal political process, and until it also emerged clearly dominant over "the extremists" in Sikh politics. It remained to be seen how, and if, this would occur, or if militancy and violence would re-escalate in Punjab.

NOTES

1. Jagdev Singh Talwandi had broken-off from the Akali Dal (Badal) shortly after the announcement of elections to be held in February 1992, and had reinvigorated the Akali Dal (Talwandi).
2. For an overview of these failed talks between the Punjab Chief Minister, Beant Singh, and Haryana Chief Minister, Bhajan Lal, see Venkitesh Ramakrishnan, "A Futile Round: Haryana Stalls Punjab Package," *Frontline*, 5 June 1992, 25–26.
3. B.R. Jaitely, "Beant Singh: 'We fought Politically, and Won'," *Indian Express*, 8 March 1992, 3.
4. Indian Express, "Punjab Problem is that of Law and Order, Says Beant Singh," *Indian Express*, 13 March 1992, 9; and Ramesh Vinayak, "Punjab: Paying the Price," *India Today*, 31 March 1992, 28.
5. Shekhar Gupta and Kanwar Sandhu, "K.P.S. Gill: 'Pakistan Has Lost'," *India Today*, 15 April 1993, 43.
6. Quoted in Venkitesh Ramakrishnan, "'Boycott has united Sikhs:' Kuldeep Singh Wadala" *Frontline*, 27 March 1992, 36.
7. Rakesh Bhandari, "Panthic Bodies for Freedom," *Hindustan Times*, 19 March 1992, 20; and The Hindu, "Six Panthic Bodies Want Beant Govt. Dismissed," *The Hindu*, 19 March 1992, 9.
8. In addition to the "moderate" Akali Dal (Kabul), the "extremist" Akali Dal (Talwandi) also did not explicitly endorse the demand for Khalistan, but did demand the full implementation of the ASR.
9. Ramesh Vinayak, "Punjab: A Separatist Surge," *India Today*, 15 April 1992, 26.
10. For example, see Venkitesh Ramakrishnan, "'For A Sovereign Sikh State:' G.S. Tohra and S.S. Mann Speak," *Frontline*, 5 June 1992, 28–29; and Tribune News Service, "Action Plan Soon: Badal," *The Tribune*, 5 May 1992, 1.

11. Satya Pal Dang, "Perspective: Now is the time for Action," *Indian Express*, 29 March 1992, 14.

12. Quoted in Venkitesh Ramakrishnan, "'For a Sovereign Sikh State:' G.S. Tohra and S.S. Mann speak," *Frontline*, 5 June 1992, 28 and 29. Both Tohra and Mann also reportedly promised to struggle for the creation of Khalistan until their "last breath." Tribune News Service, "Three Top Akali Leaders Freed,"*The Tribune*, 18 April 1992, 1.

13. For details see Tribune News Service, "Akali Plan to Meet UN Chief Goes Awry," *The Tribune*, 21 April 1992, 1 and 12.

14. See Kanwar Sandhu and Ramesh Vinayak, "Punjab: Area of Darkness," *India Today*, 15 July 1992, 25–26; and Tribune Correspondent, "No Grant for Pro-militant Panchayats," *The Tribune*, 3 June 1992, 1.

15. Kanwar Sandhu and Ramesh Vinayak, "Punjab: Area of Darkness," *India Today*, 15 July 1992, 22.

16. For an exhaustive list of militant groups including "minor" ones, see K.P.S. Gill, "Endgame in Punjab, 1988–93," in *Terror and Containment: Perspectives of India's Internal Security*, ed. K.P.S. Gill. (New Delhi: Gyan Publishing House, 2001), 81.

17. Tribune News Service, "Pressure on Militants to Mount: Gill," *The Tribune*, 24 June 1992, 1.

18. Tribune News Service, "Budhsinghwala Shot Dead," *The Tribune*, 31 July 1992, 1.

19. Tribune Correspondent, "New KLF Chief Shot Dead," *The Tribune*, 4 August 1992, 1 and 12; and Tarun J. Tejpal and Ramesh Vinayak, "Punjab: New Signs of Confidence," *India Today*, 15 September 1992, 32.

20. Tribune News Service, "Sukhdev Singh Babbar Shot Dead," *The Tribune*, 10 August 1992, 1 and 16.

21. Tarun J. Tejpal and Ramesh Vinayak, "Punjab: New Signs of Confidence," *India Today*, 15 September 1992, 32.

22. For figures on the elimination of Sikh militants during this period, see Table 3 in Joshi, "Combating Terrorism in Punjab: Indian Democracy in Crisis," in *Rivalry and Revolution in South and East Asia*, ed. Partha S. Ghosh (Brookfield, VT: Ashgate Publishing, 1997), 200.

23. Tarun J. Tejpal and Ramesh Vinayak, "Punjab: New Signs of Confidence," *India Today*, 15 September 1992, 30.

24. Ibid., 32.

25. The Tribune, "Signs of Life at Last," *The Tribune*, 31 July 1992, 4.

26. Tribune News Service, "Dal (B) Not Averse to Poll: Badal," *The Tribune*, 29 July 1992, 1.

27. K.S. Chawla, "Akalis Talk Unity, but Dals Go Their Own Ways," *The Tribune*, 28 August 1992, 1.

28. For details of these municipal elections see Ramesh Vinayak, "An Honest Election, At Last: Independents Win, Congress (I) Claims Victory," *India Today*, 30 September 1992, 24; and Venkitesh Ramakrishnan, "Punjab Paradox: For the Congress (I), Success Begets Failure," *Frontline*, 9 October 1992, 40.

29. Ibid. The Congress (I)'s "poor" performance in these elections can also be possibly explained by the fact that municipal elections are generally contested around local issues as opposed to simple partisan ones.

30. For details of these elections, see H.S. Bhanwer, "Tohra Re-elected SGPC Chief," *The Tribune*, 1 December 1992, 1 and 6.

31. P.P.S. Gill, "Akali Dal (B) Plans Parliament Gherao," *The Tribune*, 27 December 1992, 1.

32. Paul Wallace, "Political Violence and Terrorism in India: The Crisis of Identity," in *Terrorism in Context,* ed. Martha Crenshaw (College Station, PA: The Pennsylvania State University Press, 1995), 354.

33. For details, see Joshi, "Combating Terrorism," 200.

34. Manoj Joshi, "The Turnaround, Positive Signs in the Troubled State," *Frontline,* 20 November 1992, 26.

35. Venkitesh Ramakrishnan, "A Vote for Peace: The Message from the Civic Elections," *Frontline,* 26 February 1993, 15.

36. Ibid., 16.

37. Ibid., 15; and Ramesh Vinayak, "Punjab: A Victory for Hope," *India Today,* 15 February 1993, 22.

38. Venkitesh Ramakrishnan, "A Vote for Peace: The Message from the Civic Elections," *Frontline,* 26 February 1993, 15.

39. Ibid., 16.

40. Interview with senior Khalistani activist and intellectual advisor involved in the militant movement since 1986, 15 July 2002 (Interview with Author; Fremont, California [USA]).

41. U.N.I., "Manochahal Killed Near Tarn Taran," *The Tribune,* 1 March 1993, 1 and 4.

42. Kanwar Sandhu, "G.S. Manochahal: How The Trap Was Laid," *India Today,* 31 March 1993, 57.

43. Quoted in Kanwar Sandhu, "Punjab: Normal Life at Last," *India Today,* 28 February 1993, 42.

44. Kanwar Sandhu, "G.S. Manochahal: How The Trap Was Laid," *India Today,* 31 March 1993, 56.

45. Kanwar Sandhu, "Punjab: Normal Life at Last," *India Today,* 28 February 1993, 40.

11

Return of Normalcy to Punjab
and Sikh Politics (1993–1997)

AKALI DAL (BADAL)'S EMERGING
ASCENDANCE IN SIKH POLITICS

The "law-and-order" situation in Punjab seemed to be quickly on the mend in early-1993 as the government security forces appeared to be wiping out the remaining militants in Punjab's countryside, and restoring increased confidence in the official institutions of the state. *India Today* perceptively described the emerging situation as follows:

> The vendors of terror (the militants) have cleared packed up. The guns are there but they belong to the police. The militants press handouts and threatening calls to newspaper offices have ceased…Now, for the first time in a decade, …[the border districts] have not reported any terrorist strikes in the past three months.[1]

Nonetheless, political "normalcy" had not yet returned to Sikh and Punjab politics. After all, the "traditional Akali leadership" remained divided and individual leaders competed against each other by continuing to employ heated ethnic rhetoric. Furthermore, the "traditional Akali leadership" had not emerged clearly dominant over "the extremists." Until this occurred, the re-escalation of Sikh militancy in Punjab could not be definitively ruled out.

Nonetheless, the annual Holla Mohalla festival held at Anandpur Sahib (the birthplace of the Khalsa) in mid-March 1993 demonstrated the improving security situation in the state. For the first time in 13 years, the Congress (I) eagerly erected a political stage at this festival.[2] This was a notable development because, only a year earlier, the Congress (I) did not dare to participate, fearing for the physical safety of its members. The "radical" Akali Dal (Badal) and "extremist" Akali Dal (Mann), two of the most powerful Akali parties, also predictably set up stages at this gathering. The other Akali parties, which by this time had become relatively minor players in Sikh politics, were denied permission for stage platforms at this festival by the civil administration.

The Akali Dal (Badal) and Akali Dal (Mann) adopted almost identical resolutions at this conference which included demanding the dismissal of Beant Singh's Congress (I) government and an end to state repression. But, a clear ideological schism also emerged between these parties as the Akali Dal (Badal) demanded that the government implement the Anandpur Sahib Resolution (ASR), whereas the Akali Dal (Mann) stuck to its insistence for the creation of a "sovereign Sikh state."[3] The Akali Dal (Badal)'s backtracking from its demand for a "sovereign Sikh state" demonstrated that the party was starting to moderate and return to its original ideological position of the late-1970s and early-1980s. Yet, it was uncertain which Akali party—the Akali Dal (Badal) or Akali Dal (Mann)—had more political support within the Sikh community. This question promised to be answered more definitively in May 1993 with the by-election for the vacant Jalandhar parliamentary seat in Punjab.

Campaigning for this by-election ensued largely free of threats previously posed by "the militants," and party leaders flocked to the constituency to support their respective candidates. The results of this by-election were as follows: 286,922 votes for the Congress (I) candidate, 115,985 for the Akali Dal (Badal) candidate, and only 18,319 for the Akali Dal (Amritsar) candidate.[4] These results demonstrated three things. First, they indicated that the Akali Dal (Badal) was the most powerful Akali party in Sikh politics at the time. Second, they showed that "extremist" ideology, as embodied in the Akali Dal (Mann), had lost significant support within the Sikh community. In essence, being associated with separatism—whether violent or non-violent—was clearly becoming a political liability for the Akalis, whereas it had been an asset only a year earlier. Third, and somewhat paradoxically, these results demonstrated that Parkash Singh Badal was potentially vulnerable if the other Akali leaders could unite against him before he grew even stronger. After all, Badal's candidate in this by-election lost to the Congress (I) candidate by a rather large margin.

This realization prompted several of the other "traditional Akali leaders"—including Jagdev Singh Talwandi of the Akali Dal (Talwandi), Surjit Singh Barnala of the Akali Dal (Longowal), and Capt. Amarinder Singh of the Akali Dal (Panthic)—to informally "unite" in mid-1993 to try to arrest Badal's growing power. In fact, they began holding joint rallies at Sikh religious festivals. These leaders expressed their interest in coalescing around Gurcharan Singh Tohra to form a united Akali Dal against Badal, but Tohra shirked at playing this role because he feared openly challenging Badal.[5] In contrast, these leaders did not want to unite around Simranjeet Singh Mann since his "extremist" ideology was quickly losing political appeal with the Sikh community. Thus, three competing poles of power appeared to be emerging within Akali politics—the Akali Dal (Badal), the other "traditional Akali leaders," and "the extremists."

RESIDUAL ACTS OF POLITICAL VIOLENCE BY SIKH MILITANTS

After the killing of BTFK chief Gurbachan Singh Manochahal in February 1993, Punjab police chief K.P.S. Gill had confidently announced that militancy had been "crushed" in Punjab. This was largely correct, but the year of 1993 was not totally free of militant violence. In particular, "the militants" tried to reassert themselves in a spectacular way in September 1993 by exploding a car bomb outside the New Delhi office of the Youth Congress (I) leader, Maninderjit Singh Bitta, injuring him and killing several of his security guards.[6] This attack was the handiwork of the "Engineer Group" within the KLF, and it demonstrated that militant groups continued to try to confront the Indian state by targeting high-profile targets in urban areas outside of Punjab since they could no longer sustain a rural insurgency within the state.[7] The police and security forces, in fact, continued their successful operations against suspected militants and their sympathizers through late-1993, scoring a dramatic success in November 1993 when they arrested Dr Sohan Singh—the mastermind behind the once powerful Second Panthic Committee.[8]

The Sikh political spectrum at the end of 1993 looked like the following (Table 11.1):

The Akali Dal (Longowal) led by Surjit Singh Barnala and the Akali Dal (Panthic) led by Capt. Amarinder Singh were at the most "moderate" end of Sikh politics. Yet, both were relatively minor political players. The "radicals" consisted of the Akali Dal (Talwandi) and the Akali Dal (Badal). The latter included both Badal and Tohra. The "moderates" officially demanded the decentralization of the Indian Union whereas "the radicals"

Table 11.1
Sikh Political Spectrum (Late-1993)

Moderates[1]	Radicals	Extremists[4]	Militants/Separatists[5]
AD (L)[2]	AD (Badal)[3]	AD (Mann)	KLF (Engineer)
AD (Panthic)[2]	Tohra[3]	AD (Manjit)	Babbar Khalsa[6]
	AD (T)[2]	AD (Baba)	Akali Dal (Babbar)[6]
		SSF (Mehta/Chawla)	

Source: Author.

Notes: [1] The "moderate" Akali Dal (Longowal) led by Surjit Singh Barnala and Akali Dal (Panthic) led by Amarinder Singh; both demanding the decentralization of the Indian Union through non-violent means.

[2] Akali Dal (Longowal), Akali Dal (Panthic), and Akali Dal (Talwandi) united against Akali Dal (Badal).

[3] Akali Dal (Badal) and its leaders demanding implementation of the ASR by non-violent means.

[4] "The extremists" completely fractionalized; demanding either "Khalsa Raj" or the creation of a "sovereign Sikh state" through non-violent means.

[5] Most major "militant" groups defunct and based in Pakistan; remaining "militant" groups demanding Khalistan through violent means.

[6] Babbar Khalsa–Akali Dal (Babbar) combine.

continued to demand the implementation of the ASR. The "radical" Akali Dal (Talwandi) had forged "unity" with the "moderate" Akali Dal (Longowal) and Akali Dal (Panthic) earlier in the summer of 1993. The forging of "unity" between these disparate factions demonstrated that ideological differences between "traditional Akali leaders" were becoming less important than pure power considerations in an increasingly post-militancy Punjab.

The "extremists" were completely fractionalized in late-1993, and consisted of the Akali Dal (Mann), Akali Dal (Baba), Akali Dal (Manjit), and the SSF (Mehta/Chawla).[9] The Akali Dal (Mann) was clearly the most powerful "extremist" party, and its unequivocal goal was the creation of a "sovereign Sikh state" but through democratic, non-violent means. The Akali Dal (Baba), Akali Dal (Manjit), and SSF (Mehta/Chawla)— all relatively minor political players by now—shifted between demanding "Khalsa Raj" and the creation of a "sovereign Sikh state."

The "militants" had been decimated by the end of 1993. Through the year, the police had killed 794 suspected militants, arrested 970, and 379 voluntarily surrendered.[10] The most telling figure demonstrating the decline of insurgency was the relatively small number of people killed by "the militants" in 1993—only 24 civilians and 23 security force personnel. In contrast, the comparative figures for 1992 had been 1,266 and 252.[11]

The only "militant" outfits capable of armed operations at the end of 1993 were the "Engineer Group" within the KLF led by Navneet Singh Qadian and a Babbar Khalsa cell based near Chandigarh. All other militant groups were operationally defunct, and their leaders were either dead or in hiding, mostly in Pakistan.[12]

THE OTHER "TRADITIONAL AKALI LEADERS'" ATTEMPTS TO UNITE AGAINST THE AKALI DAL (BADAL)

Beant Singh's Congress (I) government in Punjab had built up a degree of legitimacy since its election into power in February 1992, but, by early-1994, its level of popular support was quickly eroding for several reasons. First, the crowning achievement of Beant Singh's government—the apparent "crushing" of Sikh militancy—was quickly fading into the background as other, mostly economic, issues were becoming more salient in Punjab's political discourse.[13] Second, corruption had become so rampant in Beant Singh's government that 25 out of his 30 cabinet ministers were either being investigated for misdeeds or were actually facing criminal charges.[14] Third, the Punjab police remained a brutal and unruly force which acted with the same ruthlessness against the general population with which it had previously acted against "the militants." In essence, it had failed to revert back to more "normal" modes of operation in increasingly post-militancy Punjab.[15] Lastly, Beant Singh was losing his unchallenged control over Punjab's Congress (I) party as new, younger leaders were quickly emerging to the forefront of the organization.

In light of this weakening of the Congress (I) party, forging "unity" became increasingly important for Akali leaders, other than Badal, who wanted to retain their quickly eroding power within Sikh politics and also effectively compete with the Congress (I). For these reasons, they renewed their efforts to forge increased "unity." This process began in earnest when Capt. Amarinder Singh, leader of the Akali Dal (Panthic), urged "acting" Akal Takht *jathedar* Prof. Manjit Singh to dissolve all Akali factions and form a united "Shiromani Akali Dal" under the leadership of Tohra.[16] Both Talwandi and Barnala also supported this idea. After all, these leaders were individually much weaker than Badal, and thus wanted to either subsume Badal under a collective leadership arrangement or collectively emerge stronger than him by unifying together. In essence, forging unity either with or without Badal was a matter of political survival for these other individual "traditional Akali leaders." In contrast, Badal, who led the comparatively strongest Akali party, had little incentive to unite with any of these other Akali factions unless they unequivocally accepted his leadership. Thus, it was becoming increasingly evident that a battle between Badal and the other "traditional Akali leaders" for supremacy within Sikh politics in apparent post-militancy Punjab was about to begin!

"Amritsar Declaration" and Formation of the Akali Dal (Amritsar) against Badal

In April 1994, the SGPC and Akal Takht *jathedar* sponsored a series of "Khalsa marches" associated with the 400th birthday of the 6th Sikh guru, Hargobind. On the last day of the Baisakhi "Khalsa march," all major Akali and Sikh leaders gathered on a common *dharmhik* (religious) stage under the supervision of the "acting" Akal Takht *jathedar*, Prof. Manjit Singh. What occurred next was largely unexpected, but it significantly altered the immediate structure of internal Sikh politics. One-by-one various Akali leaders appealed to Prof. Manjit Singh to intervene in helping forge "Panthic unity," and each presented him a handwritten letter agreeing to resign from the leadership post of his respective political party for the Panth's wider interests.[17] These leaders included Simranjeet Singh Mann, Capt. Amarinder Singh, Surjit Singh Barnala, Jagdev Singh Talwandi, Bhai Manjit Singh, and Col. Jasmer Singh Bala of the Akali Dal (Babbar). Tohra, who was engaged in an intra-party tussle with Badal at the time, also agreed to abide by any decision taken by Prof. Manjit Singh.[18]

It is uncertain whether these moves were "pre-planned" by these other Akali leaders, but, nonetheless, they put Badal into an embarrassing position in front of the mammoth Baisakhi day gathering at Anandpur Sahib. Badal responded to these other Akali leaders' overtures by agreeing to participate in any moves undertaken by the Akal Takht *jathedar* to help forge unity, but he did so only after making a long and emotional speech in which he characterized the "unity efforts" as being a part of a pre-planned conspiracy to isolate him in Sikh politics.[19] Before storming out of the gathering with hundreds of his supporters, Badal handed Prof. Manjit Singh a signed, blank piece of paper to fill-in as he wished in the best interests of the Panth. Thus, Badal appeared headed for a confrontation with the other Akali leaders and, quite possibly, with the "acting" *Jathedar* of the Akal Takht.

A few days later, the Akali Dal (Badal) officially responded to Prof. Manjit Singh's actions by sending him a formal letter which emphasized three main points. First, Badal expressed his profound respect for the

Akal Takht, but insinuated that its *jathedar* had unknowingly become a partisan player in Akali politics through the machinations of the other Akali leaders.[20] Second, Badal asked Prof. Manjit Singh to allow the Sikh *quam* to determine its own dominant leadership by waiting for the SGPC general house elections which were expected to be held within a year.[21] Third, Badal argued that "unity" could only be forged based on common principles and ideology, and pointed out that the political demands of the other Akali leaders ranged from Mann's demand for a "sovereign Sikh state" to Barnala's firm commitment to the unity of India.[22]

In response, Prof. Manjit Singh dismissed Badal's insinuations that he was acting in a partisan way by saying, "My only concern is that all the leaders should sit together and groupism should end...I have nothing to gain out of this controversy.[23] He also urged Badal to give him an official letter indicating his willingness to abide by any verdict rendered by the Akal Takht. Prof. Manjit Singh's apparent insistence on forging unity alarmed Badal who feared that the Head Priests would issue a formal *hukamnama* (edict) to this effect, thus putting him in direct confrontation with the Akal Takht. Wanting to avoid this predicament, Badal resigned from the presidency of his party and turned its leadership over to a five-member presidium committee which, in turn, voted to "dissolve" the party altogether.[24] By dissolving the party, Badal, in effect, made himself immune from any *hukamnama* issued by the Head Priests ordering all Akali parties to unite.

With the Akali Dal (Badal) supposedly defunct and out of the political scene, Prof. Manjit Singh and the Head Priests were left in a quandary about how to proceed in forging complete Akali unity. With little other recourse of action, they nonetheless decided to go ahead with their efforts without including the Akali Dal (Badal). Thus, on 1 May 1994, Prof. Manjit Singh announced the formation of a unified political party called the "Akali Dal (Amritsar)" which was to be led by a presidium of leaders including Capt. Amarinder Singh, Barnala, Talwandi, Bhai Manjit Singh, Mann, and Col. Jasmer Singh Bala.[25] Thus, the leaders of the "moderate" Akali Dal (Panthic), "moderate" Akali Dal (Longowal), "radical" Akali Dal (Talwandi), "extremist" Akali Dal (Manjit), "extremist" Akali Dal (Mann), and "extremist/militant" Akali Dal (Babbar) all found representation in this single, "unified" political party. The presidium leaders of the Akali Dal (Amritsar) subsequently signed a pledge promising to "work together for the welfare of our community after sinking all our differences," and to "abstain from mutual legpulling (undermining each other)."[26] Tohra was not given a seat in the presidium's leadership since he was not the formal head of any political party, but he was nonetheless considered to be the Akali Dal (Amritsar)'s top symbolic leader and projected to be its candidate for the chief ministership of Punjab if the party ever came into power. This arrangement actually served Tohra's interests well; after all, he did not want to be only one of potentially seven equals in the party's presidium leadership.

The Akali Dal (Amritsar)'s political ideology and goals were enshrined in its official manifesto called the "Amritsar Declaration," which was a product of mutual compromise between the ideologically-diverse constituent members of the party. The "Amritsar Declaration" read in part as follows:

> The Akali Dal being a champion of Punjabi culture based on Guru Granth Sahib reiterates its commitment for waging a struggle within democratic norms for the creation of such a separate region for the Sikhs, where they could enjoy glow of freedom...This sub-continent needs restructuring of its polity into a confederation of various cultures...If the Government of India fails to restructure the Indian polity into a federal structure, the Akali Dal would be left with no other alternative, but to wage a struggle for a sovereign Sikh state.[27]

Thus, the "Amritsar Declaration" was a "catch-all" document designed to accommodate the diverse political ideologies of each of the constituent members of the Akali Dal (Amritsar), ranging from "the moderates" to "the extremists." The demand to decentralize the Indian Union pleased both "the moderates" and "the radicals" within the party, whereas the phrase threatening to "wage a struggle for a sovereign Sikh state" placated "the extremists." Yet, the "Amritsar Declaration" purposely did not specify a timetable for when this struggle for "a sovereign Sikh state" would begin, and nor did it delineate what would constitute a sufficient restructuring of the Indian polity into a "federal structure." This vagueness was, in fact, necessary to ensure that none of the constituent members of the Akali Dal (Amritsar) were boxed into an uncomfortable ideological corner, thus potentially undermining the newly-forged "unity." The "extremist" Akali Dal (Baba) and SSF (Mehta/Chawla), both of which had informally "united" with each other, remained aloof from the collective arrangement because they refused to accept Prof. Manjit Singh as being the Akal Takht *jathedar*. Instead, they continued to claim that the Jasbir Singh Rode was the legitimate holder of this position. Thus, the vast majority of Akali factions, except for the Akali Dal (Baba) and SSF (Mehta/Chawla), had officially "united" together within the Akali Dal (Amritsar) in opposition to Badal. Yet, it remained to be seen which Akali grouping—the supposedly defunct Akali Dal (Badal) or the newly-founded unified Akali Dal (Amritsar)—had more political support within the Sikh community. The answer to this question would ultimately affect the direction of Sikh politics and the deepening sense of "normalcy" in Punjab.

INCREASING STRENGTH OF THE AKALI DAL (BADAL) AND THE CONCURRENT WEAKENING OF THE AKALI DAL (AMRITSAR) IN SIKH POLITICS

"Acting" Akal Takht *jathedar* Prof. Manjit Singh remained true to his word not to become an overtly partisan player in Akali politics; he refrained from issuing a formal *hukamnama* forcing the erstwhile Akali Dal (Badal) to unify with the Akali Dal (Amritsar). Badal took advantage of Prof. Manjit Singh's inaction in this regard by reactivating his political party, and subsequently gearing up for the upcoming Nakodar and Ajnala state assembly seat by-elections scheduled for June 1994. These by-elections would give him a chance to test his party's strength within the Sikh community. The Akali Dal (Badal)'s candidates were pitted against those of the Congress (I). In contrast, the Akali Dal (Amritsar) chose not to contest these by-elections because it supposedly lacked sufficient time to organize an effective campaign, but Akali Dal (Amritsar) activists did allegedly campaign for Congress (I) candidates in the attempt to undermine the Akali Dal (Badal).[28]

The Akali Dal (Badal) purposely avoided religious and ethnic issues during its' campaign, instead focusing primarily on secular issues such as the rising price of essential commodities, police excesses, corruption in government, and unemployment.[29] In the Nakodar by-election, the Congress (I) candidate defeated the Akali Dal (Badal) candidate by a small margin with 37,526 votes to 32,316.[30] In contrast, the Akali Dal (Badal) candidate defeated the Congress (I) candidate in the Ajnala by-election with 46,856 votes to 36,542.[31] The results of these two by-elections demonstrated that the Akali Dal (Badal) could effectively compete with the Congress (I) in electoral politics with its increasingly moderate ideology, and that it was most likely the dominant Akali party in Sikh politics. The Akali Dal (Badal)'s "success" in these by-elections in June 1994 resulted in a flood of defections from the Akali Dal (Amritsar) to the Akali Dal (Badal), alarming the other Akali leaders. After these by-elections, the Akali Dal (Badal) moderated its rhetoric and image even further by, for example, stating that one of its main goals was to unite Punjab's Sikhs, Hindus, Muslims, and Christians into a composite Punjabi identity instead of focusing exclusively on parochial ethnic issues.[32] The Akali Dal (Badal) was, in fact, successfully expanding its support base to also include Hindus while concurrently maintaining its core Sikh support base.

In contrast, the Akali Dal (Amritsar) was becoming weaker in the late-spring of 1994 due to the defection of its activists to the Akali Dal (Badal) and internal bickering between its ideologically-diverse constituent members. The main source of friction within the Akali Dal (Amritsar) was Mann who refused to give-up his insistence on the creation of a "sovereign Sikh state." This demand embarrassed the "traditional Akali leaders" in the Akali Dal (Amritsar), who wanted to compete with the Akali Dal (Badal) by portraying a more moderate and inclusive image of themselves and their party. One Akali Dal (Amritsar) leader, in fact, described Mann as being "an albatross around the neck of the party" who was ruining its electoral prospects in the state.[33] Thus, the Akali Dal (Badal) was gaining strength in Punjab and Sikh politics in mid-1994, whereas the Akali Dal (Amritsar) was concurrently getting weaker.

Renewed Interest in Forging "Akali Unity" after the September 1994 Panchayat Samiti and Zila Parishad Elections

The Akalis went into the September 1994 *panchayat samiti* and *zila parishad* polls bifurcated into the Akali Dal (Badal) and the internally-divided Akali Dal (Amritsar). These elections, the first of their kind in about 13 years, would aggregate local government in the rural areas from the *panchayat* (village council) level to both the *panchayat samiti* (blocks of about 10 to 15 villages) and *zila parishad* (district) levels. The elections involved both "direct" voting by villagers and "indirect" voting by members of village councils elected earlier in 1993.[34] The election results in Punjab's 14 districts were as follows: the Congress (I) emerged dominant in ten districts, the Congress (I) and the Akali Dal (Badal) virtually tied in another, the Akali Dal (Badal) won in two districts, and the Akali Dal (Amritsar) emerged victorious in one.[35]

The Akalis' overall "disappointing" performance in these elections was explained by two likely factors. First, the results may have been biased by the fact that village councilmen, whose "indirect" voting carried significant electoral weight, had been elected in early-1993 when Beant Singh's Congress (I) government was at the peak of its popularity. Second, Akali disunity also probably affected the poll results. Even though the Akali Dal (Badal) was clearly the most dominant Akali party, the Akali Dal (Amritsar) could still siphon off enough Sikh votes to allow the Congress (I) to win in numerous districts. For its part, leaders of the Akali Dal (Amritsar) realized that their party could not defeat the Akali Dal (Badal) in electoral politics even though it had united six different Akali factions together into a singular, "unified" organization. Thus, both the Akali Dal (Badal) and Akali Dal (Amritsar) had compelling reasons of their own to forge unity after analyzing the results of the September 1994 *panchayat samiti* and *zila parishad* elections. For this reason, representatives of both parties began "behind-the-scenes" talks with each other and the "acting" Akal Takht *jathedar* Prof. Manjit Singh to try to forge complete Akali "unity" in the late-fall of 1994.

By the end of 1994, the Sikh political spectrum consisted almost exclusively of three different Akali groupings and looked like the following (Table 11.2):

Table 11.2
Sikh Political Spectrum (Late-1994)

Moderates	Radicals	Extremists	Militants/Separatists
AD (L)[1]	AD (Badal)[2]	AD (Mann)[1]	Babbar Khalsa
AD (Panthic)[1]	Tohra[1]	AD (Manjit)[1]	
	AD (T)[1]	UAD (Baba)[3]	
		SSF (Mehta/Chawla)[3]	
		AD (Babbar)[1]	

Source: Author.

Notes: [1] Constituent members of the united Akali Dal (Amritsar) including Tohra, Akali Dal (Longowal) led by Barnala, Akali Dal (Panthic) led by Amarinder Singh, Akali Dal (Talwandi), Akali Dal (Mann), Akali Dal (Manjit), and Akali Dal (Babbar); ideology contained in the "Amritsar Declaration" demanding massive decentralization of power from the center to the states and threatening to launch a struggle for the creation of a "sovereign Sikh state" through non-violent means.

       [2] Akali Dal (Badal) demanding implementation of the ASR by non-violent means .

       [3] UAD (Baba)-SSF (Mehta/Chawla) alliance shifting between demanding "Khalsa Raj" and the creation of a "sovereign Sikh state" through non-violent means.

The first Akali party was the powerful "moderate/radical" Akali Dal (Badal). The second Akali grouping was the ideologically-diverse and internally factionalized Akali Dal (Amritsar) which consisted of six constituent members—the "moderate" Akali Dal (Longowal) led by Barnala, "moderate" Akali Dal (Panthic) led by Capt. Amarinder Singh, "radical" Akali Dal (Talwandi), "extremist" Akali Dal (Mann), "extremist" Akali Dal (Manjit), and "extremist/militant" Akali Dal (Babbar). Tohra was also a member of the Akali Dal (Amritsar) alliance. The third Akali grouping consisted of the relatively minor "extremist" UAD (Baba) and SSF (Mehta/ Chawla), both of which would eventually cease to exist in Sikh politics. The only "militant" outfit still capable of armed strikes was a small unit of the Babbar Khalsa based near Chandigarh. In an amazing statistic, there had been no militancy-related deaths in 1994—a first for the state in over 15 years!

REUNIFICATION OF THE "TRADITIONAL AKALI LEADERSHIP" INTO THE "SHIROMANI AKALI DAL" AND THE DIMINISHING STRENGTH OF "THE EXTREMISTS"

In the beginning of 1995, efforts to forge complete Akali unity intensified. These efforts were prompted by the Akali Dal (Badal) and Akali Dal (Amritsar)'s renewed interests in uniting, Prof. Manjit Singh's threat to issue a formal *hukamnama* forcing the Akalis to unite, and the desire of "traditional Akali leaders" within the Akali Dal (Amritsar) to disassociate them from Mann and "the extremists." This process gained momentum in mid-January 1995 when Prof. Manjit Singh made a public appeal to leaders of the Akali Dal (Badal) and Akali Dal (Amritsar) to hammer out their differences for the larger collective interests of the Sikh Panth. This appeal prompted Akali Dal (Badal) and Akali Dal (Amritsar) leaders, except for Mann who was in jail on charges of sedition at the time, to sign a pledge not to issue statements against each other.[36] These leaders also subsequently authorized their representatives to begin formal negotiations for forging unity. The Akal Takht *jathedar* and Head Priests contributed to these efforts by asking the various factions to "chalk out the blueprints of the constitutional, political, economic, social, and religious activities of the [new, united] Shiromani Akali Dal which will represent the 'panthic' aspirations of the Sikhs."[37]

After weeks of intense negotiations, complete Akali unity was finally forged on April 13, 1995. On this day, the Head Priests announced that a unified Akali party had been formed with Badal as its president and the Anandpur Sahib Resolution (ASR) as its official ideological manifesto.[38] This announcement stunned "the extremists" within the Akali Dal (Amritsar), including Mann and Bhai Manjit Singh; after all, they had not been privy to this decision. The "extremists" subsequently cried foul and accused the Head Priests of acting in a unilateral, partisan way in favor of the "traditional Akali leadership." The "traditional Akali leadership" within the Akali Dal (Amritsar)—Tohra, Barnala of the Akali Dal (Longowal), Capt. Amarinder Singh of the Akali Dal (Panthic), and Talwandi of the

Akali Dal (Talwandi)—had apparently struck a secret, "behind-the-scenes" deal to unite with Badal without "the extremists'" knowledge.[39] With this amazing announcement, the "traditional Akali leadership" was formally united for the first time in over 15 years since the late-1970s!

The exact organizational set-up of the unified "Shiromani Akali Dal" was determined a few weeks later when the Head Priests announced that Badal would be the party's president and that Mann would be its senior vice-president.[40] In addition, there were to be three vice-presidents—Sukhjinder Singh (a Tohra loyalist), Bhai Manjit Singh, and Gurdev Singh Badal. Tohra, Talwandi, and Capt. Amarinder Singh were all given membership in the 10-member parliamentary board.[41] Thus, every constituent member of the erstwhile Akali Dal (Amritsar) was given representation in the top leadership of the united "Shiromani Akali Dal" except for the miniscule "extremist/militant" Akali Dal (Babbar). For his part, Mann refused to join the new party because it had not accepted the creation of a "sovereign Sikh state" as its stated political goal. In contrast, Bhai Manjit Singh caved-in and agreed to join the unified "Shiromani Akali Dal," fearing being marginalized further in Sikh politics if he did not join the apparently united and dominant party. Shortly after being formed, the unified "Shiromani Akali Dal" demonstrated its electoral strength by defeating the Congress (I) candidate in the Gidderbaha state assembly by-election, and also sweeping the Delhi Sikh Gurdwara Management Committee (DSGMC) general house polls, defeating the Delhi-based Akali factions supported by the Congress (I).[42] The "traditional Akali leadership" was not only united after more than 15 years, but it was also in the process of unequivocally demonstrating its dominance within Sikh politics!

THE "PARTING BLAST" OF SIKH MILITANCY IN PUNJAB

Militancy was assumed to be dead in 1995; after all, there had been no militancy-related deaths in over 18 months. But, this was actually not the case. In late-August 1995, the last remaining cell of active Sikh militants in Punjab gave their unexpected and parting "blast" to the state by assassinating Punjab chief minister Beant Singh with a "human bomb" as he left the Punjab civil secretariat in Chandigarh.[43] Beant Singh's assassination shocked the government, and large parts of north India were immediately put on "red alert," including the Army being called-out into Punjab.[44] The government feared that "the militants" had regrouped and were on the verge of launching a series of new attacks, but this did not happen! Instead, Beant Singh's assassination was the handiwork of only a handful of Babbar Khalsa activists based near Chandigarh, who were all subsequently arrested and their cell rendered defunct.

Harcharan Singh Brar, a state cabinet minister from a mixed Congress–Akali family, was chosen by Congress (I) prime minister Narasimha Rao to be the new chief minister of Punjab. After becoming chief minister, H.S. Brar lifted many of the restrictions on political activity previously imposed on the Akalis by Beant Singh. The Congress (I) central government also unceremoniously replaced Punjab police chief, K.P.S. Gill, by the end of the year.[45] Thus, the Congress (I) leadership and state administration in Punjab was changing from one formed in the early-1990s to help crush the Sikh ethnonationalist insurgency to one more in tune with the emerging political realities of an apparent post-militancy Punjab. In this sense, political "normalcy" was deepening in the state.

The nature of Sikh politics had also changed by the end of 1995. The Sikh political spectrum at this time looked like the following (Table 11.3):

Table 11.3
Sikh Political Spectrum (Late-1995)

Moderates	Radicals	Extremists	Militants/Separatists
AD (Badal)[1]	Tohra[1]	AD (Mann)[2]	_____[3]
Badal[1]	Talwandi[1]		
Barnala[1]			

Source: Author.
Notes: [1] The "traditional Akali leadership" unified in the Akali Dal (Badal); party clearly dominated by Parkash Singh Badal and no longer making any political demands.
[2] Akali Dal (Mann) demanding creation of a "sovereign Sikh state" through non-violent means .
[3] No active "militant" groups remaining in India.

It consisted of two main Akali parties—the Akali Dal (Badal) and Akali Dal (Mann).[46] First, the "traditional Akali leadership" had united within the Akali Dal (Badal), also known as the "Shiromani Akali Dal." It included "moderates" such as Badal and Barnala and also "radicals" like Tohra and Talwandi. The party's main goal was to retain its core Sikh support base while also attracting non-Sikh, especially Hindu, votes in order to defeat the Congress (I) in electoral politics. The second major Akali party was the "extremist" Akali Dal (Mann).[47] Its ideology was enshrined in the "Amritsar Declaration," which ultimately called for the creation of a "sovereign Sikh state." At the end of 1995, there were no active "militant" groups left in Punjab. All of them had either been wiped out or were based in Pakistan. The "militants" had been crushed, but political "normalcy" had not yet fully returned to Sikh and Punjab politics. The "traditional Akali leadership" had united and moderated its ideology, but it still had not unequivocally demonstrated its dominance over "the extremists." This was necessary before the re-escalation of militancy could be definitively ruled out in Punjab.

THE "TRADITIONAL AKALI LEADERSHIP'S" HEGEMONIC DOMINANCE OVER SIKH POLITICS, FORMATION OF AN AKALI DAL (BADAL)–BJP COALITION STATE GOVERNMENT, AND THE END OF THE "PUNJAB CRISIS"

In the beginning of 1996, all political parties prepared for national parliamentary elections to be held by mid-year. The Akali Dal (Badal) began its informal election campaign by holding a massive party conference commemorating the 75th anniversary of the founding of the original "Shiromani Akali Dal." The Akali Dal (Badal) took full advantage of this conference to project an even more moderate image of it by, in part, appealing to a wide cross-section of Punjabi society, including Hindus, for support. It did this in three ways. First, the Akali Dal (Badal) proclaimed its new political goal as being the establishment of *halemi raj* (governance based on compassion and equality), thus backtracking from the regional and ethnic demands found in the ASR.[48] Second, the Akali Dal (Badal) officially opened its membership to Hindus for the first time and announced its support for the concept of *Punjabiat* (a composite Punjabi culture or nationalism irrespective of caste, creed, or religion).[49] Thus, the Akali Dal (Badal) tried to explicitly project itself as being an inclusive "Punjabi party" as opposed to an ethnic "Sikh" one. Lastly, Badal unequivocally rejected extremism by saying, "We are committed to peace in Punjab and shall not allow it to be disturbed at any cost."[50] This statement was largely designed to portray an even more moderate image of the party in order to compete more effectively in the upcoming parliamentary elections in post-militancy Punjab.

The Akalis went into the May 1996 parliamentary elections divided between the "traditional Akali leadership" found in the Akali Dal (Badal) and "the extremist" Akali Dal (Mann). The Akali Dal (Badal) aligned with the lower caste-based Bahujan Samaj Party (BSP) for these elections, and both the Congress (I) and Akali Dal (Mann) contested alone. The results of these elections were as follows: the Akali Dal (Badal) won eight seats, BSP three seats, and Congress (I) two.[51] These results provided several important political indications. First, the Akali Dal (Badal), with its united "traditional Akali leadership" and moderated image, appeared to have reaffirmed its electoral dominance within the Sikh community in Punjab, but the definitive test of this proposition would come in the SGPC general house elections scheduled for later in the year in October. Second, the Akali Dal (Badal) also appeared to have emerged as the strongest political party in Punjab overwhelming even the "catch-all" Congress (I), but this proposition would be definitively tested in the Punjab state assembly elections expected to be held in early-1997. Nonetheless, it was clearly evident that the Akali Dal (Badal) was on the rise both within the state and within Sikh politics.

At the national level, the May 1996 parliamentary elections resulted in a "hung parliament" in which no political party obtained clear majority. The BJP emerged with a plurality of seats (161) followed by the Congress with 140 and the Janata with 47.[52] In addition to the BJP's exceptional performance, the other big surprise of this election was that regional state-based parties won 128 seats, thus putting themselves into the position of helping form the governing majority in the center. This parliamentary election made it clear that the Congress (I) was on the downfall at the national level. The BJP was invited to form the central government with the support of its regional allies, including the Akali Dal (Badal), which decided to support the BJP unconditionally. "Radicals" within the Akali Dal (Badal)—namely, Tohra and Talwandi—expressed reluctance in supporting a central government led by a Hindu nationalist party but the "moderate" Badal quickly overruled them, thus demonstrating his unchallenged dominance within the party.[53] The Akali Dal (Badal)'s "unconditional" support for the BJP government also demonstrated that the party was clearly more interested in improving its governing prospects, rather than in pursuing its lingering ethnic and regional demands.[54]

The definitive test of which Akali faction, the Akali Dal (Badal) or Akali Dal (Mann), was dominant within the Sikh community came in October 1996 with the SGPC general house elections. These SGPC general house elections—the first in nearly 17 years—pitted the Akali Dal (Badal) and the Akali Dal (Mann) against each other in an exclusively Sikh electorate to elect 170 out of 190 members to the SGPC general house—the "mini-Parliament" of the Sikhs.[55] The Akali party that won a majority of seats in the SGPC general house would unequivocally be considered to be the "real" Akali Dal and the most legitimate political leadership of the Sikhs in Punjab.

It was expected that the Akali Dal (Mann) would give a strong challenge to the Akali Dal (Badal) in the exclusively Sikh electorate, but this challenge never materialized. The poll results actually surprised most political observers, as the Akali Dal (Badal) nearly swept the elections by winning 158 out of 170 seats.[56] The Akali Dal (Mann), in contrast, could win only seven seats and the remaining five seats went to unaffiliated independents. Thus, the united and moderated "traditional Akali leadership" found in the Akali Dal (Badal) had unambiguously proven its clear and unequivocal dominance over "the extremists" within the Sikh community! One political observer adroitly described these election results as being "the final burial of the hot-headed stream of Sikh politics."[57] The "extremists" stood politically marginalized!

The SGPC general elections were followed up with state assembly elections in Punjab held in February 1997. The Congress (I) contested these elections alone, the Akali Dal (Badal) allied with the Hindu-based BJP, and the Akali Dal (Mann) allied with the lower caste-based BSP.[58] The results of the February 1997 state assembly elections were as follows: Akali Dal (Badal) 75 seats, BJP 18 seats, Congress (I) 14 seats, CPI two seats, BSP one seat, and Akali Dal (Mann) one seat.[59] Thus, a Akali Dal (Badal)–BJP coalition swept into power in Punjab with an unprecedented four-fifths majority. The total seat count for the "Shiromani Akali Dal" was the highest it had ever won since the creation of the Punjabi *Suba* in 1966! The spectacular victory of the Akali Dal (Badal)–BJP combine, which had campaigned on the basis of a composite Punjabi identity irrespective of religion, represented the solidification of Sikh–Hindu *ekta* (unity) in Punjab. The "Punjab crisis" was essentially over, and "normalcy" had returned to both Punjab and Sikh politics.

When asked how he had changed from the last time he was chief minister in 1980, Parkash Singh Badal skillfully replied, "Then I had a black beard and now I have a grey [almost white] one. Of course, I have gained in political maturity."[60] After these elections, newly-appointed chief minister Badal refused to bring up militancy-related issues such as the prosecution of police officers accused of human rights violations during the insurgency or declaring a general amnesty for Sikh youth still detained in Indian jails. Instead, he promised to take "an even-handed approach [on these issues] by letting the law take its own course."[61] The united "traditional Akali leadership" wanted to look forward towards the future and not back into the past. After all, moderation, not extremism, was key to remaining dominant in Sikh politics and also to staying in power at the state level in post-militancy Punjab. Punjab and Sikh politics had, in essence, come around full circle since 1978, but only after nearly two decades of violent political strife and ethnonationalist insurgency that had threatened the very unity of India and had brutally cost over 25,000 human lives.[62]

SUMMARY AND CONCLUSION

The period under examination in this chapter analyzed the process by which political "normalcy" became re-established in Punjab and Sikh politics, and how the "Punjab crisis" definitively ended. As discussed in the previous chapter, "the militants" appeared to be "crushed" by the beginning of 1993 as a result of the culmination of several "patterns of political leadership" including their internal fractionalization and internecine competition, their loss of an effective political front in the fractionalized "extremists," and the coordinated military and political actions against them by united governing state elites. Yet, re-escalation of insurgency and separatism could not be realistically ruled out until the "traditional Akali leadership" united, moderated its rhetoric and ideology, and emerged clearly dominant over "the extremists" in Sikh politics. This chapter analyzed how these "patterns of political leadership" emerged, contributing to the definitive end of the "Punjab crisis."

To explain, the "traditional Akali leadership" was divided at the beginning of 1993 between the "radical" Akali Dal (Badal) including Tohra, the "radical" Akali Dal (Talwandi), the "moderate" Akali Dal (Longowal) led by Barnala, and the "moderate" Akali Dal (Panthic) under Capt. Amarinder Singh. A gradual trend began to emerge in Sikh politics through 1993 when the Akali Dal (Badal) proved itself to be the most popular Akali party by scoring strong electoral performances in select democratic by-elections in the state. The Akali Dal (Badal)'s apparent ascendance in Sikh politics after these by-elections prompted the other "traditional Akali leaders" to try to unite in an attempt to arrest Badal's growing power. This process culminated in the creation of the "unified" Akali Dal (Amritsar) which included the other "traditional Akali leaders"—Tohra, Talwandi, Barnala, and Capt. Amarinder Singh—and most of "the extremists" like Mann.

Even though these other Akali leaders were united, the Akali Dal (Badal) continued to grow in popularity with its increasingly moderate image in comparison to the "unified" Akali Dal (Amritsar), which also included "the extremists." Conditions for forging more complete unity between the "traditional Akali leaders" improved after both the Akali Dal

(Badal) and Akali Dal (Amritsar) performed "poorly" in local elections in September 1994 in comparison to the Congress (I). After this "mediocre" electoral performance, the other "traditional Akali leaders" realized that they could not effectively compete against either Badal or the Congress (I) even though they were united. In particular, their alliance with "the extremists" was a major liability in apparent post-militancy Punjab. For his part, Badal realized that the "unified" Akali Dal (Amritsar), even though it could not win many elections itself, could consistently siphon off enough Sikh votes to cause his party to lose in close electoral contests with the Congress (I). Thus, all sections of the "traditional Akali leadership" had an incentive to unite by late-1994. This incentive was partially facilitated by the coordinated actions of united governing state elites in both Chandigarh and New Delhi, who continued their successful military actions against the last remaining "militants" while concurrently deepening the "normal" political process by strategically holding a series of democratic elections in the state. These elections continued to prompt both the "traditional Akali leaders" and also "the extremists" to fully re-enter the "normal" democratic political process in order to avoid being marginalized within the Sikh community in an increasingly post-militancy Punjab.

Unity between the entire "traditional Akali leadership" (Badal, Tohra, Talwandi, Barnala, and Capt. Amarinder Singh) was finally achieved with the creation of the "Shiromani Akali Dal" in the spring of 1995. The "extremists," including Mann, were excluded from this arrangement and stood isolated in Sikh politics. Shortly thereafter, the "Shiromani Akali Dal" (that is, the Akali Dal-Badal) moderated its image even further by portraying itself as being a regional political party committed to *Punjabiat* (a composite Punjabi nationalism irrespective of religion) and *halemi raj* (governance based on compassion and equality) as opposed to being an exclusively Sikh ethnic party. The "Shiromani Akali Dal" subsequently proved its clear dominance over "the extremists" in Sikh politics by nearly sweeping the SGPC general house elections in the fall of 1996. It also demonstrated its ascendance in Punjab's "secular" political system by scoring a tremendous victory over the Congress (I) in the February 1997 state assembly and parliamentary elections in Punjab. The Akali Dal (Badal) subsequently formed a coalition state government with the Hindu-based BJP, which represented renewed Hindu–Sikh *ekta* (unity) in the state.

Thus, "the militants" had been completely wiped out and "the extremists" stood unequivocally marginalized within the Sikh community. In contrast, the "traditional Akali leadership" had united, moderated its ideology, and emerged clearly dominant, if not hegemonic, over "the extremists" in Sikh politics. It had also fully re-entered the "normal" democratic political process by participating in a series of local and state elections strategically held by unified ruling state elites from 1993 to 1997. This process had culminated into the formation of an Akali Dal (Badal)–BJP state government in Punjab in early-1997. The "Punjab crisis" was over after nearly two decades of political strife and ethnonationalist violence, which had threatened the unity of India and cost over 25,000 human lives.

NOTES

1. Kanwar Sandhu, "Punjab: Normal Life at Last," *India Today*, 28 February 1993, 40.
2. A.S. Prashar, "Anandpur Draft Rejected," *The Tribune*, 10 March 1993, 1 and 16.
3. P.P.S. Gill, "Dal (M) Seeks Sikh State," *The Tribune*, 9 March 1993, 1.
4. Tribune News Service, "Umrao Wins Jalandhar LS Seat," *The Tribune*, 23 May 1993, 1.
5. K.S. Chawla, "Akali Unity Around Tohra?" *The Tribune*, 9 February 1993, 1.
6. Praveen Swami, "Strategic Shift: A New Order of Threat," *Frontline*, 8 October 1993, 17–20.
7. For details about the "Engineer Group" of the KLF, see Ibid., 17–20; and Praveen Swami, "Lessons from the Mirdha Kidnapping: Disquieting Revelations," *Frontline*, 24 March 1995, 29–32.
8. Tribune News Service, "Panthic Chief Sohan Singh Held," *The Tribune*, 5 November 1993, 1.
9. Akali Dal (Baba) leader, Baba Joginder Singh, had died in October 1993. The party was subsequently led by Capt. Harcharan Singh Rode, who was Baba Joginder Singh's son and Sant Bhindranwale's elder brother.
10. Tribune News Service, "Gill Promises Peace within 3 Months," *The Tribune*, 25 December 1993, 1.
11. Paul Wallace, "Political Violence and Terrorism in India: A Crisis of Identity," in *Terrorism in Context*, ed. Martha Crenshaw (University Park, PA: Pennsylvania State University Press, 1995), 354.
12. The "Engineer Group" of the KLF would continue its sporadic, but high-profile, campaign of political violence until Qadian's death about a year later. For details, see Praveen Swami, "Disquieting Revelations: Lessons from the Mirdha Kidnapping," *Frontline*, 24 March 1995, 30.
13. Venkitesh Ramakrishnan, "A Festival of Politics: The Emerging Trends," *Frontline*, 6 May 1994, 20.
14. Ibid. Also see Ramesh Vinayak, "Beant Singh's Bugbear," *India Today*, 15 October 1994, 49.
15. Venkitesh Ramakrishnan, "The Many Faces of Terror," *Frontline*, 12 March 1993, 36.
16. Tribune News Service, "Unity if Tohra Made Chief: Amarinder", *The Tribune*, 21 March 1994, 5. Professor Manjit Singh had been appointed as "acting" Akal Takht *jathedar* in February 1993. Professor Manjit Singh was only the "acting" Jathedar of the Akal Takht because Ranjit Singh, who had been appointed to this position by the SGPC in 1990, was still in prison for the 1980 assassination of the Nirankari guru, Gurbachan Singh.

17. For details see Tribune News Service, "Akali Dals Approach Takht for Unity," *The Tribune*, 14 April 1994, 1 and 16. A good description of this entire sequence of events is also contained in Venkitesh Ramakrishnan, "A Festival of Politics: The Emerging Trends," *Frontline*, 6 May 1994, 17–24.

18. For details, see Venkitesh Ramakrishnan, "A Festival of Politics: The Emerging Trends," *Frontline*, 6 May 1994, 23–24

19. Tribune News Service, "Akali Dals Approach Takht for Unity," *The Tribune*, 14 April 1994, 1 and 16.

20. A copy of Badal's letter to Akal Takht *jathedar* Prof. Manjit Singh is contained in Kuldeep Kaur, *Akali Dal in Punjab Politics: Splits and Mergers* (New Delhi: Deep and Deep Publications, 1999), 187–90.

21. Tribune News Service, "Badal Sees Centre's Hand: Dal (B) Splits, Tohra Men Walk Out," *The Tribune*, 20 April 1994, 1.

22. See Badal's letter in Kaur, *Akali Dal*, 187–90.

23. See interview with Prof. Manjit Singh in S. Chawla, "Badal 'Should Submit before Takht'," *The Tribune*, 22 April 1994, 16.

24. Tribune News Service, "Badal Quits as Dal (B) President," *The Tribune*, 22 April 1994, 1.

25. Kaur, *Akali Dal*, 196 and Venkitesh Ramakrishnan, "Old Game, New Rules: Akali Dals Make Another Unity Bid," *Frontline*, 3 June 1994, 31.

26. Kaur, *Akali Dal*, 196.

27. An English translation of the "Amritsar Declaration" is found in Ibid., 195–96.

28. Venkitesh Ramakrishnan, "Badal's Triumph," *Frontline*, 1 July 1994, 16.

29. Ibid.

30. Tribune News Service, "Samra Elected from Nakodar," *The Tribune*, 30 May 1994, 1.

31. A.S. Prashar and H.S. Bhanwar, "Ajnala Byelection: Badal Emerges as Hero," *The Tribune*, 3 June 1994, 1.

32. Sarbjit Singh, "Dal (B) to Launch Mass Movement," *The Tribune*, 11 July 1994, 1.

33. Tribune News Service, "Akali Dal (A) Tired of Mann's Antics," *The Tribune*, 11 August 1994, 1.

34. Tribune News Service, "Congress Leads in 10 Districts," *The Tribune*, 3 October 1994, 1 and 18.

35. See ibid.; and The Tribune, "Democracy Wins in Punjab," *The Tribune*, 4 October 1994, 4.

36. Tribune News Service, "Akalis to Resume Talks on Jan 23," *The Tribune*, 12 January 1995, 1.

37. Tribune News Service, "Akali Factions Agree on Unity," *The Tribune*, 24 January 1995, 1.

38. See Varinder Walia, "Akalis Unite into Shiromani Dal," *The Tribune*, 15 April 1995, 1 and 18.

39. K.S. Chawla, "Unity of Akali Dals a Farce?" *The Tribune*, 16 April 1995, 1.

40. Tribune News Service, "Akalis Announce New Set-up," *The Tribune*, 5 June 1995, 1.

41. Ibid., 1.

42. See Tribune News Service, "Akali Dal Wins Gidderbaha Seat," *The Tribune*, 7 June 1995, 1; and Tribune News Service, "SAD Sweeps DSGMC Poll," *The Tribune*, 10 July 1995, 1 and 18.

43. For details see Tribune News Service, "Beant Singh Assassinated: Car Bomb Leaves Nine More Dead," *The Tribune*, 1 September 1995, 1; and Praveen Swami, "Back with A Blast: Terrorists Kill Beant Singh," *Frontline*, 22 September 1995, 4–13.

44. Tribune News Service, "Beant Singh Assassinated: Car Bomb Leaves Nine More Dead," *The Tribune*, 1 September 1995, 1.

45. See Ramesh Vinayak, "K.P.S. Gill: Bowing Out without a Bang," *India Today*, 31 January 1996, 36–37.

46. The Akali Dal (Baba) still existed, but was becoming an increasingly negligible force in Sikh politics.

47. The Akali Dal (Mann) continued to be interchangeably known as the "Akali Dal (Amritsar)."

48. Ramesh Vinayak, "Middle-of-the-roaders," *India Today*, 31 March 1996, 71.

49. A.S. Prashar, "Akalis May Broaden Base," *The Tribune*, 24 February 1996, 1.

50. A.S. Prashar and Varinder Walia, "SAD to Work for Federal Set-up," *The Tribune*, 26 February 1996, 1.

51. Tribune News Service, "SAD-BSP Combine Wins 11 Seats," *The Tribune*, 10 May 1996, 1. Also see Paul Wallace, "General Elections, 1996: Regional Parties Dominant in Punjab and Haryana," *Economic and Political Weekly*, 32, no. 46, 15 November (1997): 2963–69.

52. For a full breakdown of the 543 seats in parliament refer to Meenu Roy, *Elections 1998: A Continuity in Coalition* (New Delhi: National Publishing House), 26.

53. Tribune News Service, "Akalis divided on support issue," *The Tribune*, 12 May 1996, 1.

54. The BJP-led government fell in 13 days, and Janata Dal-led government called the United Front consisting of 13 national and regional parties came into power under Deve Gowda with the outside support of the Congress (I).

55. Ramesh Vinayak, "Prestige Fight," *India Today*, 15 October 1996. Fifteen of the 190 SGPC general house members are co-opted from the general house and also form the SGPC executive. The remaining five are the Head Priests who do not have voting rights.

56. Ramesh Vinayak, "Triumph of the Moderates," *India Today*, 15 November 1996, 14; and P.P.S Gill, "Big win for SAD likely," *The Tribune*, 15 October 1996, 1.

57. Ramesh Vinayak, "Triumph of the Moderates," *India Today*, 15 November 1996, 14.

58. Tribune News Service, "Wadala floats Akali Dal," *The Tribune*, 8 December 1996, 1.

59. Ramesh Vinayak and Rohit Parihar, "Punjab: A Mandate for Progress," *India Today*, 28 February 1997, 15. The corresponding percentage of votes was 37.51 percent for the Akali Dal (Badal), 26.42 percent Congress (I), 8.42 percent BJP, and 7.43 percent BSP. Praveen Swami, "Emphatic Victory: An SAD-BJB Government of Punjab," *Frontline*, 7 March 1997, 32.

60. Ramesh Vinayak, "Prakash Singh Badal: 'We will not be vindictive," *India Today*, 28 February 1997, 16.

61. Ibid.

62. Figure taken from Wallace, "Political Violence," 354. I also include the 5,000 to 8,000 Sikhs killed in the anti-Sikh riots in north India after Indira Gandhi's assassination in October 1984 in this figure.

PART V

Conclusion

12

"Patterns of Political Leadership" and Ethnonationalist Insurgency in a Comparative Perspective

OVERVIEW OF THE BOOK'S CONCEPTUAL ARGUMENTS

The number of ethnopolitical conflicts in the world, including armed movements for self-determination, increased precipitously after World War II, peaking during the late 1980s and the early-1990s.[1] During this period, 81 different countries confronted armed insurgencies of which 26 violent self-determination movements are still going on today.[2] The human significance of the violence associated with ethnopolitical conflicts is apparent by the fact that over 4 million people died as a result of it and an additional 25 million have become displaced refugees during this period.[3]

This book has attempted to make a contribution, however small, to our understanding of this important and complex phenomenon by providing a unique explanation for the rise and fall of the Sikh ethnonationalist insurgency in particular, and ethnonationalist movements in general. It has focused on the previously under-theorized explanatory variable of "patterns of political leadership." The overarching conceptual argument formulated in this book has been that *"patterns of political leadership," defined as the dynamic interaction between and amongst state and ethnic elites, significantly affect the trajectory of ethnic subnationalist movements by defining the political relationship between an ethnic group and the central state.* Three additional propositions were formulated explaining the effects of various "patterns of political leadership" on the rise, sustenance, and decline of ethnic subnationalist movements.

Regarding the rise of ethnonationalist movements, it was shown in Chapter 3 through Chapter 5 that *violent subnationalist movements arise when competing ethnic and state elites cannot resolve their political differences and ethnic militants emerge often, but not always, facilitated by either traditional ethnic elites or state elites to use in their respective intra-system struggles or against each other.* In relation to Punjab, the intense and unprincipled political competition between Indira Gandhi's Congress (I) central government and the Akali Dal during the early-1980s prompted the Congress (I) to patronize Sikh extremists/militants, including Sant Jarnail Singh Bhindranwale, in its attempt to split the Akali Dal's support base. For its part, the Akali Dal raised ethnic slogans and built alliances with Sikh extremists/militants to mobilize the community against Mrs Gandhi to try to compel the central government to concede to the party's lingering demands. Furthermore, Akali leaders such as Gurcharan Singh Tohra and Jagdev Singh Talwandi patronized Bhindranwale and other extremist elements in order to use them as allies against their comparatively more moderate rivals in internal Sikh politics—namely, Harchand Singh Longowal and Parkash Singh Badal. Intra-party competition within the ruling Congress (I) also facilitated extremism when Giani Zail Singh aided and abetted the emergence of Sikh extremists/militants in his attempt to undermine his intra-party rival, Darbara Singh. The culmination of these "patterns of political leadership" resulted in the strengthening of Sikh extremists/militants and the rise of violent Sikh ethnonationalism in Punjab from 1978 to 1984.

Regarding the sustenance of ethnonationalist movements, this book argued in Chapter 6 through Chapter 9 that, *in the absence of a negotiated settlement, violent subnationalist movements persist when ethnic militants remain "united" and retain a viable political front, while state elites become internally-divided and fractionalized traditional ethnic elites engage in competitive "ethnic-outflanking."* To explain, the Congress (I) central government under Rajiv Gandhi tried to formulate a compromise settlement for the "Punjab problem" with the Akalis after Operation Bluestar, but this Punjab Accord failed to be implemented. The Sikh ethnonationalist movement subsequently escalated. The "militants" remained largely united under the Panthic Committee, and they also retained a viable political front in the form of "the extremists" such as the AISSF (Manjit) and Akali Dal (United). Thus, internal unity amongst "the militants," amongst "the extremists," and between them helped the

Sikh ethnonationalist movement build significant popular support and legitimacy. In contrast, divisions between ruling state elites gave a fillip to militancy by stymieing the formulation and implementation of effective political and military policies on Punjab. This included both divisions within the ruling Congress (I) (that is, Bhajan Lal's incessant intransigence to compromise with the Akalis and the dysfunctional Rajiv–Buta Singh relationship) and also divisions within the ruling coalition (that is, the V.P. Singh government's reliance on the BJP and Communists, and the Chandra Shekhar government's reliance on the Congress (I) to stay in power). At the same time, the "traditional Sikh leadership" in the Akali Dal fractionalized, helping sustain violent Sikh ethnonationalism instead of dampening it. In particular, both Badal and Tohra strategically radicalized and built alliances with "the extremists" in order to undermine their intra-Akali rival, Surjit Singh Barnala, much to the detriment of peace in Punjab. These "patterns of political leadership" coalesced to help sustain the violent Sikh ethnonationalist movement through the period from 1985 to 1991.

Regarding the demise of ethnonationalist movements, this book has demonstrated in Chapter 10 and Chapter 11 that, *in the absence of a negotiated settlement or complete military victory, violent subnationalist movements decline when ethnic militants "fractionalize" and lose a viable political front, and unified state elites pursue coordinated policies prompting traditional ethnic elites to unite, moderate, and re-enter the "normal" political process.* To explain, "the militants" became increasingly fractionalized and engaged in escalating internecine violence as the Sikh ethnonationalist movement wore-on without settlement or victory. By the early-1990s, "the militants" were divided between at least three competing Panthic Committees which, in turn, contained a mushrooming number of actual armed militant groups. The "militants" also lost an effective political front in "the extremists" once the latter became completely fractionalized in the early-1990s in contrast to being united before. In addition, "the extremists'" political interests began diverging from those of "the militants" as "the gun" ("the militants") became dominant over "politics" ("the extremists"), instead of vice-versa or being mutually cooperative. These trends eroded the long-term sustainability and efficacy of the Sikh ethnonationalist movement. Concurrently, governing state elites united and formulated a coherent policy on Punjab after Narasimha Rao securely came into power in the center and his Congress (I) ally, Beant Singh, came into power in Punjab. Rao and Beant Singh successfully pursued a coordinated, aggressive "law-and-order" approach against the highly-fractionalized and politically vulnerable "militants," helping "contain" the insurgency. Unified governing elites also concurrently restarted the democratic political process, which prompted both "the extremists" and the "traditional Akali leadership" to begin rejoining electoral politics in order to avoid being politically marginalized in an increasingly post-militancy Punjab. As the democratic political process deepened, the "traditional Akali leadership" united and moderated its ideology, and eventually emerged hegemonic over "the extremists." The culmination of these "patterns of political leadership" helped definitively end the "Punjab crisis" by 1997.

CONTINUATION OF PEACE IN PUNJAB AFTER 1997: "PATTERNS OF POLITICAL LEADERSHIP" IN THE POST-MILITANCY ERA

As mentioned earlier, Punjab has seen no significant militancy related deaths since the mid-1990s. Three "patterns of political leadership" help explain the consolidation peace in Punjab during the "post-militancy" period after 1997: the continued near complete dominance of Akali moderates over the "Sikh political system," the absence of a partisan interventionist political leadership in New Delhi, and the continued weakening of "extremist" elements within Sikh politics. In many respects, these "patterns of political leadership" are mirror opposites of the trends that initially gave rise to Sikh militancy and separatism during the late-1970s and early-1980s.

Regarding the first, the "moderate" Parkash Singh Badal has consolidated and maintained his near complete dominance over the "Sikh political system" since his party's spectacular victory in the 1997 state assembly elections. The gravest threat to Badal's dominance over Sikh politics came in late-1998, about a year-and-half after the formation of his state ministry, when the "radical" SGPC president Gurcharan Singh Tohra publicly questioned Badal's leadership of the party after its loss in a key state assembly by-election to the Congress (I). Tohra criticized the Akali Dal (Badal)'s relationship with the BJP and suggested that Badal resign from his position as party president to focus on his administrative duties as chief minister.[4] Badal and his loyalists viewed these utterances as being both a direct political challenge and also an opportunity to expel Tohra from the party and remove him from the key position of SGPC president. Tohra, who had apparently miscalculated Badal's tolerance with dissention within the party, attempted to forestall his expulsion by having his loyalist, Akal Takht *jathedar* Bhai Ranjit Singh, issue a *hukamnama* (religious edict) ordering that all feuding within the Akali Dal be temporarily suspended in order to maintain the glory of the Khalsa Panth. The Badal faction ignored this edict as being inappropriate political meddling by the Akal Takht and had the SGPC executive committee, which had a slight majority of pro-Badal members, suspend Ranjit Singh from his position as Akal Takht *jathedar* in February 1999, appointing another person more loyal to the Badal faction in his place.[5] A month later, Tohra was also removed from office and replaced by another Badal loyalist as SGPC president.[6] Thus, by early-1999, the "moderate" Badal had achieved almost complete dominance over institutionalized Sikh politics by either personally holding, or having his hand-picked loyalists hold, all major focal points of power in the "Sikh political system," including the chief ministership of Punjab, the presidentship of the Akali Dal, the presidentship of the SGPC, and the *jathedari* of the Akal Takht.[7] This trend has continued virtually unabated over the past decade with the almost hegemonic leadership of Badal over the "Sikh political system." This has contributed to the maintenance of internal unity within the Akali Dal and also the structural predominance of a "moderate" ethnic leadership over Sikh politics committed to the unity of India.[8] In many ways, this dynamic is akin to the structural predominance Master Tara Singh enjoyed over Sikh politics during the post-Independence era until the mid-1960s, and that which Sant Fateh Singh enjoyed from the mid-1960s until his passing away in 1972.

A second important "pattern of political leadership" that helps explain the maintenance of peace in post-militancy Punjab has been the absence of a partisan and highly-interventionist central leadership in New Delhi. To explain, India has been largely governed during most of the post-1997 by either a BJP-led coalition, which has included the Akali Dal, or a Congress (I)-led coalition under the highly-principled prime minister Manmohan Singh during most of the post-1997 period. Regarding the former, the Akali Dal (Badal) has been a close alliance partner of the BJP in the center, contributing 9 and 2 parliamentary seats to the ruling BJP-led coalition called the "National Democratic Alliance" in 1998 and 1999, respectively. No wedge-issue has emerged to break this Akali Dal (Badal)–BJP alliance at either the state level or in the center. Thus, the BJP has had no incentive to try to undermine Badal's "moderate" leadership within the Akali Dal in Punjab by trying to foster factionalism within the party. Regarding the latter, a Congress (I)-led coalition called the "United Progressive Alliance" led by prime minister Manmohan Singh (and Congress-I party president, Sonia Gandhi) has governed India since 2004. During this period, this central Congress (I) leadership has avoided unnecessary partisan meddling and interventionism into Sikh politics in Punjab. In fact, it was reported that Manmohan Singh personally intervened to prevent intra-Sikh and intra-Akali splits during the Dera Sacha Sauda controversy in July 2007 to help avoid destabilizing Sikh politics and potentially disturbing the political peace in Punjab.[9] Earlier, it was feared that factionalism and political competition between Capt. Amarinder Singh and Rajinder Kaur Bhattal, two stalwart Congress (I) leaders in Punjab in the post-1997 period, would possibly lead to the destabilization of Akali politics and the emergence of violent Sikh extremists groups as was the case during the early-1980s with the Zail Singh–Darbara Singh feud, but this did not happen for two main reasons.[10] First, the Zail Singh–Darbara Singh feud occurred in the backdrop of the highly interventionist political leadership of Indira Gandhi who herself wanted to undermine the Akali Dal in Punjab. In contrast, neither the BJP-led "National Democratic Alliance" central government nor the Congress (I)-led "United Progressive Alliance" central government under Manmohan Singh has had any incentive to undermine the Akali Dal. Second, Zail Singh's ability to foster the emergence of violent Sikh extremist groups in the late-1970s and the early-1980s was aided by the fact that the "Sikh political system" was highly-factionalized between competing Akali leaders at the time. In contrast, it has been under the dominant control of the "moderate" Parkash Singh Badal since 1997. Thus, the absence of an overtly partisan and highly-interventionist central political leadership in New Delhi over the past decade has helped maintain the continuation of peace and political stability in Punjab.

A third "pattern of political leadership" that has contributed to the maintenance of political "normalcy" in Punjab has been the fractionalization and continuing weakening of "extremist" Sikh groups. To recap, the "militants" were completely decimated by the mid-1990s, with the possible exception of the Babbar Khalsa, and the only major "extremist" Sikh organization continuing into the late-1990s was the Akali Dal (Mann), which itself had moderated significantly and re-entered democratic politics.[11] Yet, irrespective of its attempt to moderate, the Akali Dal (Mann) has atrophied significantly both electorally and in terms of its organization during post-militancy period.[12] For example, the party won only one seat in the 1997 Punjab state assembly elections, and none in both the 2002 and 2007 Punjab state assembly elections. In contrast, the Akali Dal (Badal) won 41 and 48 and the Congress won 62 and 44, respectively, during these two elections. The Akali Dal (Mann)'s vote totals also dropped from 3.10 percent in the 1997 to a dismal 0.52 percent in 2007, signaling electoral decline.[13] The Akali Dal (Mann) received another jolt in November 2007 when Daljeet Singh Bittu—a former militant who had joined the party after being acquitted of militancy-related charges earlier in 2005—split from Mann and formed a separate "extremist" party called the Akali Dal (Panch Pardani).[14] This essentially bifurcated the already severely weakened Akali Dal (Mann) because Bittu took a large chunk of the Akali Dal (Mann)'s second-rung leaders, and potential support base, with him to the Akali Dal (Panch Pardani). Thus, the collectively weakened "extremists" remain fractionalized between the Akali Dal (Mann) and the Akali Dal (Panch Pardani), the latter of which is a member of a loose grouping of various Sikh "extremist" and religious organizations collectively known as the "Khalsa Action Committee" formed in spring 2007 to confront the Dera Sacha Sauda issue.[15] The weakening of "the extremists" and their continued fractionalization also contribute to the maintenance of peace in Punjab in the post-militancy era. These dynamics, in combination with the nearly hegemonic supremacy of the united "moderates" over institutionalized Sikh politics and the absence of a non-interventionist central leadership, provides a significant bulwark to the re-emergence of violent Sikh ethnonationalism in contemporary Punjab.

GENERALIZABILITY OF THE BOOK'S CONCEPTUAL ARGUMENTS: FOUR ADDITIONAL CASES OF ETHNONATIONALIST INSURGENCY

The conceptual arguments regarding the effects of various "patterns of political leadership" on the trajectory of violent ethnonationalist movements formulated in this book also have significant applicability to other cases of insurgency in addition to Punjab. These propositions, while not "iron-clad laws," represent strong "tendency statements" that help explain the rise and sustenance (or demise) of ethnonationalist insurgencies in general with remarkably little variation across cases.[16] The remainder of this chapter demonstrates the general applicability of the conceptual arguments formulated in this book by examining the dynamics and trajectories of the ethnonationalist insurgencies in Chechnya, Northern Ireland, Jammu and Kashmir, and Assam.

Chechnya

Chechnya was one of the several republics in the erstwhile Soviet Union. The contemporary conflict in Chechnya emerged in 1990, coinciding with the disintegration of the Soviet Union. Internal divisions within both the

Russian political elite in Moscow and the Chechen political elite in Grozny helped foster the emergence of this conflict. In particular, Boris Yeltsin and Russian reformers aligned with pro-independence Chechen leader, Johar Dudayev; whereas Mikhail Gorbachev and pro-communist elements backed the then existing Chechen government of Doku Zavgayev in their power struggle against each other.[17] For their part, Dudayev and Zavgayev sought powerful allies in Moscow for their political struggles in Chechnya. The pro-independence Dudayev eventually came to power over Zavgayev in Grozny with Yeltsin's active support, and continued to back Yeltsin in the center against the communists.

After consolidating his power in the center, Yeltsin ironically withdrew support from Dudayev who had declared Chechnya's independence from Moscow, and instead switched his loyalties to the anti-separatist, pro-Russian Zavgayev.[18] In November 1994, Chechen dissidents under Zavgayev backed by the Russian army tried to capture Grozny, but were initially repulsed by Dudayev's nationalist forces. The Russians subsequently launched a full-scale military assault on Chechnya and succeeded in capturing Grozny in the spring of 1995, sending Dudayev's forces into the mountains and beginning the contemporary insurgency. A pro-Moscow government under Zavgayev was subsequently "elected" into office in Chechnya after the fall of Grozny. Thus, internal divisions between central political elites helped facilitate the rise of a reformist ethnic leadership in Chechnya, which would eventually lead a separatist insurgency for independence from the center. In contrast, a unified Russian leadership in Moscow may well have been able to forestall the emergence of a dominant pro-independence leadership in the republic.

The subsequent sustenance of ethnic insurgency in Chechnya largely mirrors the initial continuation of the insurgency in Punjab. To explain, pro-independence rebels in Chechnya remained largely united under a popular and institutionalized political front—Dudayev's All-National Congress of the Chechen People party—much like how the Sikh militants remained united under "extremist" political organizations in Punjab. In addition, emerging intra-elite divisions within Moscow obstructed the formulation and implementation of a coherent policy to end the pro-independence insurgency in Chechnya similar to how internal divisions within the Congress Party (or within the ruling central coalitions) did in relation to the Sikh insurgency. In the Chechen case, hard-line dissident members of Yeltsin's own central government were suspected of giving tacit support to Chechen separatists to advance their own intra-system partisan interests in Moscow, resulting in the dismissal of several top Russian government and military officials in late-1995 and early-1996.[19] Thus, a section of the Russian government actually helped sustain the Chechen insurgency through its partisan competition with other competing state elites in Moscow.

In April 1996, Russian security forces killed Dudayev, but continuing disunity within the Russian political elite between hard-liners and reformers on the eve of presidential elections left the government paralyzed and forestalled effective anti-insurgency operations. As a result, Chechen rebels led by Aslan Maskhadov, the slain Dudayev's chief deputy, counterattacked and seized Grozny in the summer of 1996. Yeltsin's incoming Russian government, mired in renewed internal power squabbles, found it more feasible to compromise with the rebels rather than continue fighting a largely united and popular Chechen ethnonationalist movement. For this reason, Moscow quickly reached a "peace agreement" with Maskhadov by which the rebel government was allowed to stay in power for at least five years before the issue of Chechen sovereignty would be revisited.[20]

The two subsequent years were a period of relative calm in Chechnya, but emerging internal divisions within the Chechen government eventually raised prospects of renewed conflict between Grozny and Moscow after radical Islamist elements within the Chechen government led by Shamil Basayev began challenging the comparatively more moderate Maskhadov for governmental leadership. Basayev accused Maskhadov of being overly conciliatory toward Moscow and began pressuring Maskhadov to implement policies that would make Chechnya into an "Islamic state."[21] Instead of reaffirming Chechnya's moderate Sufi heritage, Maskhadov conceded to many of the Wahhabi radicals' demands in his attempt to preserve the government's stability. Ironically, Maskadov's catering to the radical Islamists alienated more moderate elements within his government, including Akhmad Kadyrov—a respected Sufi religious figure and powerful militia commander who would later turn against the Chechen nationalist movement and side with the Russians.[22]

Intra-elite divisions and competition between nationalist Chechen leaders took its toll in 1999 when Basayev and the radicals lost all interest in maintaining the stability of Maskhadov's government. Basayev and his loyalists subsequently launched a raid into the neighboring republic of Dagestan in a professed attempt to create a larger "Islamic republic" in the North Caucasuses—a bold action which could possibly spark a larger regional-wide conflict. Hard-line elements within the Russian government loyal to Vladimir Putin were actually suspected of encouraging Basayev's actions in order to undermine the comparatively more moderate Yeltsin and eventually justify invading Chechnya.[23] In response to Basayev's raid, Russian troops rolled into Chechnya and, by the spring of 2000, controlled most of the republic, forcing the nationalists—both moderate and radical Islamic alike—into the mountains again. This Russian recapture of Grozny subsequently re-ignited the separatist insurgency in Chechnya. Thus, intra-elite divisions and competition both within the nationalist Chechen leadership and within the ruling central leadership in Moscow helped facilitate the re-emergence of insurgency. This pattern largely mirrors the escalating phases of the "Punjab crisis" during which divisions between governing state elites (for example, Bhajan Lal's intransigence to compromise, the dysfunctional Rajiv–Buta Singh relationship, and the instability of the V.P. Singh and Chandra Shekhar coalition governments) gave a fillip to Sikh militancy, and competition between traditional ethnic elites (for example, Badal and Tohra's attempts to undermine Barnala) encouraged renewed insurgency.

Yet, new "patterns of political leadership" in both Moscow and Grozny, similar to those that eventually emerged in Punjab, soon coalesced to begin undermining the Chechen separatist insurgency. To explain, Putin's ascendance to power over the ailing Yeltsin in 2000 fundamentally altered the political dynamics within Moscow and also the central state's relationship with Chechnya. Putin was much more secure in power than his predecessor Yeltsin had ever been. For this reason, Yeltsin had been forced to shift his support back-and-forth between various regional, including Chechen, proteges to help stay in power during his tenure as Russian leader. In contrast, Putin unequivocally declared that Chechnya would forever remain a part of greater Russia shortly after gaining the presidency, and he appointed former rebel commander Akhmad Kadyrov, who had been expelled from Maskhadov's government during his Islamization campaign of the late-1990s, as its pro-Moscow president.[24] Kadyrov's defection to the pro-Russia side and his appointment to be Chechen president formally bifurcated the previously united Chechen ethnonationalist movement. Secular nationalists and moderate Sufi elements joined Kadyrov's "pro-Russian" government in Grozny, whereas the remaining Sufists and radical Islamists continued with their separatist insurgency for independence from Moscow. It was estimated that more than half of the rebel Chechen fighters defected to the pro-Russian side under Kadyrov's leadership after

Moscow offered them amnesty and positions within the official Chechen security forces.[25] This severely weakened the Chechen ethnonationalist movement.

Putin and the unified Russian elites subsequently followed up on their military "successes" against the rebels by reviving the "democratic" political process in Chechnya. This process was, in fact, similar to that which took place in Punjab under Narasimha Rao and Beant Singh during which the central and state governments effectively coordinated their military operations against the internally-divided Sikh militants, and also concurrently revived the democratic political process to wean Sikh political elements away from "the militants" and back into more "normal" modes of politics. Putin began this process by holding a constitutional referendum in Chechnya, reaffirming its status as an integral part of the Russian federation and also Kadyrov's position as Chechen president.[26] Even though Akhmad Kadyrov was assassinated by Chechen separatists in the spring of 2004, unified Russian authorities continued with their attempt to further enhance the legitimacy of the pro-Moscow Chechen government by holding parliamentary elections in the province. Voter turnout for these elections held in late-2005 was much greater than expected, and pro-Moscow parties loyal to Ramzan Kadyrov, Akhmad's son, did particularly well.[27] Ramzan Kadyrov's electoral success, in turn, facilitated a continual stream of defections from the rebels to the official Chechen government. The Chechen ethnonationalist insurgency, which continued to be internally-divided between moderate and radical factions, suffered additional major setbacks when Maskhadov and Basayev were killed in 2005 and 2006, respectively.[28] Thus, Russian military successes coincided with the central government's policy of reviving democratic elections in Chechnya in order to re-integrate more moderate ethnic elements into the "normal" political process instead of having them continue supporting separatism. The result was a consistent decline in violence and a quick dampening of insurgency after 2006.

The immediate future of the separatist movement in Chechnya portends a severely weakened insurgency which, unless predominant "patterns of political leadership" change, will resemble more of a parochial terrorist campaign as opposed to a mass-based insurgency. To explain, ruling Russian elites in Moscow and ruling Chechen elites in Grozny remain internally-united within their respective political systems and also united with each other across systems, thus helping formulate and implement coordinated policy to continue to confront ethnic separatism. The Chechen population also appears to have found Ramzan Kadyrov's moderate Chechen government to be a more viable channel for ethnic nationalism than continuing to back separatist insurgency. This is evident by the increasing levels of support in Chechnya for the state-sponsored political process.[29] Furthermore, the Chechen ethnonationalist insurgency has lacked an institutionalized political front in the region for years and the remaining armed wing of the movement remains internally-divided along ideological lines, not to mention weakened by clan-based fissures. Yet, countervailing "patterns of political leadership" will help spare the Chechen ethnonationalist insurgency from complete demise like the Sikh separatist insurgency in Punjab. In particular, current rebel leader Doku Umarov has been at least marginally successful in bridging internal ideological divisions within the armed Chechen ethnonationalist movement and coordinating the few remaining rebel groups' operational unity against Russian and pro-government forces.[30] Thus, the Chechen separatist movement may persist into the future but in a very significantly dampened form than in the past due to the culmination of the complex "patterns of political leadership" analyzed here.

Northern Ireland

The inability of the Catholic political elites and the ruling state elites in both London and Stormont to sort out their political differences provided an underlying basis for the conflict in Northern Ireland. The province of Northern Ireland was created under the 1920 Government of Ireland Act which partitioned the island into two parts—an independent south (the Republic of Ireland) containing an overwhelming Catholic majority, and the north (Northern Ireland) with a population of about 65 percent Protestant and 35 percent Catholic.[31] After partition, Protestants in the province developed a "siege mentality" by which they feared that the withdrawal of British troops would lead to internal civil war and possible republican involvement from the South.[32] As a result, Protestants, with the support of political elites in London, ignored the political and economic concerns of Catholics, and instead devised political institutions and electoral procedures to ensure lasting Protestant domination in Northern Ireland's semi-independent parliament called Stormont. Some scholars have characterized this as being a "pathological specimen of majoritarian 'democracy'" which provided an underlying basis for potential conflict.[33]

In addition to differences between Catholic and governing state elites, intra-elite competition in London also provided a catalyst for the emergence of the contemporary insurgency in Northern Ireland. To explain, the Labour Party came into power for the first time in nearly 15 years in Great Britain in 1964, but with a razor-thin majority of only 4 seats. Immediately after the 1964 parliamentary elections, incoming prime minister Harold Wilson publicly expressed his sympathy for the idea of a united Ireland, thus raising expectations for change and intensifying friction between Catholics and the Stormont regime.[34] Wilson's stance on Northern Ireland was largely predicated on the changing nature of party competition in Great Britain. Considering the Labour Party's new-found political competitiveness and the narrowness of its parliamentary majority, Wilson perceived it pragmatic to try to garner political support from Northern Ireland's Catholic community because the Conservative Party could, in contrast, rely on the Protestant-based Unionist parties in Northern Ireland, which usually won all 12 parliamentary seats in the province, to help forge majorities in London.[35] Thus, the intensification of political competition between state elites in London played a major role in increasing tensions and the likelihood of conflict in Northern Ireland.

Intra-elite competition within the Catholic community also increased the prospects for violent political conflict in Northern Ireland. To explain, the newly-created Northern Ireland Civil Rights Association (NICRA) launched a non-violent movement in 1967 to end discriminatory economic and political practices against the Catholics. The moderate Stormont prime minister, Terence O'Neil, tried to ameliorate Catholic discontent by conceding to several of the NICRA's demands after widespread peaceful protests. This prompted the NICRA to declare a temporary moratorium on demonstrations, but internal dissentions soon emerged within the NICRA which lead to its bifurcation and the emergence of a radical splinter group called the People's Democracy.[36] People's Democracy refused to honor the NICRA's moratorium on protests, thus angering Protestants who viewed O'Neil's concessions as being too accommodative and ineffective in mitigating Catholic mobilization. In January 1969, Protestant mobs attacked a People's Democracy march in Londonderry, and, instead of stopping the attackers, the Protestant-dominated police force actually joined in by indiscriminately beating Catholic residents and destroying their property. This infamous "Bogside Incident" left the Catholic community in Northern Ireland outraged, and "the Troubles" began immediately thereafter. Thus, intra-elite factionalism within the Catholic community contributed to the emergence of the violent political conflict in Northern Ireland through the process of ethnic elite "out-flanking."

Intra-elite competition between ruling Protestant leaders in Stormont also played a major role in escalating the conflict in Northern Ireland, as did competition between Catholic elites. O'Neil's decision to implement civil rights and economic reforms during the recession-inflicted mid and late-1960s was largely designed to stymie the loss of Protestant working-class support from the Unionists to the socialist Northern Ireland Labour Party.[37] Yet, O'Neil's reform package alienated more extreme elements within the Unionist Party led by Rev. Ian Paisley, who accused O'Neil of encouraging Catholic mobilization by eroding the structures of Protestant domination so effectively institutionalized since the 1920s.[38] This intra-elite schism within Northern Ireland's Protestant leadership prompted the formation of several armed Unionist paramilitary organizations in the late-1960s. These Protestant paramilitary groups subsequently capitalized on their community's fear of reforms and committed several spectacular acts of sabotage and political violence, blaming them on the Irish Republican Army (IRA).[39] In April 1969, the beleaguered O'Neil government was forced to resign from office and British troops were rushed into Northern Ireland, much to the delight of extremist Unionists. A more extreme Unionist government subsequently came into power in Northern Ireland with the support of the Conservative Party.[40] Instead of continuing with reforms, this new government opted for increased political repression in trying to deal with Catholic mobilization. This increased repression, in turn, compelled the Catholic-based IRA to resume its military campaign for reunification with the South in the winter of 1969 after several decades of dormancy, beginning the contemporary armed insurgency in Northern Ireland.

Thus, many of the "patterns of political leadership" which gave rise to the emergence of the Sikh ethnonationalism in Punjab also help explain the emergence of the violent republican movement in Northern Ireland. To explain, inter-elite competition between Catholic and state elites, intra-elite competition within the ruling establishments in both London and Stormont (for example, the razor-thin competition between Wilson's Labour Party and the Conservative Party, and the competition between the moderate O'Neil and the more extreme Paisley), and intra-elite competition within the Catholic political elite (for example, the schism between NICRA and People's Democracy) contributed to the emergence of contemporary insurgency in Northern Ireland. These "patterns of political leadership" closely resemble those found in the emerging phases of the

"Punjab crisis" during the early and mid-1980s with the inability of the Akali Dal and Congress (I) central government to reconcile their political differences, the unprincipled intra-party competition within the Congress (I) between Zail Singh and Darbara Singh, and internal factionalism and "ethnic-outbidding" between Sikh political leaders, including those in the Akali Dal.

Yet, contrasting "patterns of political leadership" help explain why the ethnonationalist insurgency in Punjab fizzled out relatively quickly, whereas the one in Northern Ireland proved to be much more sustainable. First, the dynamics of party competition within Northern Ireland have presented the British central state with a nearly insurmountable obstacle in successfully undermining or dividing the republican movement. To explain, Northern Ireland's political party system is highly-polarized along sectarian Protestant–Catholic lines.[41] The overwhelming majority of Protestants vote for either the Official Unionist Party (OUP) or the comparatively more extreme Democratic Unionist Party (DUP). On the other side of the communal divide, Catholics overwhelmingly support either the Social Democratic and Labour Party (SDLP) or the republican nationalist Sinn Fein. The only major political party which receives support from both communities is the Alliance Party, whose overall vote percentage has traditionally been in the single digits. These dynamics of party competition—which lead to ethnic bifurcation—contrast sharply with those in Punjab where the "catch-all," secular Congress (I) party has traditionally been the single largest political party in the state. Sikh support in Punjab has, in fact, been divided across the political spectrum between the Akali Dal, the Congress (I), and the two major communist parties. Furthermore, the Akali Dal has only come to power in Punjab in coalition with the Hindu-based BJP, thus further ameliorating Sikh–Hindu divisions in the state in contrast to the more rigid Catholic–Protestant chasm in Northern Ireland.

Second, the nature of political competition within Northern Ireland's Catholic community has also obstructed the central state's ability to foster the emergence of a more moderate ethnic leadership to effectively compete with the extremist Sinn Fein and help divide the republican movement. This has been the case because the Sinn Fein actually transplanted the comparatively more moderate SDLP as being the most popular Catholic political party in Northern Ireland since the beginning of "The Troubles."[42] In fact, intra-elite competition within Northern Ireland's Catholic community has produced an institutionalized, but controlled, form of "ethnic-outbidding" in which the SDLP cannot moderate too much without losing a large chunk of its support base to the Sinn Fein. Thus, moderates within Northern Ireland's Catholic community have not been able to become dominant over more extreme elements like what occurred in Sikh politics in Punjab through the early and mid-1990s. This political dynamic within Northern Ireland's Catholic community makes the republican insurgency there more sustainable than was the Sikh ethnonationalist insurgency in Punjab.

Third, in contrast to most insurgent movements throughout the world, Northern Ireland's Catholic republican movement has remained remarkably united. The unity between the IRA and the Sinn Fein has provided the republican movement with the quintessential-type of ethnonationalist organization to sustain violent insurgency. The close symbiotic relationship between the IRA and the Sinn Fein has been evident by the fact that the IRA is considered to be the "military wing" of the Sinn Fein, and the Sinn Fein is the "political arm" of the IRA. This close relationship gives the IRA a well-institutionalized political front with which to maintain support for its cause, and it gives the Sinn Fein a credible military wing for increased bargaining power vis-a-vis both Stormont and London. The IRA itself is organized into multiple 12-member "active service units" under the centralized command of a 7-member Army Council.[43] Sinn Fein leader Gerry Adams and his top lieutenant Martin McGuinness have both, in fact, been members of the IRA Army Council, thus illustrating the close and overlapping inter-relationship between the IRA and the Sinn Fein. This is in sharp contrast to the Sikh ethnonationalist insurgency during the early-1990s in which "the militants" and "extremists" became competing political entities instead of mutually-cooperative ones, thus contributing to the movement's eventual, and virtually complete, demise in Punjab.

Finally, in addition to unity between both organizations, the IRA and the Sinn Fein have also been remarkably successful in maintaining internal unity within their respective organizations, with only limited internal factionalism.[44] In particular, none of the splinter groups which have periodically emerged from either the IRA or Sinn Fein have been able to even remotely compete, either militarily or politically, with their parent organizations.[45] For example, a 2007 study by the British Ministry of Defence concluded that the IRA had not been defeated on the battlefield in Northern Ireland, and described it as being "a professional, dedicated, highly-skilled, and resilient force" in contrast to other armed republican groups which were characterized as being "little more than a collection of gangsters."[46] This lack of internal factionalism within Catholic ethnonationalist organizations has also strengthened the movement's overall political efficacy, and has made crushing or undermining it an exceedingly difficult task for the central state. This dynamic contrasts sharply with the highly-fractionalized Sikh separatist insurgency (and its multiplicity of competing "militant" and "extremist" organizations) which emerged during the early-1990s and contributed to it fizzling-out by the mid-1990s.

As a result of the "patterns of political leadership" described here, the central British state has not been able to crush the republican insurgency in Northern Ireland through either physical force, or by undermining it by promoting internal factionalism or fostering an alternative set of dominant "moderate" ethnic elites. Since neither side can achieve an overt "military" victory, resolution of the Northern Ireland conflict will invariably involve some sort of political compromise between the Sinn Fein and governing elites in both Stormont and London. For this reason, the central state entered into a series of negotiations with the republican movement starting in the mid-1980s which resulted in the 1985 Anglo–Irish Agreement, the 1993 Downing Street Declaration, and 1998 Good Friday Agreement.[47] These attempts to settle the conflict included various types of power-sharing arrangements between Catholics and Protestants in Northern Ireland, and also the increased devolution of power from London to Stormont. Yet, these agreements could not be fully implemented because of the intransigence of extremists within both major communities in Northern Ireland, especially on the Protestant side. For this reason, the Catholic republican insurgency continued intermittently through the 1990s and 2000s, with brief periods of cease-fire to allow for negotiations.

A potential breakthrough appeared to have been made in the spring of 2007 through direct negotiations between the Sinn Fein and the DUP, the first of their kind in history. As a result of these negotiations, the IRA agreed to decommission its weapons and join the "normal" political process, the Sinn Fein agreed to recognize Northern Ireland's police force, and the DUP agreed to share power with the Sinn Fein. This new agreement also allotted seats in Northern Ireland's 12-member governing council to each major political party commensurate with their strength in the provincial assembly. Yet, it remains to be seen if this agreement can hold into the future or whether it will breakdown like previous agreements.[48] If this agreement falls apart, the Sinn Fein and the IRA appear to retain the ability to renew and sustain their republican insurgency in virtually unmitigated fashion well into the future due to the "patterns of political leadership" and dynamics analyzed here.

Jammu and Kashmir

The conflict in Muslim-majority Kashmir traces its contemporary origins back to the Partition of the subcontinent during British rule and the accession of the province to India by its Hindu ruler in 1947. After Independence, the Indian-controlled state of Jammu and Kashmir was governed primarily by Sheikh Abdullah—leader of the moderate Muslim-based National Conference party—who was allowed to remain in power by the central Indian authorities as long as he did not openly contest Kashmir's accession to India. Yet, by the mid-1970s, Sheikh Abdullah became increasingly alienated from the central government in New Delhi, which he accused of systematically eroding Kashmir's special constitutional status and regional autonomy.[49] This alienation coincided with, and was accentuated by, the changing nature of political competition in the center, as a viable coalition of opposition political parties emerged to challenge the Congress (I)'s historical dominance over national politics since Independence. In light of these changing political dynamics, Sheikh Abdullah aligned with the opposition Janata coalition, which eventually came to power in New Delhi in 1977 after the Emergency. Yet, the Janata-led central government fell within about two years and the Congress (I) came back into power in 1980, thus altering Sheikh Abdullah's relationship with the center once again from being largely cooperative and symbiotic to becoming more competitive and conflictual. Incidentally, this occurred at about the same time that the relationship between the Akali Dal and the central government changed in a similar way.

Farooq Abdullah, who became leader of the National Conference after Sheikh Abdullah's death, continued with his father's post-1977 strategy of aligning with national opposition parties against the Congress (I) after assuming the chief ministership of Kashmir in 1982. Indira Gandhi and the Congress (I) sought to have an "electoral adjustment" with the National Conference in 1983 for legislative assembly elections in the state, but Farooq—who complained about the center's supposedly discriminatory treatment of Muslim-majority Kashmir—refused and instead turned to Muslim-based religious parties for electoral support.[50] The National Conference, with the assistance of Muslim religious parties, dominated these elections and came into power with an overwhelming majority in Kashmir, much to the chagrin of Mrs Gandhi and the Congress (I).

The formation of another National Conference government in Kashmir was not acceptable to Mrs Gandhi, whose position of power in the center had become much less secure after 1977 than ever before. For this reason,

Mrs Gandhi and the Congress (I) actively promoted factionalism within the National Conference and coordinated with emerging dissident National Conference leader G.M. Shah to try to undermine Farooq's ministry.[51] Farooq's ministry was, indeed, unceremoniously dismissed in July 1984 without being allowed a chance to prove its assembly majority after legislators loyal to Shah split from their parent organization. This dismissal of the popularly-elected National Conference government in such a blatantly partisan manner shocked the Kashmiri Muslim population, and massive demonstrations subsequently erupted throughout the state. For the first time in the post-Independence era, activists of pro-plebiscite Kashmiri groups also began engaging in acts of political violence against the central state, marking the beginning of the contemporary armed insurgency in the state. Thus, the intense power struggle between the regional ethnic leadership and the central state elites, internal divisions between the central elites, and internal factionalism within the regional ethnic leadership coalesced to help spark the beginnings of violent ethnonationalism in Kashmir in much the same way similar "patterns of political leadership" contributed to the initial emergence of Sikh militancy and political violence in Punjab. The ethnonationalist insurgency in Kashmir subsequently escalated precipitously through the 1990s.[52]

The dynamics of ethnic insurgency in Kashmir after its initial emergence contrast sharply to those that eventually emerged in Punjab, thus helping explain why the one in Kashmir persists whereas the one in Punjab completely declined. First, armed insurgent groups in Kashmir have maintained a relatively higher degree of unity than those in Punjab were able to maintain. To explain, the insurgency in Kashmir was initially dominated by the Jammu and Kashmir Liberation Front (JKLF), an indigenous nationalist Kashmiri group which espouses a secular ideology and demands a plebiscite to determine the constitutional status of the state. The indigenous religiously-oriented Hizb-ul-Mujahideen (HuM) also existed at the time but it attracted only limited support in comparison to the widely more popular JKLF. Yet, the nature of the insurgency began to change dramatically through the early-1990s when overtly pro-Pakistan insurgent groups emerged and became dominant within the movement.[53] Yet, even though a multiplicity of ideologically-diverse armed groups operate in Kashmir, most of them—including the JKLF and HuM—have remained largely united under the overarching and coordinating umbrella of the Pakistan-based Mutahida Jehad Council (MJC) currently chaired by Syed Salahuddin.[54] The MJC has, in particular, helped these groups maintain a relatively high degree of operational unity against the central Indian state and its security forces. For this reason, levels of internecine violence and bloodletting between Kashmiri insurgent groups have remained comparatively limited in contrast to those that emerged between the multiplicities of Sikh insurgent groups operating in Punjab under competing Panthic Committees during the latter stages of the Sikh ethnonationalist movement. Thus, the relatively successful coordinating role played by the MJC makes the insurgency in Kashmir more sustainable than was the one in Punjab, which completely declined by the mid-1990s.

Second, armed militant groups in Kashmir have retained a much more effective political front in the form of the "extremist" All-Party Hurriyat Conference (APHC) than Sikh separatists were able to maintain in Punjab. The APHC—which unites a multitude of important Kashmiri political, social, and religious organizations—has been the militants' main source of institutionalized, above-ground political support in Kashmir since 1993.[55] Even though an informal ideological schism emerged within the APHC in 2003 between a "hawk" faction led by Syed Ali Shah Geelani and a "dove" faction currently led by Mirwaiz Umar Farooq, the APHC has nonetheless maintained a strong united front on most grassroots political issues affecting the Muslim population in Kashmir. Both "ideological" factions within the APHC have also, in fact, remained united in their unequivocal refusal to participate in any elections held under the Indian Constitution.[56] This refusal to accept the legitimacy of Indian political institutions makes dividing the "political wing" of the ethnonationalist movement in Kashmir much more difficult for the central Indian state than was the Sikh ethnonationalist movement in Punjab, where "the extremists" eventually became completely fractionalized and began eagerly rejoining the government-sponsored political process in the early-1990s in their intense competition against each other. Thus, the nature and comparative effectiveness of the militants' primary above-ground political front in Kashmir with the APHC contrasts sharply, at least for the time being, to those which eventually emerged in Punjab.

Third, the dynamics of political party competition within the Muslim community in Kashmir, and the relationship of the community's two "moderate" ethnic parties with national-level political parties contrast sharply with those which eventually emerged in Punjab. To explain, a new and powerful ethnic political party, the People's Democratic Party (PDP) led by former union home minister Mufti Mohammad Sayeed, came onto Kashmir's political scene in 2002 in opposition to the dominant National Conference. The emergence of the Muslim-based PDP was largely in response to Farooq Abdullah's willingness to align his National Conference party with the Hindu-nationalist Bharatiya Janata Party (BJP) in electoral politics starting in the late-1990s. The newly founded PDP took full advantage of the National Conference's electoral relationship with the BJP by offering itself as being a viable alternative to it. In particular, the PDP began taking slightly more radical ethnic positions than the National Conference in its attempt to wean away Muslim support from the National Conference, including calling for unconditional dialog with the militants to help solve the "Kashmir problem." Yet, surprisingly, the Congress (I) proved willing to align with the PDP in electoral politics in order to more effectively compete with its primary electoral rival, the BJP, in both Kashmir and also nationally.[57] Thus, the two "moderate" Kashmiri Muslim political parties have engaged in "ethnic-outbidding," although in a controlled fashion, against each other to retain their Muslim support base and also try to win elections in the state. In addition, the two major national political parties—the Congress (I) and BJP—have been willing to tolerate this controlled "ethnic-outbidding" by the PDP and National Conference, respectively, in order to retain reliable coalition partners in their political competition against each other. Thus, a fascinating, but dangerous, dynamic in the linkage between community, state, and national politics has emerged in Kashmir that helps sustain, rather than dampen, violent ethnonationalism. In contrast, the various Akali factions in Punjab had eventually united and began engaging in the gradual process of competitive "ethnic-underbidding" instead of "outbidding" to help bring "normalcy" to that state in cooperation with ruling central state elites through the mid-1990s. Only more recently has this trend been reversed in Jammu and Kashmir with the National Conference forming a coalition government with the Congress (I) after the 2008 state assembly elections. Yet, it remains to be seen if the Congress (I) and BJP are willing to abandon either the National Conference or the PDP for ideological, as opposed to strategic, reasons in their competition with each other in the future.

The immediate future of ethnonationalist insurgency in Kashmir appears to be quite challenging for the central Indian state as long as the militant groups remain marginally united under the MJC, the extremists found in the APHC do not completely fractionalize and become internally competitive, and as long as the two "moderate" ethnic parties in the state continue to engage in competitive "ethnic-outbidding" as opposed to "ethnic-underbidding" often with the tacit support of the two main national political parties. Absent changes in these "patterns of political leadership," the central government's attempt to restore the democratic political process in the state by holding a series of democratic elections starting in early-2005 has not succeeded in ending the insurgency, although levels of political violence do appear to be declining after 2007.[58] Thus, the insurgency in Kashmir—which may periodically wax and wane somewhat—is likely to persist in the immediate future, unlike the one in Punjab which completely declined, due to the complex "patterns of political leadership" analyzed here.

Assam

The contemporary conflict in Assam emerged from two inter-related political issues dominating the state's politics in the post-Independence era—the language question and the illegal immigration of "foreigners" into the state. Regarding the former, "ethnic Assamese" resented the traditional predominance of the Bengali language in the state's governmental, administrative, and educational institutions since the colonial period. This had led to minor "language riots" between "ethnic Assamese" and Bengali-speakers in the 1960s and the early-1970s. Regarding the second issue, as many as 5 million illegal immigrants—mostly Bengali-speaking Muslims from "East Pakistan" (now known as "Bangladesh")—were living in Assam in 1971 and comprised about one-third of the state's population, thus irking the "ethnic Assamese" population.[59]

Assam had been governed exclusively by the Congress party since Independence, but this changed in 1977 when the Janata Party came to power in the center and in most of the states. The Janata government in Assam was led by Golap Borbora. In early-1979, Hiralal Patwari—a Janata Party MP—died, setting the stage for an important by-election to fill his vacant parliamentary seat. "Ethnic Assamese" organizations led by the All Assam Students Union (AASU) and the Assam Gana Sangram Parishad (AGSP) demanded that the names of "illegal immigrants" on voter lists be purged before this by-election. Borbara's government acquiesced and recommended deleting nearly two-thirds of the suspected "illegal immigrants" from voter lists, but this decision evoked a strong averse reaction from the Muslim members of his government.[60] The Congress (I) took full advantage of this controversy and, in concert with Muslim legislators within the Janata Party and also the Communists, toppled Borbora's government.[61] The AASU and AGSP responded to the toppling of Borbora's government by launching a massive agitation, including blocking the transport of crude oil out of Assam to the rest of India.[62]

As a result of this "ethnic Assamese" agitation, polling could only be held in two of Assam's 14 parliamentary constituencies in January 1980. At the national level, Mrs Gandhi's Congress (I) came back into power in New Delhi. Instead of negotiating with the AASU and AGSP, Mrs Gandhi sought to weaken and undermine the "ethnic Assamese" movement by trying to foster splits within it. In this attempt, Mrs Gandhi rebuffed the AASU and AGSP, and instead entered into negotiations with the All Assam Minority Students Union (AAMSU) in the summer of 1980 over the issue of illegal immigration.[63] The AAMSU, which had emerged earlier the same year with the support of the Congress (I), consisted mostly of Assamese Muslims and tribals who, while not disputing the seriousness of the problem of illegal immigration, were also concerned about the increasingly narrow construction of "ethnic Assamese" identity being formulated by the AASU and AGSP.[64] This angered the AASU and AGSP who reacted by expanding their agitation to include the blockage of essential bamboo, jute, and plywood out of Assam in addition to oil. In response to the AASU and AGSP's expanded agitation, Mrs Gandhi ordered the Indian Army into Assam, resulting in scores of deaths and the implementation of draconian laws by the central government to control the unrest. Shortly thereafter, the United Liberation Front of Assam (ULFA)—which had been created in 1979 but had remained largely inactive in comparison to the AASU and AGSP—escalated its campaign of sabotage and political assassinations, thus marking the beginnings of contemporary insurgency in Assam.

Thus, three "patterns of political leadership" help explain the emergence of the ethnic insurgency in Assam. First, the inability of the "ethnic Assamese" elites and the governing central elites, especially those of the Congress (I), to resolve their political differences provided an underlying basis for the conflict. Second, competition between the central elites also helped catalyze the conflict when the Congress (I) engineered the collapse of Borbora's Janata government which, in turn, prompted the AASU and AGSP to launch their massive agitation against the center. Third, divisions within the ethnic elites, partially facilitated by the central government, contributed to the rise of extremism after the AASU and the AGSP radicalized their agitation in reaction to the emergence of the AAMSU. This radicalization, in turn, invited a harsh state response and marked the beginning of political violence in the state with ULFA's active armed resistance. These "patterns of political leadership" are similar to those which coalesced during the initial phases of the Sikh ethnonationalist movement in Punjab before Operation Bluestar, including the intense political competition between the ethnic and the central state elites, competition between governing state elites, and the fractionalization of the regional ethnic leadership.

The sustenance of the ethnonationalist insurgency in Assam also bears striking resemblance to the Punjab case. In 1982, Mrs Gandhi announced that fresh state assembly elections would be held in Assam in February 1983 but under the pre-1979 voter lists. "Ethnic Assamese" organizations opposed this decision and, after negotiations over this issue broke down, "ethnic Assamese" slaughtered over 2,000 Bangladeshi, mostly Muslim, immigrants on 18 February 1983 in one of the bloodiest days of communal violence in India's history.[65] Yet, Mrs Gandhi refused to relent and state assembly elections were held later that month as scheduled. For their part, the AASU and the AGSP successfully boycotted these elections and voter turnout in constituencies dominated by "ethnic-Assamese" was minimal. As expected, the Congress (I) came into power with Hiteswar Saikia as chief minister. During this period, the ethnic insurgency in Assam continued with the highly-disciplined ULFA acting as the "military wing" of the movement, and remaining subservient to the movement's "political wing" led by the AASU and the AGSP—two organizations which closely coordinated their activities.

Instead of continuing with his mother's confrontational approach to politics, new incoming Indian prime minister Rajiv Gandhi pursued a more accommodative approach in dealing with the regional ethnic leaders, including in Assam. In August 1985, he negotiated the "Assam Accord" with the "ethnic Assamese" leaders which stipulated that illegal aliens who had entered into Assam between 1966 and 1971 would be disenfranchised for 10 years, those having entered after 1971 would be deported, and that fresh elections would be held in the state.[66] The Assam Accord was, incidentally, reached at about the same time that Rajiv signed the "Punjab Accord" with the Akali Dal in Punjab. After signing the Assam Accord, leaders of the "ethnic Assamese" movement—including those of the AASU and the AGSP—coalesced to join the government-sponsored political process and formed a new political party called the Asom Gana Parishad (AGP) to contest upcoming elections. In October 1985, the AGP came into power under former AASU president, Prafulla Kumar Mahanta.[67]

The signing of the Assam Accord and the formation of an AGP government was expected to be a definitive solution for the "Assam problem," but this was not to be the case. Much like the case with the Punjab Accord, Rajiv began to backtrack on key provisions of the Assam Accord as his power within the party and in the center started eroding.[68] In fact, instead of implementing the Assam Accord, the Congress (I) central government actually began trying to undermine the AGP government by, in part, abetting the rise of violent Bodo subnationalism in the state which demanded the creation of a separate "Bodoland"—a demand vehemently opposed by the "ethnic Assamese" organizations.[69] For its part, the AGP government, much like the Akali Dal government in Punjab at the time, became stuck between a Congress (I) central government which appeared to be reneging on its commitments and popular ethnic organizations—the AASU and the ULFA—which had placed high expectations on it.[70] The AASU's increasingly vocal criticism of the AGP government was also prompted by the emergence of a new, more radical student organization called the Asom Jatiyatabadi Yuva Chatra Parishad (AJYCP), which threatened to usurp the AASU's traditional "ethnic Assamese" support base if it too did not radicalize.[71] Problems for the Assamese ethnonationalist movement were compounded even further when, for the first time in its organizational history, the AGP became bifurcated between chief minister Prafulla Mahanta and home minister Brighu Phukan—both former high-level AASU leaders.[72] Thus, the wider "ethnic Assamese" ethnonationalist movement, especially its "political wing," became fractionalized at different levels in the mid and late-1980s. This fractionalization allowed the "militant" ULFA to move to the forefront of the ethnonationalist movement at the expense of the comparatively more moderate AGP and AASU, and levels of political violence subsequently increased markedly as a reinvigorated ULFA resumed its armed campaign through the late-1980s. Both V.P. Singh's National Front government and Chandra Shekhar's Janata government were unable to effectively confront the insurgency largely because of internal divisions within their ruling coalitions in the center.[73]

Thus, several "patterns of political leadership" coalesced during the late-1980s to re-catalyze the violent Assamese ethnonationalist movement including continuing differences between state and ethnic elites, divisions between ruling central elites and within governing coalitions, and the splintering and subsequent radicalization of the "political" wing of the Assamese nationalist movement. These "patterns of political leadership" closely mirror those which precipitated the re-emergence and escalation of the Sikh ethnonationalist movement in Punjab after Operation Bluestar, including increased friction between the Akali Dal and the central government after the non-implementation of the Punjab Accord, internal divisions within Rajiv's Congress (I) central government and the divided nature of subsequent coalition governments, and the splintering of the "traditional Akali leadership" and the rise of more extremist Sikh elements within Sikh politics.

The central Indian state was successful in dramatically curtailing levels of political violence in Assam through the early and mid-1990s, but contrasting "patterns of political leadership" in Assam have prevented the government from completely undermining the ethnonationalist movement as it did in Punjab. To explain, elections in India, including state assembly polls in Assam, were held in June 1991. The AGP was divided for these elections between the Mahanta and Phukan factions. As a result, the Congress (I) came into power in Assam with Hiteswar Saikia as its chief minister, and it also came to power in the center under Narasimha Rao.[74] Within a few months, the Rao central government, in close coordination with Saikia's state government, launched a massive Army operation against ULFA called "Operation Rhino." In contrast to earlier military operations under the V.P. Singh and Chandra Shekhar governments, ruling authorities were completely united in 1991 with the Congress (I) in power at both the center and state levels. As a result of this coordinated governmental action, a large section of ULFA's leadership and rank-and-file was arrested or killed, leaving the organization severely weakened.[75] In addition, "Operation Rhino" also caused a split within ULFA for the first time in its organizational history as a "pro-negotiation" faction emerged, which subsequently engaged in direct talks with the Indian government.[76] A subsection of this "pro-negotiation" ULFA faction eventually "surrendered" to the Indian government in exchange for amnesty and rehabilitation, and became known as (Surrendered) United Liberation Front of Assam or SULFA.[77] Rao and Saikia subsequently followed-up on their military "successes" by revamping the democratic political process in the state, including at the local level, to help build increased legitimacy for the Congress (I) state government and dampen ethnonationalist insurgency even further. This process, in fact, almost mirrored the one that took place in Punjab with the coordinated action of Rao's central government and Beant Singh's state government in Punjab which helped "turn the tide" against Sikh militancy and ushered-in increased political "normalcy" to that state.

The future of the Assamese ethnonationalist insurgency presents a mixed picture for the Indian state. To explain, ULFA has lost an effective "political front" in both the AGP and also the AASU. The AGP has, in fact, remained committed to electoral politics, and has alternated in and out of power with the Congress (I) at the state level since 1985. For its part, the AASU has largely moved away from ULFA since the mid-1990s, criticizing it for its unwillingness to compromise with the center. The AASU is, in fact, much closer to the AGP today than to ULFA. Yet, countervailing "patterns of political leadership" help sustain the Assamese ethnonationalist movement and prevent its complete demise as occurred in Punjab. For example, ULFA has managed to retain a significant degree of popular support for its armed struggle for sovereignty by formally dividing its organization into discreet "military" and "political" wings, and by creating a unified People's Consultative Group whose members include prominent journalists, human rights activists, lawyers, and academics from the "ethnic Assamese" society.[78] In contrast, Sikh militants in Punjab were unable to create an institutionalized internal political front or retain an effective external political front in the form of "the extremists," who eventually fractionalized into a multiplicity of competitive groupings and rejoined the government-sponsored political process through the early and mid-1990s. Second, and more importantly, the main ULFA faction led by Paresh Baruah has been surprisingly successful in maintaining its internal organizational unity. After all, SULFA does not actively compete with ULFA within the Assamese ethnonationalist movement nor does it confront it militarily in any significant way. Thus, the "bifurcation" experienced by ULFA is qualitatively different from the complete fractionalization and splintering of the armed Sikh militants in Punjab who had began engaging in destructive internecine warfare by the early-1990s. ULFA will most likely be able to maintain its ethnonationalist insurgency well into the future but probably in significantly dampened form in comparison to the past due to the "patterns of political leadership" analyzed here. In fact, the insurgency-related death toll in Assam bears out this assessment by showing lower levels of ethnonationalist violence since the early-1990s but its continuation nonetheless.[79]

CONCLUDING REMARKS

In conclusion, what, if anything, of significance or consequence has this book offered in explaining violent ethnonationalist movements? As discussed in Chapter 1, the main arguments formulated in this book both differ from and contribute to existing theories on the trajectory of violent ethnonationalist movements. First, there is no existing theory which analyzes the effects of "patterns of political leadership" on this phenomenon. Second, existing theories tend to explain either the rise of ethnonationalist movements or their fall, but not both phases of this phenomenon within a unified analytical framework. Third, most explanations for ethnonationalism focus primarily on underlying permissive conditions, instead of on the proximate political processes that catalyze mobilization and conflict at given points in time and foster its demise at others. This book has attempted to fill these analytical gaps in the existing literature on the trajectory of violent ethnonationalist movements.

In essence, this book has provided a general theory of how *"patterns of political leadership," defined as the dynamic interaction between and amongst state and ethnic elites, significantly affect the trajectory of ethnic subnationalist movements by defining the political relationship between an ethnic group and the central state*. It has been argued that political leaders and their dynamic interaction are largely responsible for the rise, sustenance, and/or decline of violent ethnonationalist conflicts so endemic throughout the world today. This usually involves not only inter-elite interaction between ethnic and state leaders, but also intra-elite competition within an ethnic group and within the state, including the willingness of factional leaders to build ephemeral "alliances of convenience" with unlikely partners, often to the detriment of pacific ethnic group–state relations. Thus, instead of relying on underlying permissive conditions or abstract variables to explain ethnonationalist movements, the specific arguments formulated in this book have incorporated the important role of *human agency* into their explanation and have also offered a proximate and observable *theory of action* which is applicable to ethnonationalist insurgencies in general with relatively little variation across cases. The general applicability of the propositions forwarded in this book was demonstrated by examining the trajectories of the ethnonationalist movements in Chechnya, Northern Ireland, Jammu and Kashmir, and Assam.

An important empirical conclusion emerging out of this book is that neither the rise, sustenance, and/or decline of ethnonationalist movements is inevitable. Instead, they are largely the products of the interaction between self-interested political elites, who not only react to the structural choices they face, but whose purposeful actions and decisions affect the larger political environment and ultimately the course of ethnic group–state relations. Acknowledgement of this empirical proposition holds a key to understanding the trajectory of violent ethnonationalist movements, holding self-interested political elites accountable for the consequences of their actions which often so violently affect the lives of their co-ethnic and co-nationals, and to avoiding the proverbial "fire next time," including the potential re-emergence of violent Sikh separatism in united India.

NOTES

1. For details, see Hewitt, J. Joseph, Jonathan Wilkenfeld, and Ted Robert Gurr. *Peace and Conflict 2008*, executive summary of the Center for International Development and Conflict Management report, University of Maryland, 2009, pp. 12 and 14. It is available at http://www.cidcm.umd.edu/pc/ (accessed 30 May 2009).
2. Ibid., 2 and 14.
3. Ted Robert Gurr and Barbara Harff, *Ethnic Conflict in World Politics* (Boulder, CO: Westview Press, 1994), xiii and 160–66.
4. Tribune News Service, "Battlelines Drawn in the Akali Dal." *The Tribune* (Chandigarh), 12 December 1998, online edition, available at http://www.tribuneindia.com98dec12 (accessed 15 December 1998).
5. Giani Puran Singh replaced Ranjit Singh as Akal Takht *jathedar*. Puran Singh was himself replaced by Joginder Singh Vedanti, an ardent Badal loyalist, in March 2000 because of his bickering with then SGPC president Bibi Jagir Kaur. More recently, Vedanti was forced to resign from the position of Akal Takht *jathedar* in August 2008 after making controversial remarks implicitly supporting the concept of "Khalistan" during a speech in New York, and was replaced by Giani Gurbachan Singh. For details of the latter episode, see Manish Sirindi, "Vedanti Quits, Gurbachan Singh to be Takht Jathedar." *The Tribune* (Chandigarh), August 6, 2008, online edition, available at http://www. tribuneindia.com/2008/20080806/main4.htm (accessed 11 August 2008).
6. Bibi Jagir Kaur held the position of SGPC president until November 2000 when she was replaced by Jagdev Singh Talwandi. Talwandi held this position for a short period of time after which he was replaced by the Badal loyalist, Kirpal Singh Badungar, before the ailing Tohra regained the SGPC presidency after his rapprochement with Badal in July 2003. Tohra passed away in April 2004. Bibi Jagir Kaur was subsequently again appointed as SGPC president until November 2005 when the ardent Badal loyalist, Avtar Singh Makkar, gained this post. Makkar has served as SGPC president, with Badal's personal support, ever since November 2005.
7. It should be noted that Tohra formed his own political party, the Sarb Hind Shiromani Akali Dal (SHSAD), shortly after being removed from the Akali Dal (Badal). This party existed until Tohra's rapprochement with Badal in July 2003.
8. In recent years, Parkash Singh Badal seems to be gradually transferring the leadership of the Akali Dal to his son, and former Member of Parliament, Sukhbir Singh Badal. Sukhbir had previously held the position of general secretary of the Akali Dal, but was made "acting president" of the party in March 2007. Subsequently, he was elected as Akali Dal president, with his father's blessing, in January 2008 and was also appointed to be "deputy" Chief Minister of Punjab by his father in January 2009. This gradual, orderly, and clear transition of power within the party from the "moderate" Parkash Singh Badal to Sukhbir, who is also considered to be a "moderate," has prevented factionalism and leadership struggles within the Akali Dal and has, thus, further contributed to the institutionalization of political stability in Sikh and Punjab politics.
9. For details, see Varinder Walia, "Conclave: PM's Intervention Did It." *The Tribune* (Chandigarh), 11 July 2007, online edition, available at http://tribuneindia. com/2007/20070711/punjab1.htm (accessed on 12 July 2007). The Dera Sacha Sauda controversy emerged when the leader of this "hetrodoxical" religious sect, Gurmit Ram Rayhem, supposedly mimicked the 10th Sikh guru and founder of the Khalsa,

Guru Gobind Singh, during a religious ceremony in May 2007. This incident sparked protests from Sikhs throughout India, and violence between Sikhs and members of the Sacha Sauda sect. The issue remains unresolved with continuing tension and periodic violence.

10. For an analytical discussion, see Jugdep S. Chima, "Back to the Future in 2002? A Predictive Model of Sikh Separatism in Punjab," *Studies in Conflict and Terrorism* 25:1 (January–February 2002), 31.

11. Babbar Khalsa activists have been suspected in periodic acts of "terrorism" in the post-1997 period including the bombing of a New Delhi cinema in May 2005 showing the film *Jo Bole So Nihal*, which was eventually pulled for its supposedly derogatory caricature of Sikh religious symbols; and also in alleged assassination attempts on leaders of "hetrodoxical" religious sects in Punjab, including Gurmit Ram Rayhem, Ashutosh Noormahalia, and Baba Banneriya. These periodic alleged acts of "terrorism" by select individuals hardly constitute the reemergence of insurgency or a mobilized ethnonationalist movement.

12. An exception was Simranjeet Singh Mann's victory from the Sangrur parliamentary constituency in the 1999 elections, which was the result of both his attempt to woo Hindu voters and local factionalism between loyalists of Surjit Singh Barnala and Sukhdev Singh Dhindsa—two major Akali leaders from the area.

13. Maneesh Chhibber, "SAD-BJP got 45.37% votes, Cong 40.9%." *The Tribune* (Chandigarh), March 2, 2007, online edition, available at http://www.tribuneindia. com/2007/20070302/punjab1.htm#1 (accessed on 5 March 2007). It should be noted that the "Panthic Morcha"—a conglomeration of anti-Badal Akali factions of which the Akali Dal (Mann) was a member—also won only 24 seats compared to 131 for the Akali Dal (Badal) in the May 2004 SGPC general elections, thus reaffirming Badal's clear supremacy in institutionalized Sikh politics.

14. Sanjeev Singh Bariana, "SAD(A) Formally Splits: Bittu to Head New Faction." *The Tribune* (Chandigarh), 1 December 2007, online edition, available at http://www. tribuneindia.com/2007/20071201/punjab1.htm (accessed 9 December 2007).

15. The "extremist" Dal Khalsa, which reorganized in August 2003 but publicly announced that it would work toward to goal of Sikh sovereignty and statehood through peaceful democratic means, is also a member of this "Khalsa Action Committee."

16. For a methodological discussion of "tendency statements" in political science, see James A. Bill and Robert L. Hardgrave, *Comparative Politics: The Quest for Theory* (Lanham, MD: University Press of America, 1981).

17. Gail Lapidus, "Contested Sovereignty: The Tragedy of Chechnya," *International Security* 23:1 (Summer 1998): 11 and 12; and Dmitri V. Trenin, Alesksei V. Malashenko, and Anatol Lieven, *Russia's Restless Frontier: The Chechnya Factor in Post-Soviet Russia* (Washington, D.C.: Carnegie Endowment for International Peace, Brookings Institution Press, 2004), 17 and 18.

18. Lapidus, "Contested Sovereignty," 12 and 16; and Dimitri V. Trenin, Alesksei V. Malashenko, and Anatol Lieven. *Russia's Restless Frontier*, 19 and 20.

19. For details, see Ibid., 23–25.

20. Lapidus, "Contested Sovereignty," 23; and Dimitri V. Trenin, Alesksei V. Malashenko, and Anatol Lieven, *Russia's Restless Frontier*, 28.

21. Ibid., 30.

22. Wikipedia, "Akhmad Kadyrov," available at http://en.wikipedia.org/wiki/Akhmad_Kadyrov (accessed on 13 October 2007).

23. For details, see Dimitri V. Trenin, Alesksei V. Malashenko, and Anatol Lieven, *Russia's Restless Frontier*, 34 and 35; and Wikipedia, "Shamil Basayev," available at http://en.wikipedia.org/wiki/Shamil_Basayev (accessed 13 October 2007).

24. Dimitri V. Trenin, Alesksei V. Malashenko, and Anatol Lieven, *Russia's Restless Frontier*, 36 and 40; and Wikipedia, "Akhmad Kadyrov."

25. Wikipedia, "Ramzan Kadyrov," available at http://en.wikipedia.org/wiki/Ramzan_Kadyrov (accessed on 16 October 2007).

26. Wikipedia, "Chechnya," available at http://en.wikipedia.org/wiki/Chechnya; and RFE/RL Newsline, "Russia: With Heavy Security in Evidence, Chechen Vote Comes Off without Violence," 27 November 2005, available at http://www.rferl.org/featurearticle/2005/11/41a88e3a-Oced-4639-bcf8-ef4dac1dd417.html (accessed 29 August 2006).

27. Ibid.

28. Wikipedia, "Chechnya." (accessed 16 October 2007).

29. For a discussion see RFE/RL, "Russia;" and BBC News, "Rebels' Dilemma After Basayev Death," 12 July 2006, available at http://newsvote.bbc.co.uk/mpapps/pagetools/print/news.bbc.co.uk/2/hi/europe/5168984.stm (accessed 16 October 2007).

30. For details see *Chechnya Weekly* (The Jamestown Foundation), "Dokku Umarov: Between Jihad and the Struggle for Freedom," 5 October 2006, available at http://www.jamestown.org/print_friendly.php?volume_id=3880&article_id=2371521 (accessed on 9 October 2006); and *Chechnya Weekly* (The Jamestown Foundation), "Doku Umarov's Attempts to Rebuild His Foundations," 20 September 2007, available at http://www.jamestown.org/chechnya_weekly/article.php?articleid=2373672&printthis=1 (accessed 16 October 2007).

31. Brendan O'Leary and John McGarry, *The Politics of Antagonism: Understanding Northern Ireland* (London: Athlone Press, 1993), 158.

32. For an explanation of this term see Elizabeth Crighton and Martha Abele Mac Iver, "The Evolution of Protracted Ethnic Conflict: Group Dominance and Political Underdevelopment in Northern Ireland and Lebanon," *Comparative Politics* 23, no. 2 (January 1991): 128–30.

33. Brendan O'Leary, "The Limits of Coercive Consociationalism in Northern Ireland," *Political Studies* 37, no. 4 (December 1989):, 562–63.

34. O'Leary and McGarry, *The Politics*, 159; and Adrian Guelke, "The Political Impasse in South Africa and Northern Ireland: A Comparative Perspective," *Comparative Politics* 23, no. 2 (January 1991): 151.

35. O'Leary and McGarry, *The Politics*, 159.

36. Ibid.

37. Sabine Wichert, *Northern Ireland since 1945* (New York: Longman Publishers, 1999), 73–74.

38. Ibid., 139 and 154.

39. Guelke, "The Political Impasse," 153.

40. O'Leary and McGarry, *The Politics*, 175.

41. For a detailed discussion see G. Evans and M. Duffy, "Beyond the Sectarian Divide: The Social Bases and Political Consequences of Nationalist and Unionist Party Competition in Northern Ireland," *British Journal of Political Science* 27:1 (January 1997); and O'Leary and McGarry, *The Politics*, 185–93.

42. For analysis see Stephen Farry, "Northern Ireland: Prospects for Progress in 2006?" (Special Report 173,Washington, D.C.: United States Institute of Peace, September 2006), 10–12.

43. James F. Clarity, "No End Seen to I.R.A. Power to Wage a Campaign of Fear," *New York Times*, February 25, 1996, 8.

44. The main split within both the Sinn Fein and IRA occurred in 1969–70 when the two organizations bifurcated into the "Officials" and the "Provisionals." The Official Sinn Fein and Official IRA continued to subscribe to a Marxist ideology, whereas the Provisional Sinn Fein and Provisional IRA espoused ethnic Gaelic nationalism. "The Officials" have become defunct in Northern Ireland, thus are not competitors to the Provisional Sinn Fein or Provisional IRA. For details, see Wikipedia, "Sinn Fein," available at http://en.wikipedia.org/wiki/Sinn_F% C3% A9in; and Wikipedia, "Provisional Irish Republican Army," available at http://en.wikipedia.org/wiki/ Provisional_Irish_Republican_Army (accessed 22 October 2007).

45. For a list see Wikipedia, "List of IRAs," available at http://en.wikipedia.org/wiki/ List_of_IRAs (accessed 22 October 2007).

46. BBC News, "Army Paper Says IRA Not Defeated," 6 July 2007, available at http://news.bbc.co.uk/go/pr/fr/-/hi/northern_ireland/6276416.stm (accessed 22 October 2007).

47. For discussions of the Anglo-Irish Agreement and Downing Street Declaration see Wichert, *Northern Ireland*, 191–203 and 211. The Good Friday Agreement is analyzed in detail in Farry, "Northern Ireland."

48. For details see *USA Today*, "Northern Ireland Power Sharing Begins," May 5, 2007, available at http://www.usatoday.com/news/world/2007-05-08-northern-ireland_ N.htm?csp=34 (accessed 21 October 2007).

49. For elaboration see Suranjan Das, *Kashmir and Sindh: Nation-Building, Ethnicity, and Regional Politics in South Asia* (London: Anthem Press, 2001), 35–38.

50. For details see Sumit Ganguly, *The Crisis of Kashmir: Portents of War, Hopes of Peace* (Cambridge: Cambridge University Press, 1997), 81–84.

51. Ibid., 83, and Das, *Kashmir and Sindh*, 42.

52. Farooq unexpectedly entered into a pact with Rajiv Gandhi and the Congress (I) in 1987 by which he agreed to a National Conference-Congress (I) alliance for state assembly elections in exchange for being restored to the chief ministership of Kashmir if the coalition came to power. In contrast, the increasingly popular Muslim United Front (MUF), a coalition of religious-based parties which had previously been periodically patronized by both the National Conference and the Congress (I) in their years of unscrupulous political competition against each other, was prevented from contesting these elections through preventative arrests and physical intimidation by government security forces. The National Conference-Congress (I) coalition predictably came into power, but the manner in which the open democratic political process was stifled for strictly partisan reasons further alienated the Kashmiri Muslim population. For details of these developments, see Ganguly, *The Crisis*, 96; and South Asia Terrorism Portal, Website of the Institute for Conflict Management (New Delhi), "Jammu and Kashmir Liberation Front," available at http://www.satp.org/satp.org/satporgtp/ countries/india/states/jandk/terrorist_outfits/jammu_&_kashmir_liberation_front. htm (accessed 15 July 2005).

53. For details see Kaia Leather, *Kashmiri Separatists: Origins, Competing Ideologies, and Prospects for Resolution of the Conflict* (New York: Novinka Books, 2003), 14–16; and South Asia Terrorism Portal, Website of the Institute for Conflict Management

(New Delhi), "Terrorist Groups: An Overview," available at http://www/satp.org/satporgtp/countries/india/states/jandk/terrorist_outfits/index.html (accessed 15 July 2005).

54. Leather, *Kashmiri Separatists*, 48; and South Asia Terrorism Portal, Website of the Institute for Conflict Management (New Delhi), "Muttahida Jehad Council," available at http://satp.org/satporgtp/countries/india/states/jandk/terrorist_outfits/mjc.htm.

55. Leather, *Kashmiri Separatists*, 18–19.

56. The "hawk" faction tends to be more Islamic in nature and leans in favor of Kashmir's accession to Pakistan, whereas the "dove" faction is more willing to consider solutions to the "Kashmir problem" consisting of regional autonomy or, preferably, a plebiscite to determine the status of Kashmir. For more details about this split see Kanchan Lakshman, "J&K: The Hurriyat Splits," South Asia Intelligence Review 2:8 (8 September 2003), South Asia Terrorism Portal, Website of the Institute for Conflict Management (New Delhi), available at http://www.satp.org/satporgtp/sair/Archives/2_8.htm (accessed 15 July 2005).

57. For a discussion of NC-PDP competition see S.H. Imam, "Jammu and Kashmir Assembly Elections 2002: Ending National Conference's Reign," (30 October 2002), Jammu and Kashmir: The Complete Knowledge Base website. http://www.jammu-kashmir.com/insights/insight20021030.html (accessed 18 July 2005).

58. According to Indian Defense Minister A.K. Antony, levels of violence in Kashmir declined significantly in 2007 in comparison to 2006. Yet, he expressed concern about the inability to reduce levels of violence even further, even considering the presence of nearly 500,000 troops in the state. For details see "Violence in Kashmir Down by 50 percent, Militancy Persists." Available at http://in.news.yahoo.com/071102/139/6mr9k.html (accessed 16 December 2007).

59. Sanjib Baruah, *India Against Itself: Assam and the Politics of Nationality* (Philadelphia: University of Pennsylvania Press, 1999), 118.

60. Monirul Hussain, *The Assam Movement: Class, Ideology, and Identity* (Delhi: Manak Publications, 1994), 138.

61. Ibid., 140.

62. Ibid., 114.

63. Ibid., 120–21.

64. Hussain, *The Assam Movement*, 121. The AAMSU supported the AASU and AGSP's demand that the influx of news illegal immigrants to Assam be curbed, but it also demanded that all immigrants who came to Assam before 1971 be granted full formal citizenship. Baruah, *India Against Itself*, 127.

65. Hussain, *The Assam Movement*, 141.

66. Baruah, *India Against Itself*, 137.

67. Hussain, *The Assam Movement*, 155.

68. For details, see Sanjib Baruah, "The State and Separatist Militancy in Assam: Winning a Battle and Losing the War?" *Asian Survey* 34:10 (October 1994): 871; and Hussain, *The Assam Movement*, 158.

69. Sanjoy Hazarika, *Strangers of the Mist: Tales of War and Peace from India's Northeast* (New Delhi: Viking Penguin Books, 1994), 156.

70. Udayon Mishra, *North-East India: Quest for Identity* (Guwahati: Omsons Publications, 1988), 144.

71. For details see Ibid., 150. The AJYCP was originally a constituent member of the AGSP grouping.

72. For details see, Hazarika, *Strangers of the Mist: Tales of War and Peace from India's Northeast,* 155–56.

73. For details, see Baruah, *India Against Itself,* 154–55; and Hazarika, *Strangers of the Mist: Tales of War and Peace from India's Northeast,* 198–211.

74. Ibid., 156.

75. For details of Operation Rhino, see Ibid., 217–22.

76. Ibid., 224.

77. Ibid., 218–32. For an in-depth discussion of SULFA, also see Ajai Sahni and Bibhu Prasad Routray, "SULFA: Terror by Another Name," *Faultlines* 9. http://www.satp.org/satporgtp/publication/faultlines/volume9/Article1.htm (accessed 18 March 2007).

78. For details about ULFA's internal "political wing" see Jaideep Saikia, "Autumn in Springtime: The ULFA Battles for Survival," *Faultlines* 7, http://www.satp.org/satporgtp/publication/faultlines/volume7/Fault7-JaideepSF.html. (accessed on 18 March 2007). For an analysis of the People's Consultative Group, see South Asia Terrorism Portal. "Assam Assessment 2006." http://www.satp.org/satporgtp/countries/india/states/assam/index.html (accessed 18 March 2007).

79. For the exact toll and trends, see South Asia Terrorism Portal. "Insurgency Related Killings." http://www.satp.org/satporgtp/countries/india/states/assam/data_sheets/insurgency_related_killings.htm (accessed 18 March 2007).

Glossary

Akali:	translated literally "immortal"; a member of the Khalsa order; a member or supporter of the Akali Dal.
Akali Dal:	translated literally "army of immortals"; the main Sikh political party in Punjab.
Akal Takht:	a Sikh shrine within the Golden Temple complex which is considered to be the main seat of temporal and religious authority for the Sikhs.
akhand path:	the ceremonial continuous reading of the Granth Sahib.
amrit:	the baptismal nectar consisting of water and sweets stirred with a double-edged dagger which is used to initiate an individual into the Khalsa order.
amritdhari:	a baptized Sikh and member of the Khalsa.
Baisakhi:	a festival celebrating the end of the traditional harvest season; also refers to the day (April 13) on which the Khalsa was created by Guru Gobind Singh in 1699.
bandh:	literally translated "a closure"; a strike or closure of shops and offices in an act of peaceful protest.
bhai:	literally translated "brother"; an epithet of respect used for a Sikh priest or religious person.
dhadi:	a minstrel singer.
Dharam Yudh morcha:	literally translated "the religious war agitation" or "agitation for righteousness"; refers to the peaceful Akali agitation of the early-1980's.
diwan:	a formal large gathering.
ghallughara:	massacre or holocaust.
giani:	a Sikh priest or religious scholar.

Granth Sahib:	the main Sikh religious text considered to be the "living guru" for the Sikh community.
granthi:	a Sikh priest.
gurbani:	literally "the *gurus*' words"; oral reading of the Guru Granth Sahib.
gurdwara:	a Sikh temple.
gurmata:	a collective resolution passed at a *Sarbat Khalsa* in the presence of the Granth Sahib.
Gurmukhi:	literally "from the lips of the *gurus*"; a script used for writing the Punjabi language and Sikh religious texts.
guru:	a religious teacher or leader; an term used for the founder of the Sikh religion and his nine successors and the Granth Sahib.
hartal:	a strike or peaceful protest.
hukamnama:	a supreme religious edict usually issued by the *Jathedar* of the Akal Takht in conjunction with the other Head Priests.
jatha:	a group; a band of local Akali volunteers.
jathedar:	the leader of a *jatha*; a local leader of the Akali Dal; the head of a major Sikh shrine, including heads of the Five Sikh Takhts.
kar sewa:	voluntary, community service on cleaning, repairing, and rebuilding Sikh temples.
kesdhari:	a Sikh who keeps unshorn hair, a beard, and some of the Five K's, but is not formally baptized.
Khalsa:	the militant Sikh order instituted by Guru Gobind Singh in 1699; also refers to a baptized Sikh.
kirpan:	one of the Five K's; a ceremonial dagger; a long sword.
lakh:	an Indian word commonly used for the number 100,000.
langar:	a community kitchen found in Sikh temples; the food prepared in a community kitchen.
lathi:	a long wooden or bamboo baton used by the police in India.
Lok Sabha:	literally translated, "the people's house"; the lower and representative house of the Indian parliament which is the main legislative body for India.
morcha:	a bunker or battle fortification; used metaphorically by the Akalis for their non-violent political agitations.

Nihangs:	members of a militant Khalsa Sikh sub-sect.
Panj Pyara:	literally translated "the Five Beloved"; a group of any five *amritdhari* Sikhs often considered to be a collective decision-making body in Sikh congregations.
Panth:	translated literally the "religion" or "community"; a term used for the collective Sikh community or the collective Khalsa order.
quam:	community or nation.
Rajya Sabha:	the largely ceremonial upper house of Indian parliament which has less legislative power than the *Lok Sabha.*
sahajdhari:	a follower of the Sikh religion who does not espouse the *amritdhari* or *kesdhari* identity.
sangat:	the Sikh congregation.
Sarbat Khalsa:	literally "the entire Khalsa"; a "representative" or symbolic meeting of the "entire Sikh community" called at the Akal Takht to decide important temporal matters for the Sikhs.
satyagrahis:	a term originally coined by Mahatma Gandhi for non-violent protesters.
shaheed:	martyr.
shaheedi:	martyrdom.
siropa:	a robe of honor usually presented in a *gurdwara.*
suba:	a province or state.
tankhaiya:	one who is guilty of breaking Sikh religious norms; a precursor to excommunication from the Panth.
Vidan Sabha:	state legislative assembly.

Select Bibliography

Print Newspapers

Indian Express (New Delhi)
Hindustan Times (New Delhi)
New York Times (New York)
The Hindu (Madras)
The Tribune (Chandigarh)
World Sikh News (Stockton, California USA)

Newsmagazines

India Today (New Delhi)
Frontline (Chennai)

Unpublished Documents

Wallace, Paul. Unpublished MS. 'Religious Composition of the Three Punjabs'.

Books, Chapters, and Articles

Alexander, P. C. 2004. *Through the Corridors of Power: An Insider's Story*. New Delhi: Harper-Collins.

Anderson, Benedict. 1983. *Imagined Communities: Reflections on the Origin and Spread of Nationalism*. London: Verso.

Baruah, Sanjib. 1994. 'The State and Separatist Militancy in Assam: Winning a Battle and Losing the War?', *Asian Survey*, 34(10): 863–77.

———. 1999. *India Against Itself: Assam and the Politics of Nationality*. Philadelphia: University of Pennsylvania Press.

Bates, Robert H., Avner Greif, Margaret Levi, Jean-Laurent Rosenthal, and Barry R. Weingast. 1998. *Analytic Narratives*. Princeton: Princeton University Press.

Brass, Paul R. 1974. *Language, Religion, and Politics in North India*. Cambridge: Cambridge University Press.

Brass, Paul R. 1988. 'The Punjab Crisis and the Unity of India', in Atul Kohli (ed.), *India's Democracy: An Analysis of Changing State–Society Relations*, pp. 169–213. Princeton: Princeton University Press.

———. 1991. 'Ethnic Groups and Ethnic Identity Formation', in Paul R. Brass (ed.), *Ethnicity and Nationalism*, pp 18–40. New Delhi: Sage Publications.

Breton, Albert and Gianluigi Galeotti, Pierre Salmon, and Ronald Wintrobe (eds). 1995. *Nationalism and Rationality*. Cambridge: Cambridge University Press.

Brown, Michael E. 1997. 'The Causes of Internal Conflict: An Overview', in Michael E. Brown, Owen R. Cote Jr., Sean M. Lynn-Jones, and Steven E. Miller (eds), *Nationalism and Ethnic Conflict*, pp 3–25. Cambridge, MA: The MIT Press.

Chima, Jugdep S. 2002. 'Back to the Future in 2002?: A Predictive Model of Sikh Separatism in Punjab', *Studies in Conflict and Terrorism*, 25(1): 19–39.

Crighton, Elizabeth and Martha Abele Mac Iver. 1991. 'The Evolution of Protracted Ethnic Conflict: Group Dominance and Political Underdevelopment in Northern Ireland and Lebanon', *Comparative Politics*, 23(2): 128–30.

Das, Suranjan. 2001. *Kashmir and Sindh: Nation-Building, Ethnicity, and Regional Politics in South Asia*. London: Anthem Press.

Deol, Harnik. 2000. *Religion and Nationalism in India: The Case of the Punjab*. London: Routledge.

Deora, Man Singh. 1991. *Akali Agitation to Operation Bluestar*. New Delhi: Anmol Publications.

Dhami, M. S. 1988. 'Religious-Political Mobilisation and Shifts in the Party Support Base in the 1985 Punjab Assembly Elections', in Paul Wallace and Surendra Chopra (eds), *Political Dynamics and Crisis in Punjab*, pp. 377–98. Amritsar: Guru Nanak Dev University Press.

Dhar, Maloy Krishna. 1996. *Bitter Harvest: A Saga of the Punjab*. Delhi: Ajanta Publications.

———. 2005. *Open Secrets: India's Intelligence Unveiled*. New Delhi: Manas Publications.

Dhillon, Gurdarshan Singh. 1996. *Truth About Punjab: SGPC White Paper*. Amritsar: Shiromani Gurdwara Parbandhak Committee.

Dilgeer, Harjinder Singh. 1980. *The Akal Takht*. Jullundur: Punjabi Books Company.

Evans, G. and M. Duffy. 1997. 'Beyond the Sectarian Divide: The Social Bases and Political Consequences of Nationalist and Unionist Party Competition in Northern Ireland', *British Journal of Political Science*, 27(1): 47–81.

Farry, Stephen. 2006. *Northern Ireland: Prospects for Progress in 2006?* Special Report 173 submitted to United States Institute of Peace, Washington, D.C.

Fearon, James D. and David D. Laitin. 2000. 'Violence and the Social Construction of Ethnic Identity', *International Organization*, 54(4): 845–77.

Ganguly, Sumit. 1997. *The Crisis of Kashmir: Portents of War, Hopes of Peace*. Cambridge: Cambridge University Press.

George, Alexander L. and Timothy J. McKeown. 1985. 'Case Studies and Theories of Organizational Decision Making', in Robert F. Coulam and Richard A. Smith (eds), *Advances in Information Processing in Organizations*, pp. 21–58. Greenwich, CT: JAI Press.

Gill, K.P.S. 2001. 'Endgame in Punjab: 1988–93', in K.P.S. Gill (ed.), *Terror and Containment: Perspectives of India's Internal Security*, pp 23–84. New Delhi: Gyan Publishing House.

Gill, Sucha Singh and K. C. Singhal. 1984. 'The Punjab Problem: Its Historical Roots', *Economic and Political Weekly*, 19(14): 603–08.

Government of India. 1984. *White Paper on the Punjab Agitation*. New Delhi: Government of India Press.

Grewal, J. S. 1994. *The Sikhs of the Punjab*. New Delhi: Cambridge University Press.

Guelke, Adrian. 1991. 'The Political Impasse in South Africa and Northern Ireland: A Comparative Perspective', *Comparative Politics*, 23(2): 143–62.

Gurr, Ted Robert and Barbara Harff. 1994. *Ethnic Conflict in World Politics*. Boulder, CO: Westview Press.

Hardgrave, Robert L. and James A. Bill. 1981. *Comparative Politics: The Quest for Theory*. Lanham, MD: University Press of America.

Helman, Gerlad B. and Steven R. Ratner. 1992–93 'Saving Failed States', *Foreign Policy*, 89 (Winter): 3–20.

Hewitt, J. Joseph, Jonathan Wilkenfeld, and Ted Robert Gurr. 2009. *Peace and Conflict 2008*. College Park, MD: Center for International Development and Conflict Management (University of Maryland).

Hussain, Monirul. 1994. *The Assam Movement: Class, Ideology, and Identity*. Delhi: Manak Publications.

Islam, Syed Serajul. 1998. 'The Islamic Independence Movements in Patani of Thailand and Mindanao of the Philippines', *Asian Survey*, 38(5): 441–56.

Jones, Kenneth W. 1973. 'Ham Hindu Nahin: Arya-Sikh Relations, 1877–1905', *Journal of Asian Studies*, 32(3): 457–75.

Joshi, Manoj. 1997. 'Combating Terrorism in Punjab: Indian Democracy in Crisis', in Partha S. Ghosh (ed.), *Rivalry and Revolution in South and East Asia*, pp. 187–222. Brookfield, VT: Ashgate Publishing.

Kapur, Rajiv. 1988. *Sikh Separatism: The Politics of Faith*. New Delhi: World Book Centre.

Kaur, Jaskaran. 2004. *Twenty Years of Impunity: The November 1984 Pogroms of Sikhs in India*. London: Nectar Publishing.

Kaur, Jitinder. 1986. *The Politics of Sikhs: A Study of Delhi Sikh Gurdwara Management Committee*. New Delhi: National Book Organization.

Kaur, Kuldeep. 1999. *Akali Dal in Punjab Politics: Splits and Mergers*. New Delhi: Deep and Deep Publications.

Kohli, Atul. 1997. 'Can Democracies Accommodate Ethnic Nationalism? Rise and Decline of Self-Determination Movements in India', *The Journal of Asian Studies*, 56(2): 325–44.

Kumar, Ram Narayan. 1997. *The Sikh Unrest and the Indian State: Politics, Personalities, and Historical Perspective*. Delhi: Ajanta Publications.

Lapidus, Gail. 1998. 'Contested Sovereignty: The Tragedy of Chechnya', *International Security*, 23(1): 5–49.

Leather, Kaia. 2003. *Kashmiri Separatists: Origins, Competing Ideologies, and Prospects for Resolution of the Conflict*. New York: Novinka Books.

Leaf, Murray J. 1985. 'The Punjab Crisis', *Asian Survey*, 25(5): 475–98.

Madhok, Balraj. 1985. *Punjab Problem: The Muslim Connection*. New Delhi: Hindu World Publications.

McAdam, Doug. 1982. *Political Process and the Development of Black Insurgency, 1930–1970*. Chicago: University of Chicago Press.

Mishra, Udayon. 1988. *North-East India: Quest for Identity*. Guwahati: Omsons Publications.

Mitra, Subrata K. 1995. 'The Rational Politics of Cultural Nationalism: Subnational Movements of South Asia in a Comparative Perspective', *British Journal of Political Science*, 25(1): 57–77.

Morris, Aldon D. and Carol McClurg Mueller (eds). 1992. *Frontiers in Social Movement Theory*. New Haven: Yale University Press.

Nayar, Kuldip and Khushwant Singh. 1984. *Tragedy of Punjab*. New Delhi: Vision Books.

Nayar, Raj Baldev. 1966. *Minority Politics in the Punjab*. Princeton: Princeton University Press.

Newman, Saul. 1991. 'Does Modernization Breed Ethnic Political Conflict?', *World Politics*, 43(3): 451–78.

Nordlinger, Eric A. 1972. *Conflict Regulation in Divided Societies*. Cambridge, MA: Center for International Affairs-Harvard University.

O'Leary, Brendan. 1989. 'The Limits of Coercive Consociationalism in Northern Ireland', *Political Studies*, 37(4): 562–63.

O'Leary, Brendan and John McGarry. 1993. *The Politics of Antagonism: Understanding Northern Ireland*. London: Athlone Press.

O'Neill, Bard E. 1980. 'Insurgency: A Framework for Analysis', in Bard E. O'Neill, William R. Heaton, and Donald J. Albert.(eds), *Insurgency in the Modern World*, pp. 1–26. Boulder, CO.: Westview Press.

Pettigrew, Joyce. 1984. 'Take Not Arms Against Thy Sovereign', *South Asia Research*, 4(2): 102–23.

———. 1995. *The Sikhs of the Punjab: Unheard Voices of State and Guerilla Violence*. London: Zed Books.

Popkin, Samuel L. 1979. *The Rational Peasant: The Political Economy of Rural Society in Vietnam*. Berkeley: University of California Press.

Posen, Barry R. 1993. 'The Security Dilemma and Ethnic Conflict', *Survival*, 35(1): 27–47.

Purewal, Shinder. 2000. *Sikh Ethnonationalism and the Political Economy of Punjab*. New Delhi: Oxford University Press.

Puri, Harish K. 1988. 'Akali Politics: Emerging Compulsions', in Wallace and Chopra (eds), *Political Dynamics and Crisis in Punjab*, pp. 299–321. Amritsar: Guru Nanak University Press.

Rabushka, Alvin and Kenneth Shepsle. 1972. *Politics in Plural Societies: A Theory of Democratic Instability*. Columbus, OH: Charles E. Merrill Publishing.

Ribeiro, Julio F. 1998. *Bullet for Bullet: My Life as a Police Officer*. New Delhi: Penguin Books.

Roy, Meenu. 1999. *Elections 1998: A Continuity in Coalition*. New Delhi: National Publishing House.

Sandhu, Ranbir Singh. 1999. *Speeches and Conversations of Sant Jarnail Singh Khalsa Bhindranwale*. Dublin, Ohio: Sikh Educational and Religious Foundation.

Sharma, D. P. 1995. *The Punjab Story: Decade of Turmoil*. New Delhi: APH Publishing Corporation.

Singh, Anurag (trans. and ed.). 1999. *Giani Kirpal Singh's Eye-Witness Account of Operation Bluestar: Mighty Murderous Army Attack On the Golden Temple Complex*. Amritsar: B. Chattar Singh Jiwan Singh Publishers.

Singh, Devinder. 1993. *Akali Politics in Punjab, 1964–1985*. New Delhi: National Book Organisation.

Singh, Gur Rattan Pal. 1979. *The Illustrated History of the Sikhs, 1947–78*. Chandigarh: Akal Printmatics.

Singh, Gurharpal. 1987. 'Understanding the "Punjab Problem"', *Asian Survey*, 27(12): 1268–77.

———. 1991. 'The Punjab Problem in the 1990's: A Post-1984 Assessment', *The Journal of Commonwealth and Comparative Politics*, 39(2): 175–91.

Singh, Gurharpal. 1996. 'Punjab Since 1984: Disorder, Order, and Legitimacy', *Asian Survey*, 36(4): 410–21.

———. 2000. *Ethnic Conflict in India: A Case-Study of Punjab*. New York: St. Martin's Press.

Singh, Gurmit. 1989. *History of Sikh Struggles*. New Delhi: Atlantic Publishers and Distributors.

———. 1991. *History of Sikh Struggles*. New Delhi: Atlantic Publishers and Distributors.

———. 1992. *History of Sikh Struggles*. New Delhi: Atlantic Publishers and Distributors.

Singh, Harbans (ed.). 1995. *The Encyclopaedia of Sikhism*. Patiala: Punjabi University.

Singh, Sangat. 1996. *The Sikhs in History*. New Delhi: Uncommon Books.

Suri, Surinder S. and Narinder Dogra. 1988. 'A Study of the SGPC Elections, March 1979', in Paul Wallace and Surendra Chopra (eds), *Political Dynamics and Crisis in Punjab*, pp. 123–34. Amritsar: Guru Nanak Dev University Press.

Teleford, Hamish. 1992. 'The Political Economy of Punjab: Creating Space for Sikh Militancy', *Asian Survey*, 32(11): 969–87.

Trenin, Dmitri V., Alesksei V. Malashenko, and Anatol Lieven. 2004. *Russia's Restless Frontier: The Chechnya Factor in Post-Soviet Russia*. Washington, D.C.: Carnegie Endowment for International Peace, Brookings Institution Press.

Tully, Mark and Satish Jacob. 1985. *Amritsar: Mrs. Gandhi's Last Battle*. New Delhi: Rupa and Company.

Van Dyke, Virginia. 1996. 'The Anti-Sikh Riots of 1984 in Delhi: Politicians, Criminals, and the Discourse of Communalism', in Paul R. Brass (ed.), *Riots and Pogroms*, pp. 201–20. London: MacMillian Press Limited.

Varshney, Ashutosh. 2003. 'Nationalism, Ethnic Conflict, and Rationality', *Perspectives on Politics*, 1(1): 85–99.

Wallace, Paul. 1981. 'Religious and Secular Politics in Punjab: The Sikh Dilemma in Competing Political Systems', in Paul Wallace and Surendra Chopra (eds), *Political Dynamics in Punjab*, pp. 1–32. Amritsar: Guru Nanak Dev University Press.

———. 1990. 'Religious and Ethnic Politics: Political Mobilization in Punjab', in Francine R. Frankel and M. S. A. Rao (eds), *Dominance and State Power in Modern India: Decline of a Social Order*, pp. 416–81. Delhi: Oxford University Press.

———. 1993. 'The Regionalization of Indian Electoral Politics 1989–90: Punjab and Haryana', in Harold A. Gould and Sumit Ganguly (eds), *India Votes: Alliance Politics and Minority Governments in the Ninth and Tenth General Elections*, pp. 144–48. Boulder CO: Westview Press.

———. 1993. 'India's 1991 Elections: Regional Factors in Haryana and Punjab', in Harold A. Gould and Sumit Ganguly (eds), *India Votes: Alliance Politics and Minority Governments in the Ninth and Tenth General Elections*, pp. 403–27. Boulder, CO: Westview Press.

———. 1995. 'Political Violence and Terrorism in India: The Crisis of Identity', in Martha Crenshaw (ed.), *Terrorism in Context*, pp. 352–409. University Park: The Pennsylvania State University Press.

———. 1997. 'General Elections, 1996: Regional Parties Dominant in Punjab and Haryana', *Economic and Political Weekly*, 32(46) (November): 2963–69.

Wichert, Sabine. 1999. *Northern Ireland since 1945*. New York: Longman Publishers.

Wood, John R. 1981. 'Secession: A Comparative Analytical Framework', *Canadian Journal of Political Science*, 14(1): 107–34.

INTERNET WEBSITES

British Broadcasting Corporation, available at www.news.bbc.co.uk

Jammu & Kashmir: The Complete Knowledge Base, available at www.jammu-kashmir.com

Radio Free Europe/Radio Liberty, available at www.rferl.org

South Asia Terrorism Portal, available at www.satp.org

The Jamestown Foundation, available at www.jamestown.org

The Tribune, available at www.tribuneindia.com

USA Today, available at www.usatoday.com

Wikipedia, available at www.wikipedia.org

Yahoo News, available at news.yahoo.com

Index

About the Author

Jugdep S. Chima currently holds the position of Associate Editor for South Asia with *Asian Survey* (Institute of East Asian Studies) at the University of California, Berkeley. He previously held the positions of Visiting Scholar and Research Fellow with the Center for South Asia Studies at the same institution during 2005–06 and 2003–05, respectively. His research articles have been published in *Asian Survey, Journal of Commonwealth and Comparative Politics, Review of International Studies, Small Wars and Insurgencies,* and *Studies in Conflict and Terrorism.*

About the Author